Irish Famines
before and after the
Great Hunger

To all who have suffered due to hunger, famine and pandemics.
They are remembered.

Irish Famines
before and after the
Great Hunger

Edited by

CHRISTINE KINEALY
and **GERARD MORAN**

QUINNIPIAC UNIVERSITY PRESS
CORK UNIVERSITY PRESS

Published by:
Quinnipiac University Press
275 Mount Carmel Ave
Hamden, CT 06518-1908
www.quinnipiac.edu
for

Ireland's Great Hunger Institute:
www.qu.edu/institutes-and-centers/irelands-great-hunger-institute/
Cork University Press:
www.corkuniversitypress.com

ISBN: 978-0-578-48498-3

Cover Image: "The State of Ireland—Evicted," *Illustrated London News*, 20 March 1880
Designed by the Office of Integrated Marketing Communications

Typesetting by Marsha Swan
Printed in Villatuerta, Spain, by GRAPHYCEMS

Contents

MAKING HISTORY VISIBLE

ACKNOWLEDGEMENTS

While the fleet only sails as fast the slowest boat, we have been fortunate that each of the contributors to this collection have completed their works on time and with few complications. We acknowledge their commitment and dedication, especially as the final stages were undertaken at a time of social isolation and lockdown at the onset of the Coronavirus pandemic.

Many of the chapters were part of a conference hosted by Ireland's Great Hunger Institute, which brought together an impressive range of Irish famine scholars. A special feature of the conference was an exhibition dedicated to Quaker philanthropist, James Hack Tuke, who worked selflessly on behalf of the Irish poor during the Great Famine and the Forgotten Famine of 1879-82. We were delighted to welcome a number of descendants from his emigration scheme in the 1880s. To all who made the conference a success, we express our appreciation.

Quinnipiac University has established a reputation as a centre of excellence for research on the Great Hunger and we acknowledge all who have made this possible. Uniquely, the university has an Irish Institute, a Special Collection based in the Arnold Bernhard Library, and a museum, all dedicated to understanding poverty, hunger, disease, dislocation and famine. Our work has benefited greatly from working with our associates in Ireland and Canada. The Institute has a partnership with the Irish Heritage Trust and the National Famine Museum at Strokestown Park and we value their continued co-operation and assistance. We have benefitted from our associations with Maynooth University and University College Cork, resulting in many fruitful and ongoing exchanges between scholars, librarians and students. We are also delighted to continue our collaboration with Cork University Press, and with all involved in the production of this publication.

We are indebted to Maureen Murphy, Ray Gillespie, Francine Sagar, Rebecca Abbot and Donna Pintek for reading earlier drafts of these chapters and their thoughtful comments. The editors take responsibility for any remaining mistakes. Writing is a solitary, and sometimes selfish, pursuit. The greatest thanks are due to the families of each of the contributors to this volume, for their selfless support and understanding.

BRIEF TIMELINE OF FAMINES IN IRELAND

1271 A 'great famine' killed many people

1315–17 Food shortages following invasion by Edward Bruce

1434 Severe frost led to famine referred to as *Samha na mear-aithne*, meaning the 'Summer of slight acquaintance' due to high mortality

1478 A 'big wind' killed many cattle, resulting in food shortages

1492 Heavy rainfall destroyed the corn crop

1497 Famine through the country, accompanied by inflated food prices

1500 Inclement weather destroyed the wheat crop

1523 Heavy rainfall led to extensive flooding

1541 Severe frost and snow led to a bad harvest

1545 A 'great dearth' throughout the country

1568 Drought in south west of country

1572 Elizabethan Vagrancy Act allowed for Irish beggars in England to be punished and returned to Ireland

1574 Extreme hailstorm destroyed the crops

1575 Drought from May to August

1581 Constant wind, rain and lightening

1586 Food shortages in the southern counties

c. 1596 English poet, Edmund Spenser, published *A View of the Present State of Ireland*, suggesting Ireland be subdued through a scorched earth policy of famine

1600 Wind and floods

1602–1603 Extreme cold in northern counties. Disease killed approximately 10 percent of the population

1620–23 Poor harvests

1628–30 Food shortages resulted in licenses being granted to allow grain imports

1641 Irish Rising led to a decade of warfare, dislocation and hunger

1674 Localized famines

1690 Localized famine

1698 Act for additional duty on wool exports (10 William III c. 5)

1703 House of Industry (poor house) opens in south Dublin

1708–1709 Famine throughout Europe, including Ireland. Fever in Cork

1716–1717 A drought resulted in a poor grain harvest, especially severe in the north

1721–22 Poor harvest leads to food shortages

1727–1728 Severe famine caused by failure of grain harvest; most severe in Dublin and rural Ulster

1729 Jonathan Swift's *A Modest Proposal For preventing The Children of Poor People in Ireland From being a Burden to Their Parents or Country, and for making them Beneficial to the Publick*
Act for the more effectual punishment of vagabonds (3 Geo. II c. 17)
Act for the encouragement of tillage, and better employment of the poor, etc. (the first of many such acts) (3 Geo. II c. 3)

1735 House of Industry opens in Cork

1739 Onset of mini Ice Age in Europe

1740 Great Frost continues
May: bread riots in Dublin
October: Dublin Castle imposes an embargo on all food exports
Conolly's Folly in County Kildare, commissioned by Katherine Conolly, is commenced to provide employment to the local poor. The completed monument stands 140 feet high

1741 December: Lord Lieutenant renews the embargo.

1741–1742 An estimated 480,000 die. Remembered as 'the year of slaughter' or *blaidhain an áir*

1742 13 April: first performance of Handel's *Messiah* at the Music Hall in Fishamble Street, Dublin. Proceeds are for local poor
June: famine obelisk on Killiney Hill near Dublin is commissioned as a relief project by wealthy Catholic, John Mapas

1757 Potato and corn crop fails throughout Europe, coinciding with a depression in the linen industry in Ireland
The British government banned the export of grain from England

1765 Act to prevent the export of corn for a limited time (5 Geo. III c. 4)
First Magdalene asylum (for Protestant girls) opens in Dublin

1766 Depression in linen industry. Emigration to Colonial America increased

1767 Harvest failure: impact lessened by corn exports and distillation stopped

1770 Widespread distress, especially severe in Dublin and the north

1771 Act to punish people who attempt to prevent the export of corn (11 Geo. III c. 4)

1773 House of Industry opens in north Dublin

1774 House of Industry opens in Limerick
Belfast Charitable Society opens

1783–1784 Exceptionally cold winter results in bad harvests

1785 Act preventing the export of hay for a limited time (25 Geo. III c. 57)

1795 Poor harvests
Act against exporting starch (35 Geo. III c. 26)

1796 Act permitting the prohibition of bread and biscuit if price of corn increases above rates of exportation (36 Geo. III c. 43)
Act for the further advancement of agriculture, and a steady supply of corn for the city of Dublin, by extending the export bounties on corn and flour to the said city, and discounting all inland, canal and coast bounties thereto (37 Geo. III c.24)
Act to enable the lord lieutenant and council to prohibit the export of corn, grain, meal, malt, flour, bread, biscuit, peas, beans, potatoes, starch and hair powder for a limited time (36 Geo. III c. 8)

1799–1800 Bad harvest combined with wartime inflation

1800 Act to prohibit the making of malt, and the distilling of spirits for a limited time (40 Geo. III c. 6)
Bonus incentives to bring food to Dublin

1816 Abnormally cold weather – 'the year without the summer'

1817 June: Poor Employment Act
September: establishment of National Fever Committee

1818 Select Committee on Contagious Fever in Ireland appointed

1821 Poor harvest

1822 Widespread distress
Mansion House Committee formed in Dublin
Tavern Committee formed in London

1823–25 Peter Robinson scheme assists emigration from north Munster to Canada

1831 Distress in the west
Mansion House Committee reconvened
Tavern Committee reconvened
Board of Works established

1835 Distress in the west

1838 Introduction of the Poor Law

1839 Night of the Big Wind (*Oíche na Gaoithe Móire*), widespread distress

1842 Widespread distress

1845–1852 The Great Famine (*An Gorta Mór*)

1861–1863 Poor harvest and turf crop as a result of exceptionally wet weather

1862 Mansion House Committee reconvened

1861–1865 Lancashire Cotton Famine

1867 Localized distress in the west of the country; two-thirds of potato crop in Connemara fails.

1869 Localized distress in the west of the country

1876 Localized distress on islands off Connemara, especially Inishboffin

1879 December: Duchess of Marlborough Committee established

1880 Mansion House Committee reconvened

1879–1881 The forgotten famine, or the mini-famine (*an Gorta Beag*)

1880 March: Distress Act allows guardians to give relief to those holding land
March: the U.S. Department of Navy dispatches the *U.S.S. Constellation* to Ireland with more than 3,300 barrels of foodstuffs, plus clothing
Potato Crop Committee to consider alternative varieties of seed potatoes provided by various charities

1880–1883 Vere Foster assists 18,000 young women to emigrate

1882–1884 The James Hack Tuke assisted emigration schemes from Connemara and Mayo to North America

1885–1886 Potato failure in Connemara and west Mayo leads to seed potatoes having to be supplied

1887 Distressed Unions Bill

1888 Potato harvest deficient in County Donegal
Irish Distressed Ladies' Fund formed

1890 Distress in the west
American Irish Famine Fund established

1897 Poor harvests in the west of Ireland, particularly County Mayo

1898 Mansion House Committee reconvened
Maud Gonne travels to Mayo to assist with relief and resisting evictions
Irish Distressed Ladies' Fund reformed
Comité de Secours Aux Irlandais established in France
Manchester Committee established to feed children in the west

1900 Queen Victoria visits Ireland for the fourth and final time; Gonne describes her as 'The Famine Queen'

1916 Food shortages in Dublin in the wake of the Easter Rising

1925 Poor harvests and political upheaval led to famine conditions in the western counties and islands of the new Free State

1932 Mass unemployment in Northern Ireland (where the Poor Law was still operative) led to an 'Outdoor Relief Strike'

1945–60 Over 500,000 people left the newly named Republic of Ireland

1985 Irish man, Bob Geldof, organized, 'Live Aid,' a dual-venue benefit concert for famine-stricken Ethiopia

1991 As a result of two decades of conflict and emigration, the population of Northern Ireland had fallen

2017 The Republic of Ireland named the country best able to feed its inhabitants in a global food security index, while the U.S. had stagnated

2020 The World Health Organization and Global Citizen held "One World: Together at home," concert to support healthcare workers in the fight against the COVID–19 pandemic, curated by pop artist, Lady Gaga.

INTRODUCTION

Christine Kinealy and Gerard Moran

Famines, subsistence crises and food insecurity have been a constant feature throughout history, with no country being exempt. In 2020, the world's population stood at an estimated 7.8 billion, and was predicted to increase rapidly, especially in less developed nations. Coupled with the dual—and interlinked—threat of climate change, it appears inevitable that famines and food shortages will reoccur due to the familiar issues posed by population pressure, disease, war, political priorities, distribution failures, disenfranchisement, economic equalities, lack of entitlement, etc.[1] The outbreak of the coronavirus in late 2019, with its catastrophic impact on both people and markets, has made global crises even more likely.[2] Coronavirus may be "novel" but are many of the same patterns of preventable hunger, disease and death repeating themselves? Can history teach us any lessons for our present-day problems?

Defining or measuring hunger and famine is challenging? The United Nations and the World Health Organisation, academics and individual experts, NGOs and aid workers, have all attempted to explain what constitutes a famine, but there has been little consensus on a definition. The United Nations has drawn a distinction between a food crisis and a famine, defining the latter as "when at least 20 per cent of households in an area face extreme food shortages with a limited ability to cope; acute malnutrition rates exceed 30 per cent, and the death rate exceeds 2 persons per day per 10,000 persons."[3] A number of scholars have applied the principles of "intensity" and "magnitude" to add a more nuanced approach to the various phases and categories of famines, ranging from minor famine, to moderate famine, to major famine, to great famine, to catastrophic famine.[4] Again, excess mortality is a key indicator. For historians, however, such quantifiable measures are difficult to apply to situations where statistical records do not exist. Moreover, even when available, differing interpretations of data can lead to diverse conclusions. This was evident during the Ireland's Great Famine of 1845 to 1852. The British government, who governed the country from London, repeatedly refused to allow information relating to the number of deaths to be collected, regardless of frequent requests to do so.[5] Consequently, historians have utilized other sources, primarily the census returns, which themselves are not complete.[6] However, using what remains of the 1841, 1851 and 1861 census returns, the estimate of excess mortality during the Great Famine has varied from half-a-million dead to one-and-a-half million.[7] Such discrepancies suggest a politization of famine and of famine deaths.[8]

While the Great Famine, or Great Hunger, of the 1840s is generally accepted as a watershed in modern Irish history—and "Great" due to its longevity and lethalness—up to 1995, it was subject to little scholarly research. Other periods of hunger and famine received even less attention. The sesquicentenary of the Irish Famine coincided with a number of developments that favoured a reappraisal of Ireland's history in general, and the Famine in particular; they included unprecedented economic growth and a Peace Process that ended 30 years of conflict on the island. The resulting large number of academic publications focussed on the Great Hunger have led to a greater understanding of what happened during this period. Moreover, interest in the tragedy not only had a global reach, but was examined from multiple disciplinary perspectives, not simply by historians, but by economists, sociologists, musicologists, art historians, geographers, poets, nutritionists and scientists etc. While interest in the Famine of the 1840s shows no sign of abating, it has tended to overshadow the other periods of famine and subsistence crises. Few publications have dealt with famines from the earliest times, rare exceptions including Margaret E. Crawford's edited, *Famine: The Irish Experience, 900–1900* (1989) and Cormac Ó Gráda, 'Famine in Ireland, 1300–1900 (2015) and Christine Kinealy and Gerard Moran's edited collection of primary sources, *Fallen Leaves of Humanity: Famines in Ireland Before and After the Great Famine* (2018).[9]

Writing in 1918 about the economic history of Ireland in the 18th century, Irish historian George O'Brien stated:

> To give particular dates as the occasions of famine years is, to some extent, to create a wrong impression of the Irish situation, the truth being that the country lived in a chronic state approaching famine, and that the particular years which are mentioned by historians as famine years were simply the years in which the chronic symptoms became acute.[10]

Several factors were responsible for the famines and food crises that occurred in Ireland throughout the centuries, which frequently had a devastating impact on communities, regions and the country. These included inclement weather, wars, crop failures, unsympathetic legislators, unviable land holdings, high dependency on one food source and a growing population that could not be supported on the country's under-developed resources. The reasons for the perennial crises were noted by people who toured Ireland and those who lived in the country. Some commentators regarded famine as a way of limiting the population, as explicated by Thomas Malthus, while others argued that Ireland's development had been hampered by centuries of colonial misrule.[11] The Great Hunger, however, with its massive human toll, did not bring an end to famines in Ireland, demonstrating that the size of the Irish population was not the problem. In a debate in the British House of Commons in 1901, one member pointed out: "Without touching on the famine of 1846–47, the question of distress was brought up before the House from 1831 to 1898 in 27 different years."[12] No decade had been free from local or regional famines, and a number, for instance, from 1860 to 1862 and from 1879 to 1881, had been particularly severe.

While the Great Famine of 1845–52 had a transformative impact on Irish society, poverty, destitution, crop failures and famines were a recurring theme in Ireland. William Wilde, eye surgeon, folklorist and census commissioner in 1841 and 1851, defined Ireland in the wake of the Great Hunger as a land of famines.[13] Wilde's painstaking compilation of deaths points to the existence of sources prior to this date. For example, he identifies a source from 964, when the country experienced "A great miserable dearth in Ireland that the father sould [sic] his sonn [sic] and daughter for meat."[14] The cause of pre-1500 crop failures was frequently severe weather and war, and they were generally followed by plague, pestilence and epidemics.[15] Ungenial weather conditions continued to play a role in subsequent famines.[16] Bad weather alone, however, did not cause famines, and while environmental factors clearly played a part in each crisis, understanding the socio-political context is crucial. Ireland's subservient position as a colony, a position that did not change until the 20th century, meant that, in the period leading up to the Great Famine, in the words of David Dickson, the country was "by contemporary European standards, lightly governed, materially poor, and socially polarised."[17] Moreover, famines are processes, not events, and a key to understanding their frequency in Ireland was the on-going vulnerability of the poor. In Ireland, there was no state or centralized provision for giving relief to the most vulnerable in society. Unlike England, Scotland and Wales, where structures had been in place since the reign of Elizabeth I, Ireland possessed no national system of poor relief until 1838. The legislation then introduced, although loosely modelled on the "new" English Poor Law of 1834, was premised on the belief that the poor in Ireland were less deserving of relief than their counterparts elsewhere. The 1838 Act, therefore, only permitted relief within the confines of a workhouse and denied the Irish poor a legal entitlement to relief.[18] Overall, the new legislation indicated a harshening of attitudes towards the poor, and a new stringency in the way in which relief was provided.[19] The inappropriateness of the system was obvious by the end of 1846. Although an amended Poor Law was introduced in 1847, which allowed outdoor relief, it saved neither lives nor livelihoods—the burden of poor rates increasing evictions, homelessness and bankruptcy. In both 1847 and 1849, the *Illustrated London News* sent Cork-born artist, James Mahoney, to west Cork and to County Clare. The iconic images that he sent back were shocking, but just as powerful was the text that accompanied them:

> Kilrush, which gives its name to a Poor-law union, will be celebrated in the history of pauperism. With Clifden, Westport, Skibbereen, and other places, it forms one of the battle-fields of Ireland, in which property, under the guidance of legislation, has fought with poverty ... The board agreed yesterday to petition the Poor-law Commissioners on the state of the Union, and said that the guardians would not be morally responsible for the deaths that may occur through starvation ... The present condition of the Irish, we have no hesitation in saying, has been brought on by ignorant and vicious legislation.[20]

This volume provides research on aspects of famine and hunger over seven centuries. The frequency and distinctiveness of each subsistence crisis makes it impossible to include details on each one, but the following chapters are indicative of the part famines have played in Ireland's history. The publication commences with a chapter by Brendan Smith examining famines in Ireland throughout the late medieval and early modern periods, that is, *c*.1400 to *c*.1641. Extreme weather conditions were often the cause of the frequent crop failures, but, as Smith also shows, intermittent periods of violent warfare destroyed the food and livelihood of the native population.

The famine of 1740–41 has dominated the historiography of 18th-century shortages, but historian James Kelly has estimated that, during this century, the country underwent "serious dearth on twelve occasions," four of which he characterizes as famines, eight as subsistence crises. The difference in nomenclature is defined by Kelly in terms of demographic impact.[21] In 1708–1709, extreme weather conditions caused crop failures throughout Europe. In Ireland, the impact was mitigated by the intervention of the Privy Council which placed an embargo on grain exports.[22] In 1716 and 1717, there was a drought that was particularly severe in the north of the country and caused the corn crop to fail. One response was emigration, from all parts of the country, including the north.[23] Between 1725 and 1729, there was a series of bad harvests in Ireland. The Irish government responded with highly interventionist measures—imposing price controls and importing grain from overseas. Nonetheless, there was excess mortality, most notably in Dublin and rural Ulster.[24]

Peter Murphy's chapter focuses on a member of the Protestant Ascendancy, Jonathan Swift, who saw beyond the short-term responses of the government to recurring famines. In "A Modest Proposal," published in 1729, Swift challenged, through his deft use of wit and irony, the structural vulnerabilities within Irish society. Legislation from both the London and the Dublin parliaments had repeatedly undermined the position of Catholics in the country, economically, politically, socially and culturally.[25] More generally, trade restrictions imposed by the Westminster parliament served to reinforce Ireland's subservient and colonial status.[26] The Navigation Acts of 1661, 1671, 1685 and 1696 banned the direct exportation of most Irish products to the colonies, requiring that they first travel to English ports, on English vessels.[27] The Wool Act of 1699, also passed by the Westminster parliament, favoured the English trade by deliberately restricting the Irish one.[28] These fault-lines hindered Ireland's ability to respond to the famines that beset it throughout the 18th and 19th centuries.

The famine of 1740–41 has been remembered in folk memory as "'the year of slaughter" or *blaidhain an áir*. The crisis was precipitated by extreme weather conditions. In Ireland, the winter of 1739–40 was the coldest it had been for half a millennium.[29] While most of Europe experienced freezing conditions in 1739, in 1740, it was less widespread.[30] The freezing of the ports meant it was impossible to import coal, or anything else, from overseas.[31] At this stage, potatoes were the subsistence crop of many of the poor in the west and south, and the extreme cold not only destroyed these and other crops, but it also killed livestock as well as wild animals and birds. In the absence of a national system of welfare it was left to local elites and private charity to provide relief. For historian John Post, it was the weaknesses in Ireland's social structure and the lack of welfare provision that made the suffering so acute.[32] Not for the last time, private charity partly filled the gap.[33]

Karen Sonnelitter's chapter explores "the extraordinary wave" of private philanthropy that was put in place between 1739 and 1741. Some of the measures predate the exceptional charitable outpouring that accompanied the Great Hunger a century later and, and as Harvey Strum and Catherine Shannon show, re-emerged after 1879. In the mid-18th century, even as anti-Catholic restrictions remained in place, some of those in power were recognizing that poverty could be a greater threat to the stability of the country. The 1740–41 famine bears similarities with the tragedy of a century later in terms of massive excess mortality, although the earlier one may have claimed as many as 38 percent of the population. However, unlike in the later, more famous famine, there was no mass emigration. This tragedy demonstrated the need for a national welfare and a hospital system in Ireland, although it took almost a further 100 years before a network of workhouses, each with an infirmary, was established.

The fact that the north of the country was in the forefront of the suffering during many of the subsistence crises of the 18th century conforms with Patrick Fitzpatrick's assertion that "the interconnecting themes of poverty, hunger and migration were very much central to an Ulster Protestant, and particularly Presbyterian, historical experience."[34] More specifically, Ian McBride has found that in the half century before 1760, the province of Ulster experienced multiple famines or near-famine conditions.[35] One consequence was large-scale emigration of people who became known as the "Ulster-Scots" to Colonial America.[36] These Protestant famine emigrants preceded by a century the exodus triggered by the Great Famine.

As Robert Smart's chapter shows, the fears and uncertainties that permeated Irish society in the 18th century, and led to mass emigration, did not remain in Ireland but were sometimes taken overseas, most notably to North America. Even in their new homes, the traditional religious fault-lines emerged. It was not just people who travelled across the Atlantic, but also ideas. Echoing some of the themes explored in Murphy's chapter, Smart shows how literature became a platform for "cultural resistance." Gothic literature, in particular, became an early form of post-colonial discourse that was common to both Ireland and America.

A feature of relief in the late-18th century, was the high level of government intervention in the market-place. During the widespread distress of 1756 the British government responded by banning grain exports from England.[37] In later periods of shortage in Ireland, similar legislation was enacted by the Irish parliament, most notably in 1765.[38] Only a short time after, however, in 1771, an act was passed to punish people who attempted to stop corn being exported.[39] The most serious food shortages since the 1740s occurred from 1782 to 1784. The Irish government, based in College Green, intervened directly in the movement of food both in and out of the country. In 1783, the ports were closed temporarily to keep food in the country, while a bounty was offered to merchants to import additional foodstuffs.[40] Significantly, during the 1790s, when Britain was at war with France and feared an alliance between its two traditional enemies, multiple acts were passed to prevent many items of foodstuffs from leaving Britain or Ireland.[41] Again, in the wake of the poor harvests in 1799 and 1800, the official response was swift and comprehensive and included importing additional provisions to Dublin and banning malting (until October 1801) and distilling (until January 1802).[42] Such interventions helped not only to provide additional food resources, but also to stabilize prices. Additional legislation ensured that the people of Dublin would have a constant supply of food, through the offering of bounties.[43] Charles Thorp, the Lord Mayor of Dublin in 1800, threatened to punish any tradesperson who exploited the food shortages in order to increase their profits.[44] His actions were praised for saving the city from starvation:

> The natural visitation of scarcity, aggravated by the arts of wicked and avaricious men, had almost affirmed the form of determined Famine, and to your Lordship's indefatigable exertions, aiding the wise and honest felicitude of superior power, it is principally owing that the streets of the Metropolis did not become the Golgotha of its poorer inhabitants.[45]

Nor was the town of Belfast immune from periodic food shortages. The crop failure of 1799 had an immediate impact on the local population, leading to the establishment of a soup kitchen committee, funded by subscriptions, based on the system that had been established in 1740.[46] Also, as early as November 1799, gruel was given to the "badged begging poor."[47] Less than 50 years later, during the Great Famine, these types of intervention were viewed as a dangerous meddling in the market-place, which would have disastrous results. The success of such interventions in earlier periods of crisis were conveniently forgotten.

The ending of the long-running Napoleonic War in 1815 plunged much of Europe into a trade depression. In Ireland, this was followed by months of inclement weather, with the summer of 1816 being unusually cold and wet, and snow and severe frost appearing as early as November in many parts of the country.[48] In Belfast, the early snow-fall led the town's elites to call on the wealthy citizens to make some provision for the poor, "because the case is urgent."[49] Moreover, snow, wind and freezing weather continued until March 1817, leading to poor potato and corn harvests. The prolonged bad weather left the poor not only without food, but also without fuel.[50] In response to the widespread appearance of "famine" fever, in September 1817, a National Fever Committee was created in Dublin, but it was overwhelmed by the scale of the outbreak. In April 1818, the British House of Commons responded to the epidemic by appointing a Select Committee to enquire into the spread of contagious fever in Ireland and to suggest measures to stop its spread.[51] Regardless, the typhus fever continued into 1819 when it disappeared as quickly as it had appeared. During that time, an estimated one and a half million people had been infected, resulting in 65,000 deaths.[52]

In 1821, the potato crop failed again.[53] Although the resultant distress was widespread, it was most severe in counties Clare, Cork, Galway, Kerry, Leitrim, Limerick, Mayo, Roscommon and Sligo. By July 1822, an estimated one million people in these areas were living on the edge of starvation.[54] Whereas earlier shortages had been dealt with promptly and directly by using imaginative and effective measures to provide the people with cheap food, a new approach to dealing with the poor was emerging regarding the responsibility of the government towards providing poor relief, whether permanent or emergency. In 1819, William Gregory, Under Secretary in Dublin Castle from 1813 to 1831, had articulated the philosophy behind this new approach:[55]

> I am adverse to the plan of sending Potatoes to the South in the Manner you propose, not from any doubt of the great partial distress but from the principle that the government are not on all occasions to be the first resort when any pressure occurs without the Gentry contributing to the relief of their impoverished tenantry.[56]

To some extent, Gregory's concerns were justified because, in 1822, as in later famines, absentee landlords contributed little to relief, thus throwing an even greater burden on those who were resident.[57] However, during a debate in the House of Commons in May 1822, the Prime Minister, Lord Liverpool,[58] reaffirmed the changing role of the government during periods of distress, when he informed his fellow politicians:

> The government of Ireland had resorted to measures for the purpose of obtaining information as to the state of Ireland, both politically and with regard to the supply of food. It was found, that at that period there was a great abundance of articles of food, and at low prices, and no apprehensions were entertained of any scarcity. He thought it right here to observe that great delicacy and difficulty were necessarily involved in any question of interfering with regard to the supply of food; as such interference tended to do much mischief by interfering with individual speculations, and enhancing the price of articles of the first necessity.[59]

Moreover, Liverpool made a point of criticizing the intervention in trade by the Dublin government in 1800, when, amongst other things, they had offered bounties on the importation of grain, stating, "all were now agreed that that measure did more harm than good, as the grain would have been sold at a cheaper rate, had the bounty not been given."[60] The comments by leading members of the British government, suggested that Parliament—now centred in London—did not accept its moral responsibility to saving Irish lives during a famine.

Food shortages occurred sporadically in Ireland throughout the 1830s. The poor harvest in 1831 was attributed to a series of turbulent storms in the Atlantic in August and September 1830, which damaged the new harvest. They also disrupted the usual deposits of sea-moss, which was widely used as manure for the potatoes, while supplies of fish were much reduced.[61] Regardless of the welcome interventions of private charity, there was a feeling that the government was not doing enough and appeals were made to them by Irish MPs to be more interventionist.[62] As was the case in other periods of shortages, food continued to be exported from areas in which the people were starving, adding to the desperation of the poor. In Newport in County Mayo, for example, there was an attempt to raid the ship on which oats were being carried to England. This action was prevented by the intervention of the local priest, Father James Hughes.[63] Ciarán Reilly's chapter on the largely overlooked famine of 1831 is a reminder that during subsistence crises, traditional codes of behavior could break down, pitting neighbor against neighbor in the struggle for survival. Reilly shows how the incidents of crime and the retribution that accompanied the food shortages could vary from parish to parish. Some of these themes are revisited in Mark McGowan's chapter.

Reporting on the widespread starvation in the county, a local newspaper, the *Telegraph and Connaught Ranger*, criticized the apathy of the government and asked, "Are not the Irish peasantry entitled to the protection of the Government? !!"[64] The question was a prescient forewarning of events that would unfold 15 years later. In addition to the usual outbreaks of fever and other diseases that traditionally accompanied periods of famine, a fresh enemy appeared in Ireland in 1832, cholera. This deadly disease reached the ports first, appearing in Dublin and Belfast in March 1832 and Cork in April. By early 1833, it had reached all parts of Ireland and was reappearing in some of the original locations.[65] The epidemic added to the existing hardship of the poor and added a new spike in deaths. While it is hard to gauge excess mortality resulting from the cholera epidemic, the *Medical Gazette* reported in September 1833, that it was finally declining; deaths in the previous week had numbered 69, compared with almost 200 deaths a fortnight earlier.[66]

The 1830s was also the decade in which the question of poverty, and how to alleviate it, was at the centre of political debate within the United Kingdom. Within the union, Ireland was unique in having no national Poor Law. In addition to the intermittent periods of distress, compelling evidence of the widespread poverty and repeated hunger of the Irish poor was provided by a three-year-long Poor Enquiry Commission, which sat between 1833 and 1836. Although appointed by the British government, the Commission's final report on the extent and perennial nature of poverty in Ireland, and their comprehensive programme of solutions, did not conform to orthodox views on why the poor were poor. Consequently, the report was bypassed.[67] Instead, the British government chose to rely on the Poor Laws to provide relief throughout the United Kingdom. While these debates resulted in major changes in the provision of poor relief in England, Wales and Scotland, in Ireland they led to the introduction of a Poor Law in 1838.[68] Tellingly, the Poor Laws that were adopted in Britain allowed for a combination of indoor and outdoor relief and recognised that the poor had a legal right to relief. The more draconian Irish Poor Law only allowed for indoor relief and, pointedly, did not recognize a right to relief. In 1846 and 1847, the consequences of these limitations were to prove disastrous. Although the 1838 legislation was intended to be implemented swiftly, the building and opening of the country's new 130 workhouses took a few years to complete. In the absence of a national system of poor relief, therefore, it was left to a combination of special government measures, interventions by private individuals and philanthropists, to respond to the localized distress in 1839 and 1842.

The final year of the 1830s closed with another famine, which was largely due to extreme weather conditions. The Night of the Big Wind (*Oíche na Gaoithe Móire*) commenced on 6 January 1839, when Ireland experienced the most devastating gales in memory.[69] Throughout the country, houses and cabins were destroyed, trees were toppled and rivers broke their banks, while stacks of grain were blown away.[70] Turf, flax and hay crops were also scattered, and livestock killed. Numerous fishing boats and ships were destroyed.[71] The heavy falls of snow that had preceded and followed the hurricane added to the misery of the poor in particular.[72] Appeals for outdoor relief to be provided in 1839 and 1840, utilizing the administrative machinery of the new Poor Law, were rejected by the Poor Law Commissioners on the grounds that:

> They cannot direct or sanction any action having for its object the administration of outdoor relief, that being a description of relief which the law not only does not sanction, but expressly prohibits.[73]

The determination to separate "ordinary" from "extraordinary" relief, and not to permit outdoor relief however great the evidence of distress, was adhered to in 1842 and again in 1845 and 1846.

The famine of the 1840s is one by which famines in Ireland before 1845 and after 1852 are compared. Moreover, studies of famines elsewhere in the world often reference what occurred during those years. However, the deadly impact of the Famine was not confined to Ireland but proved to be transnational. The role of Canada, as a famine frontier beyond the island of Ireland, is explored from four different perspectives by Laura Smith, Jason King, Mark McGowan and Timothy Forest. Their use of previously unexplored sources offers a more complex understanding of Canada's multi-faceted response to the crisis occurring 3,000 miles away. While the United States was the main destination of Irish emigrants during the 19th century, up to and during the Great Hunger, the majority of those leaving Ireland headed to Canada because of cheaper passenger fares. Through a careful analysis of the little-used records of the Emigration Service Fund from 1843 to 1847, Smith reaches several interesting conclusions about migration and settlement patterns in the Canadas between 1843 and 1847. By taking this longer view, she is able to posit the question, "To what extent did Famine disrupt the well-documented chain migration patterns amongst the Irish in Canada." Interestingly, by looking at emigrant's luggage, Smith challenges the idea that these immigrants were the poorest of the poor.

The chapters by King and McGowan deal with one of the most notorious episodes involving Irish emigrants during the Great Hunger, that is, the sending of 1,490 people from the Mahon estate at Strokestown. Their findings serve to complicate further what is already known about the scheme. King shows how rumor and misinformation, both in the transatlantic press and in the British parliament, effectively sealed the fate of Major Denis Mahon. His assassination in November 1847, provided an early example how "fake news" could have a deadly outcome, while propelling an incident in a small town in the west of Ireland, into the international spotlight.

Using previously little-used sources—including the Mahon papers at the Strokestown Park archive and the neglected *Berean*, a historic newspaper from Quebec—McGowan's essay questions the approach of some historians to the scheme and to Major Denis Mahon's role in it. Contrary to traditional interpretations, these sources indicate that the landlord had a more philanthropic approach to his tenants, providing them with maize during the Famine and assisting the better-off tenants who applied to leave. The tragedy that occurred on the passage to Canada, it appears, may have been more the fault of his agent, John Ross Mahon, and the shipping agent, Robinson, who wanted to keep expenditure low rather than care for the passengers' welfare. Smith's chapter also uses previous under-utilized sources to show the complexity of the internal transport system when Irish immigrants arrived in Canada. In addition to providing new insights into settlement patterns, like McGowan,

Canada is also the focus of Timothy Forest's contribution, which examines the Canadian government's proposal in 1880 to establish a "New Ireland" colony in the recently opened lands in Manitoba and bring in large numbers of families from the west of Ireland. His chapter is a reminder that the 1840s were not the last time that Canada would come to the rescue of Ireland's starving poor. However, the reasons were not totally altruistic, but motivated party by a desire to counteract the growing influence of French Canadians and to hinder the approaches of First Nations people. The scheme, however, was opposed because of hostility to the Irish and their religion, and a preference for German and Scandinavian settlers. Another factor was a dispute between the Canadian and British governments in the event of the Irish settlers' failure to make the repayments for their resettlement.

Recovery from the catastrophe of the Great Famine proved to be slow, with mass emigration continuing into the mid-1850s. Although emigration continued to Canada, after 1847, America became the favoured destination for Irish emigrants. After 1861, however, she was engaged in a bloody civil war that would last for four years, making her a less desirable destination for Irish emigrants. Its impact in England, mainly in the industrialized north west, led to a period of shortages and unemployment, which was known as "the Cotton Famine."[74] The use of the word "famine" in an English context is particularly interesting, at a time when there was a reluctance amongst British politicians to use it in the Irish context. In Ireland, the opening years of the 1860s coincided with another period of food shortages. Again, weather played a part in exacerbating the distress. Prolonged and heavy rainfall put a stop to outdoor work and prevented the collection of peat. During a debate in Westminster, the Chief Secretary of Ireland, Sir Robert Peel (son of Sir Robert Peel, British Prime Minister during the first year of the Great Famine), provided statistics of rainfall in parts of the country: 57 inches had fallen in County Galway, with 24 inches falling in the traditionally drier months of July, August and September.[75] Regardless of an acknowledgment of widespread distress, the government was reluctant to provide any additional relief, other than that offered by the Poor Law. The London *Times* even challenged the Irish people to prove that they were starving, adding, "then and not till then, will it be proper for the government to exercise that power which you treat as its particular function."[76] In contrast, 3,000 miles away, despite being in the midst of war, the *New York Times,* quoting from Irish letters and newspapers, informed its readers that "'famine in Ireland' is doomed to represent an appalling fact this year". It added, "This will carry sharp grief to the millions in America who are connected by the closest tie of kindred and affection with those in the Green Isle."[77] As was the case so often in the 18th and 19th centuries, private charities stepped in to fill the void.[78]

The Forgotten Famine of 1879–82 had the potential to be every bit as devastating as that of the Great Hunger. A combination of factors led to the crisis: there was a decrease in remittances from agricultural work in Britain due to the mechanization of British agriculture; the kelp industry, which had been the mainstay of coastal communities along the western seaboard, was in decline due to the emergence of cheaper chemical fertilizers from Germany; and banks and shop-keepers were withdrawing credit and also drawing in loans. The major issue was the failure of the potato crop, which remained the main food source for large sections of the population along the western seaboard. The continuous summer rains in 1879 led to the blight reappearing with over half of the crop destroyed, resulting in a yield averaging only 1.4 tons per acre, the lowest since 1847. Mitchel Henry, a landowner in Connemara, wrote, "Blank despair is settling down upon the district, and the efforts of the few in this locality who can give a little employment, are but a drop in the ocean of misery around."[79] An estimated one million people out of 2.5 million survived on the aid provided by relief organizations such as the Mansion House Relief Committee, the Duchess of Marlborough Relief Committee, the *New York Herald* Relief Committee and the Land League. The British government, in contrast, refused to acknowledge there was a crisis stating the claims were exaggerated and that these communities were always poor and looking for external support. Only 15 of the 350 families on Richard Berridge's estate at Rosmuc were able to support themselves, while the journalist, Bernard Becker, described the people in the villages of Cusheen and Derryinver, who were suffering with fever, as having "high cheek bones and hollow eyes."[80] While mortality levels were not as high as those during the Great Hunger, deaths from famine did occur. The chairman of the Inverin Relief Committee, Father P. Mannion, told the Mansion House Relief Committee in May 1880, that the destitution in his parish was so great that "in a short time several families must inevitably die of starvation unless aided from some source or other."[81]

Gerard Moran's essay indicates that James Hack Tuke's remedy was the removal of the surplus population to North America where there was a demand for labour, while at the same time farms would be consolidated into economic holdings for those who remained. While the scheme was radical, it did have a significant impact not only on those who left for the United States and Canada, but also for those who remained in Connemara and Mayo. During famines and economic crises, emigration became the safety valve for many people attempting to avoid hunger and deprivation. In Ireland, people left for Canada, the United States, Britain, Australia and other destinations. People can only emigrate when they have the means, through their savings or assistance from friends and relations. During the Forgotten Famine many in the west of Ireland did not possess the funds, but there were those who were prepared to pay their passage to a better life. Jane Kennedy's essay on the Connemaras deals with one such scheme, pioneered by Father James Nugent from Liverpool, who was so moved by the reports from Connemara that he established a fund to send 369 people to Minnesota, where Bishop John Ireland of St Paul had agreed to provide them with farms at Graceville. Were these emigrants suited to a farming life on the prairies having been subsistence dwellers in Connemara? Within a year, John Ireland was forced to repatriate most of these emigrants to St Paul, where they resided in an area known as "the Connemara Patch," which existed up till the

1950s. Margaret Lynch's contribution also deals with assisted emigrants from the Belmullet and Newport Poor Law Unions who left between 1883 and 1884 and settled in Cleveland. Many came from Achill Island and were joining friends and relations already in Cleveland, who were prepared to provide them with support. This trans-migration study indicates the importance of the chain process for Irish emigrants.

The intervention of governments, local elites, the international community and private charities in the provision of relief and aid was an important component in counteracting food shortages and famine. Questions have been asked of the British government's inadequate role in the provision of relief and food during periods of crises as witnessed during the Great Hunger and the Forgotten Famine of 1879–82. On both occasions, it was left to private agencies such as the Society of Friends, the Mansion House Relief Committee and others to intervene and provide support to vulnerable people. The role of the international community was particularly important during the various crises in the 19th century. For example, when it became known that Ireland was facing another calamity in 1879, the Mayor of Adelaide in Australia contacted the Mayor of Dublin, Edmund Dwyer Gray, and asked "Does present distress in Ireland warrant action being taken here for its relief?"[82] Within days, a relief committee had been established in Adelaide and aid was sent to Ireland. While precise amounts are difficult to compute, in excess of £400,000 was sent to Ireland by the international community in 1879–80. As the Mansion House Relief Committee pointed out, "the money collected in remote cities in Australia and New Zealand one week was feeding the famished peasants of Connemara the next."[83] The Mansion House Relief Committee received a total of £94,916 from Australia, while £26,875 was received from North America and £32,156 from Europe.

Harvey Strum's essay highlights how the American public came to the assistance of the starving Irish, the most notable action being the sending of a cargo of food on the U.S.S. *Constellation* to Cork in April 1880. This "errand of mercy" mirrored the *Jamestown* arriving with food from the United States in 1847. Catherine Shannon extends this theme by showing how individuals, together with the Catholic Church in Massachusetts, mobilized to send subscriptions to Ireland after 1879 to help ward off famine. Many were either immigrants or the children of Irish immigrants. Significantly, women were at the heart of this philanthropic endeavor.

Christine Kinealy explores famines in the west of Ireland in the final decade of the 19th century, by examining the role of one woman, Maud Gonne, who combined hands-on activism with a life-long commitment to social justice. Her actions not only inserted her amongst the pantheon of notable Irish republican women but placed her within an inventory of selfless individuals who risked their own lives to assist the starving Irish. The visit of Queen Victoria to Dublin in 1900, the eponymous "Famine Queen" of Gonne's polemical article, brought to a close a century of famine and mass emigration.

Eileen Moore Quinn takes the story of Irish hunger and famine overseas, but eastwards to Scotland. Her findings, based on interviews with female "tattie-hokers," provides a powerful insight into the role of seasonal migration in providing an economic safety net. It is also a reminder of the multi-faceted function of women emigrants. Art Historian, Niamh Ann Kelly, examines how two women Irish artists, namely Lilian Lucy Davidson and Muriel Brandt, responded to the centenary of the Great Famine by "imaging" and reimagining hunger. Significantly, in addition to creating a number of powerful works of art, they were offering an important commentary on the socio-economic realities of food politics in early-20th-century Ireland.

The early decades of the 20th century in Ireland were dominated by the quest for independence, and the latter ones, by bitter conflict in the north of the country; each resulted in the loss of thousands of Irish lives. Much of the century was also marked by hunger, poverty and emigration throughout the island. In the newly created Free State, the early years of independence were marked by unrelenting rainfall and poor harvests in 1923 and 1924. By the middle of the latter year, it was reported that 75 percent of people in Connemara had no potatoes, still their staple diet, with people surviving on shell-fish or anything else they could find.[84] In an attempt to assuage panic and minimize negative media, Patrick Hogan, the Minister for Lands and Agriculture repeatedly denied the existence of famine. In December 1924, he issued a statement that:

> There was no famine in any part of the country in the strict sense of the word, and scare statements that there was a fuel famine or a potato famine were inaccurate and misleading. There was a shortage of potatoes in limited districts, and it might be that potatoes generally would not keep as well. He himself believed they would keep. The real fear was not a shortage or the danger that the potatoes would not keep, but that in some areas where there was extreme poverty, the people might use the potatoes which they should keep for seed, and that, as a result, there would be a shortage of seed next year. That was the real problem at the moment.[85]

Such reports and responses were redolent of 1847 and 1880.

The rapid economic growth that commenced in the mid-1990s proved to be as dramatic as it was short-lived, with the Irish economy plunging into recession—and austerity—after 2008.[86] Within less than ten years though, the Irish economy had turned around, demonstrating its traditional ability to overcome periods of adversity. In 2017, the Republic of Ireland was rated as number one in the world in terms of food security, that is, in relation to "affordability, availability, and quality and safety of food and food systems." Although in 2018, it had dropped to second place, it marked an overturn of centuries of perennial poverty and famines.[87] Nonetheless, in Ireland as elsewhere, systemic economic inequalities ensure that those with low, or no, income, remain vulnerable, if sometimes, invisible. The final chapters show how hunger continued to shape lives, whether as a lived experience or as a haunting memory.

The importance of immediate and direct international intervention during periods of famine are as important today as they were in the 18th and 19th centuries. Irish relief organisations such as Concern and Goal play an important role in long-term, as well as short-term, relief in those areas of the world where help is required. While the provision of immediate aid is essential during periods of crises, the need for more permanent solutions is also necessary to provide a more sustainable future for the affected areas. Moreover, although famines might grab headlines, food security, even in some of the richest countries in the world, remains a serious if sometimes invisible aspect of contemporary society. This volume concludes with a timely and thought-provoking chapter by Mary Corcoran, undertaken when she was a Fulbright Visiting Scholar at Ireland's Great Hunger Institute in 2018. The challenge of finding sustainable solutions to food supplies is the theme of Corcoran's contribution, which she examines in relation to present-day New Haven. The city is home to the "Ivy League" college, Yale University, thus privilege and extreme poverty exist cheek by jowl. This situation is replicated throughout the United States. As Corcoran reminds us, however, lessons from the Great Famine and other subsistence crises, which remain relevant today, are repeatedly ignored. Instead, the poor continue to be blamed for their poverty.[88]

Making history more visible and accessible has been at the center of the mission of Ireland's Great Hunger Institute at Quinnipiac University and of their partner, the Irish Heritage Trust at Strokestown Park. To this end, the final chapters by Alan Singer and Robert Young show how, in two different ways, information about Irish famines are being made available and relevant. Singer has achieved this through his contribution to New York's Great Famine Curriculum, which, like his teaching at Hofstra University, is firmly grounded in universal ideas about social justice. Young, who looks after the extensive Irish Collection at Quinnipiac University, provides an overview of a special and unique holding, known as The Poverty Collection.

Shortly after these chapters were completed, the world found itself at war with a new, deadly enemy, Coronovirus, a virus that led to a pandemic of respiratory illnesses, designated "COVID—19." Its spread and impact were swift. The people and government of the Republic of Ireland—a country familiar with adversity—won early praise for their handling of the crisis.[89] Unfortunately, in the United States, the inequalities referred to in Mary Corcoran's chapter, appeared to leave the many lower income families vulnerable and hungry. A report in early April 2020 stated that the number of people experiencing food insecurity in the country, from its existing base of 37 million people, had risen by 40 or 50 percent within the previous month, and was continuing to climb.[90] Headlines such as "Food banks are overrun, as surging hunger meets dwindling supplies" were reminiscent of scenes from the Great Hunger and other famines.[91] Moreover, in the U.S. and elsewhere, deaths were disproportionately higher amongst the poorest groups, most especially minority and other traditionally disadvantaged groups.[92] Other parts of the world, especially developing areas, experienced similar inefficiencies with food supplies and distribution, resulting in a similar outcome.[93] Unusually though, while historically hunger has exacerbated the spread of disease, during this catastrophe, disease has compounded the problem of hunger.[94]

The COVID–19 pandemic has presented a watershed moment in international history, while its legacy—just as with the Great Hunger—is likely to be transgenerational.[95] Although some of the problems associated with this pandemic are new, issues of social justice, discrimination, entitlement to assistance, unregulated markets and economic inequalities, remain relevant to minimizing its impact and spread. The same disparities and discriminatory practices were evident during each of Ireland's numerous famines. Ireland's long history of poverty, famine, disease and death, provide a poignant reminder of resilience in the face of tragedy.

NOTES

1. "World Population: 2020 Overview," *YaleGlobal Online* at: https://yaleglobal.yale.edu/content/world-population–2020-overview.
2. "Deep Global Recession in 2020 as Coronavirus Crisis Escalates," *Fitch Ratings*, 2 April 2020, at: www.fitchratings.com/research/sovereigns/deep-global-recession-in–2020-as-coronavirus-crisis-escalates–02–04–2020.
3. "When a food security crisis becomes a famine," United Nations, 2011, www.un.org/apps/news/story.asp?NewsID=39113.
4. See, Paul Howe and Stephen Devereux, "Famine Intensity and Magnitude Scales: A Proposal for an Instrumental Definition of Famine," in *Disasters*, 28 Jan. 2005 (4), 353–72; Alex Dewaal, "Historic famines and episodes of mass intentional starvation," 12 Oct. 2015, at: https://sites.tufts.edu/reinventingpeace/2015/10/12/historic-famines-and-episodes-of-mass-intentional-starvation/.
5. See the various debates in the British House of Commons in 1847 when opposition MPs, including William Smith O'Brien, Lord George Bentinck and Benjamin D'Israeli,

repeatedly asked that returns of death be kept for each parish in Ireland: DEATHS (IRELAND), House of Commons Debates, 9 March 1847, vol. 90, cc. 1101–3. Christine Kinealy, *the Great Irish Famine: Impact, Ideology and Rebellion* (Houndmills: Palgrave, 2002), pp 49–50.

6. The first national census was taken in Ireland in 1821 and every ten years thereafter. With few exceptions, the returns for 1821, 1831, 1841 and 1851 were destroyed in 1922 in the fire at the Public Record Office at the beginning of the Civil War, and the original census returns for 1861 and 1871 were destroyed shortly aftethe censuses were taken.
7. Since S.H. Cousens addressed the issue in 1960, the debate about mortality has continued. In an article published in 2010, the author concluded that there was significantly more emigration and significantly less mortality in Ireland than has been commonly believed: *H.P.H. Nusteling*, "How many Irish potato famine deaths? Toward coherence of the evidence," *Historical Methods*, 42:2 *(2009)*, 57–80.
8. Frank Rynne, "The Great Famine in Nationalist and Land League propaganda 1879–1882" (La Grande Famine dans la propagande des Nationalistes et de la Ligue agraire 1879–1882), in *Mémoire(s), identité(s), marginalité(s) dans le monde occidental contemporain* (2015), at: https://doi.org/10.4000/mimmoc.1864; for a discussion on the revisionist distortion of mortality etc. during the Great Famine, see Christine Kinealy, "*Beyond Revisionism*: Reassessing the Great Irish Famine," in *History Ireland*, vol. 3, no. 4, Winter 1995, 28–34.
9. Margaret E. Crawford (ed.), *Famine: The Irish Experience, 900–1900* (Edinburgh, 1989); Cormac Ó Gráda, "Famine in Ireland, 1300–1900," UCD Centre for Economic Research Working Paper Series, May 2015; Christine Kinealy and Gerard Moran, *Fallen Leaves of Humanity: Famines in Ireland Before and After the Great Famine* (London: Routledge, 2018).
10. George O'Brien, *The Economic History of Ireland in the Eighteenth Century* (Dublin: Maunsell and Co., 1918), p. 102.
11. Contemporary observers of the Great Famine, who represented the extremes of these interpretations, were Charles Trevelyan (author of *The Irish Crisis* in 1848) and John Mitchel (author of *The Last Conquest of Ireland (Perhaps)* in 1864).
12. This statement was made during a debate on Congested Districts in Ireland, in *The Parliamentary Debates*, fourth series, vol. xc, February to March 1901 (London: HMSO, 1901), p. 1436.
13. William Wilde's "Table of Irish Famines," in *The Census for Ireland for the Year 1851*, part v, Table of Deaths. Wilde identified 1,000 years of famine in Ireland.
14. Wilde's "Table of Irish Famines."
15. Mary Lyons, "Weather, famine, pestilence and plague in Ireland, 900–1500," in E. Margaret Crawford (ed.), *Famine: The Irish Experience 900–1900* (Edinburgh: John MacDonald, 1989), pp 31–74.
16. S. Engler, F. Mauelshagen, J. Werner and J. Luterbacher, "The Irish famine of 1740–1741: famine vulnerability and 'climate migration,'" in *Climate of the Past*, 9, 1161–1179, 2013, at https://doi.org/10.5194/cp-9-1161-2013, 2013.
17. David Dickson, *Arctic Ireland: The Extraordinary Story of the Great Frost* (Belfast: White Row Press, 1997), p. 16.

18. *An Act for the more effectual Relief of the destitute Poor in Ireland*, 31 July *1838* (1 and 2 Vic. c. 56).
19. Christine Kinealy, "The operation of the Poor Law during the Famine," in John Crowley, Michael Murphy and William Smyth (eds), *The Atlas of the Great Irish Famine 1845–52* (Cork University Press, 2012).
20. "Condition of Ireland: Illustrations of the New Poor-Law (from our own correspondent)," *Illustrated London News*, 15 Dec. 1849.
21. James Kelly, "Scarcity and poor relief in eighteenth-century Ireland: The subsistence crisis of 1782–84," in *Irish Historical Studies*, xxviii, 109 (May 1992), 38–62.
22. James Kelly, "Famine and harvest crisis in Ireland before the Great Famine" (Unpublished Paper, 1995). See chapter by Brendan Smith.
23. There is a memorial in Larne that commemorates the departure of the *Goodwill* in May 1717. No mention is made that the ship had first picked up emigrants in Dublin. For more on this, see Patrick Fitzgerald, "Irish Hunger, migration and denomination, 1550–1850," in Patrick Fitzgerald *et al.* (eds), *Irish Hunger and Migration: Myth, Memory and Memorialization* (Quinnipiac University Press, 2015), p. 22.
24. James Kelly, "Harvests and hardship: Famine and scarcity in Ireland in the late 1820s," in *Studia Hibernica*, xxvi (1991–1992), 87–93.
25. The Penal Laws were was mostly directly at Catholics ("papists"), but some restrictions applied to other non-conformist groups.
26. The "Glorious Revolution" of 1688 to 1689 resulted in the deposition of Catholic King James II and his replacement with his son-in-law, Protestant champion, William of Orange. In Ireland, the revolution was regarded as a victory of Protestantism over Catholicism; in England, it was regarded as a victory of parliament over absolute monarchy.
27. The Navigation Acts were passed by the English parliament at the end of the 17th century, to regulate the lucrative trade with the colonies in favour of England.
28. The Wool Act of 1699 was passed by the English parliament (11 Will. III c. 13).
29. David Dickson, "1740–41 famine," in John Crowley *et al.* (eds), *Atlas of the Great Irish Famine* (Cork University Press, 2012), p. 23.
30. Engler *et al.*, *Climate*.
31. Dickson, *Arctic Ireland.*
32. John D. Post, *Food Shortage, Climatic Variability, and Epidemic Disease in Preindustrial Europe: The Mortality Peak in the Early 1740s* (Cornell University Press, 1985), pp 269–270.
33. Christine Kinealy, *Charity and the Great Hunger: The Kindness of Strangers* (London: Bloomsbury, 2013), pp 16–17.
34. Fitzgerald, "Irish Hunger, migration and denomination," pp 17–28.
35. Ian McBride, *Eighteenth-Century Ireland: The Isle of Slaves* (Dublin: Gill and Macmillan, 2009), p. 106.
36. Fitzgerald, "Irish Hunger, migration and denomination," pp 17–28.
37. A Citizen of Waterford, *Letters on Ireland to refute Mr George Barne's Statistical Account* (Waterford: William Smith, 1813), p. 73.
38. *Act to prevent the export of corn for a limited time* (5 Geo. III c. 4).
39. *Act to punish people who attempt to prevent the export of corn* (11 Geo. III c. 4).

40. Kelly, "Scarcity and poor relief," pp 38–62.
41. *Act* to enable the lord lieutenant and council to prohibit the export of corn, grain, meal, malt, flour, bread, biscuit, peas, beans, potatoes, starch and hair powder for a limited time, 1796 (36 Geo. III c. 8).
42. Adrian Randall and Andrew Charlesworth, *Markets, Market Culture and Popular Protest in Eighteenth-Century Britain and Ireland* (Liverpool University Press, 1996), pp 172–173.
43. Act for the further advancement of agriculture, and a steady supply of corn for the city of Dublin, by extending the export bounties on corn and flour to the said city, and discounting all inland, canal and coast bounties thereto, 1797 (37 Geo. III c.24).
44. "Address to the Late Lord Mayor, Alderman Charles Thorp," *Freeman's Journal*, 17 Oct. 1801.
45. "Corporation of Hosiers," *Freeman's Journal*, 1 Oct. 1801.
46. Ian Budge, *Belfast: Approach to Crisis: A Study of Belfast Politics 1613–1970* (London: Macmillan, 1973), p. 15.
47. Randall, *Markets, Market Culture,* p. 173.
48. No title, *Belfast News-Letter*, 12 Nov. 1816; Ibid., "Diary of the weather," 17 Jan. 1817.
49. Ibid., "Provision for the poor," 12 Nov. 1816.
50. "Provincial intelligence," *Freeman's Journal*, 14 March 1817.
51. The Select Committee produced two reports, in 1818 and 1819.
52. Hugh Fenning, "Typhus epidemic in Ireland, 1817–1819: Priests, ministers, doctors," in *Collectanea Hibernica*, 41 (1999), 117–152, p. 17. See, William Harty, *Historic Sketch of the Causes, Extent, and Mortality of Contagious Fever Epidemic in Ireland in 1741: And During 1817, 1818, and 1819; Together With a Review of the Causes, Medical and Statistical, Productive of Epidemic Fever in Ireland* (Dublin: Hodges and Smith, 1820).
53. The historiography on the 1822 famine is limited. Exceptions are, T. P. O'Neill, "The Famine of 1822," MA Thesis (National University of Ireland, 1966), and the excellent local study by Gerard MacAtasney, *The Other Famine: The 1822 Crisis in County Leitrim* (Dublin: The History Press, 2010).
54. Conor McNamara, 'Pray pity your poor people . . . the Mahon papers and the famine of 1822 in the west', *History Ireland*, 19.5 (Sept./Oct. 2011), pp 26–27.
55. William Gregory (1766–1840), whose family seat was Coole Park in County Galway, served in the Irish parliament from 1798 to 1800. He was grandfather of William Gregory (1816–92) who was responsible for the introduction of the draconian Gregory Clause in 1847.
56. W. Gregory to C. Grant, 1819 (n.d.), in Lady Gregory (ed.), *Mr Gregory's Letter Box, 1813–30* (London: Smith, Elder and Co., 1898), p. 217.
57. Stephen A. Royle, "Irish Famine relief in the early nineteenth century: The 1822 Famine on the Aran Islands," in *Irish Economic and Social History*, 11 (1984), 44–59, p. 46.
58. Robert Banks Jenkinson, 2nd Earl of Liverpool (1770–1828) served as Prime Minister from 1812 to 1827. He was noted for his repressive response to riots in England in 1819,and in Ireland in 1822 and 1825.
59. Earl of Liverpool, Distress in Ireland, *Hansard*, House of Lords Debates, 17 May 1822, vol. 7, c. 671.

60. Ibid.
61. *Report of the Committee Appointed at the Mansion House in London ... 24th March, 1831 for the Purpose of Adopting Measures for the Temporary Relief of the Distress ... in the West of Ireland, Together With an Appendix* (London: George Taylor, 1831), p. 3.
62. F.L. Blosse, 5 May 1831, Irish Distress Committee, p. 27.
63. "Famine in Mayo," Connaught Telegraph, 1 June 1831.
64. Ibid.
65. Hugh Fenning, "The Cholera Epidemic in Ireland, 1832–3: Priests, Ministers, Doctors," in *Archivium Hibernicum*, vol. 57 (2003), 77–125; "Reappearance of Cholera in the South of Ireland," *Morning Post*, 4 Jan. 1833.
66. Quoted in, "Decline in Cholera," *Freeman's Journal*, 10 Sept. 1833.
67. The "Whately Commission" after its Chairperson, Archbishop Richard Whately, was officially titled *The Royal Commission for Inquiring Into the Condition of the Poorer Classes in Ireland* (London: HMSO, 1836). It consisted of three reports.
68. Christine Kinealy, *A Disunited Kingdom: England, Ireland, Scotland and Wales, 1800–1949* (Cambridge University Press, 1999 and re-printed, 2008).
69. Peter Carr, *The Night of the Big Wind* (Belfast: White Row Press, 1991).
70. "The storm in Newry," *Freeman's Journal*, 10 Jan. 1839.
71. "Awful and destructive storm," *Freeman's Journal*, 8 Jan. 1839.
72. "The storm," *Freeman's Journal*, 9 Jan. 1839.
73. "Relief of temporary distress in Ireland," in *Annual Report of the Poor Law Commissioners* (London: Poor Law Commission Office, 1840, vol. 6), p. 58.
74. The Lancashire Cotton Famine arose from the blockade of the Southern Confederacy, the major supplier of raw cotton to the mills in northwest England. One-quarter of a million people who engaged in cotton manufacture were out of work and dependent on relief or charity. There was international sympathy for the Lancashire poor, see, *New York Times*, 26 Nov. 1862.
75. Sir Robert Peel in, "Distress in Ireland," *Hansard*, House of Commons Debates, 21 Feb. 1862, vol. 165, cc. 548–592.
76. Reprinted in "The Famine in Ireland. England Reluctant to Afford Extraordinary Relief," *New York Times*, 29 Dec. 1861.
77. Ibid., "The Famine in Ireland," 5 Dec. 1861.
78. See, Kinealy and Moran, *Fallen Leaves of Humanity*, pp 37–40, 185–338.
79. Mitchel Henry, "The distress in Ireland," in *Dublin Review* (April 1880), p. 467.
80. Brendan O'Donoghue, *Activities Wise and Otherwise: The Career of Sir Henry Augustus Robinson* (Dublin: Irish Academic Press, 2015), p. 18; Bernard Becker, *Disturbed Ireland: Being the Letters written during the Winter of 1880–81* (London: MacMillan and Co., 1881), p. 57.
81. Father P. Mannion to the Mansion House Relief Committee, 30 May 1880 (Dublin City Archives, Mansion House Relief Committee papers, ch1/260/28).
82. *The Irish Crisis of 1879–80: Proceedings of the Mansion House Relief Committee* (Dublin: Browne and Nolan, 1880), p. 24.
83. Ibid.

84. Peter Cunningham, "The forgotten famine and how it put the fledging Irish Free State on the brink," *Irish Times* podcast, 9 April 2020.
85. "The Minister for Lands and Agriculture," *Freeman's Journal*, 6 Dec. 1924. He was challenged by Hugh Colohan, Labour TD for the Kildare-Wicklow constituency, who warned of the imminent danger of starvation.
86. Michael Böss, "The Collapse of 'Celtic Tiger' Narrative," *Nordic Irish Studies,* vol. 10 (2011), 119–135.
87. "Ireland slips to second in the world for food security," *Irish Independent*, 10 Oct. 2018.
88. Similar attitudes towards poverty, which informed British policy makers in the mid-nineteenth century, were recently articulated by American politician, Paul Ryan, *The War on Poverty: A Progress Report* (Washington, DC: House of Representatives, 2013).
89. "Ireland has strategy to 'break the chains' of coronavirus. WHO's Mike Ryan," *Irish Times,* 2 April 2020; "Mixed Approval Rating Fortunes for World Leaders During Covid–19," *Leaders' League*, 10 April 2020; "How a Pandemic has raised the Political Image of Ireland's Leader," *New York Times*, 11 April 2020.
90. "COVID–19 crisis heaps pressure on nation's food banks," *NBC News,* 7 April 2020.
91. This was a headline in the *New York Times*, 8 April 2020.
92. Rev. Al Sharpton, "Coronavirus deaths in the U.S. reveal a startling truth about America's 'two pandemics,'" in *Think,* 10 April 2020.
93. "Eye on Africa: Sahel food insecurity: WFP warns coronavirus disrupting supplies," 3 April 2020, www.france24.com/en/eye-on-africa/20200403-sahel-food-insecurity-wfp-warns-coronavirus-disrupting-supplies
94. "Lockdown: Hungry people more dangerous than COVID–19, Nigerians cry out," *Vanguard*, 11 April 2020; "Instead of Coronavirus, the Hunger Will Kill Us.' A Global Food Crisis Looms," 22 April 2020.
95. Oonagh Walsh, "'An invisible but inescapable trauma:' Epigenetics and the Great Famine" in Christine Kinealy, Jason King and Ciarán Reilly (eds), *Women and the Great Hunger* (Quinnipiac University Press and Cork University Press, 2016), pp 173–84.

Early Famines

CHAPTER ONE

FAMINE AND POVERTY IN LATE-MEDIEVAL AND EARLY-MODERN IRELAND

Brendan Scott

In 2011, a group of archaeologists, exploring caves in Moneen, close to Ballyvaughan in County Clare, discovered prehistoric pottery, an antler hammerhead and a human skull. Subsequent excavations uncovered the human skeleton to which the skull belonged.[1] In 2013, an announcement was made that there was a strong possibility that these remains belonged to a person who had lived in the 16th or 17th century. The small size of the skeleton and its underdevelopment led the team of archaeologists to suspect that it was that of a pre-pubescent child, probably female. Subsequent analysis revealed that the remains belonged to a male who had died around the age of 14 to 16-years-old. There was evidence of stunted growth, almost certainly a result of malnutrition and hunger. Osteoarchaeologists confirmed that this young man's short life had been hard, punctuated with periods of malnutrition and severe hunger. These human remains and the story that they tell, bring into sharp focus the harsh reality of famine and deprivation and the devastating effects such conditions had on people in Ireland at this time.

Famine and its effects are obviously important themes in Irish historiography but surprisingly little has been written on the topic as it pertains to the early-modern period. Certain aspects of famine are mentioned in various studies, especially in relation to the Desmond Rebellion (1579–83), but few other publications have delved into this period in any great detail.[2] Indeed, the monumental *Atlas of the Great Irish Famine*, which contains over 90 short articles, only includes one essay that discusses famine in Ireland pre–1800.[3] Occasionally, scholars have investigated in greater detail early-modern famines, but these generally focus on specific events, rather than taking an overview of a longer time period. Studies by Raymond Gillespie and more recently by this author, for example, discuss the harvest failures of the 1620s and 1630s and the resultant food shortages.[4] Colin Rynne has also discussed in some detail the devastating effects that the Desmond Rebellion had on the Munster populace.[5] The excellent collection of essays dealing with atrocity in early-modern Ireland, edited by David Edwards, Pádraig Lenihan and Clodagh Tait, and published in 2007, contains some important details on famine during this period, but, by its nature, presents this material in a fragmented fashion, scattered throughout a selection of the essays.[6] Indeed, an article by James Kelly dealing with harvest failures and food shortages in the 1720s is the first detailed study of famine in Ireland at such an early point.[7] It is the intention of this chapter, therefore, to survey the causes and course of famine in Ireland throughout the late medieval and early modern periods (*c.*1400–*c.*1641), and discuss the effect that they had on Ireland's population.

The various annalistic sources are an important point of reference when searching for evidence of food shortages and famine in Ireland, particularly during the late medieval period. There are numerous references in the annals to famine in Ireland from the 15th century onward, normally through natural causes (i.e., not man-made through war or civil unrest). The *Annals of the Four Masters*, for instance, noted in the summer of 1434 a famine that was called for a very long time afterward, "Samha na mear-aithne," meaning the "Summer of slight acquaintance," so-called because, as the annalist recorded, "no one used to recognise friend or relative, in consequence of the greatness of the famine."[8] It seems that people were starved beyond recognition, but it is also unlikely that one season of famine could have caused this level of change to those affected, and it is more probable that 1434 was when a recurring famine and its consequences reached its peak, or rather its nadir. This appears to be the case as, in 1433, Mairgréag Ní Chearbhaill, a woman from a prominent Gaelic Irish clan in what is now County Offaly, invited large numbers of those affected by the hunger to a feast in Killeigh, County Offaly, "bestowing both meate and moneys with all other manner of guifts, wherinto gathered to [receive] gifts[,] the matter of two thousand and seauen hundred persons."[9]

The reason for this famine is not given in the Four Masters, but the *Annals of Ulster* records that 1434 was the year of the Big Frost and that "great destruction was inflicted upon the fowl of Ireland" during that harsh winter. It seems likely, therefore, that the cold conditions were at least partially responsible for the conditions endured by the people.[10] Another famine, just over 40 years later, occurred in late December 1478, but this time resulting from what the annalists termed a "big wind," which led to the deaths of a high number of Ireland's cattle, with predictably disastrous consequences.[11] This misfortune was followed in 1492 by further bad weather; a deluge of rain throughout the summer and autumn leaving the "corn crops of Ireland decayed," and the vulnerable, starving and in need.[12] A similar occurrence had taken place much earlier, in 1294, when, on 20 July, a great storm destroyed the corn crops "so that many people perished of the hunger."[13] The 1490s was a particularly harsh decade of unsettled weather. In 1497, it was recorded that there was: "Great famine through all of Ireland in this and the following year, so that people ate of food unbecoming to mention, and never before heard of as having been introduced on human dishes."[14] The *Annals of Ulster* reported:

> A very great, grievous famine throughout Ireland this year [1497], to which the folk of this time saw not the equal, nor like; for there was scarce an angle or recess in all Ireland wherein died not many persons of that hunger.[15]

Both the *Annals of the Four Masters* and the *Annals of Ulster* reported in 1500, in what were almost identical entries, that:

> There was continual rain and much inclement weather in this year from the festival of the Cross in Autumn till after the festival of St Patrick, so that the crops, particularly the wheat, were injured.[16]

Although it was not specified, localized famine likely occurred as a result of this latest crop failure.

Famine continued at various points during the 16th century, obviously climaxing in the horrors of war during the late Elizabethan period, but there were at least eight harvest failures between 1550 and 1600, which were not caused by warfare.[17] Studies of tree rings have demonstrated that there was an above-average level of precipitation between 1520 and 1630, which would have made crop cultivation difficult,[18] and the various annals record heavy rains and flooding in 1523.[19] Weather conditions continued to play a part in food shortages and, in 1541, it was reported that "there was much severe weather, frost and snow, the beginning of this year, which prevented tillage and ploughing from being properly done."[20] But in 1545, a "great dearth" prevailed, leading to significant inflation, so that sixpence of the old money was being charged for a cake of bread in Connaught, or six white pence in Meath.[21] Although we do not know how much these items cost normally, the increase was obviously enough for the compilers to mention it in the annals. This was not the first time that famine had caused such inflation in food prices—a similar situation had been recorded in 1497, which only served to exacerbate an already serious situation.[22] The extreme and changeable weather conditions of the 16th century continued to play havoc with Ireland's food supply, it being reported in 1574 that a severe shower of hailstones had fallen, unseasonably, on 1 May, which affected the grain supply in varying degrees around Ireland. Although primarily pastoral in nature, the Irish economy nevertheless did rely on arable produce, particularly in hard times.[23] Some areas were not affected too seriously, whereas in other unspecified parts of the island, the annalists noted that "The fields of green corn, which had been sown a quarter or half a year before, were left by this shower bare and barren places without corn or blade."[24]

It is also important to appreciate that famine did not always impact upon the entire island of Ireland—it was reported in 1586, that, unlike the south of Ireland, Inishowen, in north County Donegal, "had much flesh meat," so the people there did not suffer as much as others did.[25] Moreover, much of our information regarding these events come from the annals, which were mainly compiled in the Gaelic north-west of Ireland, and therefore lay much of their focus on that part of the island. The poor weather conditions continued and 1575 saw further disaster befall Ireland's food supplies as a severe drought hit the island with no rain falling from 1 May to 1 August, resulting in an "extreme drought." To exacerbate an already challenging situation, this drought was accompanied by a bout of the plague.[26] Further calamity again struck between 1581 and 1582 as "great wind, constant rain, lightning and much tempestuous weather, prevailed."[27] What is striking about many of these incidents is the wide range of extreme weather conditions—it is not just one type of weather event occurring—rather, many types are recorded, in all of their extremes, from floods to droughts. Severe weather events were not uncommon during the late 16th century and in 1585 it was reported that, "There was much rain ... so that the greater part of the corn crop of Ireland was destroyed." This was followed in the next year by "wet weather and unproductive corn" with "great mortality among the cattle," along with a "great destruction of corn," noted again in 1587.[28] Ireland's wet weather was noted by Lord Deputy Mountjoy's secretary, Fynes Moryson, who remarked how Ireland in 1600 was "open to winds and floods of rain."[29] The Little Ice Age affected not only the average temperatures and precipitation patterns, but also played a part in the increase in both severity and frequency of extreme weather events.[30] The inclement weather was commented on by many of the deponents in the 1641 Rising[31] and a generation earlier, Josias Bodley, a military engineer, complained of the cold he experienced in Ulster during the winter of 1602–1603. Bodley also noted the lack of food in the province, remarking that in Newry, "nor was there any bread, except biscuits, even in the governor's house."[32]

Table 1: Weather conditions and famine, 1433-1587

Years of Famine	Cause
1433-34	Frost
1478	Wind
1492	Rain
1497	Unknown
1500	Rain
1541	Frost & Snow
1545	Unknown
1574	Hail
1575	Drought
1581-82	"Great wind, constant rain, lightning and much tempestuous weather"
1585-87	Rain

Obviously, inclement weather conditions or other such natural causes were not the only reasons for famine during this time. The weaponization of famine, or at the very least the threat of famine, grew more popular as a military tactic in Ireland as the 16th century wore on, but it was not a new experience in Ireland. The years 1315–17, during Edward Bruce's invasion of Ireland, witnessed widespread famine as armies made their way across the island.[33] Even earlier, in 1271, what was described as a "great famine" was so severe that "multitudes of poor people died of cold and hunger and the rich suffered hardship."[34] It was no surprise that this hardship also coincided with civil disturbance in Ireland.[35] For almost 40 years of the 15th century, mention is made in the *Annals of the Four Masters* of crop burnings and raids on cattle or other goods by various Gaelic clans on their rivals, or occasionally by the English on the Irish. It has been recently estimated that the main occupation of roughly 20 percent of Gaelic Irishmen at the beginning of the Tudor period was military in nature.[36] These sporadic attacks were often one-offs, but resulted in some degree of localized famine, and people would do what they could to avoid such debilitating raids. For example, in 1475, the O'Donnells received gifts from the inhabitants of Mullingar in order to dissuade them from raiding the town, "the country on all sides of it having been already destroyed."[37] The O'Donnells and MacMahons led joint raids into east Breifne (modern-day County Cavan) in 1496, which along with a prolonged period of bad weather, resulted in crop destruction, and cattle disease, and spelled disaster for the people there in the inevitable famine that followed.[38] These raids increased during the 16th century and David Edwards has noted that by 1500 almost every Gaelic incursion noted by the Four Masters was accompanied by land and crop burning.[39] In 1541, the O'Donnells were again raiding, this time attacking the islands on Lough Erne, "so that he left them in want of corn for that year," a situation not helped by the adverse weather conditions experienced that year.[40] In 1568, the earl of Desmond led a raid into Kerry, causing most inhabitants to flee with whatever cattle they could bring with them. Desmond besieged the town of Lixnaw in Kerry, and the siege, coupled with, "Intense heat of the air, sultriness and parching drought," meant that the people and their livestock were "obliged to drink the brackish water of the river, in consequence of the intensity of their drought and the oppressiveness of their thirst."[41] The English engaged in similar tactics in Ireland, resulting in severe hardship for the people. The *Four Masters* noted the arrival in 1414 of John Stanley as lord deputy, describing him as a man who subjected as many as he could to "cold, hardship and famine."[42]

Table 2: Cattle raids in the 15th century

References to cattle raids/crop burnings	Years
Annals of the Four Masters	1408, 1409, 1410, 1412, 1414, 1415, 1417, 1418, 1419, 1421, 1422, 1423, 1424, 1428, 1430, 1431, 1432, 1434, 1444, 1445, 1446, 1449, 1451, 1458, 1461, 1464, 1466, 1468, 1471, 1473, 1475, 1477, 1483, 1485, 1486, 1487, 1488, 1489, 1490, 1499

How did famine and warfare affect Ireland's population? Around 1300, the population was estimated to be about one million—but, by the 15th century, that number had been greatly reduced by the disorder and plague that had hit Ireland in the 14th century. By the late 15th century, the population may have been as low as 500,000, with a rise beginning from around 1470 onward, although some have estimated it to be not far below 750,000 in 1500. From 1534, this rise was halted and began to decrease in some areas, with an estimate of 750,000 by 1600, although the most recent literature places the figure closer to 1.4 million. The plague epidemic of 1602–1604 may have reduced Ireland's population by up to 10 percent, although it did rise again after that, especially with the influx of British settlers into Ulster following the Plantation.[43]

The unsettled and violent events of the late 16th century contributed greatly to famine and general destitution and loss of life throughout Ireland, particularly in Munster and Ulster. Food shortages do not necessarily lead to famine, but, in this case, the joint blows of crop failure and food destruction led inexorably to such an outcome. During the hostilities between Shane O'Neill and the earl of Sussex in the 1550s and 1560s, Sussex slaughtered 4,000 cattle in Tyrone and sacked Armagh, seizing all of the food that his army could take and destroying everything else. This scorched earth tactic, and the starvation that inevitably followed, was, Sussex believed, the surest way of quickly bringing O'Neill to heel, but hundreds of innocent bystanders suffered and died as a result.[44] In 1573, Castlemaine in County Kerry was besieged by the president of Munster for three months, who finally took it "through the want of provisions, not at all for want of defence."[45] Much of the famine was due to the warfare triggered by the second Desmond Rebellion (1579–83) and the scorched earth tactics carried out by the various armies, both English and Irish, marauding around Ireland during this extraordinarily violent period. In 1579, both Desmond's sons and the English destroyed large swathes of cornfields so that "the country was left one levelled plain, without corn or edifices."[46] The Desmond Rebellion and the English reaction led to much of this violence, famine and death in the south-west. In early 1580, Nicholas Malby, then governor of Connacht, was spending much of his time chasing a supporter of Desmond named Richard-an-Iarainn Burke. Burke fled to Achill Island and was soon seeking terms with Malby. Bad winds left Burke and his retinue stranded on Achill, "during which time he sustained great misery by hunger and cold, whereby 100 of his people were dead and starved within the Islands."[47] In the summer of 1580, Richard Bingham, who later was appointed governor of Connacht, was a senior naval officer patrolling the Munster coast. Thousands of livestock belonging to the Gaelic Irish were confiscated and later killed, which had disastrous consequences for the Irish in the south-west. Although massive numbers of livestock were slaughtered, when the head of the fleet, Admiral Winter, came ashore at Kerry, there "came to him a hundred poor people of the country beseeching him for God's sake to bestow upon them some of that cattle to feed them." Many more livestock were slaughtered than saved, resulting in the deaths from starvation of many of the local populace.[48] Both sides utilized scorched earth tactics and Desmond's followers in 1581 managed to steal 7,000 cattle from their enemies, John Fitz Edmund of Cloyne and the Fitzgeralds of the Decies. This bolstered their supplies while impoverishing and weakening those who remained loyal to the Crown.[49] Lord Justice Pelham recorded that "the poor people that live only upon labour and fed by their milch cows offer themselves with their wives and children to be slain by the army than to suffer the famine that now in extremity is beginning to inch them."[50]

It was Edmund Spenser, then a secretary to Lord Deputy Arthur Grey, who later presented a notorious account of the famine being experienced by the Gaelic Irish and their suffering. Familiarity with this text does not diminish its ability to shock the reader:

> Out of every corner of the woods and glens they came creeping forth upon their hands, for their legs could not bear them; they looked like anatomies of death, they spake like ghosts crying out of their graves, they did eat the dead carrion, happy where they could find them, yea, and one another soon after in so much as the very carcasses they spared not to scrape out of their graves; and I they found a plot of water-cresses or shamrocks, there they flocked as to a feast for the time, yet not able long to continue therewithal; that in short space they were none almost left and a most populous and plentiful country suddenly left void of man or beast; yet sure in all that war, there perished not many by the sword, but all by the extremity of famine, which they themselves had wrought.[51]

Grey's tenure as lord deputy was especially violent and he was regarded by many as "a bloody man who regarded not the life of subjects more than dogs."[52] Nor was the spectre of cannibalism referred to by Spenser far away during the Nine Years' War (1594–1603). Fynes Moryson recorded stories of people eating the flesh of the deceased near Newry and William Farmer, a field army surgeon, later recounted how he came across children roasting and broiling the flesh of their dead mother. When questioned about this by the troops, the children replied that they would otherwise die as other solders had driven away their cattle. Asked if they would rather have meat or money for relief, the children cannily replied that they would rather have both. In one of the rare examples of compassion displayed by any side in the conflict, the commander of the English forces left food with the children, and the troops then went on their way.[53] Tyrone, the seat of O'Neill's power, was marked for destruction by the English and the O'Hagan chief in that area related that the remains of 1,000 people lay unburied along a 20 mile stretch and how more than 3,000 had starved in Tyrone. This was confirmed by Moryson who wrote of the poor state of Tyrone, "wherein we found everywhere men dead of famine."[54]

The loss of life continued as deprivation and destruction escalated. In April 1582, it was recorded that an average of 50 people a day were dying in Cork city and more than 30,000 had died of famine in Munster in the previous half year.[55] In 1582, as a result of the violence in the region, "it was commonly said, that the lowing of a cow, or the voice of the ploughman, could scarcely be heard from Dunqueen (west County Kerry) to Cashel in Munster."[56] St. Leger wrote that there was "such a famine among the people here, as it is to be feared this province, or the greatest part thereof will ere it be long be unpopulated."[57] The situation continued to deteriorate in Munster. In 1584, Kerry and Limerick were especially underpopulated, "consumed, what with the sword, and by justice, but chiefly by famine."[58] The massive population drop was regarded as a positive development in the eyes of the English—Sir Henry Wallop, who surveyed the lands of the Desmond rebels following the cessation of violence in 1583, remarked approvingly on the high mortality rates and recommended that the province could be repeopled with "a better race and kind of people than the former were."[59]

Although hostilities had ceased by the early 1580s, another island-wide harvest failure in 1585–86 further exacerbated the privations already being experienced by most of the population.[60] The population drop at this time has traditionally been viewed through the prism of the violence in the south-west, some historians estimating that Ulster's population was halved from the 1580s to 1607.[61] The Nine Years' War saw further famine, exacerbated by the military activities in Ireland. On 9 August 1597, Henry Harrington wrote of the difficulties facing the people in Cavan. He noted that as a result of "famine and extremity," the people there were forced to "eat horses, a qua[r]ter of a bad garron is sold for five shillings, their stud mares, their best relief."[62] Even spoiled horse meat was selling, so great was the need in the county. Fynes Moryson, writing about the Nine Years' War, also described the effects of food shortages: "Multitudes lay dead in the ditches of towns and other waste places, with their mouths all coloured green by eating nettles, docks and all things they could rend above ground."[63]

On 15 August 1597, the English soldiers' provisions were running low and "flesh indeed was already scarce." If they continued to go without meat, the military commanders believed that their best course of action would be to "break in amongst the rebel's creaghts, and so be furnished; or if the worst came, they had plenty of biscuit, and, for so great a service, their horses would supply the want of beeves."[64] County Galway was described in 1598 as being:

> In a manner unpeopled by reason of the spoyles committed in the last rebellion, partlie by the rebell and partly by the souldier, and the great famine that followed thereupon, which hath so wasted this countie that scarce the hundereth men or hous is to be found now that was several years ago.[65]

The local populace was suffering from the presence of the various armies in Ireland during the 1590s. Lord Mountjoy reported how in 1600, following a foray into Wicklow as part of his attempts to starve out the rebels, he "spoiled and ransacked the countries of Ranelagh and Cosshay, swept away the most part of the cattle and goods, burnt all their corn and almost all their houses, leaving them little or nothing that might relieve them."[66] The previous year, Mountjoy had carried out similar attacks in counties Laois and Offaly, noting again, that '"heir [the rebels'] country [was] spoiled, and their corn and houses burned."[67] Sir Henry Docwra reported in 1610 his attack on the MacSweeney Fanad clan on Inch Island in Lough Swilly—there, Docwra claimed, his men had destroyed about £3,000 worth of corn and driven off 2,000 sheep, 250 cattle and 200 small horses, known as garrons.[68] As a result of this famine, people began to travel to Wales and England in the hope of finding peaceable conditions where they could work and live, much to the displeasure of the English privy council, who ordered that they be returned to Ireland. This migration had begun in earnest from Munster in the 1580s.[69]

The early 17th century again was a difficult period for those living throughout Ireland. Inclement weather and onerous taxes were making life difficult in, and it was reported in 1603 that "an intolerable famine prevailed all over Ireland," which was somewhat precipitated by harvest failures between 1600 and 1603 and exacerbated by the Nine Years' War. This particular famine resulted in the death of vast numbers of people in north-west Ulster from cold and famine, a mortality rate accelerated by the theft of thousands of cattle during Gaelic cattle raids.[70] Poor harvests were again experienced between 1620–23, and in Leitrim in 1622, Cahell Grone McHugh referred to:

> the utter undoing of the petitioner, his wife, brothers and their 25 poor children who god knows have neither food to sustain their poor and hungry want, only in summer and in harvest but shamrock and farvell, in winter and spring water, grass and foghell.[71]

These setbacks were followed by widespread harvest failures in 1627 and 1628. The failing harvests of the late 1620s led to the granting of numerous licences in Ireland for the import of grain. By April 1629, the situation was dire, and the lord deputy wrote to the privy council in England, asking for an end to restrictions on the export of grain to Ireland, claiming that existing food supplies there would be depleted by June of that year.[72]

Acts of God such as harvest failures were obviously out of the government's hands (England experienced its share of harvest failures during this period also), but the problems experienced by the population in Ireland were made worse by payments due to Charles I from Ireland as a result of an agreement between the king and his Irish subjects, popularly known as "The Graces." As part of this agreement, counties were required to pay for the upkeep of soldiers billeted in each county. The final straw for many counties came with a demand in 1629 from the privy council to pay the tax due.[73] One county which had been stretched beyond its capability was Cavan, which was expected to pay £334 *5s. 6d.* On 7 July, the county sheriff Philip Reilly presented the order of payment to the justices of the peace at the quarter sessions and read it to the commonality, which refused to pay any of the monies demanded. Wishing to explain their position, the people of Cavan who were liable for this payment wrote a letter defending their stance, which Reilly sent to the lord deputy.[74] The letter described in graphic detail the famine conditions, which the signatories claimed were being experienced in Cavan. There is no indication whether the scarcity was being experienced throughout the entire county or just in certain areas, but the letter included signatories based from Virginia all the way through to west Cavan, virtually the length of the county, implying that it was a county-wide problem. The signatories claimed that, having paid similar taxes for the previous three years, they could pay no more. This, they stated, was a result of the situation described in the letter that it "is nowe come to passe that yᵉ dead burie the dead for hee that burieth the dead this day lyeth dead in yᵉ fields himselfe for want of foode."[75] Other sources point to a serious famine underway throughout all of Ireland at this time, and William Bedell, the Church of Ireland bishop of Kilmore, noted in a letter dated 24 May 1629 that "many are dead, the residue have no bread; horse and dog's flesh is eaten." He also claimed that 1,000 people had left his diocese for England to escape from the privations, and that extra assizes were being held to prevent the starvation of prisoners in custody.[76] This migration of people from Ireland to England was not a new issue—by the Elizabethan period, Irish vagrants were landing in England by the shipload, and the 1572 vagrancy act ordered that they be punished and returned to Ireland.[77] Between 1628 and 1631, another significant migration of people from Ireland to England, Wales and Continental Europe occurred. On 27 August 1628, the English privy council complained about the "great numbers of poore Irish people" who had landed in Wales, and ordered that they be returned to Ireland, with heavy penalties exacted from those who transported them. More Irish beggars, described as "great nombers of strong and sturdie Yrish beggars" were noted in Scotland, in November 1629, with particular emphasis being laid on their insolence.[78]

Those who remained in Cavan (and Ireland in general) during this period were not helped by the onerous charges exacted from the populace of which, according to Bedell, the Catholics were "paying double tithes to their own clergy and to ours, from the dearth of Corn and the death of their Cattle these last years, with the Contributions to their Souldiers and their Agents."[79] Consequently, the privations caused by an act of nature were being exacerbated by the actions of both the government and the Church of Ireland. There were attempts by individuals to alleviate the suffering which they saw around them, and in 1628, one Sir James Goghe left in his will malt, oats, barley and wheat to a poorhouse.[80] Some were not so charitable, however, and in Belfast in 1620 and Youghal in 1630, the corporations ordered the inhabitants not to take new lodgers without first receiving their permission. Dublin corporation issued similar decrees in 1623 and 1634, indicating that the possibility of the potential lack of essential food and supplies was of concern to those charged with governing urban areas.[81]

Cavan was not alone, however, in protesting against these payments.[82] Along with Cavan, similar letters from Armagh, Offaly, Westmeath, Donegal, Tyrone, Monaghan Kilkenny, Dublin and Wexford were also sent to Dublin. The language and tone of the letters varied from county to county, but they were united in agreeing that they could not pay this onerous charge during the current economic climate. Those writing from Wexford claimed that "trade [was] ruined by war, and many people in the town are dead with famine," and the petitioners in Monaghan went so far as to warn that enforcing the payment would "drive many of them into rebellion."[83] Worse was to come, with loss of life becoming commonplace during the decade following the 1641 Rising when a population which had reached between 1.8 million and 2.1 million, fell to 1.3 million by 1652, the dead being victims of intermittent war, plague and famine.[84]

Extreme and adverse weather conditions, added to internecine Gaelic warfare and brutal English military tactics, led to significant levels of excess mortality in Ireland throughout the 15th, 16th and 17th centuries. Lack of charitable institutions—one of the consequences of the monastic dissolutions carried out under Henry VIII and continued by his successors—also resulted in further suffering for those affected by food shortages, although private individuals, such as Mairgréag Ní Chearbhaill, did assist those suffering the most. Harsh weather conditions and violent military activities led, on more than one occasion, to perfect storm conditions, which resulted in catastrophic famines during Ireland's late medieval and early modern periods, but especially during the latter part of the 16th century. The philosopher Thomas Hobbes, writing in the 1650s, described life for anyone who lived on the margins of society in this period as "nasty, brutish and short." Certainly, in the case of the young boy found in the cave in County Clare, it is an assessment that is difficult to dispute.

My thanks to Professor Christopher Maginn for his comments on an earlier draft of this chapter, to the Moore Institute, NUI Galway, for granting me a fellowship in 2019 during which I undertook much of the research for this chapter and to Tom Sullivan, former Cavan County Librarian, Cavan County Council, and the Creative Ireland Programme 2019 for enabling my participation in the conference from which this volume is drawn.

NOTES

1. Marion Dowd, "About a boy: excavations at Moneen Cave in the Burren," *Archaeology Ireland*, 27:1 (Spring 2013), pp 9–12.
2. Anthony McCormack, *The earldom of Desmond, 1463–1583: the decline and crisis of a feudal lordship* (Dublin: Four Courts Press, 2005).
3. John Crowley, William J. Smyth & Mike Murphy (eds), *Atlas of the Great Irish Famine* (Cork University Press, 2012). My thanks to Dr. Patrick Fitzgerald for this point.
4. Raymond Gillespie, "Harvest crises in early seventeenth-century Ireland," *Irish Economic and Social History*, 11 (1984), pp 5–18; *idem*, "Meal and money: the harvest crisis of 1621–24 and the Irish economy" in Margaret Crawford (ed.), *Famine: the Irish experience, 900–1900* (Edinburgh: John McDonald, 1989), pp 75–95; Brendan Scott, "Select document: petition of the inhabitants of Cavan to the lord deputy and council, 8 July 1629," *Irish Historical Studies*, 43 (163) (2019), pp 111–25.
5. Colin Rynne, "Famine and displacement in Plantation-period Munster" in James Lyttleton & Colin Rynne (eds), *Plantation Ireland: settlement and material culture,* c.*1550*–c.*1700* (Dublin: Four Courts Press, 2009), pp 132–9.
6. David Edwards, Pádraig Lenihan and Clodagh Tait (eds), *Age of atrocity: violence and political conflict in early modern Ireland* (Dublin: Four Courts Press, 2007), especially essays by David Edwards and John McGurk.
7. James Kelly, "Harvests and hardship: Famine and scarcity in Ireland in the late 1720s," *Studia Hibernica*, 26 (1992), 65–105.
8. *Annála ríoghachta Éireann: annals of the kingdom of Ireland by the Four Masters from the earliest period to the year 1616*, ed. John O'Donovan, 7 vols (Dublin: Royal Irish Academy, 1851) [hereafter *AFM*], *s.a.* 1434.
9. Bernadette Cunningham, *Medieval Irish Pilgrims to Santiago de Compostela* (Dublin: Four Courts Press, 2018), p. 142.
10. W.M. Hennessy and B. MacCarthy (eds), *Annála Uladh: annals of Ulster*, 3 vols (Dublin: Royal Irish Academy, 1895) [hereafter *AU*], *s.a.* 1434.
11. *AFM*, *s.a.* 1478; *AU*, *s.a.* 1478.
12. *AFM*, *s.a.* 1492. The Annals of Ulster place this event in 1491: *AU*, *s.a.* 1491.
13. Richard Butler (ed.), *The Annals of Ireland by Friar John Clyn and Thady Dowling* (Dublin, 1849), p. 10.
14. *AFM*, *s.a.* 1497.

15. *AU*, *s.a.*, 1497.
16. Ibid., *s.a.* 1500; *AU*, *s.a.* 1500. The festival of the cross is 14 September.
17. Raymond Gillespie, "Harvest crises in early seventeenth-century Ireland," *Irish Economic and Social History*, 11 (1984), 5–18, p. 8.
18. Francis Ludlow & Arlene Crampsie, "Environmental history of Ireland, 1550–1730" in Jane Ohlmeyer (ed.), *The Cambridge history of Ireland, volume II: 1550–1730* (Cambridge University Press, 2018), 608–37, p. 612.
19. Ibid., p. 618, fn. 35.
20. *AFM*, *s.a.* 1541.
21. Ibid., *s.a.* 1545.
22. *AU*, *s.a.* 1497.
23. See Raymond Gillespie, "Economic life, 1550–1730" in Ohlmeyer (ed.), *The Cambridge history of Ireland,* vol. II, pp 531–54.
24. *AFM*, *s.a.* 1574.
25. Ibid., *s.a.* 1586.
26. Ibid., *s.a.* 1575.
27. Ibid., *s.a.* 1582. It was also recorded, however, that "there was a great abundance of nuts also in this year."
28. Ludlow & Crampsie, "Environmental history of Ireland, 1550–1730," p. 620.
29. Fynes Moryson, *An itinerary*, 4 vols (Glasgow: James Maclehose and Sons, 1907–8), iv, p. 192.
30. Ludlow & Crampsie, "Environmental history of Ireland, 1550–1730," p. 609.
31. There are numerous examples of deponents who mentioned the harsh winter experienced that year, including: TCD, MS 837, fos 4r, 36v–r; TCD, MS 830, fo. 40r.
32. Ludlow & Crampsie, "Environmental history of Ireland, 1550–1730," p. 631.
33. Robin Frame, *Colonial Ireland, 1169–1369* (Dublin: Four Courts Press, 2012), pp 128–9.
34. Seán Mac Airt (ed.), *The annals of Inisfallen* (Dublin, 1951), p. 371.
35. James Lydon, "A land of war" in Art Cosgrove (ed.), *A new history of Ireland, II: Medieval Ireland, 1169–1534* (Oxford University Press, 1987), 240–71, p. 257.
36. Christopher Maginn & Steven G. Ellis, *The Tudor discovery of Ireland* (Dublin: Four Courts Press, 2015), p. 37.
37. *AFM*, *s.a.* 1475.
38. *AU*, *s.a.* 1496, 1497.
39. David Edwards, "The escalation of violence in sixteenth-century Ireland" in Edwards, Lenihan & Tait (eds), *Age of atrocity*, 34–78, p. 45.
40. Ibid., *s.a.* 1541.
41. Ibid., *s.a.* 1568.
42. Ibid., *s.a.* 1414.
43. Gillespie, "Economic life, 1550–1730," p. 539; R.A. Butlin, "Land and people, *c.*1600" in T.W. Moody, F.X. Martin & F.J. Byrne (eds), *A new history of Ireland, III: Early modern Ireland, 1534–1691* (Oxford: Oxford University Press, 1976), pp 142–66 at p. 147; R.E. Glasscock, "Land and people, *c.*1300" in Cosgrove (ed.), *A new history of Ireland, II*, pp 205–39 at p. 212. Although Kenneth Nichols suggests that half a million may be closer to

the true population throughout the sixteenth century, "Gaelic society and economy," in Cosgrove (ed.), *A new history of Ireland, II*, 397–438, pp 408–9.

44. Edwards, "The escalation of violence in sixteenth-century Ireland," pp 76–7.
45. *AFM*, *s.a.* 1573.
46. Ibid., *s.a.* 1579.
47. David Edwards, *Campaign journals of the Elizabethan Irish wars* (Dublin: Irish Manuscripts Commission, 2014), p. 138.
48. Ibid., pp 127–32.
49. McCormack, *The earldom of Desmond,* p. 154.
50. Rynne, "Famine and displacement in plantation-period Munster," pp 134–5.
51. A. Hadfield & W. Maley (eds), *Edmund Spenser: A view of the state of Ireland* (Oxford University Press, 1997), p. 102.
52. Colm Lennon, *Sixteenth-century Ireland: The incomplete conquest* (Dublin: Gill and Macmillan, 1994), p. 227.
53. John McGurk, "The pacification of Ulster, 1600–3" in Edwards, Lenihan & Tait (eds), *Age of atrocity*, 119–29, pp 123–4.
54. Quoted in McGurk, "The Pacification of Ulster, 1600–3," p. 124.
55. Michael MacCarthy-Murrough, *The Munster Plantation* (Oxford University Press, 1986), p. 26.
56. *AFM*, *s.a.* 1582.
57. Quoted in Rynne, "Famine and displacement in plantation-period Munster," p. 136.
58. MacCarthy-Murrough, *The Munster plantation*, p. 29; Rynne, "Famine and displacement in plantation-period Munster," p. 136.
59. Quoted in Nicholas Canny, *Making Ireland British, 1580–1650* (Oxford University Press, 2001), p. 109.
60. Rynne, "Famine and displacement in plantation-period Munster," p. 136.
61. William Smyth, *Map-making, landscapes and memory: a geography of colonial and early-modern Ireland,* c.*1530–1750* (Cork University Press, 2006), p. 349.
62. *HMC Salisbury*, vii, p. 340.
63. Quoted in Gráinne Henry, "Ulster exiles in Europe, 1605–1641" in Brian Mac Cuarta (ed.), *Ulster 1641: aspects of the rising* (Belfast: Institute of Irish Studies at Queen's University, 1993), 37–60, p. 37.
64. *Cal. S.P. Ire., 1597*, p. 383.
65. *Description of Ireland, 1598*, pp 138–9.
66. *Cal. S.P. Ire., 1600–01*, p. 178.
67. Ibid.
68. McGurk, "The pacification of Ulster, 1600–3," p. 122.
69. Henry, "Ulster exiles in Europe, 1605–1641," p. 39.
70. *AFM*, *s.a.* 1603; Ludlow & Crampsie, "Environmental history of Ireland, 1550–1730," p. 612.
71. Brian Mac Cuarta, "The plantation of Leitrim, 1620–41," *Irish Historical Studies*, 32:127 (2001), 297–320, p. 314.

72. Gillespie, "Harvest crises in early seventeenth-century Ireland," 7–11; "The lord deputy and council to the English privy council," 4 April 1629 (T.N.A., S.P. 63/248, f. 181).
73. See Scott, "Select document: petition of the inhabitants of Cavan to the lord deputy and council, 8 July 1629."
74. "Philip Reilly (sheriff of Cavan) to the lord deputy," 8 July 1629 (T.N.A., S.P. 63/249, f. 63).
75. "Petition of the inhabitants of Cavan to the lord deputy and council," 8 July 1629 (T.N.A., S.P. 63/249, ff 65–6).
76. E.S. Shuckburgh (ed.), *Two biographies of William Bedell* (Cambridge University Press, 1902), pp 297–8.
77. See Patrick Fitzgerald, "Poverty and vagrancy in early modern Ireland, 1540–1770," PhD, QUB, 1994. My thanks to Dr. Fitzgerald for loaning me a copy.
78. Henry, "Ulster exiles in Europe, 1605–1641," p. 39.
79. Gilbert Burnet, *The life of William Bedell* (London: Richard Chiswell, 1692), p. 46.
80. Fitzgerald, "Poverty and vagrancy in early modern Ireland, 1540–1770," p. 31.
81. Ibid., pp 54–6.
82. There had been protests in autumn 1628 against payments towards the disbanding of an army regiment: Hunter, *The Ulster plantation in the counties of Armagh and Cavan*, p. 166.
83. "Robert Forte [sheriff of the Co. Monaghan], to the lord deputy," 17 July 1629 (T.N.A., S.P. 63/249, f. 78); "Richard Chevers, mayor of Wexford, to the lord deputy," 21 July 1629 (T.N.A., S.P. 63/249, f. 80).
84. Smyth, *Map-making, landscapes and memory*, pp 160–1. By 1652, William Petty reckoned that Ireland's population had dropped to 40 percent of its pre-war level, Gillespie, "Economic life, 1550–1730," p. 546.

CHAPTER TWO

"SUCH FREQUENT WANTS AND FAMINES"

Philanthropy and the Famine of 1739-41

Karen Sonnelitter

In the 1741 pamphlet "The Groans of Ireland," an anonymous writer powerfully recorded the impact of the devastating famine that was then ravaging the country. This individual described witnessing "the most miserable scene of universal distress, that I have ever read of in History: want and misery in every face; the rich unable almost, as they were willing, to relieve the poor." The writer placed the blame for the catastrophe not on the extreme and unexpected frost that had first struck in 1739 and destroyed crops, but rather on the country's tillage laws which, in their view, meant that, "this Country, one of the most fertile in the World, is subject to such frequent Wants and Famines."[1] The famine of 1739–41 gave rise to an extraordinary wave of private philanthropy, but at the same time tensions existed between those who chose to focus on relieving the immediate distress and those who argued that time and resources were better spent on agricultural and economic improvement projects.

Eighteenth-century Ireland is often seen as a period of relative stability. There were no major rebellions until 1798 and, for most of the century, the Protestant Anglo-Irish Ascendancy seemed to rule unchallenged. But it was also the century of *Blian an Áir*, or "the year of the slaughter," a devastating frost and famine that struck the country from 1739 to 1741. Within the Ascendancy there was real fear that crises, like *Blian an Áir*, along with more endemic problems, such as poverty, represented a threat to the stability of Protestant rule in Ireland. In June 1746, the Earl of Chesterfield, then Lord Lieutenant of Ireland, wrote to Thomas Prior, the founder of the Royal Dublin Society, warning, "be as much upon your guard against poverty as against popery, take my word for it, you are in more danger of the former then of the latter."[2] Famines were a particular challenge since they exacerbated pre-existing social issues and tensions. Throughout the 18th century, the Protestant elite feared that any famine could lead to insurrection. In this period, members of the Anglo-Irish Ascendancy founded a range of voluntary societies and undertook a variety of philanthropic projects designed to reform Ireland socially, religiously, and economically. These projects can best be understood as part of a broad culture of improvement.[3] The famine that struck Ireland in 1739 revealed an inherent tension within this emerging movement between those who organized broad charitable relief efforts and those, such as the author of "The Groans of Ireland," who argued that alleviating the current famine was not enough. They believed that only through organized and rational political intervention, including changes to tillage laws, could famines, and the social threats associated with them, be alleviated or eliminated.

Famines were a regular occurrence in pre-modern Ireland; in general, they resulted from periods of war or adverse weather conditions. In the 17th and 18th centuries, Ireland experienced famines stemming from both causes. Years of difficult growing seasons led to famines in 1674, and again in 1690, the harvests failed in 1708–9, in 1721–22 and 1728–29.[4] The famine from 1739–41 was by far the most severe. It was regarded as the "worst human disaster" to hit Ireland in 100 years, and while demographic data is incomplete, David Dickson has argued that it had a higher death rate and greater impact on population than even the Great Hunger.[5] Based on hearth tax returns, Dickson theorized that the 1739–41 famine killed approximately 310,000 to 480,000 people out of a population of about 2.4 million. He concluded that there was excess mortality ranging from 13 to 20 percent. While the Great Famine killed significantly more people and led to mass emigration, it was also affecting a population that was three times larger.[6]

The crisis of 1739–41 was caused by unusual weather conditions. Generally a temperate country, Ireland was hit by a severe frost in 1739. The frost was followed by two years of unusually cold, dry weather.[7] Katherine Conolly, the wealthy widow of the politician James Conolly, wrote in January 1740 that, "such severe weather was never known" and "I am close by the fire yet a freezing."[8] General James Oughton, at the time a young Coronet, recalled that "The River Liffey was frozen over in a few hours' time, so that the crews of ships which were either driven in there or at anchor, walked ashore on the ice."[9] This extreme, unseasonable cold, followed by months of unusual weather patterns, caused massive crop failures. Potatoes, which had provided a cushion against catastrophic famine, were frozen and once thawed were inedible.[10] International wars and a continent-wide harvest failure meant that there was no external food supply to import.[11] Food prices rose so dramatically that even the very wealthy grew concerned. Conolly complained in March 1741 of the prices that she was paying for beef and veal, and worried throughout the crisis that her less wealthy sister, Jane Bonnell, was suffering. In 1740 she wrote to her, "I beg you do not starve yourself, which I believe you are apt to do."[12] The *Dublin Journal* reported in the spring 1740 that, "there is now as great Scarcity of Provisions in this City as ever known, and it is much to be feared all over the Kingdom, every Kind of Food being at vast high Prices."[13]

The author of 'The Groans of Ireland" provided a graphic description:

> ... the most miserable scene of universal distress, that I have ever read of in history: want and misery in every face; the Rich unable almost, as they were willing to relieve the poor; the roads spread with dead and dying bodies; mankind of the color of the docks and nettles which they fed on; two or three, sometimes more, on a car going to the grave for want of bearers to carry them, and many buried only in the fields and ditches where they perished ... whole Villages were laid waste by want and sickness, and death in various shapes.[14]

That writer estimated that between 200,000 and 400,000 people had perished from both hunger and the associated diseases. It was a loss that was, "too great for this ill-peopled country to bear."[15] Another anonymous pamphlet writer noted:

> ... it is computed by some, and perhaps not without reason, that as many people have died of want, and disorders occasioned by want, within these two years past, as fell by the sword in the massacre and rebellion of forty one. Whole parishes have in some places been almost desolated and the dead have been eaten in the fields by dogs, for want of people to bury them.[16]

Sir Richard Cox described the breakdown in cultural traditions that accompanied the famine:

> Mortality is now no longer heeded; the instances are so frequent. And burying the dead, which used to be one of the most religious acts amongst the Irish, is now become a burthen: so that I am daily forced to make those who remain carry dead bodies to the churchyards, which would otherwise rot in the open air; otherwise I assure you the common practice is to let the tree lie where it falls, and if some good natured body covers it with the next ditch, it is the most to be expected. In short, by all I can learn, the dreadfullest civil war, or most raging plague never destroyed so many this season.[17]

Suffering of this magnitude required some sort of response for both humane and practical reasons. Food riots broke out in cities and rioting descending into revolutionary unrest was a significant fear of the Protestant population. Charitable intervention began almost immediately and focused at first on providing heating fuel for the poor. In February 1739, the *Belfast News-Letter* reported on the efforts of local clergymen who were undertaking house collections to provide for the poor in Belfast. In Dublin meanwhile, "charitable persons" purchased large quantities of coal and meal to be delivered to the city's parishes and distributed among "poor and indigent creatures."[18]

Charity struggled to keep pace with the scale of the crisis, hence the writer of "The Groans of Ireland" lamented that "the rich unable almost as they are willing to relieve the poor."[19] In March 1740, residents of Dublin attempted to break open a bakery to steal bread, an event that was only prevented by a party of soldiers who arrested seven rioters.[20] Events like these explain why only five years later, the Lord Lieutenant regarded poverty as a greater threat than Catholicism. To prevent this sort of social disorder, government authorities stepped in. In Cork, city officials bought grain and meal in bulk to resell at subsidized rates. In all of the larger towns, local government began to regulate the size of bread loaves to prevent bakers from defrauding the public.[21]

Ireland in the 18th century lacked a statutory poor law. In practice, Church of Ireland parishes still attempted to provide for the needs of the poor within their parishes, but they lacked the income provided by a regular poor rate. Most Church of Ireland parishes were overburdened financially and struggled to provide poor relief in regular years and, during times of famine, that situation only worsened. In urban areas, ministers and vestry councils ran local committees that received donations and organized distribution.[22] A few cities had poorhouses, the oldest was the Dublin Workhouse, which had been founded in 1703 and partially funded by a tax on houses in the city. It was founded in large part to respond to increasing problem of beggars who were regarded as a nuisance.[23] Most poor relief during this famine was funded by voluntary donations, with even the Dublin Workhouse relying on private fundraising to feed the city's poor, so there was little impetus within Ireland to create statutory poor relief as it existed in England.

As with other famines, one result of the 1739–41 famine was mass vagrancy. In calamitous times, people left small farms and made their way to more populated cities and towns in search of food and work. Events like famines contributed to the changing demographic make-up of Dublin. Between 1685 and 1725, the city's population more than doubled in size, from 45,000 people to 92,000. It continued to grow throughout the 18th century and, for the most part, these new residents, many of them migrants from the countryside and many of them Catholic, were unwelcome. Jonathan Swift complained in 1737 that Dublin was "infested" with "strollers, foreigners, and sturdy beggars."[24] The Lord Mayor of Dublin lamented that the city had "become the common receptacle of objects disfigured and frightful, as well as pretending to be miserable from all parts of the kingdom."[25] This situation worsened between 1739 and 1741. Even at the height of the famine, *The Dublin Journal* complained that "strolling beggars" were "a real Burthen and Nuisance to the Publick."[26]

The severity of the famine revealed the complicated contemporary attitudes towards begging. While much was done to relieve the distressed, a general distrust of the practice of begging still pervaded. A 1740 performance sponsored by the Charitable Musical Society announced that it sought to relieve those who suffered privately, "Numbers of whome in this City as is too manifest, daily pine away for want of Food, thinking it worse than Death to beg from Door to Door."[27] A scheme by several local gentlemen in King's County in the winter of 1740 sought to relieve poor tenants who were ashamed to beg and therefore "greater objects of charity than common beggars."[28] There was discussion in Dublin of feeding the elderly and infirm at convenient locations in each parish, because the central relief operated out of the Dublin Workhouse was thought to encourage the nuisance of strolling beggars.[29] Famine motivated an increase in charitable giving, but it did not break down the traditional boundaries between the deserving and the undeserving poor. These attitudes might explain why during the years of this famine, there was widespread charitable giving in Ireland, but there was no major initiative to drastically reform poor relief. The central mechanism for poor relief in Dublin in 1739 was the workhouse, which was located on the south side of the River Liffey near St James Street. By 1739, it had become increasingly concentrated on the care of foundling children and would remain so for the rest of the century. Even when there was not a famine, the workhouse and Foundling Hospital faced severe budget shortfalls and struggled with mismanagement.[30] It was not until 1773 that the House of Industry opened in the north side of Dublin to provide another receptacle for the poorest residents of the city.[31] Most poor relief came from individual benefactors who did a lot of good, but many came to feel that working individually was not enough.

The 18th century saw a general trend towards the establishment of clubs and societies that served a variety of purposes—religious, political, entertainment, intellectual and scientific. It seemed a natural extension to establish voluntary societies that were devoted to charitable impulses. Organized philanthropy in the form of voluntary societies was only beginning to emerge in 1740, with the number of charitable societies increased greatly after this famine.[32] For the most part, emergency relief in 1739–41 was of the same basic nature that it had always been: voluntary efforts by the Church and local elites. During the famine of 1729, most relief efforts came from either the parish level, or individuals. The same was true in 1740–41. Among the wealthier classes of Ireland there was an awareness of the link between hunger and social disorder in towns, and this fear, along with humanitarian concerns, motivated elites into action. For example, early in the crisis a local landowner, William Conolly, distributed meal, coal and bread to the poor of the parish of Leixlip.[33] Most efforts were similar to Conolly's, involving either the subsidized or free distribution of food, or employment schemes.[34] One anonymous local lady sent three pounds of beef and bread to poor debtors in Marshalsea.[35] These ad hoc efforts, both individual and collective, were praised widely at the time. As a young army officer stationed in Ireland during this crisis, James Oughton lauded the response by Dublin's elites:

> It would be endless to enumerate the calamities occasioned by the intense frost which prevailed at this time oval off the northern parts of Europe. The humane and benevolent dispositions had a large field to assert itself in; and the Irish Gentry showed on this occasion, that their charity was not inferior to the hospitality they are so justly famed for. Exclusive of very extensive private charities, upwards of 1500 miserable wretches were fed three time a week with wholesome food by voluntary subscription in the city of Dublin, gentlemen of distinction superintending the provision and attending the distribution in person. And when the subscription began to fall short...the Primate made up the deficiency for several weeks at the expense of near £200 a week.[36]

The *Dublin Journal* also linked charity with Irish hospitality arguing in January of 1739 that:

> This country, which hath ever been remarkable for its great Hospitality and Charity, will no Doubt at this Time exert itself, and set an Example to the World, that although we are not as rich as other Nations, yet we shall endeavor to vye with them on this melancholy occasion.[37]

The writer of the pamphlet "The Judgement of God Upon Ireland" attributed the famine to God's punishment for Ireland's national sins, but still gave thanks to God for "raising up a spirit of charity" in the country.[38]

Katherine Conolly funded several building projects as part of a famine relief scheme at her County Kildare estate. She decided to employ the poor and hungry to build a huge obelisk on the northwest skyline a mile from her stately Castletown House, now known as Conolly's Folly. The obelisk, however, was erected by mistake on land belonging to her neighbor, the Earl of Kildare. She later funded the building of a large stone barn, called the Wonderful Barn, which served to provide employment during its construction and to store grain for future famines.[39] Conolly also donated food. She wrote that she sent 80 loaves of bread a week to Castletown and that 100 people were fed at her home in Dublin every day. Yet she worried about her ability to keep up with the need, "if this weather continues long I believe we will be all poor, for no charity can hold out."[40] A year later, in March 1741, she worried in a letter to her sister that, "Not a day but I hear of such dismall things from the highest to the lowest and the poor a starving. The great collection and great charities given here, but everything so dear that hardly poor or rich can buy bread."[41]

It was a challenge to maintain such consistent and sustained charitable giving, particularly given the longevity of the famine. In December 1740, the *Dublin Journal* urged the poor to be patient to "melt the hearts of compassionate people to relieve their necessities." While newspapers praised the beneficence of the elites, they also did not flinch from describing the harsh realities of the famine. Earlier in that same edition the paper had reported that large numbers of the poor were dying daily of flux due to poor nutrition. They also explicitly critiqued the continued excesses of the wealthy by writing:

> A poor Woman, with two infants crying over her, was found starved to Death in a ware-house in Dirty-Lane, Thomas-Street. If our people of Quality and Fortune would retrench their Number of Dishes, and many superfluities, what Numbers of Poor might be relieved![42]

Relief efforts during the 1739–41 famine exhibited a greater level of coordination and administration than earlier famines. Town authorities intervened in food markets in an attempt to control food prices and maintain order. Cork, in particular, had suffered from severe unrest during the famine of 1729. Nonetheless, there was rioting in some areas as residents attacked those thought to be keeping food in bulk, bakers being a frequent target. In December 1740, *The Dublin Journal* reported that in Youghal and other parts of the country the populace "will not suffer any Corn to be taken out of their Towns, either by Sea or Land."[43] The Corporation of Cork bought grain and meal in bulk in order to sell it at subsidized rates. The Lord Lieutenant prohibited the export of grain to any destination except Britain, which was an unprecedented move. In Dublin, relief efforts were centralized out of the Dublin Workhouse, where *bonafide* residents of the city were entitled to free basic rations, a measure which contributed to Dublin's relatively low mortality rate during the crisis. Hugh Boulter, the Archbishop of Armagh, acting on his own, launched a fund that would underwrite the cost of an emergency feeding program out of the Dublin Workhouse.[44] At its height, the institute supported up to 9,000 people, making it likely the largest relief program undertaken between 1739–41.[45] Other cities and dioceses saw similar interventions. Local gentlemen in Galway combined to feed 200 of the cities' poor, while in Tuam, Archbishop Edward Synge personally paid for food and medicine for all who requested them.[46]

Pre-existing voluntary societies struggled financially to respond to the crisis, but the impulse to respond through organized societies seemed to strengthen.[47] Boulter's fund for the Dublin Workhouse relied on funds from other anonymous gentlemen.[48] The Charitable Musical Society began to expand through organized performances, such as a 1740 performance of a play called "The Twin Rivals," the proceeds of which were used to relieve the poor of Dublin. The newspaper advertisement noted that the society had subsisted for three years out of its own private funds but now sought new subscribers, "it is hoped all charitable persons will exert themselves to be the happy instrument of so universal a good."[49]

One of the largest and most ambitious voluntary societies in 18th-century Ireland was the Incorporated Society for Promoting English Protestant Schools. Founded in 1733, the charter schools were intended as a nationwide network of charity schools with an evangelizing mission. They focused on admitting the poor children of Catholic families. Those children would receive a basic academic education, be taught a trade and, most importantly, be introduced to the Protestant faith. The Incorporated Society was able to ride out the famine of 1739–41 with what seems like relative ease and it may even have benefited from this situation. But the organization did struggle financially as a result of rising food prices. In its 1742 report, the charity praised the "uncommon spirit of charity" of the previous two years while noting that the schools were running a deficit because of increased operating expenses. Ideally, the charter schools were meant to support themselves at least in part through agriculture, a plan that generally did not succeed even in good years. The central committee of the society operating in Dublin had to increase food allowances to each school, fearing that if they did not, children would have deserted and returned to their parents. They also complained of increased competition for donations, "What has therefore increased the demand upon the society, has at the same time been a means of preventing a proportionate supply."[50] Children in the schools were spared the worst catastrophes of the famine because they, at least, had food. In a 1740 letter to their Corresponding Society, the secretary noted that charter school children were "better nourished than others of their low rank" that they had managed to avoid the diseases which "like a pestilence have swept away incredible numbers of the poor of this kingdom." They wrote that "the Destroying Angel has passed over the charter schools." This fortunate development was attributed to "the distinguishing favor and protection of the almighty."[51] Reports from local school committees said the same, noting the "healthy and vigorous state of all the children in this school, especially when compared with others of the same rank in the whole side of the country." They pointed out that while the rest of the region had been beset by a fever, the children of the local charter school remained untouched, a fact which they attributed to the "goodness and regularity of their diet, clothing, and the universal cleanliness of the children of the house."[52] In its correspondence, the society acknowledged that the relatively good conditions in the charter schools discouraged children from escaping. It seems likely that desperate economic conditions also led to an increase in admissions. While the charter schools were intended to educate children from Catholic families, they often had difficulty with this, and, in reality, many admitted children had at least one Protestant parent, and many were orphaned. The Catholic Church was understandably opposed to the charter schools and priests were said to refuse absolution to parents who sent their children to them. The famine allowed some Catholic families to overcome the fervent objections of priests. The society itself claimed in 1743 that it had 19 schools and could easily fill 10 times that number.[53] The registry of children did not survive for the first decades of operation so it is impossible to determine the truth of these claims and whether the famine did lead to an increase in Catholic children being admitted.

The impetus for improvement in 18th-century Ireland was not just about responding to immediate crises, there also was a desire and a belief that the causes of the famines, which seemed to strike Ireland so regularly, needed to be addressed. Charity work was to be praised, but it was also inadequate. The author of a 1741 pamphlet on tillage wrote:

> Had not the gentry, clergy, and corporate towns given liberally to the relief of the poor, at those calamitous seasons, those who perished must have been followed by as many more. But daubing and patching up all evils of this kind with late, and ineffectual alms, is a poor, desperate necessitous expedient. Are we never to think of preventing them? Are not the lives of so many people worth saving? Are they not our countrymen, our tenants, our flesh and blood? Shall we idly wish a remedy for such general calamities only while they continue to afflict or frighten us, but as soon as ever they abate, never once think of providing against them for the future?[54]

There was no shortage of blame to go around for the 1739–41 famine. The author of "The Groans of Ireland" blamed tillage laws and a lack of strong guidance on agricultural reform government, "the particulars left to the weak guidance or their private opinions, go astray, and wander in a maze of absurdities and mistakes; and 'tis from the want of them, that this country, one of the most fertile in the world, is subject to such frequent wants and famines."[55] There was a general sense amongst these writers that Irish agriculture was deeply and fundamentally flawed. Charitable giving during times of crisis was to be praised, but the best use of the resources of the wealthy was economic and agricultural reform designed to prevent famines.

It was this belief in part which fueled the foundation of the Royal Dublin Society in 1731, for "improving husbandry, manufacturing, and other useful arts."[56] Thomas Prior, the founder of the society, was particularly aware of the issues with Irish agriculture. Prior had been in Ireland during the famines of the 1720s and, as a land agent and a landowner, he was well acquainted with the devastating impact crop failures could have on the population. The same could also be said of the other founders of the society, most of whom were wealthy Anglo-Irish landowners who were involved in multiple charity societies. The society was prominent enough that membership became almost socially obligatory for members of the Anglo-Irish elite.[57]

The establishment of the Royal Dublin Society demonstrated that issues with the Irish economy were apparent well before the famine of 1739–41. Samuel Pierson argued in 1728 for a new method of plowing that would increase land production and improve yields. He argued this would help to prevent the "common calamity," (i.e., famine) from which Ireland suffered.[58] Thomas Prior, who had also established a reputation for his several pamphlets on Ireland's economic situation, largely attributed to the prevalence of absentee landlords and the country's relationship with Britain.[59] An anonymous pamphlet from 1737 warned that the country was dangerously reliant on imported foodstuffs.[60] The crisis after 1739 proved that to be correct. Prior agreed that action had to be taken, writing in 1741:

> supplies out of all proportion larger than at any other times were then charitably distributed for the relief of the poor, yet famine stared us everywhere in the face ... it is of much more importance to think of preventing the like misfortunes for the future than to lament those that are past.[61]

Prior's solution to Ireland's famine problem was to encourage the establishment of a system of public granaries. He argued that government owned public granaries, which would purchase the surplus, were essential to preventing future famines and would encourage farmers to continue grain cultivation by always ensuring them a market.[62] Public granaries were a popular solution to subsistence crises, but many authors argued that greater reforms were needed to stall Ireland's "declining languishing condition." The author of "A Dissertation on the Inlargement of Tillage" supported the establishment of a system of public granaries, but also argued for legislative intervention to increase tillage and the creation of a workhouse system.[63] Interestingly, while the writer argued for Parliament to intervene with regards to public granaries and tillage laws he did not support the creation of a national poor rate in Ireland.

Instead, he argued for a system of parish-based workhouses to reform and profit from the "able-bodyed strollers who make a trade of begging by day, and of robbing or stealing by night."[64] Poor relief efforts during the 1739–41 famine all indicate a similar fear over the consequences that expanding poor relief might accidentally encourage an increase in the number of vagrants.

Granaries were not the Dublin Society's only plan to prevent future famines. Throughout the 18th century, the society supported a number of schemes designed to improve agriculture in Ireland from increasing the amount of land under tillage to encouraging the growing of different crops. The society's charter from 1750 references large amounts of uncultivated land, although it placed the blame for this on the inhabitants of Ireland lacking the necessary skills or industry to improve cultivation.[65] The charter praised the society's efforts to encourage the draining of bogs and the cultivation of flax.[66] The Dublin Society also sought to encourage the growth of various industries which they argued would make the island more prosperous, and less prone to famines. The Dublin Society proved to have great energy throughout the 18th century for proposing solutions. In 1740, it began offering premiums for agricultural experiments and manufacturing.[67] However, premiums went entirely to schemes designed to improve agriculture and manufacturing and not to reforming the system of poor relief.

Eventually, by 1741, famine eased. In June, five ships carrying grain from America landed in Galway and grain prices began to decline. By the fall, the harvest was returning to normal. Katherine Conolly wrote in September 1741 that, "we have the finest weather I ever say and great plenty in the country."[68] The country slowly began to recover from the devastation of the previous two years. The famine of 1739–41 was not the last famine to hit Ireland in the 18th century, although it was by far the most severe to occur in that period and caused the largest reaction. By the later 18th century, Ireland's economic situation had improved and so later food shortages were not nearly as devastating.[69] During the crisis, many in Ireland worked to ease the immediate suffering caused by the frost and accompanying food shortages. Even after it had passed, that energy was redirected towards several voluntary charitable societies that worked to alleviate poverty and its symptoms around the country, at least for those regarded as deserving of poor relief. Others sought to address the root causes of Irish famines through improvements to Ireland's economy and agricultural systems, which they hoped would prevent future famines. Both trends illustrated that the Anglo-Irish Ascendancy believed, as the Earl of Chesterfield had warned, that poverty posed a greater threat to them than Catholicism. However, despite this common belief, they were unable to agree on how to respond.

NOTES

1. Anonymous, "The Groans of Ireland: In a Letter to a Member of Parliament" (Dublin: George Faulkner, 1741), p. 3.
2. Public Record Office of Northern Ireland (PRONI), T3228/1/26.
3. Karen Sonnelitter, *Charity Movements in Eighteenth-Century Ireland: Philanthropy and Improvement* (Woodbridge: Boydell Press, 2016), p. 2.
4. S.J. Connolly, *Religion, law, and power: The making of Protestant Ireland* (Oxford: Clarendon Press, 1992), pp 47–8; "William Wilde's Table of Irish Famines, 900–1850," in E. Margaret Crawford (ed.) *Famine: The Irish Experience, 900–1900* (Edinburgh: J. Donald, 1989), pp 11–13.
5. David Dickson, "The Gap in Famines: A Useful Myth?" in Crawford, *Famine: The Irish Experience,* p. 97.
6. David Dickson, *Arctic Ireland: The Extraordinary Story of the Great Frost and Forgotten Famine of 1740–41* (Belfast: White Row Press, 1997), pp 69–72.
7. David Dickson, "The Other Great Irish Famine," in Cathal Póirtéir (ed.), *The Great Irish Famine* (Dublin: Mercier Press, 1995), pp 53–4.
8. "Katherine Conolly, Dublin, to Jane Bonnell, 29 Jan. 1739," in Marie-Louise Jennings and Gabrielle Ashford (eds), *The Letters of Katherine Conolly, 1707–1747* (Dublin: Irish Manuscript Commission, 2018), pp 190–1.
9. National Army Museum (NAM), Chelsea: 1988–08–36.
10. National Library of Ireland: MIC p4679.
11. Dickson, "The Other Great Irish Famine," p. 97.
12. "Katherine Conolly, Dublin, to Jane Bonnell, 10 May 1740," p. 195.
13. *The Dublin Journal,* 12 April 1740.
14. "Groans of Ireland," p. 3.
15. Ibid, p. 4.
16. "The Necessity of Tillage and Granaries in a Letter to a Member of Parliament" (Dublin: s.n., 1741), pp 36–7.
17. Armagh Public Library: Lodge MSS, 1741.
18. *Belfast News-Letter,* 5 Feb. 1739.
19. "Groans of Ireland," p. 3.
20. *Dublin Journal,*7 March 1740.
21. Dickson, *Arctic Ireland,* pp 19, 24–5.
22. Ibid., p. 18.
23. Sonnelitter, *Charity*, p. 78.
24. Jonathan Swift, *A Proposal for Giving Badges to the Beggars in All the Parishes of Dublin* (Dublin: George Faulkner, 1737), pp 5–6.
25. J.T. Gilbert (ed.), *Calendar of Ancient Records of Dublin in the possession of the municipal corporation of that city* (Dublin: J. Dollard, 1896), vol. 11: pp 523–4.
26. *Dublin Journal,* 10 Jan. 1740.
27. Ibid.

28. Ibid., 6 Dec. 1740.
29. Ibid., 10 Jan. 1740.
30. Sonnelitter, *Charity*, p. 152.
31. Ibid., p. 165.
32. James Kelly, "Charitable Societies: Their genesis and development," in James Kelly and Martyn J. Powell (eds), *Clubs and Societies in Eighteenth-Century Ireland* (Dublin: Four Courts Press, 2010), p. 91.
33. *Dublin Journal,* 19 Jan. 1739.
34. Dickson, "The Other Great Irish Famine," pp 57–8.
35. *Dublin Journal,* 13 Dec. 1740.
36. NAM, 1988–08–36.
37. *Dublin Journal,* 10 Jan. 1739.
38. *The Judgement of God Upon Ireland, or Sickness and Famine God's Visitation: For the Sins of the Nation,* 2nd edition (Dublin: s.n., 1741), p. 40.
39. Dickson, *Arctic Ireland,* p. 42.
40. "Katherine Conolly, Dublin to Jane Bonnell, 29 Jan. 1739/40," pp 190–1.
41. "Katherine Conolly, Dublin to Jane Bonnell, 21 March 1740/1," p. 206.
42. *Dublin Journal,* 13 Dec. 1740.
43. Ibid.
44. Dickson, *Arctic Ireland,* pp 18–19; Dickson, "The Gap in Famines," p. 106.
45. James Kelly, "Coping with Crisis: The response to the Famine of 1740–41," in *Eighteenth-Century Ireland,* 27 (2012), pp 115–6.
46. Ibid, p. 116.
47. Kelly, "Charitable societies," p. 92.
48. Kelly, "Coping with Crisis," p. 115.
49. *Dublin Journal,* 10 Jan. 1740.
50. *A Continuation of the Proceedings of the Incorporated Society in Dublin for Promoting English Protestant Schools in Ireland* (Dublin: George Grierson, 1742), pp 3–4.
51. Trinity College Dublin: MSS 5302.
52. *Proceedings of the Incorporated Society*, p. 13.
53. Joseph Robins, *The Lost Children: A Study of Charity Children in Ireland, 1700–1900* (Dublin: Institute of Public Relations, 1980), p. 69.
54. "The Necessity of Tillage and Granaries in a Letter to a Member of Parliament," pp 36–7.
55. "Groans of Ireland," p. 4.
56. Royal Dublin Society Minute Books, vol. 1.
57. Sonnelitter, *Charity*, pp 103–5.
58. Samuel Pierson, *Further Considerations for the Improvement of the Tillage in Ireland* (Dublin: George Grierson, 1728), p. 6.
59. Thomas Prior, *A View of the Present State of Affairs in the Kingdom of Ireland : in three discourses* (London: Weaver Bickerton 1730).
60. *Some Thoughts on the Tillage of Ireland: Humbly Dedicated to the Parliament* (London: T. Cooper, 1737), pp 5–6.

61. Thomas Prior, *A Proposal to Prevent the Price of Corn from Rising Too High, or Falling Too Low, by the Means of Granaries* (Dublin: s.n., 1741), p. 2.
62. Ibid, pp 1–7.
63. *A Dissertation on the Inlargement of Tillage* (Dublin: S. Powell, 1741), pp 5–7.
64. Ibid, p. 63.
65. *The Royal Charter of the Dublin Society to which are added, the Society's by-laws and ordinances, for the good government of the corporation* (Dublin: S. Powell and Son, 1766), pp 1–2.
66. Ibid., p. 2.
67. Sonnelitter, p. 112.
68. "Katherine Conolly, Castletown to Jane Bonnell, Writtle, 22 Sept. 1741," p. 213.
69. Kelly, "Coping with Crisis," p. 122.

CHAPTER THREE

A MODEST PROPOSAL

Jonathan Swift's Solution to Famine

Peter Murphy

By the late 1720s, centuries of political, economic and religious struggles between England and Ireland had reduced the latter to a colony in reality as well as name. Laws passed throughout the latter half of the 17th and early 18th centuries had relegated the majority Catholic population to a subservient and oppressed position in Irish society. Nearly all rights—from voting to owning land, practicing religion, holding public office, possessing weapons, studying law or medicine, or speaking or reading Gaelic—were denied to them. Catholics were not permitted to attend schools, including Trinity College. The Popery Act of 1704 took away nearly all of their rights regarding the inheritance of land. By 1700, Catholics, who constituted nearly 90 percent of the population, owned less than 15 percent of the land. Other acts had all but ruined the economy of Ireland. Ireland was prohibited from trading with other nations or colonies, such as North America; all shipping had to be done on English merchant ships; cattle could not be exported to England; and the woolen industry was all but eliminated when the Wool Act of 1699 prohibited any exports anywhere.[1] Poor harvests during this period made it increasingly difficult for tenants to pay their rent. Many starved while thousands more emigrated to North America, both to flee hunger and poverty and to avoid further religious, political and economic oppression.[2]

During the previous decade, Jonathan Swift, the 18th-century satirist, essayist, political pamphleteer and poet, had led a relatively quiet existence, writing little that was intended for public consumption. Swift had spent the years 1710 to 1714 in England, trying to further his political influence by obtaining an appointment to an

English bishopric. However, with the death of Queen Anne in 1714, Swift's hopes for an appointment were forever dashed. He was appointed the Dean of St. Patrick's Church in Dublin, a position he was not overly enthusiastic about taking. His views on living in Ireland were reflected in letters that he wrote to friends in which he referred to his "perfect hatred to this place"[3] and expressed his deep dislike of "this scurvy country."[4] He had remained silent in the hope that a more preferred appointment would be forthcoming and therefore he did not wish to draw the ire of the English authorities. Silence was not a characteristic of his nature and he had soon returned to writing pamphlets and essays.

By 1720, with conditions worsening, Swift began writing about various economic issues as he witnessed oppression and poverty throughout Ireland. In a pamphlet titled "A Proposal for the Universal Use of Irish Manufacture," Swift, in an act of defiance, urged the Irish people to buy and wear only garments made in Ireland. England's restrictive trade laws were ruining the local economy and Swift saw this as a way to fight back. Leo Damrosch, a Swift biographer, makes two important points about this pamphlet: first, since the Irish were not being treated fairly by the English, their best hope of resisting exploitation was to boycott English goods; and second, Swift was helping to create a new national self-awareness, from which an independent Ireland would eventually emerge.[5] In 1729, Swift composed an essay entitled "A Modest Proposal: For Preventing the Children of Poor People in Ireland from Being a Burden to Their Parents or Country and for Making Them Beneficial to the Publick," one of his most known and analyzed works. As one Swiftian scholar has noted, "'A Modest Proposal' remains probably one the most infamous and widely-read of all works in the pamphleteering genre in English."[6] Swift's essay was written in response to the terrible poverty and hunger that Ireland was experiencing in the 1720s, along with the political, economic and religious conflicts that existed between Ireland and England. Many years later, Swift described what he had witnessed on a tour through Tipperary, "which is like the rest of the whole kingdom, a bare face of nature, without houses or plantations; filthy cabins, miserable, tattered, half-starved creatures, scarce in human shape."[7]

George Wittkowsky, writing three-quarters of a century ago, lamented the "almost complete absence of sustained scholarship on the subject of Swift's 'A Modest Proposal,'" adding that one searches in "vain for a serious critical article on this pamphlet".[8] If Wittkowsky were alive today, he would be pleasantly surprised how over the past several decades there has been an explosion of interest in Swift, with several biographies published, papers written, and seminars offered, including a three-day gathering in Dublin, in 2019.[9] There have been many different interpretations of "A

Modest Proposal," with scholars examining what may have influenced Swift. Others have looked at Swift's use of irony, satire and other literary devices. This chapter will examine the historical context and the economic conditions of Ireland in the early 18th century, along with Swift's use of irony and satire, especially in relation to the work of a contemporaneous figure, Bernard Mandeville. His attacks on the economic theories will be reviewed, focusing on mercantilism, the prevailing economic theory during that period. What perhaps makes Swift's essay so compelling and enduring is that there are so many perspectives the reader can take in appreciating this great work of satire.

In the late 1600s, during the reign of King William III and Queen Anne, the minority Protestant Parliament of Ireland passed the first in a series of laws, known as the Penal Laws, which greatly restricted the rights of Catholics. Many of these laws were already in place from earlier in the 17th century and "represented less the implementation of coherent policy than a by-product of new constitutional assumptions and of a new set of political relationships."[10] In a 1729 letter to his friend, the great English poet Alexander Pope, Swift wrote, "Imagine a nation the two-thirds of whose revenues are spent out of it, and who are not permitted to trade with the other third, and where the pride of the women will not suffer them to wear their own manufactures even when they excel what come from abroad: This is the true state of Ireland in a very few words."[11]

The late 1720s proved a difficult time, both for Ireland and for Swift personally. It was during this period that Swift lost the love of his life, Esther Johnson, who he referred to as "Stella." In early 1728, at the age of 39 and after a protracted illness, possibly tuberculosis, she succumbed. Swift was so distraught over her passing that he would not attend her funeral service at St. Patrick's, blaming his health. There has been considerable speculation as to the true nature of Swift's relationship with Stella. Were they lovers or just very close friends? Were they in fact married? In the final months of Stella's illness, Swift was often at her bedside, reciting prayers he wrote for her. Upon her passing, Swift spent three long nights penning a memoir entitled *On the Death of Mrs. Johnson.* In it, he wrote of her "gracefulness, somewhat more than human, in every motion, word and action. Never was so happy a conjunction of civility, freedom, easiness, and sincerity."[12] Her death led Swift to close himself off from friends and he ate little in the days following her passing. He did not see her die nor did he attend her service three days after her death. Forever afterward, whenever he spoke of Stella, his words were accompanied by a sigh.[13] Swift's mood was becoming increasingly more despairing as he grieved over the loss of Stella and the impoverished conditions that he witnessed while walking the streets of Dublin.

Swift's despair was clearly evident in a pair of letters he wrote to Lord Bolingbroke: "I find myself disposed every year, or every month, to be more angry and revengeful" and a few weeks later, "I never wake without finding life a more insignificant thing than it was the day before."[14]

Swift's "Modest Proposal" followed a decade of writings that attacked the economic system that Ireland had been laboring under, which included "advocating consumption of domestic products, challenging the existing political structures and criticisms of absenteeism and other dysfunctional aspects of the land tenure system."[15] The South Sea debacle led Swift to continue his attacks on "basing an economy on credit rather than on property—or, in contemporary parlance, on 'money' rather than on 'land.'"[16] The ensuing London stock market crash was felt throughout Ireland and England as thousands of investors, including Swift, had invested tremendous sums of money in what had looked like a "sure thing."[17] Swift penned in 1724–25, once again under a pseudonym, "Drapier's Letters," which led to the downfall of Wood's half-pence, an attempt by the Whig government's plan to make up for the shortfall of coinage in Ireland by minting copper coins. The critique of Wood's plan was really about more than the value of a copper coin: "It was about the status of Ireland as a kingdom."[18] At the beginning of the letter, Swift wrote, "A people long used to Hardships, lose by Degrees the very Notions of Liberty; they look upon themselves as Creatures at Mercy; and that all Impositions laid on them by a stronger Hand, are, in the phrase of the Report, legal and obligatory."[19]

By the late 1720s, the economic condition in Ireland had worsened as a succession of poor harvests, caused in part by unusually bad weather conditions, brought famine and disease to Ireland. This led to an increase in emigration to the American colonies for those who could afford to leave, but for the poor, poverty or death was often the result. People had started eating their potato crops earlier than usual as there was a shortage of oats in the summer of 1727. Therefore, by winter, when they would normally rely on potatoes as their primary food staple, the supply had diminished greatly. Hugh Boulter, Archbishop of the Church of Ireland, from his base in Armagh wrote to several ministers in 1727:

> As the winter subsistence of the poor is chiefly potatoes, this scarcity drove the poor to begin with their potatoes before they were full grown, so that they have lost half the benefit of them, and have spent their stock about two month sooner than usual, and oatmeal is at this distance from harvest in many parts of the kingdom three times the customary price, so that this summer must be more fatal to us than the last, when I fear many hundreds perished by famine.[20]

Boulter campaigned for emergency legislation to limit the conversion of arable land to pasture, and for compulsory transfers of corn to the north from the south.[21]

In the summer of 1728, Swift acted upon an earlier invitation from his friends, Sir Arthur Acheson and his wife, Lady Anne, to come visit them at their country home at Market Hill (now Gosford Castle) in County Armagh. Sir Arthur was an Ulster baronet and a member of the Irish Parliament. This area was mostly populated by Scottish Presbyterians (often referred to as Dissenters), as the local Catholic population had been driven off their lands by planters and previous oppressions. Swift witnessed for himself the devastating effects so vividly described by Archbishop Boulter. He stayed with the Achesons for eight months and what he saw in Ulster "informed much of the pathos and descriptive horror of his political writings during this period."[22] It is entirely plausible that his time in Armagh influenced his thinking on the state of the poor and led to his composing "A Modest Proposal." In a letter to his friend Pope, he spoke to the despair and dismal situation: "As to this country, there has been three terrible years dearth of corn, and every place strowed with beggars, but dearths are common in better climes, and our evils here lie much deeper."[23]

Through the haze of depression over losing his dearest Stella, and the economic malaise and political oppression that plagued Ireland, Swift sat down to compose "A Modest Proposal." According to John Stubbs, "The depression and famine he witnessed in the late 1720s stirred Swift to write his indignant Modest Proposal in the voice of a psychopath suggesting that poor Irish children could be farmed as livestock."[24] His own personal despair was expressed in a letter to Lord Bolingbroke:

> I never wake without finding life a more insignificant thing than it was the day before: which is one great advantage I get by living in this country, where there is nothing I shall be sorry to lose. But my greatest misery is recollecting the scene of twenty years past, and then all on a sudden dropping into the present.[25]

In one of the ironic twists of the timing of his essay, it was published in October 1729, in a year when the harvests had returned to normal after three years of a truly catastrophic hunger. While many members of the population were feeling better and a bit more optimistic, Swift chose to "castigate rather than cheer."[26]

Swift's essay has been viewed from a variety of perspectives, including his use of irony and satire. Swift introduces a spokesman in the essay, who has been referred to as the "Projector" or the "Modest Proposer." "A Modest Proposal" begins innocuously enough by describing the problems of beggars and homeless children in Ireland:

> It is a melancholy Object to those, who walk through this great Town, or travel in the Country, when they see the Streets, the Roads, and Cabbin-doors crowded with

> beggars of the female sex, followed by three, four, or six Children, all in rags, and importuning every Passenger for an Alms. These Mothers, instead of being able to work for their honest livelihood, are forced to employ all their time in strolling to beg Sustenance for their helpless infants who, as they grow up, either turn Thieves for want of work, or leave their dear native country ...[27]

The first-time reader is lured into thinking perhaps that this is a serious analysis of the economic conditions plaguing Ireland at that time. Swift initially misleads the reader into believing that this is an empathetic individual who is proposing an altruistic solution to the problem of poverty and homelessness. The proposal appears modest at first, being introduced with terms such as, "I shall now therefore humbly propose my own thoughts..." and "I do therefore humbly offer it to publick consideration..."[28] Swift's use of "modest" to describe the proposal, when it is in fact a horrific and unacceptable solution, is an early example of his use of irony to shock his audience.

In utilizing a projector in this way, Swift is following an ancient classical rhetorical tradition, which is an "important constituent of Swift's irony," relying on one of Aristotle's three kinds of proof: the ethical proof. Charles Allen Beaumont, a mid-20th-century Swiftian scholar, wrote that "within the ironic inversion, the projector is humane, self-confident, reasonable, competent, and somewhat exhausted in his attempts to improve his native kingdom."[29] The Proposer first says that:

> My intention is very far from being confined to provide only for the children of professed beggars: it is of a much greater extent, and shall take in the whole number of infants at a certain age, who are born of parents in effect as little able to support them, as those who demand our charity in the streets.

The benevolent irony is later expressed when he suggests that:

> there is likewise another great advantage in my scheme, that it will prevent those voluntary abortions, and that horrid practice of women murdering their bastard children, alas! too frequent among us, sacrificing the poor innocent babes, I doubt, more to avoid the expense than the shame, which would move tears and pity in the most savage and inhuman breast.

A short while later, after using demographic statistics to build an argument, he turns the earlier empathy on its head by stating clearly and unambiguously what his idea actually is:

> I have been assured by a very knowing American of my acquaintance in London, that a young healthy child well nursed, is, at a year old, a most delicious, nourishing and wholesome food, whether stewed, roasted, baked, or boiled; and I make no doubt that it will equally serve in a fricassee, or a ragout.

Swift's Proposer first expresses apparent sympathetic concern for these poor, destitute, hungry children, and then, using a series of economic arguments, completely dehumanizes the children in a gruesome manner. Initially, the reader might think that Swift is commiserating with the educated Irishman regarding the problem of the poor, but "it is not until the details of Swift's actual solution are displayed, encased within the same, former overtones of gravity, that the reader realizes that he is being mocked."[30] By using statistics to make his argument seem legitimate, he is instead satirizing Sir William Petty, a 17th-century English economist, who used "political arithmetick" [sic] to consider human beings as commodities. An ironic twist that Swift exploits here is that if the reader is so repulsed by the idea of cannibalism of one-year old children, why are they not equally horrified by the mass starvation that was occurring throughout Ireland and indeed, right outside their doors on the streets of Dublin? Swift's use of a narrator allows him to be removed from what the narrator is proposing, which in effect makes the narrator unreliable and therefore ultimately easier to disbelieve. An unreliable narrator "differs markedly depending on how far and in what direction they depart from the author's norm."[31] This allows Swift to take the side of the reader, and the reader, sensing that the narrator is unreliable, sees that the proposal is not a serious one. He is clearly not seriously suggesting that the Irish eat their young, as any sane person would find that notion morally reprehensible. While Swift was being ironic, he was also expressing his moral outrage and intolerance. As one contemporary biographer has noted:

> There is no contradiction between irony and what we might now take as pure intolerance. He was not at all a tolerant person. Swift's irony instead very often expresses the anger of a moral authority who is presented with the standards of a debased majority and illustrates their corruption by speaking for a moment as if he accepted and shared it."[32]

Swift was displaying his anger and using the proposal to attack the status quo and the institutions that allow the tragic and sad state of affairs to persist. During this time, Swift wrote to Knightley Chetwode, a local squire, of the "universal complaints and despair of all people."[33]

A question that intrigues many Swiftian scholars is where the idea of cannibalism for Swift emanated. There have been many different suggestions as to this gruesome and desperate act appearing in Swift's work. During 1729, Swift and his close friend Thomas Sheridan were editing a weekly periodical titled *The Intelligencer.* In issue 17, Sheridan related a story told by the Elizabethan chronicler, Fynes Moryson, of Tyrone's Rebellion. Moryson was traveling throughout Ireland in 1602 when he witnessed:

> A most horrible spectacle of three children (whereof the eldest was not above ten yeeres old) all eating and knowing with their teeth the entrals of their dead mother, upon whose flesh they had fed twenty days past, and having eaten all from the feete upeard to the bare bones, rosting it continually by a slow fire.[34]

Moryson related another story of an old woman who lured her children to a fire in her field and one by one killed them and ate them.[35] Another source of cannibalism that Swift could have drawn upon was from tales from Peru. According to Ian Higgins, a Swiftian scholar at the Australian National University, the "particular idea of a cannibal economy producing babies was not wholly new as the Modest proposer claims" and, furthermore, the old, barbaric tales from Peru "had been a rich mine in which Swift's imagination had worked before he came to write A Modest Proposal."[36] There have been other tales of cannibalism from various parts of the world for thousands of years.

Swift has often been described as one of the great satirists in literature. His use of mockery and his bitter indignation were two hallmarks of a specific form of satire known as Juvenalian satire. Juvenalian satire is defined as follows:

> The character of the speaker is that of a serious moralist who uses a dignified and public style of utterance to decry modes of vice and error which are no less dangerous because they are ridiculous, and who undertakes to evoke from readers contempt, moral indignation, or an unillusioned sadness at the aberrations of humanity.[37]

Many scholars have approached "A Modest Proposal" as a polemic on the famine conditions that prevailed in Ireland in the early 17th century, while others have looked at it as a satire "against a set of theories and attitudes which rendered such conditions possible."[38] Swift's use of cannibalism can also be viewed as a metaphor for the devouring of the Irish by the English. As he sardonically points out, "I grant this food will be somewhat dear, and therefore very proper for landlords, who, as they have already devoured most of the parents, seem to have the best title to the children." The suffering and multi-generational poverty of much of the population lies at the crux of what Swift is attacking. He summed up their fate towards the end when he posed this rhetorical question:

> I desire those politicians who dislike my overture, and may perhaps be so bold to attempt an answer, that they will first ask the parents of these mortals, whether they would not at this day think it a great happiness to have been sold for food at a year old, in the manner I prescribe, and thereby have avoided such a perpetual scene of misfortunes, as they have since gone through, by the oppression of landlords, the impossibility of paying rent without money or trade, the want of common sustenance, with neither house nor clothes to cover them from the inclemencies of the

> weather, and the most inevitable prospect of intailing the like, or greater miseries, upon their breed for ever.

Swift is often compared to another satirist, Bernard Mandeville, an Anglo-Dutch philosopher who lived during the same period. Mandeville argued (satirically) that the answer to economic prosperity was man's vice, such as public, state-controlled prostitution, introduced in his 1724 essay, "Modest Defence of Publick Stews." Renee Prendergast of Queen's University in Belfast, who has written extensively on both Swift and Mandeville, points out that while their use of the word "Modest" in both essay titles might seem an obvious link, the word was not uncommon in the pamphlet literature of the 17th and 18th centuries. What Prendergast did emphasize, however, in citing another scholar, Richard Cook, "is their use of the word modest in works which advocate shocking violations of accepted moral practice." She adds further that they use a similar methodology that stresses that the benefits of their schemes—selling babies for the purpose of being eaten (Swift) and state-controlled prostitution (Mandeville)—to advance the public good of the country. She emphasizes that both writers pay a good deal of attention to what was later called "incentive compatibility."[39] A mechanism is considered "incentive-compatible" if all of the participants can achieve the best outcome for themselves just by acting according to their true preferences. In Swift's proposal, the mother, who was breeding the baby to be ultimately sold, and the wealthy, who were buying the baby to be eaten, were both open about their aims, so the proposal worked. In Mandeville's pamphlet, both the courtesans and the customers would prefer to use the public stew rather than a private one and that courtesans infected with venereal disease would have an incentive not to conceal it.[40]

Both satirists were very likely aware that their proposals would greatly offend their readers but that the readers would also realize that the outcome was worth the price. They were both satirically applying an approach that would become known as "consequentialist reasoning,"[41] which determines the rightness or wrongness of an act solely based on its consequences; in other words, the ends justify the means. Mandeville knew that his subject matter was likely to offend but since it, prostitution, was widely practiced anyhow, why not get some good out of it. Mandeville reiterated his earlier position when, in 1729, he wrote in his best-known work, *The Fable of the Bees*, that "Private Vices by the dextrous Management of a skilful Politician may be turned into Publick Benefits."[42] While Swift never tacitly acknowledges Mandeville, there is reason to believe that he was aware of his works as there are some similarities in their writings. It is very likely that Swift was influenced by "Modest Defence" when he wrote "A Modest Proposal" and, in fact, Swift beats "Mandeville at his own game by showing that there were really no bounds on what could be justified by consequentialist reasoning." In effect, Swift uses consequentialist reasoning to "justify a course of action which is grotesque and barbaric."[43] While their solutions to Ireland's poverty were different, there are similarities. Both satirists were advocating a "scheme that outraged public decency by challenging accepted moral values in order to achieve a material good, or set of goods."[44]

While Swift possessed a strong understanding of economic issues, his real strength was his "grasp of the essential features of the emerging market economy and the social relationships underlying it."[45] He recognized that others had examined Ireland's economic and social problems, through the lenses of mathematical analysis, while completely ignoring the moral implications. There were several prevailing economic theories and solutions being offered during this period that Swift viciously attacked through satire. The prevailing economic theory in the early 1700s was mercantilism, which the English deployed to expand their empire, enrich the ruling elites, and exploit their colonies. Since early in the previous century, England's wealth and power had grown tremendously. Mercantilism was predicated on several fundamental tenets: that a nation's wealth and power were achieved by trade, which emphasized exports and limited imports, the accumulation of gold and silver, forbidding trade to be carried in foreign ships, high tariffs and export subsidies, and restricting trade between the colonies and other nations. From 1651 onward, the English Parliament passed several Navigation Acts that reinforced its dominant position in world trade. The Wool Act of 1699 prevented domestic wool production the English colonies of Ireland and North America, in order to protect and promote English wool exports. The effect was to crush the Irish wool industry and impoverish many Irish farmers.

Another tenet of mercantilism was the idea that a nation's wealth was measured by the number of productive people it encompasses; in other words, the number of people, regardless of age, who were working. Sir William Petty, wrote that, "Fewness of people, is real poverty; and a Nation wherein are Eight Millions of people, are more than twice as rich as the same scope of Land wherein are but Four."[46] Petty also attempted, through political arithmetic, to "estimate the 'value' of the population, as part of the aggregate national wealth."[47] Josiah Child, another 17th-century economist, wrote, "That whatever tends to the Depopulating of a Kingdom, tends to the impoverishment of it."[48] While this belief was widespread, Swift disagreed when he wrote in "An Answer to a Paper":

> But, why all this concern for the poor? We want them not as the country is now managed; they may follow thousands of their leaders and seek their bread abroad. Where the plough has no work, one family can do the business of fifty, and you may send away the other forty-nine. An admirable piece of husbandry, never known or

> practised by the wisest nations, who erroneously thought people to be the riches of a country![49]

Mercantilism regarded all labor as a commodity, and this includes the youngest of children. From the perspective of today, the "ideal of economic activity was nowhere expressed so peculiarly as in the question of child labor" and in the "mercantilist view, no child was too young to go into industry."[50] It is important to note that charity towards the poor had undergone a fundamental change from earlier times. Mandeville wrote of the "unreasonable vein of petty reverence for the poor... and arises from a mixture of pity, folly, and superstition."[51] Swift sets up his proposal by suggesting that anyone who could find a solution to these mothers and their three, four or six children "would deserve so well of the publick, as to have his statue set up for a preserver of the nation."

The Elizabethan Poor Laws, enacted when Englishmen still felt a sense of responsibility toward the unfortunate, divided objects of public charity into three groups: the aged and impotent, children, and persons able to work but unemployed.[52] Swift believed strongly that reducing Ireland's population would make the country richer, a theme that permeates "A Modest Proposal." He again satirizes the then-common practice of "political arithmetic," attributed to Petty, who applied his mathematical methodology to Ireland when he was directed by Oliver Cromwell to make a survey of the land and people of Ireland in the early 1650s. Petty's "political arithmetic" was used to "legitimate previous property seizures,"[53] which was in fact a way to justify the land seizure that occurred during the Cromwellian era. Swift used numbers throughout to make the proposal appear legitimate:

> The number of souls in this kingdom being usually reckoned one million and a half, of these I calculate there may be about two hundred thousand couple, whose wives are breeders; from which number I subtract thirty thousand couple, who are able to maintain their own children, (although I apprehend there cannot be so many under the present distresses of the kingdom) but this being granted, there will remain a hundred and seventy thousand breeders. I again subtract fifty thousand, for those women who miscarry, or whose children die by accident or disease within the year. There only remain a hundred and twenty thousand children of poor parents annually born."

Later he adds that, "of the hundred and twenty thousand children, already computed, twenty thousand may be reserved for breed, whereof only one fourth part to be males."[54]

Petty's analysis of Ireland's population tended to make out the population to be nothing more than a commodity, which is doubtless the underlying theme to Swift's use of babies as a food source. Swift's proposal was in effect to address the problem of poverty in Ireland, in part by reducing the population as 100,000 babies annually would be sold as a food source. Reducing the population in Ireland flew in the face of the then commonly accepted wisdom that the country was underpopulated and that was the source of her poverty. Towards the end of the proposal, Swift references a possible difficulty: "I can think of no one objection, that will possibly be raised against this proposal, unless it should be urged, that the number of people will be thereby much lessened in the kingdom."

Readers of Swift had gotten an earlier indication of his attitude towards this commonly accepted maxim that "people are the riches of a nation" when he penned *Maxims controlled in Ireland*. He makes the argument that Ireland had far too many people, many of whom were unproductive members of society:

> And I will grant it to be so far true, even in this island, that if we had the African custom, or privilege, of selling our useless bodies for slaves to foreigners, it would be the most useful branch of our trade, by ridding us of a most unsupportable burthen, and bringing us money in the stead.[55]

This appears to be a satirical swipe at Mandeville's idea of state-run prostitution to make the marginalized citizens contribute to the productivity of the nation, thereby enriching the state. There is also irony in Swift's suggestion of selling off bodies as slaves to reduce the overpopulation and then later suggesting selling babies as food to accomplish the same goal. "In effect, Swift is maintaining that the maxim—people are the riches of a nation—applies to Ireland only if Ireland is permitted slavery or cannibalism."[56]

What Swift was trying to say in this masterpiece of satire and irony has intrigued scholars and readers for nearly 300 years and may likely continue to do so. Prendergast summarizes her argument thus:

> In utilizing the language of political arithmetic and the employment of consequential forms of reasoning to argue for something so obviously immoral would seem to indicate that Swift was pointing to something very wrong with the methods of measurement and/or the consequential evaluation.[57]

It is evident that Jonathan Swift was a hero to the Irish through his writings, which attacked the economic, political and religious persecution and subjugation that England was imposing on her colony:

> By his forcible and unflinching assertion of the constitutional rights of the Anglo-Irish colony Swift had made himself a national hero. And by 1730 he was already well on the way to becoming a legendary figure. To his restless mind Irish problems presented a series of challenges and, while striving to drive home the injustice of

> England's behaviour towards Ireland, he tried to shock and goad his countrymen into exerting themselves.[58]

George Wittkowsky, writing nearly 80 years ago, summed up Swift's contribution succinctly: "Looked at from the angle of the literary critic, it is a superb work of art which happens to be saturated with economic theory."[59]

NOTES

1. The Navigation Act, 1660 (12 Cha. 2 c. 18), or *An Act for the Encourageing and increasing of Shipping and Navigation*, was intended to strengthen restrictions on colonial imports and exports by placing restrictions on the ships and their crews, to the benefit of England. This act was amended in 1663. The Navigation Acts were repealed in 1849, prompted by the Great Famine, but also by the orthodoxy of *laissez-faire*.
2. Patrick Fitzgerald, "Irish Hunger, Migration and Denomination, 1550–1850," in Patrick Fitzgerald, Christine Kinealy, Gerard Moran (eds), *Irish Hunger and Migration. Myth, Memory and Memorialization* (Hamden, CT: Quinnipiac University, 2015), pp 17–28.
3. Swift letter to Robert Cope, 9 July 1717. Walter Scott (ed.) *Works of Jonathan Swift* (Edinburgh: Archibald Constable and Co., 1814), vol. XVI, p. 318.
4. Swift letter to Charles Ford, 3 May 1719. J.A. Downie, *Jonathan Swift Political Writer* (Abingdon: Routledge, Kegan & Paul, 1984), p. 215.
5. Leo Damrosch, *His Life and His World* (New Haven, CT: Yale University Press, 2013), pp 342–3.
6. Ian Higgins, "The Afterlife of a Modest Proposal," presented at the Dean Swift Seminar, 17–18 Oct. 2009, at the Deanery of St. Patrick's. Higgins has written and researched extensively on the life and works of Jonathan Swift. He is the founding general editor of *The Cambridge Edition of the Works of Jonathan Swift*.
7. Swift to Dean Brandreth, 30 June 1732.
8. George Wittkowsky, "Swift's Modest Proposal: The Biography of an Early Georgian Pamphlet," in *Journal of the History of Ideas* 4, no. 1 (1943), 75–104. doi:10.2307/2707237.
9. "The Jonathan Swift Festival," Dublin, 21 to 24 Nov. 2019, https://jonathanswiftfestival.ie/
10. S.J. Connolly, *Divided Kingdom Ireland 1630–1800* (Oxford University Press, 2008), p. 199.
11. Swift Letter to Alexander Pope, 11 Aug. 1729, "The Works of the Rev. Jonathan Swift," vol. 14.
12. Jonathan Swift, *On the Death of Mrs. Johnson*, Jan. 1728.
13. John Earl of Orrery, *On the Life and Writings of Jonathan Swift, Dean of St. Patrick's, Dublin; In a Series of Letters to His Son, The Honorable Hamilton Boyle.* Second Edition (London: MDCCLII), p. 18.
14. Swift to Lord Bolingbroke, 21 March 1729 and 5 April 1729. Reprinted in *Letters between Dr. Swift, Mr. Pope & From the year 1714 to 1736* (ECCO: Eighteenth Century Collections Online Print Editions).

15. Renee Prendergast, "The Political Economy of Swift's Satires and other Prose Works," Economia, 4–4 (2014) pp 593–619.
16. John Stubbs, *Jonathan Swift The Reluctant Rebel* (London: W. W. Norton, 2016), p. 430.
17. For a more detailed understanding of the South Sea Bubble of 1720, see, Patrick Walsh, *The South Sea Bubble and Ireland: Money, Banking and Investment, 1690–1721* (Boydell and Brewer, 2014). See also, Walsh, "The South Sea Bubble: a parable for our own time," *History Ireland*, issue 2, March/April 2009.
18. Stubbs, p. 474.
19. Jonathan Swift, *Drapier Letter IV: A Letter to the Whole People of Ireland* (vol. IV of the Author's Works containing a Collection of Tracts, Relating to Ireland; Among which are The Drapier's Letters to the People of Ireland, Against Wood's Half-pence (Dublin: George Faulkner, MDCCXLII) pp 120–121.
20. Hugh Boulter, "Letters written by His Excellency Hugh Boulter, D.D. Lord Primate of All Ireland to Several Ministers of State in England, and Some Others. Containing, An Account of the Most Interesting Transactions which passed in Ireland from 1724 to 1738" (Printed for George Faulkner and James Williams, Dublin, MDCCLXX), vol. I, p. 178.
21. Stubbs, p. 506.
22. Ibid., p. 522. For a more detailed description of his stay at Market Hill, see pp 521–527. According to some accounts, Swift became taken with Lady Acheson, who he found to be interested in books and sprightly conversation, unlike her husband, whom he found somewhat dull. For additional insights into his three visits at Market Hill see, Leo Damrosch, "Jonathan Swift His Life and His World" (New Haven, CT: Yale University Press, 2013) pp 435–442.
23. Swift Letter to Alexander Pope, 11 Aug. 1729, "The Works of the Rev. Jonathan Swift," vol. 14.
24. Stubbs, pp 22–3.
25. Swift Letter to Lord Bolingbroke, 5 April 1729, "The Works of the Rev. Jonathan Swift," vol. 14.
26. Stubbs, p. 530.
27. David Hayton and Adam Rounce (eds) *The Cambridge Editions of the Works of Jonathan Swift. Irish Political Writings after 1725. "A Modest Proposal" and other Works* (Cambridge University Press, 2018), pp 146–59.
28. Arushi Mather, "Jonathan Swift's Use of Irony in 'A Modest Proposal,'" *O Captain! My Captain*, an online journal of literature.
29. Charles Allen Beaumont, "Swift's Classical Rhetoric in *A Modest Proposal*," *The Georgia Review* 14, no. 3 (1960), 307–17.
30. Xiaojue Hu quoted in The Victorian Web, at: http://www.victorianweb.org/previctorian/swift/hu1.html.
31. Wayne C. Booth, *The Rhetoric of Fiction* (University of Chicago Press, 1983), p. 159.
32. Stubbs, p. 569.
33. Swift to Knightley Chetwode, F. Elrington Ball, *The Correspondence of Jonathan Swift, D.D.* (London: G. Bell and Sons, 1913), pp 81–2.

34. "The Itinerary of Fynes Moryson," vol. III (University of Glasgow Press, MCMVIII), pp 282–83.
35. Ibid.
36. Higgins, "The Afterlife of A Modest Proposal."
37. M.H. Abrams & Geoffrey Galt Harpham, *A Glossary of Literary Terms* (Boston: Wadsworth Cengage Learning, 2009. Ninth ed.), p. 321. The term is named after the first-century Roman poet, Juvenal, known for his satirical poems, the Satires.
38. Wittkowsky, p. 76.
39. According to Leonid Hurwicz, a mechanism is said to be "incentive-compatible" if every participant can achieve the best outcome for him/herself by revealing his or her true preferences, or openly acting on his or her preferences without cheating. Dr. Hurwicz was co-awarded the Nobel Prize in Economics in 2007 for his work on Mechanism Design. At: www.leonidhurwicz.org/incentive-compatible/
40. Renee Prendergast, "Swift's Critique of the 'Economic' Way, of Thinking," presented at the "Dean Swift and 18th Century Economic Thought" Conference at St. Patrick's Deanery, Dublin, 16–17 Oct. 2010.
41. The term "consequentialism" first appeared in Elizabeth Anscombe's article "Modern Moral Philosophy," in *Philosophy*, vol. 33, no. 124 (Jan. 1958), 1–19.
42. Bernard Mandeville, *The Fable of the Bees, or Private Vices, Publick Benefits* (London, 1725), p. 428.
43. Prendergast, "Swift's Critique."
44. Hayton and Rounce, p. lxxvii. For further discussion of comparisons between Swift and Mandeville, see Claude Rawson's, "Mandeville and Swift" in *Swift and Others* (Cambridge University Press, 2015), pp 51–69.
45. Renee Prendergast, "The Political Economy of Swift's Satires and other Prose Works," in *Economia*, 4, 4, 2014, p. 595.
46. Sir William Petty, "The Economic Writings of Sir William Petty, together with The Observations upon Bills of Mortality," more probably by Captain John Graunt (ed.), Charles Henry Hull (Cambridge University Press, 1899), 2 vols. See: https://oll.libertyfund.org/titles/1677. For a more in-depth examination of this topic see: Louis A. Landa, "'A Modest Proposal' and Populousness" in *Modern Philology* 40, no. 2 (1942), p. 162. Landa quotes Petty in his paper. Petty came to Ireland in 1652 during the reign of Oliver Cromwell. He reformed Ireland's medical services and in 1654 undertook the first scientific cartography of Ireland. He has been referred to as the founding father of political economy. See, Wittkowsky, pp 80–81.
47. Eli F. Heckscher, *Mercantilism* (London: George Allen and Unwin, 1955), p. 190. Also quoted in Wittkowsky, p. 83.
48. Josiah Child, *A New Discourse of Trade* (London, 1692), p. 179.
49. "The Works of the Rev. Jonathan Swift," vol. 9; "An Answer to a Paper called a Memorial of the Poor Inhabitants, Tradesmen, and Labourers of Ireland": https://en.wikisource.org/w/index.php?title=The_Works_of_the_Rev._Jonathan_Swift/Volume_9/An_Answer_to_a_Paper_called_a_Memorial_of_the_Poor_Inhabitants,_Tradesmen,_and_Labourers_of_Ireland&oldid=7470639.

50. Eli F. Heckscher, *Mercantilism*, II, p. 155.
51. Mandeville, *Bees*, p. 357.
52. Dorothy Marshall, *English Poor in the Eighteenth Century* (London: Geo. Routledge & Sons, 1926), p. 23.
53. Sean O. Moore, *Swift the Book and the Irish Financial Revolution* (Baltimore: Johns Hopkins University Press, 2010), p. 3.
54. Hayton and Rounce, pp 146–59.
55. Louis A. Landa, "A Modest Proposal and Populousness," *Modern Philology* 40, no. 2 (1942), 161–70, p. 161.
56. Ibid., p. 162.
57. Prendergast, "Swift's Critique."
58. R.B. McDowell. *The English Historical Review* 72, no. 282 (1957), 182–83.
59. Wittkowsky, p. 104.

CHAPTER FOUR

THE "VITAL BLOOD" OF IRISH COLONIALS IN AMERICA AND THE FORMATION OF THE NEW NATION

Robert Smart

> Ghosts can be very fierce and instructive. They cast strange shadows, particularly in our literature.
>
> Flannery O'Connor (1960)

Long before the agitation that led to the Declaration of Independence in 1776, Irish-born writers were publishing in the colonies, and they introduced to their new home two literary traditions that became central to the larger current of American writing—the literary Gothic and political satire. Satire was the early preference among colonial readers, focused on both local politics and on regional trade issues, but the Gothic tradition remained strong and pronounced throughout the colonial and Federal periods until it fully flowered in the early 19th century. The new country lacked the ruined castles and monuments of Ireland, but it did have two features that drove the Gothic imagination of this first generation of Gothic writers: dark, forbidding forests and a native population that left burial mounds and abandoned villages throughout the colonial landscape.[1] None other than Thomas Jefferson, in his *Notes on the State of Virginia* (1781) conducted archaeological surveys of Indian burial mounds that dotted the greater Virginia landscape and considered them evidence of a previous unknown civilization that haunted the new citizens of the young country.[2] His long fascination with fossils, such that he instructed explorers, Meriwether Lewis and William Clark, to unearth and ship back to Monticello any and all fossil evidence of previous habitations in the new country,[3] drove his conviction that Americans lived their lives atop buried layers of previous civilizations.[4]

Critic Leslie Fiedler, in *Love and Death in the American Novel* (1960),[5] argued that there were only two truly Gothic countries in the world, Ireland and America.[6] For our purposes, the case could truly be made that the Gothic roots of American literature were inherited from these early Irish settlers and not just cultivated indigenously.[7] The cultural conflict as Fiedler saw it during this period of American literary history was between the sentimental tradition in English literature, and the rougher, often seditious forms of popular literature that served as *sub rosa* forms of cultural resistance in Ireland for centuries. Here is Fiedler's then-radical explanation of the "cultural work" of the Gothic genre:

> The guilt which underlies the gothic and motivates its plots is the guilt of the revolutionary haunted by the (paternal) past which he has been striving to destroy; and the fear that possesses the gothic and motivates its tone is the fear that in destroying the old ego-ideals of Church and State, the West has opened a way for the inruption of darkness ... Through the pages of the gothic ... the soul of Europe flees its own darker impulses.[8]

For Fiedler, the powerful New World influence of Gothic forms was crucial to the "invention" of America itself:

> [America is] a world without a significant history or a substantial past; a world which had left behind the terror of Europe not for the innocence it dreamed of, but for new and special guilts associated with the rape of nature and the exploitation of dark-skinned people;[9] a world doomed to play out the imaginary childhood of Europe.[10]

He concluded his exegesis by claiming that America itself was an "event in the history of the European [i.e., Irish] spirit—as, indeed, is the very invention of America itself."[11] Fiedler's "history" of the new country found few champions when it was first published in 1960, but has since received a number of second looks from critics less interested in doctrinaire chronologies of colonial history and who are more interested in the tectonic cultural history of the colonies and the eventual creation of a new nation of immigrants. Jefferson's search for cultural precedents at the same time as the new nation was stretching its boundaries westward reflects this idea that America was as much "invented" as it was founded, and that its prevailing cultural ethos was driven by a Gothic understanding at this moment of invention. In other words, the earliest immigrants to the new nation brought the past with them as part of the nation's invention and founding. This ethos was wrought by the country's earliest Irish settlers and found fertile ground among those writers struggling with the cultural and natural inheritances of the new country.

Scribed along these terms, then, what discursive province follows this approach to the foundation story of America? First of all, it would suggest that the European imagination as it had been shared by the inhabitants and writers of England's oldest colony was brought to American shores early in the 18th century, initially after 1717 when many Scotch Irish planters lost their leases in the north of the island because of persistent poor harvests and, in even greater numbers, during the 1740–41 famine, "The Year of the Slaughter," which may have been as destructive in human terms as the first years of the Great Hunger.[12] The most salient forms of that immigrant literary imagination also found root here, most significantly, the Gothic as it emerged in Ireland to become its first post-colonial discourse.[13] As Jarlath Killeen explains, this origin point for the Gothic in Ireland derived from the island's long characterization as "Celtic lands as zones of the weird."[14] In the same discussion, Killeen notes that "Gothic can perhaps be called the only true [American] literary tradition," something that is "even more the case with Irish literature."[15]

This point is what led Fiedler to claim that these two countries were the only "truly Gothic" countries in the world, and that lineage invites us also to claim that America's "invention" proceeded on these terms and had at its core the work of those early Irish Gothicists. If America was indeed a Gothic nation, then it was Gothic by virtue of it being significantly Irish at that moment of invention. As critic Charles Fanning noted, by 1790 "there were over 400,000 Irish Americans spread across all the new states of the American republic" in that year of the first American census.[16] This literary genealogy, then, follows Lawrence "Bloody" Sweeney to Charles Brockden Brown to Edgar Allen Poe, descended from his great-grandfather, David Poe from County Cavan, and culminating in America's true Gothic geniuses, William Faulkner, also of Irish descent, and his fellow Southerner, Flannery O'Connor.

"Bloody Sweeney" earned his moniker by publishing risqué tales of violent encounters between native tribes and colonials during the French and Indian Wars, complete with detailed descriptions of torture, decapitations and by implication (as with all captivity narratives from this period) implications of rape and sexual slavery. Published a bit later, Poe's most famous story, *The Fall of the House of Usher* (1839), has been compared to the fall of the big houses in Ireland:[17] aristocratic castles wrecked by generations of decay and incest. Additionally, Charles Brockden Brown's early novels featured suspect Irishmen who arrived in the colonies as revolutionaries hopeful that they might sow similar seeds of discord and sedition across the Atlantic in England's newest colony. In fact, in *Edgar Huntley, Or, Memoirs of a Sleepwalker* (1799) Brown created a subterranean world of hidden caves and passages—much in keeping with Jefferson's surmises about the new American landscape—in which tigers, Irish political exiles and a white captive woman all vie for the attention of our naïve hero. No surprise, then, that Brown supported President John Adams' Alien and Sedition Acts of 1798, which were drafted at least in part with the Irish in mind. He also supposedly marched up to the White House while Jefferson was still in office to personally hand the outgoing president a copy of *Wieland; Or, The Transformation* (1798) in which he warned Americans about seditious imports from the old countries of Germany and Ireland.[18]

Incidentally, this occasionally violent debate over the proper response of the new nation to open immigration (an issue that still resonates) produced one of the more interesting and relatively unknown documents in the long relationship between Ireland and America. In the summer of 1798, a group of Irish American citizens in Philadelphia published "The Plea of Erin," a direct response to White House support for Congressional passage of The Alien and Sedition Acts.[19] The specific reference that informed the 10-page document came early: "the president of 1798 [John Adams] was a member of the committee of congress of 1775 who deliberately prepared, and reported the touching address to Ireland, which openly excited them to approve, to assist, and to imitate the American struggle." This was followed by a quote from the 1775 document that specifically offered beleaguered Irish republicans asylum in the colonies. Moreover, the disastrous 1798 Rebellion in Ireland was supposedly, in no small part, to have been inspired by the American struggle. The Plea ended poignantly:

> Half our supplications have already been granted, by the favour of Divine Providence; *for you have been made free* [italics in the original]. Suffer us then to enjoy among you, the peace, liberty and safety, which our gallant countrymen have helped to establish.

Why seek to expel, the document asks, those who have worked for the success of the American Revolution when they still yearn for their own liberation from perfidious Britain?

Practically, then, when newspapermen and pundits in the Middle Atlantic colonies worried that colonial unrest and agitation for independence would bring renewed strength and purpose to Great Britain, there were others, mostly concentrated in New England, who used this same Gothic register to describe England's aims toward the colonies. In the *Connecticut Courant* of 26 August 1765, several partisan voices asked whether, "Great Britain had plundered Ireland for 200 years avaricious London was now about to attempt to 'drink your [the colonies'] vital blood."[20] Again, in 1773, the Sons of Liberty in Boston "alleged that Britain's victimization of Ireland—long since bled white by 'pensioners and placemen,'" characterized the struggle of the colonies to both avoid Ireland's fate and align their political and cultural interests with Britain's oldest colony.[21] These Gothic references in the public record reflect similar claims in Irish politics from the same period, the mid-to-late-18th century, starting with Theobald Wolfe Tone who, in 1790, used those very Gothic images to characterize the perfidy of English legislators and commissioners who enriched themselves at Ireland's expense:

> Our benches were filled with English lawyers; our Bishoprics with English divines; our custom-house with English commissioners; all offices of state filled, three deep, with Englishmen in possession ... busily and actively employed against that country on whose vitals and in whose blood they were rioting in ease and luxury.[22]

By 1798, that unfortunate year of revolution, Tone had sharpened his Gothic rhetoric, claiming that:

> The Temple of your liberties is filled with buyers and sellers, with ... with placemen and pensioners, those unclean and ominous harpies, gorged with public spoil, and sucking still, like insatiable Vampires, the last drainings of the vital blood of their country.[23]

We can see just how closely political writings in the old country were being read in the new republic and vice versa, allowing those writing in Hartford, Connecticut and in Boston to echo Tone in their alarums about English perfidy.[24]

What all this means is that at the moment when the nascent literary and public discourses of America were being shaped, the presence of Irish political and literary writing was decisive, hence the claim earlier that when speaking of an early American literature, we are really describing a contested tradition of letters that was heavily influenced by writing in country and from abroad in Ireland by Irishmen. The earliest contributions to the literature of the colonies and the new republic from the growing Irish émigré population fleeing famines and crop failures—notably in 1717 and 1740–41—were predominantly satiric, often self-deprecating. Flourishing alongside this more popular strain of Irish American writing was the Gothic tradition inherited from those writers in Ireland who used the rhetoric from this seditious strain of letters to comment on political affairs on both sides of the Atlantic.[25] After the 1798 Rebellion, much of this Gothic rhetoric and imagery featured in popular historical tracts published in New England that touted the heroics of Irish patriots and detailed the atrocities of the British regulars who quelled the rebellion. William James MacNeven and Thomas Addis Emmet—both exiled United Irishmen—published in 1807 a detailed history of the failed rebellion in which the focus on dismembered and despoiled bodies of those who were punished after the fighting was over is central. By 1828, in a strange Boston publication by "A Lady of Boston" (later revealed to be Rebecca Warren Brown), *Tales of the Emerald Isle; or, Legends of Ireland,* blended history, folklore and fiction to produce a true Gothic literature, complete with tales about ruined castles and great houses after the Battle of the Boyne, against which doomed lovers tried to navigate the strife that followed that historical defeat. It is not difficult to see in these stories outlines for Poe's most famous Gothic work, *The Fall of the House of Usher*. In fact, a growing awareness of the parallels between 19th and 20th century Ireland and the American South, ante and post bellum, among cultural critics has made this important thematic resonance a mainstay of American literary criticism.[26]

By the time of Poe's ascendance as the most important Gothic writer of the new country in the first half of the 19th century, the American Northeast had replaced England as the villainous antagonist in the minds of many Irish who had moved to the southern states, and it was ranged against the racially-based and self-fashioned aristocracy of Southern cotton culture. Faulkner's work, most especially his Gothic masterpiece *Absalom, Absalom!* reveals in these contours the shape of the Irish Gothic inheritance in 20th century American literature.[27] The Anglophilia of King Cotton South (made possible by the invention of the cotton gin by Eli Whitney of Connecticut) reflected the growing political divide between the increasingly industrialized Northeast and the agrarian South, which saw itself as more aligned culturally and politically with the Anglo-Irish Ascendancy. David Gleeson has argued persuasively that the adoption of Southern attitudes towards the increasingly abolitionist North and Northeast was "the key to their survival and prosperity."[28] Clearly, British colonial hegemony over Ireland, contested unsuccessfully for centuries, had produced a Gothic response that reflected the political and cultural repression of the island's mostly Catholic inhabitants, and that place was taken up in the American South by generations of slaves who arrived in the New World almost at the same time as the first white settlers in Virginia. While the number of Irish who settled in the Southern states was never equal to the numbers that moved into cities in the Northeast, they did form a considerable body of white settlers who harbored no antipathy to the "peculiar institution" that propped up Southern prosperity.[29] The inevitable conflict produced by this regional separation was, of course, the American Civil War, in which thousands of Irish immigrants escaping the aftermath of the Great Hunger fought and died in the service of both sides of the conflict. Moreover, the plantation culture that stubbornly persisted in antebellum memory provided the ruins that would dominate so called "Southern Gothic."

It is important to note that these emerging sentiments and alliances followed sectarian fault lines brought to the new nation from Ireland. The term "Irish" in

American parlance prior to the Famine decade of 1840–50, identified both Protestant and Catholic Irish, but following the huge influx of poor Catholic Irish (and the concomitant rise in anti-Catholic sentiment in the country), *Scotch-Irish* became the customary term to describe Protestant families of Irish descent.[30] Culturally and historically, then, after the 1840s and the immigration of 1.5 million mostly Catholic Irish to America, "the label *Irish* would identify Irish Catholics exclusively."[31] Throughout the ante- and post-bellum decades of the 19th century and the first half of the 20th century, this sectarian inheritance became more pronounced and produced some interesting developments across the American South and West. In 1842, Daniel O'Connell, the Liberator and hero of Frederick Douglass, enjoined his countrymen who had fled or who planned to flee to America "to treat the colored people as your equals, as brethren." By the 1840s, "the Irish had aligned themselves with the Democratic Party, which was proslavery."[32] In fact, efforts by public figures in Ireland such as O'Connell were received coldly in America, leading American leaders in the Irish community, including Bishop John Hughes of New York, to characterize such efforts as "foreign interference in American affairs."[33]

One should not, therefore, be surprised to find many profound contradictions in this part of the national story, starting with the founding mythology of the American experiment in democracy. Begin, perhaps, with the fact that a nation founded by a collection of *philosophes* on the principles of reason, rational decision-making in a world unmoved by divine hands has the Gothic as its national literature, wherein the irrational past always threatens to intervene in the present to subvert any progressive future. One of the few points of consensus among Americanist critics is that Herman Melville's *Moby-Dick* (1851) is the likeliest candidate for the title of "Great American Novel," or of America's national epic. In it, an obsessive amputee chases a great white whale to his death at sea amid floating coffins, while his ship and nearly all his crew are lost. It is difficult to ignore the strong racial dimensions of the novel—something also reflected in the last, incomplete magnum by Melville's near contemporary, Poe, in *The Narrative of A. Gordon Pym of Nantucket* (1838) in which the main character and his comrades land on an island of black natives for whom the color white is alien because it does not exist on the island. Even the natives' teeth are black. The narrative ends abruptly at the point when Pym drifts into a white fog never to be seen again. The influence that this earlier "color narrative" might have had on Melville's work has been the focus of literary debate for over a century. Both of these major works arose at the moment in the country's history when the question of whether an American literature in fact exists, separate from English literature, and the fact that both works are Gothic in nature and obsessed with the defining issue of race is not insignificant. Nobel

Laureate Toni Morrison described this entanglement accurately in *Playing in the Dark* (1992) as "the shadow that is companion to ... whiteness—a dark and abiding presence that moves the hearts and texts of American literature with fear and longing."[34]

A second perhaps more profound contradiction falls along the racial lines that Fiedler and others have correctly identified as one of the main Gothic themes of the American canon, this one involving Irish migration more directly. In earlier accounts of Irish influence on the development of American literature, the focus has been on simplifying rather than deepening our understanding of just how the complexities that these men and women left behind them in Europe did not just disappear when they arrived in the colonies. As the country itself followed shifting axes of cultural identification in the months and years leading to the Civil War, so too with the fate of Irish immigrants and writers who found themselves having to choose sides in the looming conflict. One might expect that Irish Republicans and agitators for Irish freedom would most naturally align themselves with the Northern struggle for the abolition of slavery, but the realities were not that simple. David Gleeson's summary of these antipathies is stark: "The Irish supported African slavery in the South. Wealthier Irish men had no qualms about buying slaves, and those too poor to purchase chattel did not oppose the institution."[35] Frederick Douglass might have found a ready, sympathetic audience during his 1845 visit to Ireland and in his admiration for Daniel O'Connell, but the Young Irelander, John Mitchel, escaped from Van Diemen's Land only a few years later and founded a pro-slavery newspaper in Tennessee.[36] Two of his sons died for the Confederacy and his advocacy for the Southern cause remained unabated until his death in 1875. In an interesting turn of phrase from the long Anglo-Irish history of colonization, it has been said of the Irish who migrated to the American South that "they eventually became more southern than the southerners themselves."[37] That Mitchel saw the abolitionist movement in the North as more akin to British interferences in Ireland than to the independence efforts in Ireland is telling and powerful, and it made him notorious enough post-Civil War to be imprisoned in Fortress Monroe, along with Jefferson Davis and Confederate Senator Clement Clay, as one of the "great triumvirate of 'Rebel' public enemies."[38]

To move this argument closer to the end of the 20th century, in 1976, historian Michael Shaara published an historical novel based on the battle of Gettysburg in mid-1863, *The Killer Angels*.[39] The piece was an example of what Shaara termed "hot history," in which the scenes and dialogue were taken directly from the published memoirs, letters and reports from the time by the various principals. So, in Shaara's words, "I have not consciously changed any fact," and when the language men spoke and wrote seemed too "windy," "I have changed some of the language."[40] There is one problem: one of the central characters in the constructed narrative is an Irishman named Buster Kilrain, whose explanations for why he is fighting for the Union underline Shaara's main thesis that this was a fight for freedom and the dignity of human beings regardless of their race and not simply a contest over states' rights. Kilrain never existed; he is a complete fabrication, meant no doubt to contextualize and heighten the speechifying of the main character, Joshua Lawrence Chamberland, the hero of Little Round Top. Why invent an Irishman to play such an important role in an otherwise historical account of this central battle in the American Civil War? (of necessity, Kilrain does not survive the battle) Kilrain's words echo, remarkably, the language in The Plea of Erin, in that the struggle for liberty in the States reflects the long struggle for liberty in Ireland. When this once obscure novel caught fire in the wave of renewed interest in the Civil War leading to its 150th anniversary, the reissue of the novel and the subsequent epic movie version funded by CNN mogul, Ted Turner, made this little bit of cultural fictionalizing a central part of the discussion, an indication of just how sub-lingua this portion of the Irish-American saga had become.

William Faulkner's famous Joycean line about history from *Requiem for a Nun* (1951), "The past is never dead. It's not even past," provides a possible concluding stratagem for this particular historical complexity.[41] The Gothic arose in Irish literature and history as a mostly post-colonial discourse, accelerated by the events of the Great Famine of the 1840s, which were continuously occluded in official versions of those events written by English reporters.[42] The Gothic in Ireland was mostly written by the Anglo-Irish, partly as an expression of fear concerning the large Catholic majority that had suffered the most profoundly during the Famine.[43] Thus, in Gothic texts like Sheridan LeFanu's *Carmilla* and Bram Stoker's *Dracula,* there are myriad and sometimes not so subtle references to famine, famine ruins, abandoned villages, etc. These were paralleled in nonfiction writing about the Famine by witnesses like James Mahoney and Asenath Nicholson, whose descriptions and drawings of the hardest hit areas during those horrid years rival the fictional descriptions in their evocation of haunting suffering, silent and often unmarked graves and living ghosts wandering the countryside. The parallel experience in the American South is the plight of enslaved Africans, whose suffering did not abate following the Civil War; if anything, the rise of Jim Crow and the KKK moved that violent repression into the cultural fabric of the region and away from the vicious clashes that had marked the region before and during the war. The fears of the minority Anglo-Irish regarding the Catholic majority that surrounded them in Ireland is paralleled in the Southern Gothic by fears of a slave uprising, heightened by actual uprisings like those led by Nat Turner and Desmond Vesey.

By the time of Poe's ascendance as America's leading Gothic writer, the African presence in that literature surpassed the indigenous figure of the Indian as the immediate source of danger and threat, especially with the increasing industrialization of the greater northeast of the country. Southern regional writers like Henry Clay Lewis and Rose Terry Cooke exploited white southern fears of the large black population of slaves in their stories, working less obliquely than contemporaries like Poe and Melville, to create an overarching canopy of cultural fear that white civilization would be violently overthrown by former slaves. Add to this the post-war experience of this one region of America that had ever experienced military defeat, and the parallels to the Irish experience post-Famine begin to clarify. John Mitchel's political and cultural identification with the agrarian American South makes some sense in this context,[44] as does the central argument of this essay, that the Irish Gothic tradition became an essential part of both the larger American cultural identity and fed what most critics now accept as the main branch of the new country's literature. Move the focus past Faulkner in the American Gothic canon and the Irish presence is impossible to miss. Writers like Flannery O'Connor, Eugene O'Neill, Cormac McCarthy and John O'Hara deepened the regional boundaries of American Gothic to parallel the rapid expansion of the republic itself. In the words of Kieran Quinlan, the present state of Gothic affinity between the American South and Ireland grew from "an impoverished [and defeated] South after the war and a retrenched Ireland after the famine."[45] Finally, the recent skirmishes between culture warriors of various stripes over Confederate monuments throughout Southern cities, and the existence of "ghost estates" and "zombie banks"[46] that followed the collapse of the Celtic Tiger in Ireland would indicate that, indeed, when it comes to the Gothic, "the past is never dead."

NOTES

1. After the American Civil War, the image of the ruined plantation becomes a more than adequate substitute for the ruins of Europe, featured in such emblematic texts and films as *Gone with the Wind,* where the plantation is aptly named "Tara."
2. Karl Lehmann-Hartleben, "Thomas Jefferson, Archaeologist," in *American Journal of Archaeology,* vol. 47, No. 2 (April-June 1943), pp 161–163.
3. The expedition was led by Captain Meriwether Lewis and his friend, Second Lieutenant William Clark. It took place between May 1804 and September 1806, starting in Pittsburgh in Philadelphia and ending at the Pacific Coast.
4. Jefferson brought many of these artifacts into the still unfinished White House, displaying them in a curio cabinet as guests came through the Entrance Hall into the residence of the President of the United States.
5. Leslie Fiedler, *Love and Death in the American Novel* (Mclean, Ill: Dalkey Archive Press, 1966).

6. He has also said regarding the American Gothic strain that "our classic literature is a literature of horror for boys," ibid., p. 29.
7. G. Richard Thompson explained this distinction in his long essay exegesis on the Gothic, "Gothic Fiction of the Romantic Age: Context and Mode," in *Romantic Gothic Tales, 1790–1840* (New York: Perennial Library, 1979), p. 31.
8. Fiedler, *Love and Death*, p. 129; Toni Morrison addresses the same point decades later in *Playing in the Dark* (1992) when she asks: "Why should a young country repelled by Europe's moral and social disorder, swooning in a fit of desire and rejection, devote its talents to reproducing in its own literature the typology of diabolism it wanted to leave behind," p. 36.
9. This point would become important in the sorting out of Irish racial fidelities post-Civil War, especially when tempered by sectarian divides that had been exasperated by the influx of so many Irish Catholics post Famine.
10. Fielder, *Love and Death*, p. 31.
11. Ibid.
12. Jay P. Dolan, *The Irish Americans: A History* (New York: Bloomsbury Press, 2008), p. 6.
13. See Robert Smart, "Mapping the Imperial Body: Body Image and Representation in Famine Reporting," in David Valone (ed.) *An Gorta Mór: Relief, Representation and Remembrance* (New York: University Press of America, 2009).
14. Jarlath Killeen, *The Emergence of Irish Gothic Fiction: History, Origins, Theories* (Edinburgh University Press, 2014), p. 9.
15. Ibid., p. 12.
16. The population was 3,929,214; Charles Fanning, *New Perspectives on the Irish Diaspora* (Carbondale, IL; Southern Illinois Press, 2000), p. 7.
17. For example, Margaret Hallisey, *Understanding Contemporary Irish Fiction and Drama* (Chapel Hill, NC: University of North Carolina Press, 2016).
18. See, for example, Sydney J. Krause, "Charles Brockden Brown and the Philadelphia Germans," in *Early American Literature*, 39, 1 (2004), 85–119, p. 85. Brown gave up his place as America's first professional writer of fiction to focus exclusively on broadsides and pamphlets that pleaded his sometimes paranoid brand of politics.
19. The full title is informative: "The plea of Erin. Or, the case of the natives of Ireland in the United States, fairly displayed in the fraternal address of the first congress, in the year 1775; and in the respectful memorial of the republican Irish, who had, consequently, sought 'an asylum' in America, addressed by them to the congress of the year 1798. Philadelphia." At: www.loc.gov/resource/rbne 14901200.
20. John Ferling, *A Leap In The Dark: The Struggle to Create the American Republic.* (Oxford University Press, 2003), p. 42.
21. Ibid., p. 97.
22. Quoted in Robert Smart and Michael R, Hutcheson, "The 'Unborn and Unburied Dead': The Rhetoric of Ireland's *An Gorta Mór,* in David Valone and Christine Kinealy (eds), *Ireland's Great Hunger: Silence, Memory and Commemoration* (New York: University Press of America, 2002), p. 69.
23. Ibid., pp 69–70.
24. For more insight into the rhetorical uses of Gothic imagery throughout this period of Irish history and through the Famine half a century later, see Smart and Hutcheson, 'The Unborn and Unburied Dead,' pp 65–83.

25. For example, Jarlath Killeen, *Gothic Ireland: Horror and the Irish Anglican Imagination in the Long Eighteenth Century* (Dublin: Four Courts Press, 2005). "Gothic is disturbing because it challenges the way we think, questions the way we divide up reality, and threatens to discard our grades of meaning," p. 16.
26. One of the best of these studies is Kieran Quinlan, *Strange Kin: Ireland and the American South* (Baton Rouge, LA: LSU Press, 2005).
27. Within the same 12-month period—1936–37—two novels that explored the post-bellum inheritance of this Southern Anglophilia were published—Margaret Mitchell's *Gone with the Wind* and William Faulkner's *Absalom! Absalom!*—with Mitchell's 1,000 plus page tome completely overshadowing Faulkner's novel. *Gone with the Wind* features an Irish rebel, Gerald O'Hara, who longs to be both a slave owner and a landed gentleman and achieves both on a plantation named Tara, while few American novels have so completely captured the boundedness of land and blood as does *Absalom! Absalom!*
28. David T. Gleeson, *The Irish in the South 1815–1977* (Chapel Hill, NC: University of North Carolina Press, 2001), p. 121.
29. Just shy of a 90,000 total by 1960, having seen a 55% increase after 1845. Ibid., p. 27.
30. Dolan, *Irish Americans*, p. x.
31. Ibid., p. xi.
32. Ibid., p. 53. See, Christine Kinealy, *Daniel O'Connell and Anti-Slavery. The Saddest People the Sun Sees* (London: Routledge, 2010).
33. Douglas C. Riach, "Daniel O'Connell and American Anti-Slavery," in *Irish Historical Studies*, vol. 20, no. 77 (March 1976), 2–25.
34. Toni Morrison, *Playing in the Dark: Whiteness and the Literary Imagination* (New York: Random House, 1992), p. 33.
35. Gleeson, *Irish in the South*, p. 121.
36. In 1846, Young Ireland broke away from O'Connell's Repeal movement, abolition of slavery being one topic on which they differed. During the American Civil War, other prominent Young Irelanders, notably Thomas Francis Meagher, fought on the side of the Union.
37. Quinlan, *Strange Kin*, p. 8.
38. David T. Gleeson, "The Forgotten Nationalist: John Mitchel, Race, and Irish American Identity," in *Reviews in American History,* vol. 38, No. 4 (Dec. 2010), 658–663, pp 660–61.
39. Michael Shaara, *The Killer Angels* (New York: Ballantine Books, 1974).
40. Ibid., p. xvii.
41. The corresponding line from Joyce, of course, is spoken by Stephen Dedalus in *A Portrait of the Artist*: "History is a nightmare from which I am trying to awake."
42. For example, Robert Smart, *Black Roads: The Famine in Irish Literature* (Quinnipiac, CT: Cork University Press, 2015).
43. An exception to this generalization is the poetry of James Clarence Mangan.
44. This sentiment was echoed by Oscar Wilde, in a New Orleans newspaper interview in 1882, "The case of the South in the civil war was to my mind much like that of Ireland today. It was a struggle for autonomy, self-government for a people." Quoted in Quinlan, *Strange Kin*, p. 73.
45. Quinlan, *Strange Kin*, p. 238.
46. Jarlath Killeen expressed similar sentiments in the *Irish Times*, "How Celtic Tiger's Death led to a Gothic Revival," 28 April 2017.

CHAPTER FIVE

"A HALF-STARVED NATION"

Famine and Crime in Ireland in 1831

Ciarán Reilly

> Ye landlords of Ireland, listen to these accusing facts; and if the Lord Limericks of a half-starved nation object to legislative interference for its rescues, because to relieve the poor Irishman by law would be to rob the rich one, we trust in a British legislature to reply, that to rob—though it were a robbery, which restitution is not—but to rob the rich by hundreds is a less crime than to murder the poor by thousands; and that the aggravation of famine by defective laws, is equivalent to an act of murder.[1]

Frequent failure of the potato crop was an almost annual feature of early 19th-century Ireland, particularly following the end of Napoleonic Wars in 1815. Failed harvests in the years 1816–17, 1821–22, 1830–31 and 1839–40 led to localized famine and perhaps as the writer William Carleton claimed, no year in Irish history was without famine.[2] Additionally, in the early decades of the 19th century, there were several outbreaks of cholera and typhus; 1817 and 1832 were among the worst, which seriously added to the plight of the lower orders.[3] Each of these potato failures was short-lived and usually followed by a bumper harvest, nonetheless, they caused severe distress. Almost inevitably, these periods of dearth led to increased levels of crime and violence. In 1821, Sir Edward O'Brien of Dromoland Castle, County Clare, despaired of the fact that "poverty, famine and distress of every kind" were "staring them in the face." For O'Brien and others, the failure of the potato would almost certainly bring about "evil" on the part of the peasantry.[4] Much of the distress in 1821 centred on counties Galway and Mayo, where it was suggested that public works be established to alleviate distress and quell unrest. John Killaly, an engineer in County Clare, suggested alternatives to conventional public works schemes that would serve the people better. They included "reclamation of waste land or the rescuing [of] ground from the Sea, or from rivers."[5] Such work was regarded as preferable to menial tasks, as they could be managed more effectively and, it was argued, would quell rural disquiet. The potato failure in 1826 and 1827 again raised these fears, testing the resolve of the police and the Dublin Castle authorities. For the clergy and the gentry another season of famine would drive the poor to acts of "desperation and violence."[6]

In 1831, Ireland starved, most notably in the west of Ireland where counties Donegal, Galway and Mayo reported high levels of distress and hunger.[7] The failure of the potato crop in August 1830 would have devastating consequences throughout Ireland as 1831 dawned, although the famine had very different local origins. The lack of seaweed in Erris and other coastal communities in County Mayo, for example, in 1829–30 exacerbated the problem for a large part of the population there. Seaweed was widely used to fertilize the potato crop and when it did not arrive the people planted crops late, resulting in a poor yield of potatoes. Coupled with other factors including subdivision and overpopulation, in Mayo quickly became the epicentre of the 1831 shortages. Reports of hunger and distress depicted large numbers of people on the verge of starvation.[8] The winter of 1830–31 suggested that those starving would quickly turn to crime as a means of survival. This chapter examines the extent to which they did, and more importantly, it considers the motives for such crime.[9]

Amid the growing number of reports of distress and a starvation in Mayo in early 1831, also came reports of crime. Hunger drove many to partake in the interception of goods and it soon became difficult to transport anything throughout the county. In Belmullet, the merchants of the town sought protection to their shipping trade against attacks by the "banditti."[10] Attacks on property increased and, in many instances, arson was the favoured method. In February, one such attack on the house of a farmer near Westport was widely condemned and only for the exertions of his neighbors, the entire house would have been destroyed. However, the outbuildings were lost to fire and the charred remains of several animals were said to have presented a "disgusting spectacle."[11] The perpetrators of these crimes usually belonged to secret societies, who through fear of retribution by fellow members, operated with impunity in the Irish countryside. At Newport, James Hughes, the parish priest, lamented that huge numbers were engaged in attending illegal gatherings and swearing oaths. The focus for many of the societies were estate personnel, including the Earl of Lucan's wood-ranger, who was savagely beaten at his home in January.[12] These agrarian conspirators were also responsible for the liberation of animals and crops which had been taken for the non-payment of rent. In February, the animal pound at Cloghans near Ballina was broken open and cattle, which had been taken by the Earl of Limerick, removed.[13] In the same month, two pounds, in Killasser and Bohola, near Swinford, were razed to the ground for the same reason.[14] The police met with some success and, by April, the number of committals to jails in Mayo had risen from 152 to 800, the largest increase in Ireland. A range of crimes were committed as indicated by the breakdown of cases brought before the summer assizes in Mayo. On this occasion, 101 persons stood trial for:

> Administering oaths and appearing armed by night (24); burglary and robbery (4); robbery of arms (10); abduction (3); rape (4); sheep stealing (14); horse stealing (1); murder (2); forgery (1); cow stealing (4); larceny (12); passing base coin (2); assault and robbery (4); levelling houses (10) and miscellaneous (6).

Of course, these were only a fraction of the number of crimes committed as most of the culprits went undetected, while a host of other crimes were not reported to the authorities.[15]

By early summer, the effects of famine were evident everywhere. According to James MacHale, parish priest of Kilcommon, over 3,800 individuals in his jurisdiction were without either "horse, cow or sheep or any provisions." In Foxford, it was estimated that close to 800 families would be without provisions by mid-July.[16] The distress of the poor was magnified by the onset of a "malignant" fever which ravaged the county and claimed among its victims two Catholic clergy, Father Prendergast of Clifden and Rev. Hughes of Crossmolina.[17] There was widespread anger towards the plunder of meal that was transported through the county. At the Mayo Central Relief Committee meeting, following the plunder of meal near Swinford, it was suggested that the parish where this occurred should forfeit their supply in an effort to deter other poor from similar actions.[18] Such suggestions proved ineffective. At Kilbree, near Westport, where a party of soldiers from the 34th Regiment of Foot were attacked by "an immense number of persons," eight cart loads of goods were taken.[19] When the ship "Fame," with a cargo of potatoes, was stranded between Clare Island and Innisturk, the famishing population procured about 100 boats from the neighbourhood, in an attempt to seize the potatoes.[20] Part of this may have been opportunism, but it also reflected the determination of the lower classes to prevent the shipping of foodstuffs from the county.[21] Indeed, there was widespread annoyance at reports that the markets of Ballina and Killala were well supplied with provisions and that export of grain continued steadily.[22] The hoarding of food was widely condemned and mirrored what the writer William Carleton would depict more than a decade later, during the Great Famine:

> We say then, that any man who now forestalls meal and potatoes—and such persons, it is said are to be found even in Castlebar and Westport—are inhuman beings ... who would grow wealthy upon the ruin of the poor, and make the surrounding famine a source of opulence. These wretches must be thwarted in their infamous machinations.[23]

In what was familiar criticism, many blamed "absentee" Irish landlords who, it was argued, "preferred the clubs of London, Bath or Cheltenham" to attending to their Irish estates and tenants.[24] However, the charge was not always founded. The Mayo Central Relief Committee, for example, was headed by Sir Francis Lynch Blosse and included a number of landowners in the county. This body was responsible for overseeing the mammoth task of providing relief to a huge population. For the week ending 25 July, the committee relieved just over 224,000 people at a cost of just under £5,000.[25] Other landowners initiated schemes of their own. The Marquis of Sligo undertook "a mission of charity" to help the poor, while George Moore of Moorehall was a regular contributor to local relief schemes, winning praise for providing employment to his tenants.[26] Many landowners backed plans for public work schemes including land reclamation and the construction of new roads to create employment of the poor.[27] It was argued that these schemes would counteract the need for prolonged provision of relief gratis, which promoted idleness among the poor. As a body, Mayo landowners were at pains to emphasize that the famine was not of their making. Signed by 64 individuals in March 1831, they petitioned the government for help during this time of extreme distress.[28] According to Lynch Blosse, the conditions of the people were worse than they had been in 1822, but still "the Government continue to turn a deaf ear to the various appeals made to them."[29] By the middle of the summer some, like Thomas Parnell, feared that there would be more bloodshed if relief was not provided for the "suffering peasantry" of the west of Ireland.[30] Commenting on a mission to England to secure relief, undertaken by Mayo priest, Rev. Lyons, the *Morning Chronicle* hoped that someone would come to their aid. Would it be natural, they asked, that in an "age boasting of humanity and civilisation, thirty thousand British subjects perished of absolute want?"[31] Aid was provided from many quarters. In an effort to provide relief, theatres in Dublin gave performances on behalf of "the distress in Connaught,"[32] and a number of the leading gentlemen and merchants of Dublin petitioned the city's Lord Mayor to call a meeting to help with the distress in Mayo.[33] However, the distress of the poor was not confined to the west of Ireland. In Dublin, large numbers were on the brink of starvation and a great number out of work due to the severity of the weather.[34] The city also suffered from the influx of wandering poor and would-be emigrants from other counties, ensuring that the local almshouses were soon at capacity. Similarly, in Cork there were "frightful details of the progress of pauperism in that city," and in the city's house of industry, over 1,400 paupers were huddled together.[35]

While the failure of the potato had devastating consequences for the large portion of the population that relied solely on it, other factors contributed to the plight of the lower orders in 1831. The collapse of cottage industries in the wake of the Napoleonic Wars and the continued growth in population exacerbated the competition for land. By the early 1830s, the hunger for land was said to be so great that people were willing to pay well above market value for even the smallest patches of ground.[36] Repeated subdivision since the late 18th century had exacerbated this problem, with many landowners moving to counteract it. In 1832, for example, the Earl of Fitzwilliam's agent in County Wicklow, Robert Chaloner, sought to ban the subdivision of land "except in the most urgent necessity as the larger class of farms is at present too small."[37] However, there was an added complication—in doing so, large tracts of land were rented to middlemen on long leases. Until these leases expired there was nothing that could be done. When they did expire, it was often the smallholders who suffered most. In 1831, the expiration of a middleman's lease resulted in the eviction of 28 families in Strokestown, County Roscommon, prompting Thomas Conry, agent of the Mahon estate, to write:

> In all my life I never performed so disagreeable a duty, the poor creatures quit it with extreme reluctance, still they were perfectly obedient to the law. It will remain tenantless for the year as no person would venture to take it.[38]

While Conry praised the obedience of the Strokestown tenants, the fact that no person would take the land indicated a more menacing character amongst the people. Given the tensions that were bubbling below the surface, it was hardly surprising then that, with the onset of famine in 1831, the number of outrages associated with land rose. This was confirmed by a House of Commons report in 1832, which noted that small farmers believed that agrarian outrages were necessary to prevent them losing their lands on the expiration of their leases.[39] No one, it seemed, was immune from agrarian outrage. In Scariff, County Clare, a priest received a threatening notice to quit 30 acres of land by a group styling themselves "Terry Alts." In the same village, the local doctor was ordered to quit his holding or else "prepare a coffin."[40] In County Limerick, the favored method of outrage was the digging of land and driving cattle off it. In April 1831, at least seven different properties near the village of Bruff were dug up over the course of a couple of nights; one report stated that almost 800 men had dug up several acres of land during the night destroying the crops and making graves. In other areas, laborers were driven out of the fields by armed men, houses were attacked, and animals maimed in disputes over access to land.[41]

Outrages occurred in Mayo and elsewhere that attempted to coerce tenants to combine to withhold the payment of rent or to support the "system of swearing to pay only a certain proportion."[42] Naturally, fear among landowners and the authorities grew and many believed that a rebellion would soon commence. In King's County (now Offaly), J.W. Armstrong, a magistrate, reported that a "party practising some military exercise" was terrorising the countryside.[43] In County Sligo, "nightly attacks" and raids for arms were taking place, with only few arrests made.[44] In was the same in Ballina, County Mayo, where Rev. James Burrowes reported that Ribbonmen, the generic name given to secret societies, had made incursions into the neighborhood searching for arms and threatening violence.[45] In County Limerick, fire-arms were stolen while people were attending Sunday worship. The agrarian societies within the county stated their determination at "turning out all strangers." At Rathkeale in the same county, a "tumultuous" crowd assembled with the intention of ridding the area of outsiders.[46] Threatening notices appeared elsewhere. Many of the writers assumed a nom-de-plume; in County Clare it was "Lady Clare," or "Leady Cleare," who issued these menacing letters.[47] Lynch Blosse in Mayo alluded to about 400 men, assembled for the purpose of intimidating the tenants of Colonel Browne.[48] In April and May, gangs of men roamed County Galway, forcing shepherds to give up their flocks.[49] In the same month, there were reports that the "gentry are deserting their mansions, and seeking refuge in the neighbouring towns," amid threats to life and property.[50] This was not just a west of Ireland phenomenon. In County Louth, a mob gathered in the parish of Termonfeckin with "large clubs" to stop several men engaged in ploughing.[51] At Templemore in County Tipperary, tenants at Captain Butler's estate were driven off the land by a large group of men.[52] In the village of Inagh in County Clare, a man planting potatoes was severely beaten by a group of five men.[53] Indeed, such was the intimidation in Clare that many people had not bothered to till the ground in preparation for the coming season.[54] In other instances, and even in times of hunger when people starved, animals were mutilated and crops burned in revenge for some perceived wrong doing.[55] At Edenderry in King's County, the mutilation of animals was rife, while in the neighbouring barony of Carbury in County Kildare, Protestant farmers were targeted.[56] These outrages suggest a sectarian motive to several of the incidents. On 12 July 1829, Edenderry had been the scene of riots when Orangemen assembled there, close to where the River Boyne rises, which was an important location for the Orange tradition.[57] The following year, local magistrates alarmed at the increase in large assemblies at night that were attended by armed men, appealed for a better police force to be sent to the town. According to Dr. Richard Grattan, the authorities were "totally inadequate to make any resistance consisting of only about 5 Policemen." It was later suggested that much of the agitation around Edenderry was being stirred by a Catholic priest, Father Richard Cullen, who was described as "a very violent man."[58] Cullen and his colleague, Father James Colgan, were engaged in a battle with the local land agent Thomas Murray, who they labelled a "jackal' for intimidating the tenantry.[59] There was similar sectarian tension in Mullingar, County Westmeath, where people were warned not to have any dealings with Protestant merchants and shopkeepers.[60]

As the outrages continued to mount, memories of the 1798 rebellion were revived. In County Carlow it was claimed that "chests" of pikes were being sent to Wexford in advance of a rebellion and the likely massacre of Protestants.[61] Likewise, in Newmarket, County Cork, it was claimed that the Catholic population were preparing for "a struggle for independence."[62] In Dublin, many feared the "rising of O'Connell's rebellious mob."[63] Some of these fears centred on paranoia that all public gatherings were a conspiracy to commit crime. In County Clare, Tomkins Brew believed the lower orders were meeting nightly in public houses, to "plan who are to be plundered & who are to be murdered."[64] However, talk of a rebellion were dismissed from some quarters. Despite the level of outrage across the country James Dombrain, Inspector General of the Coast Guard who later played a prominent role during the Great Famine, dispelled any notion that there would be a rising, claiming that the people were displaying "fortitude and forbearance" in the face of want.[65]

While Dombrain was right in his assertion that a rebellion would not take place, he was wrong in the belief that the people, and the lower orders in particular, would remain quiet. The number and nature of murders committed in 1831 reflected this, with little value being placed on life. In January, the murder of William Blood, a magistrate in County Clare, was described as the "most revolting" to have taken place in living memory. Having broken into his home near Corofin, Blood was killed as he tried to fend off his attackers. Escaping from the house after seeing off his initial attackers, he was met by more of the party, "one of whom knocked him down with a scythe." According to the *Clare Journal*, the "head of the unfortunate gentleman presented in the morning a most frightful appearance. It was literally broken to pieces and the brains scattered about."[66] Blood's servant was tied up while the house was "rifled" of its contents. The murder created "confusion and excitement" in the locality, as landowners worried about their own safety.[67] This particular part of Clare was greatly troubled and when Edward Synge impounded cattle in lieu of rent the following month, an attempt was made on his life.[68] It was difficult to police the county owing the vastness of the terrain. Moreover, it was claimed that armed parties roamed about "without any disguise" and had a large number of firearms in their possession.[69] In April, an attack on a house in the parish of Kilfarboy by a large gang of armed insurgents[70] was followed by the murder of Daniel Hastings, the steward to John Scott Vandeleur of Newmarket.[71] Causing a sensation in the county, Hastings' crime was attributed to the work he did for his employer, which made him "obnoxious to the peasantry." Land stewards were targeted in other parts of the country. At Listowel, County Kerry, Maurice Shea, land steward at the Fitzmaurice estate, was murdered on his way from the fair in the town.[72] In May, another land steward, William Eason, was murdered at Ballinasloe, County Galway. Eason had previously received a notice to quit but had paid little heed to the threat.[73] At Cluggin, County Limerick, a land agent, Milo Burke, was murdered "within 200 yards of his own house."[74]

This period of dearth and anarchy also provided the opportunity for many to settle old scores. In August, Thomas Gregory, a landowner and attorney, was murdered at Newtown in Queen's County (now Laois) having given evidence in a land dispute in the local courts.[75] In the same county a man named Brophy was murdered at Knockaroe, near Borris-in-Ossory, when upwards of 40 men descended upon his house, most of whom were armed.[76] At Kedrah, near Cahir in County Tipperary, a man named Fitzgerald, the father of nine children, was murdered with his own spade. An earlier dispute over land between Fitzgerald and two men named Harty was said to have been the reason for the murder.[77] Nothing, it seemed, prevented these crimes from being committed. At Castlecrine, County Clare, a man named Hegarty was murdered when he returned from selling corn in the town. As the murder was committed, his young son who accompanied him was placed in a hedge.[78] Likewise, in County Carlow a man was "stoned to death" after being waylaid on the public road with many witnesses present.[79] In September, near Dundalk, County Louth, a poor fisherman named Philips was murdered—"his skull, face, nose and jaws were broken to atoms."[80]

Apart from land-related issues and settling old scores, the motive for many attacks and murders was attributed to the payment of tithes, which in a year of famine became more detestable to those who were starving. Both tenant farmers and cottiers considered it unjust that, in addition to paying their rent, they should be forced to pay an annual tax on the produce of their land, known as the tithe, towards the upkeep of the minority Established Church. The tithe varied from district to district and was paid in kind, mostly in corn or potatoes. No part of the country was spared from agitation.[81] In the southeast of the country, in Carlow and Wexford, it was claimed that under the cover of hurling matches, meetings had been organized to oppose the payment of tithes.[82] In County Donegal, Nassau Forster, a magistrate, reported that "a very bad spirit" existed amongst the lower orders in the parishes of Templecrone and Lettermacaward, where agitators warned people not to pay rents or tithes.[83] In Dunfanaghy in the same county, there were several disturbances over the collection of tithes,[84] while in nearby parishes, several of the clergy feared that there would be "violent opposition."[85] In Stradbally, Queen's County, it was reported that there was a "desperate degree of opposition" to tithes.[86] In County Longford, it was claimed that people were warned against paying a tax, which only supported the "monstrous bloated Bishops."[87] The valuation of tithes became a dangerous task and many were attacked in the course of doing so. In County Tipperary, Denis O'Shaughnessy was murdered while valuing tithes near the village of Dundrum.[88] Likewise, at Bennetsbridge in County Kilkenny a process server named Drohan was murdered as he carried out his duties.[89] County Kilkenny, it was claimed, was in a constant state of alarm, where, despite protection, it proved impossible to collect tithes.[90] This opposition would manifest itself most publicly in what became known as the "Battle of Carrickshock" when, in December 1831, 17 people were killed over opposition to tithes.[91] This was but one of several "battles" which took place in 1831—Newtown Barry (now Bunclody) in County Wexford and Castlepollard in County Westmeath being the scene of other deadly affrays.[92]

As 1832 dawned, the arrival and spread of cholera added to the social woes of Ireland. By summer, not a single town in Ireland had escaped the ravages of the disease. In Sligo, a town particularly badly affected, some 40 to 60 deaths per day were reported.[93] In early July, reports from Dublin suggested that more than 1,200 deaths had occurred there, while in Cork the figure was over 800.[94] Elsewhere, the figures testified to large numbers dying from the disease, including in Galway (295); Drogheda (367); Tullamore (150); Ennis (131) and Belfast (83)—all figures which would undoubtedly rise before the end of the year. Terence Shanley, medical attendant for the Tarmonbarry and Kilglass dispensary in County Roscommon, noted that the majority of the poor were living in habitual disease, lingered from day-to-day in fear of dying. In the space of three years, he estimated that he had attended to over 10,000 people, in whom "fevers of almost every type, affections of the chest, rheumatism, small-pox, measles, whooping cough, croup, dysentery, diarrhoea and cholera" prevailed.[95]

The fears of government officials and landlords that a year of famine would bring about a rise in crime and violence in Ireland was well founded. This violence, as has been demonstrated, was exacerbated by issues of land and tithes, problems that would continue to play a major role in rural unrest. The opening days of January 1832 saw a continuation of violence. In Mountrath in Queen's County, a man named Phelan was stabbed with a pitchfork as an armed party tried to enter his brother's house looking for firearms.[96] At nearby Graigue, a young woman was found in the River Barrow and the deep wound on the back of neck and marks of violence across her back suggested she had met a vicious end.[97] In County Clare, at Ballycorick, a man was savagely murdered by "cutting the roof of the skull, inflicting three wounds on the back of the head, and cutting him almost in two across the back."[98] It was these crimes and the litany of outrages which had preceded them in 1831 that prompted the Earl of Roden to comment in the House of Commons in July 1832 that Ireland was "almost overwhelmed with misery and crime."[99]

NOTES

1. *Dublin Morning Register*, 20 July 1830.
2. William Carleton, *The Black Prophet: A Tale of Irish Famine* (London: Simms and M'Intyre, 1847), p. 175.
3. For the impact of cholera see Tim. P. O'Neill, "Cholera in Offaly in the 1830s," in *Offaly Heritage*, 1 (2003), 96–107.
4. Sir Edward O'Brien, Dromoland Castle, Newmarket on Fergus, County Clare to Charles Grant, Chief Secretary, Dublin Castle, 24 Nov. 1821 (National Archives of Ireland (NAI), CSORP, 1821/1103).
5. Ibid., John Killaly, Ennis, County Clare to William Gregory, Under Secretary, Dublin Castle, 29 June 1822 (1822/315).
6. Ibid., for example, Nathaniel Taylor, Noan, County Tipperary to William Gregory, Under Secretary, 20 May 1827 (1827/778).
7. *Chutes Western Herald*, 24 Feb. 1831. My thanks to Brendan Hoban for bringing this to my attention.
8. For a sample of the reports of famine in Mayo see *Freeman's Journal,* 16 Feb. 1831, 5 July 1831; *Connaught Telegraph*, 8 June 1831.
9. See *Select committee on disturbed state of Ireland*, HC, 1831–32 (677).
10. "File of documents arising from the disturbed state of the neighbourhood of Belmullet and Binghamstown, County Mayo, due to a lack of provisions, 7 Nov. 1830, 11 Feb 1831" (NAI, CSORP/OR/1831/38).
11. *Chutes Western Herald,* 28 Feb. 1831.
12. *Freeman's Journal*, 22 Jan. 1831.
13. *Kerry Evening Post*, 23 Feb. 1831.

14. *Southern Reporter and Cork Commercial Courier*, 3 March 1831.
15. *Roscommon & Leitrim Gazette*, 23 July 1831.
16. Rev. James MacHale to Henry William Paget, Lord Lieutenant, Dublin Castle, 10 June 1831 (NAI, CSORP, OR, 1831/1139). There were similar numbers reported in neighbouring County Galway. For example, Rev. Patrick Hughes to Dr. John James Bodkin, 29 June 1831 (Ibid., 1831/1821).
17. *Dublin Morning Register*, 6 June 1831.
18. *Connaught Telegraph*, 13 July 1831.
19. "File of documents on local fatalities arising from the theft of provisions sent for the relief of the starving in County Mayo, 10 June 1831–8 Aug. 1831" (NAI, CSORP, OR/1831/1139).
20. Ibid.
21. Ibid., "File of documents arising from the disturbed state of the neighbourhood of Belmullet and Binghamstown, County Mayo, due to a lack of provisions," 7 Nov. 1830–1 Feb. 1831 (1831/38).
22. Ibid., Gregory Haines, Deputy Commissary General, Commissary General's Office, Dublin, to an unnamed recipient [but likely the Chief Secretary's Office] (1831/967).
23. *Freeman's Journal*, 9 June 1831. For Carleton see *The Black Prophet*, p. 67.
24. *Dublin Morning Register*, 13 June 1831.
25. *Connaught Telegraph*, 27 July 1831.
26. Ibid., 8 June 1831.
27. *Dublin Morning Register*, 2 Aug. 1831. See also Martin Joseph Howley, Ballina, County Mayo to Lieutenant Colonel Sir William Gosset, Under Secretary, Dublin Castle, 3 March 1831 (NAI, CSORP, 1831/1078).
28. Ibid., "Memorial of the landed proprietors and clergymen of the parishes of Dunferry [Doonfeeny] and Kilbride, County Mayo, to Henry William Paget, Lord Lieutenant, 28 March 1831 (1831/967).
29. Ibid., Sir Francis Lynch Blosse to Edward Geoffrey Smith Stanley, Chief Secretary, Dublin Castle, 23 May 1831 (1831/1560)
30. Ibid., Thomas Parnell to Alexander Mangin, 5 July 1831 (1831/1650).
31. Quoted in *Dublin Morning Register*, 4 March 1831.
32. Ibid., 28 June 1831.
33. See *Freeman's Journal*, 4 April 1831.
34. *Dublin Morning Register*, 7 Feb. 1831.
35. Ibid., 22 Jan. 1831.
36. *Times*, 7 July 1837.
37. "Memoranda dealing with tenancies, 1796–1841" National Library of Ireland (NLI), Fitzwilliam papers, MS 4948.
38. Ibid., Thomas Conry to Baron Hartland, 10 Dec. 1831, Pakenham Mahon papers, MS 10,099, 2.
39. Questioning their use in the first place, the Earl of Glengall of Cahir, County Tipperary, queried whether "any tenant in Ireland perform the covenants in his lease towards a landlord?" See Earl of Glengall to Lord Charleville, n.d. (1838–9), PRONI, Charleville papers, T/ 3069/ D/ 22.

40. *Chutes Western Herald*, 25 April 1831.
41. "Memorial from the magistrates, clergy and inhabitants of the town and district of Athleague, County Roscommon, 3 May 1831" (NAI, CSORP, OR/1831/19).
42. Ibid., Major Samson Carter, Castlebar, County Mayo, to Edward Geoffrey Smith Stanley, Chief Secretary, Dublin Castle, 24 Jan. 1831 (1831/107).
43. Ibid., J.W. Armstrong, magistrate, Ballycumber, King's County to the Chief Secretary's Office, Dublin Castle, 20 Jan. 1831 (1831/4).
44. Ibid., John Armstrong, James Wood and Thomas Fenton, [magistrates], Ballymote, Tobbercurry, County Sligo, to Edward Geoffrey Smith Stanley, Chief Secretary, Dublin Castle, 7 Feb. 1831 (1831/8).
45. Ibid., Rev. James Burrowes, Killanley Glebe, Ballina, county Mayo to Edward Geoffrey Smith Stanley, Chief Secretary, Dublin Castle, 24 Jan. 1831 (1831/45).
46. Ibid., John S. Brown, Rathkeale, County Limerick, 16 June 1831 (1831/117).
47. Ibid., George Browne, Chief Constable, Killaloe, County Clare to Lieutenant Colonel Sir William Gosset, Under Secretary, Dublin Castle, 6 Dec. 1831 (1831/153).
48. Ibid., Sir Francis Lynch Blosse to the Chief Secretary's Office, nd [1831] (1831/41).
49. Ibid., "File of documents arising from an investigation of an attack on the dwelling of Sir John Burke of Marblehill in County Galway, 9 April 1831–28 May 1831" (1831/85).
50. *The Morning Post*, 12 April 1831.
51. Sir John Byng, Commander of the Troops in Ireland, Royal Hospital, Dublin, to Lieutenant Colonel Sir William Gosset, Under Secretary, Dublin Castle, 28 Jan. 1831 (NAI, CSORP, OR/1831/47).
52. Ibid., Thomas Brereton to the Under Secretary, Dublin Castle, 26 Jan. 1831 (1831/60).
53. *Kerry Evening Post*, 6 April 1831.
54. Ibid., 23 Feb. 1831.
55. See for example *Leinster Express*, 22 Oct. 1831.
56. *Sligo Journal*, 17 June 1831.
57. For example, William Peel, Whitehall, London, to Francis Leveson Gower, Chief Secretary, Dublin Castle, 27 July 1829 (NAI, CSORP, 1829/2251).
58. Ibid., Arthur Hill, 3rd Marquis of Downshire, Easthampstead Park, Bracknell, England to Sir William Gosset, Under Secretary, Dublin Castle, 17 April 1832 (1832/1560); ibid., Thomas Murray, Edenderry, King's County to Sir William Gosset, Under Secretary, Dublin Castle, 13 Apr 1832 (1832/2127).
59. Rev. Richard Cullen to Robert Cassidy, 24 March 1832 (NLI, Cassidy papers).
60. *Westmeath Journal*, 20 Jan. 1831.
61. "Anonymous letter to Henry William Paget, Lord Lieutenant, Dublin Castle 20 July 1831" (NAI, CSORP, OR/1831/26).
62. Ibid., Home Office, Whitehall, London to Richard Earle, Irish Office, London, 20 May 1831 (1831/30).
63. Ibid., R. Cathcart, 65 Upper Stephen Street, Dublin to Edward Geoffrey Smith Stanley, Chief Secretary, Dublin Castle, 7 Jan. 1831 (1831/53).
64. Ibid., Tomkins Brew, Chief Magistrate, Ennis, County Clare, to Lieutenant Colonel Sir William Gosset, Under Secretary, Dublin Castle, 3 June 1831 (1831/52).

65. Ibid., James Dombrain, Comptroller General of the Coast Guards in Ireland, Limerick, to Edward Geoffrey Smith Stanley, Chief Secretary, 15 June 1831 (1831/1467).
66. *Clare Journal*, 24 Jan. 1831. See also *Kerry Evening Post*, 26 Jan. 1831.
67. Robert Armitage, Corofin, County Clare, to Edward Geoffrey Smith Stanley, Chief Secretary, Dublin Castle, 22 Jan. 1831 (NAI, CSO/RP/OR/1831/3).
68. Ibid., Rev [James] Hastings Allen, Curate of Corofin, Roxton, County Clare, to Lieutenant Colonel Sir William Gosset, Under Secretary, Dublin Castle, 18 Feb. 1831 (1831/10).
69. Ibid., Andrew Bedient, County Clare to Henry William Paget, Lord Lieutenant, Dublin Castle, 10 June 1831 (1831/23).
70. Ibid., Lieut. Col. George Tovey, 5th Regiment of Foot, Ennistymon, County Clare to Sir Frederick Stovin, Military Secretary, Royal Hospital, Dublin, 11 April 1831 (1831/21).
71. *Chutes Western Herald*, 28 April 1831.
72. *Tralee Mercury*, 10 Dec. 1831.
73. *Freeman's Journal,* 9 May 1831.
74. *Roscommon & Leitrim Gazette*, 1 Aug. 1831.
75. *Kerry Evening Post*, 27 Aug. 1831.
76. Lieut. Col. Daniel O'Donoghue, Portarlington, Queen's County to Lieutenant Colonel Sir William Gosset, Under Secretary, Dublin Castle, 6 April 1831 (NAI, CSORP, OR/1831/84).
77. *Kerry Evening Post*, 5 Nov. 1831.
78. Ibid., 28 Sept. 1831.
79. *Tralee Mercury*, 12 Nov. 1831.
80. *Freeman's Journal*, 22 Sept. 1831.
81. Quoted in Michael O'Hanrahan, "The tithe war in county Kilkenny, 1830–1834" in William Nolan and Kevin Whelan (eds), *Kilkenny history and society: interdisciplinary essays in the history of an Irish county* (Dublin: Geography Publications, 1990), p. 483.
82. For example, Lieut. James Battersby, Sub-Inspector, Carlow, County Carlow, to Col. Sir John Harvey [Inspector General of Police], Jan. 1831, (NAI, CSORP, OR/1831/51).
83. Ibid., Nassau Forster to an unidentified recipient [but likely the Chief Secretary's Office], 15 Jan. 1831 (1831/355)
84. Ibid., Lieut. Finlay Ash, Dunfanaghy, County Donegal, to Richard Cane, General Agent, Yeomanry Department, Dublin Castle, 8 Jan. 1831 (1831/2).
85. Ibid., "File of letters from Rev John Barrett, Inniskeel House, Narin, County Donegal, regarding resistance to the collection of tithes, 9 Jun 1831–31 Aug 1831" (1831/112).
86. Ibid., Lieut. Hugh Boyd Wray, Sub-Inspector, Maryboro, Queens County, to Col Sir John Harvey, Dublin, 18 Aug. 1831 (1831/131).
87. Ibid., Samuel Alworthy, Ballymahon, County Longford, to Lieutenant Colonel Sir William Gosset, Under Secretary, Dublin Castle, 25 Nov. 1831 (1831/34).
88. *Roscommon & Limerick Gazette*, 1 Aug. 1831.
89. *Chutes Western Herald*, 28 March 1831.
90. Francis Blackburne, Attorney General, Leinster Street, Dublin, to Lieutenant Colonel Sir William Gosset, Under Secretary, 31 March 1831 (NAI, CSORP, OR/1831/78); ibid., "Anonymous letter from a Church of Ireland clergyman, Cheltenham, England to Edward Geoffrey Smith Stanley, Chief Secretary, Dublin Castle, 15 Aug. 1831" (1831/28).

91. *Kilkenny Journal*, 17 Dec. 1831.
92. For an in-depth account of the Tithe War in County Kilkenny see O'Hanrahan, "The tithe war in county Kilkenny 1830–1834," pp 481–505. For Castlepollard, see Eoghan Ó hAnnracháin, "Massacre at Castlepollard, 1831: socio-political aspects" in *Ríocht na Mídhe*, 22 (2011), pp 150–78; for Newtown Barry see *Report of Brigade Major Bushe to the lord lieutenant on the Newtownbarry affray*, H.C. 1831 (241) xv. 487.
93. *Tralee Mercury*, 1 Sept. 1832.
94. Ibid., 4 July 1832.
95. *First report from His Majesty's commissioners for inquiring into the condition of the poorer classes in Ireland*, supplement to appendix B, part 1, 1835 (369), p. 12.
96. *Newry Telegraph*, 3 Jan. 1832.
97. *Dublin Morning Register*, 20 Dec. 1831.
98. *Limerick Chronicle*, 4 Jan. 1832.
99. Quoted in the *Belfast News-Letter*, 10 July 1832.

Canada—a famine frontier

CHAPTER SIX

"WE HAVE SCATTERED THEM FAR AND WIDE"

Transporting Indigent Irish Emigrants in the Canadas, 1843–1847

Laura J. Smith

As the extraordinary migration year of 1847 wound to a close, James Bruce, Earl of Elgin and Governor General of Canada, included three newspaper clippings in his regular correspondence to Henry George, Earl Grey and Secretary of State for War and the Colonies.[1] The third, an unattributed clipping simply titled "Hamilton," is particularly noteworthy. In addition to making it across the Atlantic to the Colonial Office, the piece, which was from the *Hamilton Gazette*, was widely reprinted throughout British North America. It highlighted issues of concern for the Canada West city in the wake of the 1847 migration season (which saw 16,000 newcomers overwhelm the nascent city of 7,000), but also pointed to trends in the migration and settlement, particularly of "indigent" migrants, the majority of whom were Irish, to Canada West in the 1840s more broadly. Reporting on the imminent closure of the government-run emigrant hospital and sheds in that city, the newspaper predicted the development would "bear particularly hard on this city, which seems to have been made a sort of rallying point for those who cannot get employment in this section of the country." As winter set in, Hamilton was already overrun with the sick and the destitute thousands of whom were "huddled together in damp cellars without food or clothing." This was "not all the evil," the *Gazette* reported, for "every day poor emigrants are seen coming into the city to seek that shelter for the winter which they cannot find in the country." Blaming the imperial government for overwhelming the colony with "disease and poverty" the paper predicted, "unparalleled misery, starvation, crime, will be the consequences of leaving the wretched emigrants to their fate" and called on the Crown to "relieve us from this pecuniary infliction."[2]

At first glance, the "Hamilton" article evokes familiar images of destitute Irish Famine migrants huddled in urban dwellings, their plights made all the more distressing with the onset of a brutal North American winter, but it also highlights elements of the Canadian migration context that have been largely ignored in the historiography. The migrants huddled in the damp cellars of Hamilton had not come straight from the wharf, but many, during their short time in the country, had already traveled to other parts of the colony, often at public expense, in search of employment or reunification with family and friends. The persistence of migrants in the port towns and cities on the north shore of Lake Ontario was not a phenomenon of 1847, but a perennial problem not confined to solely to "indigent" emigrants, as those requiring government assistance were termed.[3] In 1840, the *Toronto Colonist* reported that the emigrants of that season who were of a "better class, and paid their own expenses," were resisting the authorities' efforts to "scatter" them into the country, but were returning to Toronto, some via the United States.[4] This chapter explores the effort by emigration authorities to "scatter" migrants, an effort that apparently had little effect in Toronto in 1840, and failed spectacularly in Hamilton in 1847.

The authorities were A. J. Buchanan, the chief emigrant agent for the united Canadas, based in Canada East at Quebec, and his designate in Canada West, Arthur Hawke (based primarily in Kingston). Hawke oversaw a network of emigrant agents posted along the St. Lawrence and in the port cities on the north shore of Lake Ontario. Emigrant agents superintended the reception of new arrivals to the province, provided assistance in the form of food, temporary shelter, and medical assistance to those who were without means, and facilitated the inland transportation of migrants out of their final port of disembarkation.[5] This chapter draws upon the financial records generated by Hawke and his Canada West-based agents between 1843 and 1847. The Emigrant Service Fund records are essentially receipts for the expenses paid by the agents administering the arrival, reception, dispersal and settlement of indigent emigrants, the majority of whom were Irish.[6] Throughout the 1840s, considerable government funds and energy were spent in transporting emigrants not only from the quarantine station at Grosse *Île* to Quebec, but further west to Montreal and ports in the upper province. At each port, agents facilitated the transport of emigrants away from the city and into rural townships. The assistance, ostensibly offered to only those lacking the means to transport themselves, was premised on the notion that emigrants stood a better chance of finding work in rural settings than in urban. That emigrants were dispersed over multiple jurisdictions rather than concentrated in one, was another unstated benefit (and source of criticism) of the program. Thus, the return to Hamilton of thousands of destitute migrants in 1847 highlighted the apparent failure of a central plank of emigration policy.

The financial records shed light on a critical period of Irish migration to Canada and broaden the usual scholarly focus from the summer of 1847 to consider much of the decade. Relatively consistent record keeping means a demographic picture of who sought assistance in Canada West can be constructed. The records also move migrants past the wharf, and provide, in their continued movement, evidence of emigrant dynamism and agency, adding further nuance to what is known about the rural nature of Irish settlement in Canada in the 19th century.[7] While the emphasis of the provincial government was on rural settlement, and facilitating the transition of migrants into settlers, implicit was an acknowledgement that destitute migrants could not acquire land in the short term, and were unlikely to do so in the long term.[8] Yet the work of the emigrant agents also made it clear that indigent migrants, by offering much needed labor, particularly for agricultural and public works, were integral to the province's development.

Contemporaries, including emigrant agents, regarded the process of moving emigrants through the province as a random dispersal rather than a calculated distribution. Though he spoke of using his funding and networks to further emigrant journeys, Hawke likened emigrant transportation to a "scattering."[9] In 1847, he was particularly anxious to move emigrants out of port cities, sensitive to criticisms that the government was allowing them to "accumulate" in the colony's cities.[10] Of Kingston he noted, "with the exception of those emigrants in hospital and a few in the sheds waiting on the recovery of those in hospital, we have not an emigrant hanging loose in society ... we have scattered them far and wide."[11] As that season came to a close, he conceded that migration that year had been "a calamity to the province." Only the owners of steam ships had profited Hawke noted and, ironically given his role, "there is no denying that they [emigrants] have scattered disease and death to a fearful extent wherever they have congregated in any considerable number."[12]

Observers were critical of what they perceived as a careless way to introduce emigrants into the province, particularly in 1847. The Toronto-based *Examiner* complained that newcomers "have been hurried off in every direction by vessels or carriages to any locality where there was the smallest probability of their meeting with acquaintances, friends or employment."[13] The Irish-run *Mirror* likened emigrants to weeds, who in being removed from the port cities, "are all thrown out of our garden into our neighbour's fields, to die or to take root as heaven pleases."[14] Larratt Smith, a Torontonian, wrote to his uncle that after a brief stay at the sheds, new emigrants were "carried off 'willy nilly' some 16 or 20 miles North, South, East & West and quickly put down, leaving the *country* to support them by giving them employment."[15] Early historiographical treatments reinforced the perception that emigrants were passive and their distribution unintentional. A discussion of the reception of Famine emigrants in 1847, invokes crowds of Irish paupers "aimlessly waiting" in the province's ports while government officials flailed about with apparently no infrastructure in place to grapple with the onslaught.[16] More recent treatments have acknowledged the Emigration Office's work in providing inland transportation, but provide few details of the process.[17] The relative obscurity of the Emigration Service Fund records explain, in substantive detail, the considerable time and money spent on dispersing emigrants inland in the historiography.

Directing the flow of migrants was a central function of the Emigration Office. Emigrants' movements were subject to government control immediately upon arrival in British North America, first with quarantine at Grosse *Île,* and then as they were directed west to Quebec and beyond.[18] As they progressed along the maritime transportation route, they were subject to scrutiny and control at each port. The sick were removed and transported to local hospital facilities if they existed; the healthy who could prove that they had friends or relatives in the vicinity were allowed to disembark; those without local support were left to wait, often confined to the sheds, until they could be transported further west. While waiting, their movements were curtailed, whether by the requirement that they reside in the sheds to receive rations, or by more coercive measures such as those enacted in 1847. At Montreal, for example, the police were instructed to prevent emigrants from moving beyond a strict boundary around the sheds, which were located on swampy land at a distance from the city.[19] In Toronto, the city's Board of Health issued an edict forbidding migrants to leave the wharf without the permission of the emigrant agent.[20] Such measures were intended to prevent the spread of disease, but had the added benefit of preventing emigrants from loitering in the city while facilitating their eventual efficient removal.[21]

Providing emigrants with inland transportation away from Lake Ontario appears to have been exceptional, dispensed on a case-by-case basis, but it quickly became a central element of the system.[22] Newcomers to Canada often sojourned in one place to raise the necessary funds for the next stage of their journey; government assistance was often part of their overall migration strategy.[23] In 1841, Hawke noted that it was increasingly common for emigrants to exhaust their resources before reaching Upper Canada. As many were destined to become "actual settlers," he argued that help to complete their journey should be "invariably given."[24] Later, as the scale of indigent migration to the colony increased, he cautioned that free passages and a supply of food should be given to indigent emigrants only when "imperatively necessary" and only if it allowed an emigrant to "proceed to such parts of the country as is likely to afford them employment."[25] But the scope of the Emigration Service Fund transportation records belies this caution, indicating that Hawke's emigrant agents saw transportation assistance, particularly if it sent emigrants toward an employment opportunity or facilitated a reunion with settler friends and family, as a worthwhile expense.

It is not surprising that as immigration to the colony increased, the expense of transporting emigrants grew, accounting for approximately two-thirds of the Emigration Office's budget in 1846 and 1847.[26] Transportation was a significant portion of a local agency's budget. Not surprisingly, transportation expenses made up 25 percent of the £2,800 spent by the Hamilton agency in 1847. Only the eponymous "hospital expenses including funerals" was a larger category, namely 68 percent.[27] Imperial officials pushed back these expenses, arguing that too much assistance would invite abuse and retard the industriousness of those who might be able to support the emigration of needy friends and relatives.[28] Earl Grey cautioned the Governor General in 1847 that emigrants, "especially when you have to deal with the Irish," were liable to abuse any generosity on the part of the government: "it is far better to do too little than too much, and rather to allow a good deal of suffering to take place than to take away the motive to exertion by attempting to relieve everybody."[29] The Governor General countered that defraying transportation costs prevented emigrants "from accumulating in excessive numbers near the ports of disembarkation" and encouraged them to stay in the province rather than proceed to the United States.[30] Buchanan also defended the expenses as entirely justifiable and necessary.[31] From Canada West, Hawke argued that offering transportation to all emigrants, not just indigent ones, would encourage Upper Canadians to "put their shoulders to the wheel" to facilitate their relatives' emigration, whether by funding the transatlantic passage, or by offering shelter or employment assistance once in Canada.[32]

To understand the possibilities posed by the Emigrant Service Fund records, a sample of transportation documents, for at least one emigrant agency for each year, was compiled. Hamilton figures prominently in the years 1843 to 1846, and Toronto was sampled for 1847. Further work into other locations and for other years will reveal some of the nuances of particular agencies, agents and migration years. There is some variation in the information included in the transportation receipts, but they generally include the name of the emigrant agent, the teamster, the names of single emigrants, the heads of households, the number of their party and their destination. Often, a calculation of the baggage carried by each party, or by the group as a whole, was included, though the way in which it was quantified varied and has not been included in this study.[33] The number of passages associated with each emigrant party was usually calculated to determine the costs of transportation. This often differed from the number of people noted to constitute a party. Children were counted as a half passage, while adults constituted a full passage.[34] Given the temporal and geographic range of the records, the relative consistency of recordkeeping is remarkable. This consistency allows a comparison of demographic trends between agencies or ports and between years. A sample of documents from the five years covered by the records suggests interesting trends in the demographics of migration, particularly of those "indigent" who required and sought assistance. Agents grouped emigrants with their travel companions and the relationship of each to the "head of the household" was usually indicated. The head of a travelling party was always identified by name. In many cases the head, as was convention, was the oldest adult male in a family. In other cases, the status may have been determined by who spoke on the group's behalf or was simply determined by the emigrant agent himself. A summary is shown in Table 1. The samples gleaned names for 1,101 emigrants and counted 5,268 emigrants. The ratio each year between named and unnamed emigrants was roughly 1:4. For example, in the receipts generated by the Hamilton agency in 1846, 198 emigrants were named compared to 1,258 who were not. This indicates the extent to which emigrants who sought assistance for transportation, maintained and preserved familial groups, despite the dislocation and chaos of the trans-Atlantic and inland voyages and the frequency of illness and quarantine.

Conjugal families consisting of a mother, father, and dependent children were the most common demographic given assistance in the mid-1840s. Just over half of the named emigrants at Hamilton in 1843, 1844, and 1845 were heads of conjugal families. In Toronto in 1847, the percentage of conjugal families assisted was slightly lower at 44 percent, with a greater proportion of men and women travelling alone, and single men and women with dependents seeking assistance. Further study will illuminate the extent to which the 1847 emigration differed from its predecessors and the extent to which other ports deviated or replicated Toronto's demographics.[35] Of note, is the relative lack of extended families. Where families included other relatives, they were mostly a "sister" or "sister-in-law." Only on rare occasions did a family include the "mother" of the head of the family and no fathers were found in the samples studied. The absence of elderly parents is indicative of the relative youth and health of the emigrants who made it across the Atlantic.

The transportation receipts indicate that a significant number of women traveled to the Canadas in the mid-1840s. The prevalence of conjugal families in the sample data, meant that the majority of adult women traveled with their husbands and dependent children.[36] Women who traveled with adult men were not identified by name, but by their relationship to the head of the party: "wife," "sister" or, occasionally, "mother." Other women were identified as "daughters" presumably to distinguish them from children, or to indicate their relatively advanced age and their dependence, at least for the duration of the journey, on their parents.[37] Inconsistency across documents, particularly relating to marital status, makes it difficult to determine the dynamics of a woman's relationship to the children. For example, on 5 June, Nelly Harrington with seven children, and Mary McBride and 10 children, were sent from Cobourg to the Township of Emily. The agent at Cobourg often identified women as "Mrs." or "Widow" and thus the absence of either identifier for Harrington or McBride is notable, but not a conclusive indication that they were both unmarried.[38]

While most women traveled as part of families, a significant proportion did so without adult men.[39] When an adult woman was identified as the head of a party, in the absence of an adult male, she was usually identified by a first and last name. If a widow, only her last name was recorded.[40] Named female emigrants consistently accounted for between 13–25 percent of all named emigrants (see Table 1) indicating that female-headed groups were a significant portion of those assisted. A subtle increase in Toronto in 1847 to 26.9 percent and an extraordinary 80.7 percent in Port Hope the previous year, suggest local nuances that require further exploration, but may indicate demographic changes wrought by the onset of widespread famine in Ireland.[41] Widows and orphans were grouped together and singled out as deserving government support. Orphans, by virtue of separate relief measures, are not visible in the Emigration Service Fund transportation records; widows, on the other hand, appear with some frequency.[42] In 1847, Hawke commented on the volume of widows "with large families" and "no friends in America" sent out by landlords and local relief committees.[43] In Kingston, newspapers solicited donations of clothing for widows and orphans residing in the city's emigrant sheds.[44] In Toronto, a dedicated Widows and Orphans Asylum was established in September 1847, operating until 1848.[45]

The sampled records suggest widows were assisted frequently and consistently. Widows made up on average one-third of named female emigrants in the sample (see Table 1), but outnumbered other named women only in 1847.[46] Widows rarely traveled without dependents or other companions.[47] Drawing on statistics for Kingston, Cobourg, and Bytown, Hawke estimated that widows migrating in 1847 brought with them an average of three children.[48] Statistics for the combined Port Hope and

Table 1: Compiled demographics for assisted emigrants receiving transportation from sample Canada West ports, 1843–1847

Year	City	Total Emigrants in Sample	Named Emigrants	Conjugal families	Named Women	Named women alone	Named women with dependents (not widows)	Widows	Named men alone	Named men with dependents (no wife)	Children
1843	Hamilton	801	176	103	23	4	8	11	24	17	519
1844	Hamilton	730	147	83	36	11	17	8	3	15	460
1845	Kingston	414	128	n/a	22	4	11	7	1	0	n/a
	Hamilton	963	213	117	46	12	21	13	13	9	559
1846	Port Hope	431	83	11	67	4	44	19	0	3	291
	Hamilton	1258	198	n/a	26	3	13	10	3		488
1847	Toronto	671	156	69	42	14	9	19	26	24	405

Cobourg agency for 1846 indicate widowed mothers traveled with an average of four children. The considerable presence of widows offers a corrective to the contemporary impression that most ended up as inmates of charitable institutions. Rather, widowed women drew on the transportation offered just as other adult women and men did, journeying to locations where they might procure employment and shelter for their dependents.

Women travelling alone, or with no discernable dependents, appeared with far less frequency than those with family members. They accounted for an average 20 percent of named females, with a high of 40.5 percent assisted at Toronto in 1847. Such women were often grouped together on travel tickets. In August 1847, Mary Crowley, Betty Brown, Catharine Sullivan and Nancy Hurley traveled north from Toronto with two families to Brampton.[49] It is not clear if their grouping indicates self-selection to preserve preexisting relationships, or reflects a choice on the part of the emigrant agent to keep individual females together for their protection or for propriety's sake. When women traveled with other women to whom they were related, it was most often their sisters. Mary, Catharine, and Ann McTaggart went to Caledon from Toronto in August 1847. Less common were instances of women travelling with their brothers. On 7 June 1846, Ellen Carney and her two brothers, and Mary Rooney and her three sisters (one of whom was a child), were transported from Port Hope to the Township of Otonobee.[50]

The prevalence of conjugal families and the extent to which adult women rarely traveled without dependents, is indicative of the extent to which the trans-Atlantic migration of this period was dominated by dependent children.[51] Buchanan noted in 1847 that families, and consequently children, made up a larger share of the migrant population than was usual. The increased number of children, he believed, increased the number of emigrants unable to support themselves.[52] The Emigration Service Fund records suggest that children were a significant feature of the annual arrival of emigrants for most of the 1840s. Emigrant agents mostly indicated how many children were in a party, though there is some inconsistency. In Kingston in 1845, Hawke simply noted that a named emigrant traveled with "family." In such cases, the number of passages attributed to a group might shed light, though limited, on the number of individuals in the party.[53] Figure A indicates that children amounted to 60 percent or more of the total emigration in each sample, with the exception of Hamilton in 1846. There, children accounted for less than 40 percent, though the proportion of conjugal families was lower in Toronto in 1847, the proportion of children did not accordingly decrease, suggesting a greater portion of children traveled with single parents that year.

Orphans are not visible in the Emigration Service Fund records. Emigrant agents rarely provided details about a child's relationship to the adult with whom they traveled, nor were unaccompanied children found in the sampled records. Yet children without adult guardians, orphaned or not, were transported. In July 1847, the Board of Health in London, Canada West, reported that three sisters had recently "been sent here from Quebec" where their parents had taken ill. Of the sisters, the two eldest were "almost too young to be able to take care of themselves much less of the youngest which is only about four years old. The [youngest] has consequently been neglected and there are very small hopes of its recovery."[54] Children traveling alone also featured in the sundry expenses recorded by Buchanan at Quebec. In 1846, he remitted 12 shillings 6 pence to a "poor German child going to her parents."[55] A child whose mother had been confined to the Beaufort Lunatic Asylum was nursed and clothed for almost a year, costing the Quebec emigrant agency £132.[56] In 1844, the same agency spent over £8 lodging Patrick and Mary Sullivan, a brother and sister from Limerick, whose father had drowned on his way to meet them in Quebec.[57]

Finally, the relative lack of men travelling alone was apparent. Assisted men overwhelmingly traveled in conjugal families. The number of unaccompanied men was equaled and frequently exceeded by women doing so. Men with dependent children and no adult females in their party were an even smaller subset of the sampled data. (See Table 1) Sons or brothers were virtually nonexistent (despite the occasional daughters or sisters) suggesting that young adult men were less inclined to travel with their relatives. Perhaps single men did not feel the need to be assisted or failed to meet the qualifying criteria. Did the city offer more opportunity than a rural township for a young single man? Further study will determine the extent to which the patterns discerned in these records are indicative of broader trends for migration. The relative lack of single men also raises questions about a central goal of emigrant transportation—providing employment opportunities. Prejudices about the competence of the Irish for agricultural labor were rampant in Upper Canada.[58] But so too was the perception that labour was in short supply and emigrants, regardless of origins, were needed to support the development of the province, particularly by laboring on public works.[59] It was assumed that employment was plentiful and wages good if emigrants proved willing to take up the work.[60] That emigrants were too picky about the wages was the perennial complaint of colonial observers, while the loss of labor, particularly of assisted emigrants to the United States, was a perpetual bone of contention.[61]

It did not follow that the existence of positions led to employment. In 1840, Hawke had sent several parties of laborers to Hamilton despite warnings from the local agent that there was little work. Hawke complained that the local Road

Commission's unwillingness to take advantage of the men's readiness to work meant that they had been "lost to the province," instead going to the United States.[62] Nor did the relocation of emigrants result in positions. Writing to his uncle in summer 1847, Toronto resident Larratt Smith recounted an amusing anecdote: "woe betide anyone from friendly feelings advertising for labour! John Gamble advertised for 50 for the Vaughan plank road, and hardly were the placards out, than the Corporation bundled 500 out and set them down"[63] In other cases, emigrants were simply unwilling to follow the agent's directives. In 1840, Hawke sent a large group of men to St. Catharines, with the expectation that their employment chances were good on the nearby Welland Canal. Instead, many crossed the Niagara River into Lockport, New York.[64] Regrettably, the records do not give the reason for an emigrant being sent to a given place, and thus are a poor source for evaluating the success of agents in finding employment for newcomers, or of reuniting them with Canadian family and friends.

It is clear that government assistance and support from friends and family were key ingredients facilitating the migration and settlement of new arrivals, and not just of those who were destitute.[65] In June 1841, the *Chronicle and Gazette* noted that upwards of 3,000 emigrants had landed at Kingston that season. The emigrants, who seemed to "belong to the better class of labourers," had little capital. About half had already left the city bound for Cobourg, Port Hope, Toronto and Hamilton "to join their friends"; a "great many" had received assistance for the journey. The others remained in Kingston, seeking employment to allow them to "proceed to the upper ports to join their friends and relations."[66] The Emigration Office supported emigrant journeys if they facilitated reunions with friends and family willing and able to support the newcomers.[67] Hawke advised Canadians eager to assist to put what resources they had toward the transatlantic passage on the assumption that the Emigration Office would then provide the necessary transportation from Quebec.[68] Emigrant agents also offered assistance when reunions failed. Sundry expenses generated by Buchanan detail a number of these. In June 1845, Buchanan paid for Ellen McTaggart's passage to Londonderry. McTaggart, aged 60, had gone to Toronto in search of a son who had emigrated previously, but having "no tidings of him" sought the emigrant agent's assistance to return to County Tyrone.[69] In other cases, Buchanan facilitated reunions. In 1845, he sent Bridget Coulton and her daughter from Quebec to Bonaventure on the Gaspé Peninsula where another daughter was settled. The agent at Hamilton, J.H. Palmer, rarely offered details about individual emigrant's circumstances, but, in rare cases, was willing (and able) to fund a journey. In August 1844, he hired teamster Samuel Shelton to transport Margaret Borden 106 miles from Hamilton to Goderich. Borden had "arrived ill" and spent time at the Hamilton Emigrant Hospital with fever and smallpox. Her "delicate" health had induced Palmer to assist her to her final destination with food and lodging for the three-week trip.[70] Such details are unusual, however, as most emigrants were transported to centers peripheral to the port and then expected to complete their journey themselves.

The transportation receipts provide interesting information about the distribution of assisted emigrants out of three sampled ports (Toronto, Hamilton, and Port Hope/Cobourg). These emigrants traveled in summer, their movements determined by the existing roads infrastructure.[71] The limits of available routes meant that they were directed from each place to accessible peripheral towns or regional centers. Emigrants leaving Toronto often traveled north along Yonge Street to Newmarket, Bradford, Gwillimbury and to Holland Landing at the northern terminus of the 56-kilometer-long route (see Figure 1). Forty-five percent of emigrants in the 1847 Toronto sample went to Holland Landing. A bustling settlement, Holland Landing offered steamboat access, by way of the Holland River, to Lake Simcoe and to Barrie, where the Penetanguishene Road went north to Georgian Bay. Though emigrant agent Edward McElderry did not record destinations, transportation to Holland Landing likely represented a good portion of those intended to make only a temporary stop.

Figure 1: Distribution of Emigrants Transported from Toronto Emigration Office, 1847

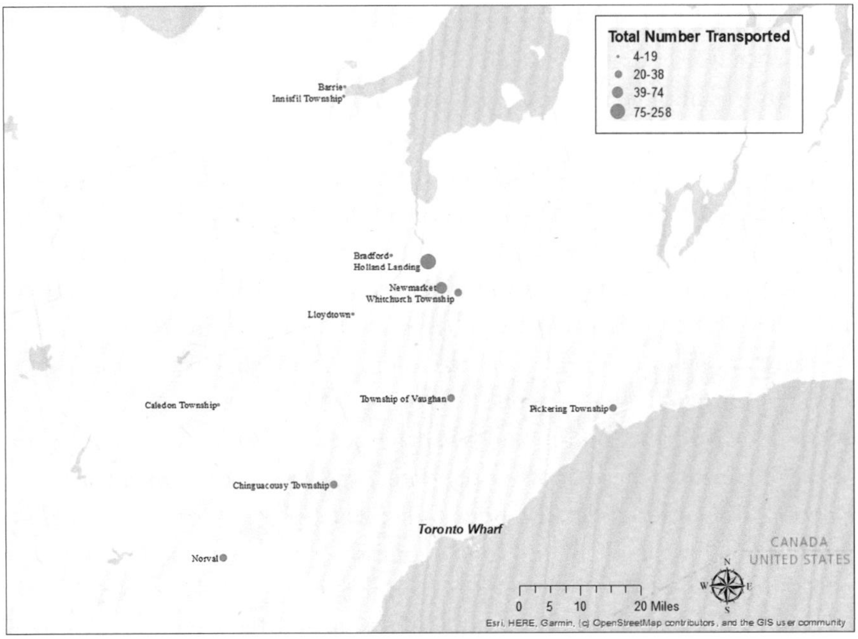

Similarly, from Port Hope, the overwhelming majority of assisted emigrants (78 percent in the sample) went to Peterborough, over a road that was "hilly, stony, or stumpy, with the exception of about a mile of swamp traversed by bad corduroy."[72] (See Figure 2). A place of significant Irish settlement from its inception in 1825, Peterborough was "flourishing" in 1846. It probably offered more employment opportunities for emigrant women (the majority in that sample) than in the much smaller Port Hope.

Figure 2: Distribution of Emigrants Transported from Port Hope/Cobourg Emigration Office, 1846

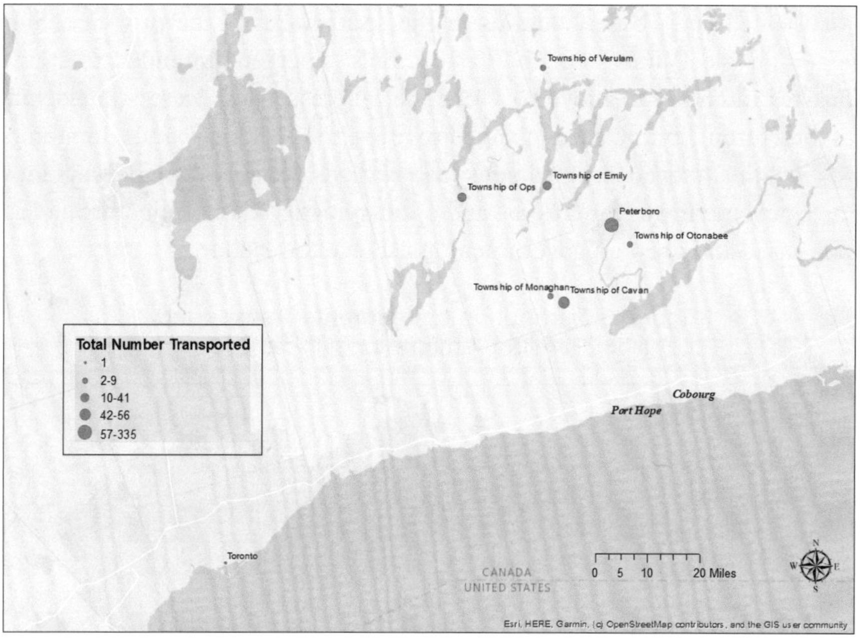

Occasionally, deviations from the standard set of destinations appear in the records suggesting a particular intention on the part of emigrants. In July 1843, a family of five went from Hamilton to Waterdown, a small settlement atop the Niagara escarpment. Despite its proximity to Hamilton, Waterdown was not a traditional destination. A few of the females sent out of Port Hope in 1846 went to rural townships with significant Irish settlement such as Cavan, Monaghan, Ops and Emily. These women probably had friends and relatives awaiting their arrival. Occasionally, a more specific address in a township was recorded. In 1847, James Wilson and four family members were transported from Toronto to the sixth concession in Pickering

Township. In October 1847, William Wilton received £2 to take Henry Downey, his wife and two children, and the Widow Miles and her three children to the Third Concession of West Gwillimbury. Emigrants leaving Hamilton often traveled to Brantford 28 km to the southwest, or to Preston 25 miles to the northwest, both linked by macadamized roads.[73] (See Figure 3 for 1843). In 1843, Palmer reported that those assisted to Brantford and Preston had then proceeded to the London, Huron, Brock, and Talbot districts in the southwest of the province.[74] Remarkably, in 1844, Palmer had the foresight to record the place to which he had sent a group or family and their ultimate destination. Of the 302 people sent to Brantford that year, only 14 percent had named it their intended destination. Instead, most chose London, Paris or Oxford and Essex Counties in the south-west of the province. Similarly, of the 267 people Palmer sent to Preston, only 3 percent intended to stay there. One-quarter intended to move to Goderich where settlers were still flocking for land in the Huron Tract. Others planned to move to the agricultural communities of Fergus, Guelph and Stratford. Palmer's 1844 records demonstrate the ways in which emigrant movement was intentional and opportunistic. Many emigrants had a destination in mind and drew on government assistance to reach it.

Figure 3: Distribution of Emigrants Transported from Hamilton Emigration Office, 1843

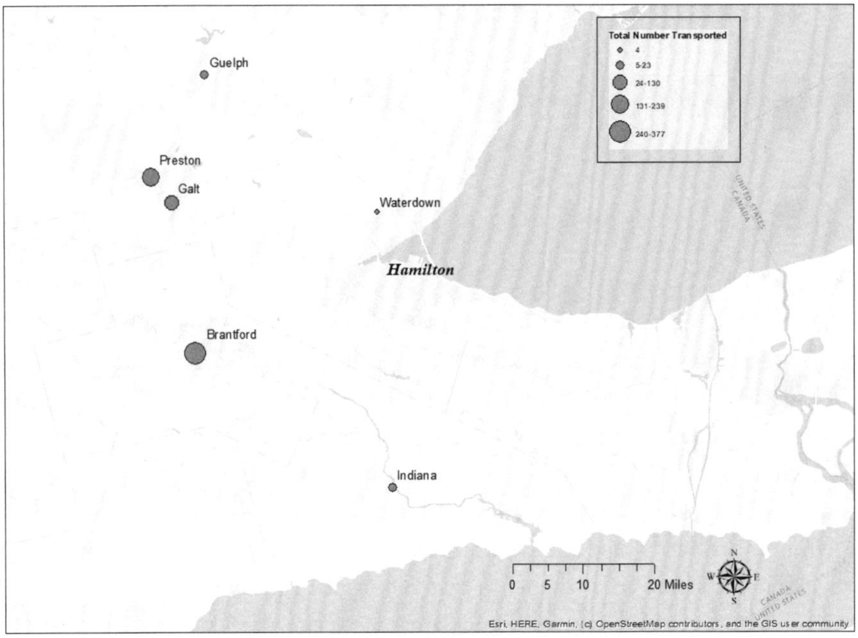

The ramifications of inland transportation assistance were felt in jurisdictions beyond the north shore of Lake Ontario. The arrival of emigrants prompted many communities to establish Boards of Health, and to petition the provincial secretary for funding and advice. Communities such as Peterborough, Brantford, Guelph, and Newmarket grappled with how to support destitute, and often sick, arrivals. Despite having received transported emigrants the previous season, Peterborough was caught off guard by the arrival in late June 1847, of a "large number" of emigrants, "several" of whom immediately died of starvation.[75] Brantford responded by establishing a temporary emigrant hospital. Local memory suggests wagons from Hamilton arrived daily with "all sick except the driver."[76]

Other cities beyond the range of assisted transportation notified the colonial government that they were dealing with unexpected influxes of emigrants. Hawke dismissed claims from Woodstock that those offering medical assistance should be compensated: "If the cases become too numerous for private relief the patients should be sent to the next station ... Woodstock is not more than three hours journey from Brantford—where there is a Board of Health hospital ... sick emigrants have been sent to the hospitals at Kingston and Toronto from a greater distance."[77] Barrie petitioned for a Board of Health in early July.[78] There was no doctor at River Trent at the head of the Bay of Quinte to treat the sick emigrants landed there in June 1847.[79] London also sought assistance, complaining of the "want of proper nurses" to tend to feverish emigrants, and the insufficiency of rations and accommodation for emigrants.[80] More than 200km from Hamilton, Chatham engaged in interminable correspondence with various government officials, as it sought, but was denied, permission to use abandoned barracks to house emigrants. The local sheriff was tasked with investigating who had funded the transportation of a "large body" of emigrants there.[81]

Fears about emigrants spreading disease into the rural townships and elsewhere abounded in the press, sparking fears about their return to the cities. In September, the *British Whig* reported that around Kingston, "sickness is still extremely great, and much loss of valuable life is the consequence."[82] The Toronto-based *Examiner* cautioned in August 1847, "The suffering and death away in the interior of the country arising from the want of shelter from the weather is, we believe, unknown."[83] Despite officials' best efforts to "scatter them widely" emigrants did return to the city. Some were sick and required medical attention; others simply sought the employment and shelter they were unable to find in the rural townships.[84] The main impediment to travel and employment that summer was "sickness and debility,"[85] with numerous emigrants deemed healthy enough to be transported away from a port city, succumbing to illness later. Many were too weak to do physical labor.[86] In June

1847, Hawke assured the provincial secretary, Dominick Daly, that the oncoming harvest would provide sufficient employment for the season's emigrants. Only days later, he confided to Buchanan that he was no longer confident. Demand for labor had not changed, but many emigrants deemed healthy at Grosse Île were too weak to labour in the hot weather, with many admitted to an Emigrant Hospital with fever.[87] The incubation period for typhus meant that seemingly healthy emigrants could import illness to an unsuspecting employer.[88] As the "calamitous" 1847 season wound to a close, Hawke reported that the majority of emigrants had been "diseased in body ... very few of them are fit for farm servants and as there is but little demand for labourers on public works, it will be very difficult to dispose of them, so they will be able to earn their bread."[89] The volume of migrants in 1847 meant their presence in Canada West cities was particularly noticeable as winter set in.[90] Residents of Kingston complained that they were begging in the streets.[91] In November, the Hamilton Board of Health reported "one thousand persons sick and destitute within the limits of the city," many of whom had returned from failed sojourns in the rural townships. Lamenting this "evil" development, the *Hamilton Gazette*, predicted contagious disease would soon effect every resident: "the wealthiest and healthiest will have to take his chance with the poor and weakly."[92]

The government's role in scattering emigrants throughout the province was highlighted as jurisdictions grappled with influxes of homeless emigrants. Concerns in Toronto about emigrants "infesting the streets of that city" were blamed on the "shameful conduct of those who keep pouring the sick by hundreds into the city, thus making Toronto a general Lazaretto."[93] Without a shred of irony, Hawke rejected claims for financial compensation, explaining that the government, "has done all that could be expected" and could not "bring relief to the Emigrant in all his wanderings after he has left the point at which assistance is ascertained."[94] With the onset of winter, "many will no doubt be thrown back upon the towns for support. NO plan that the government can adopt for their relief can reach claims scattered over so wide a surface."[95] Hawke acknowledged the burden to other jurisdictions, but asked for "duty due to humanity, for the communities in which they reside to render them assistance. Food is cheap and plentiful everywhere for the harvest in Upper Canada has been a most bountiful one."[96]

A bountiful harvest, and appeals to humanity, were cold comfort for jurisdictions that could not support a large, needy population. Critics pointed to the lack of support. "True our large towns have been kept well weeded; but the weeds are all thrown out of our garden into our neighbour's fields, to die or to take roots as heaven pleases" wrote the Irish-Catholic editor of the Toronto-based *Mirror*. Throughout the rural districts, the *Mirror* contended, one could "see the dying emigrants perishing by the roadsides, rotting in the woods, or languishing, unsheltered on bare earth, untended and unmourned."[97] Emigrants had been too quickly and carelessly "dropped down upon the highway to be taken up by the humane or to starve, sicken, and die," wrote the *Examiner*.[98] Consequently, settlers, "generally dread the appearance of newly arrived emigrants, and shun them as they would the pestilence," and "in some cases ... had them conveyed back to the city."[99] It was little wonder that migrants often returned to the city against the wishes of government officials.

The ending of the sailing season prompted the Colonial Office to press for the close of emigrant agencies and for considerable cuts to spending. The Governor General resisted, arguing, "it will hardly be possible to get rid during the winter of those who were in hospital when the winter set in, for to turn them out at this season is to consign them to destruction."[100] Hawke attempted to close all but the Toronto and Kingston agencies, but met considerable local resistance. In Hamilton, the government-run Emigrant Hospital was the sole medical facility in that city, continuing to operate throughout winter. Hawke initially suggested transporting any remaining sick from Hamilton to Toronto but reversed the decision quickly. Of the widows and orphans, "we have hundreds [in Toronto]" and "they would stand a better chance of obtaining places at Hamilton than at Toronto" he reasoned.[101] Hawke did not mince words as he reflected on the 1847 season on the province:

> upon the whole I am obliged to consider the migration of this year a calamity to the province. It has no doubt been the cause of much benefit to the ship and steamboat proprietors as well as to those interested in furnishing supplies for the subsistence of the immigrants. But on the other hand, there is no denying that they have scattered disease and death to a fearful extent.[102]

Perhaps not surprisingly then, as the 1848 sailing season approached, Hawke notified his agents that the transport system had ended. The "excessive" expense of the previous year had necessitated the change, though Hawke was certain that the "peculiar circumstances" of 1847 were unlikely to reoccur.[103] Emigrants were now to "endeavour to reach their place of destination ... with the assistance of their friends."

Fittingly, 1847 also marked the end of the extant Emigration Service Fund records. The data samples in this study offer only a glimpse of the possibilities offered by these rich records, including details of apparently "excessive" expenses. Among fees charged for passages are fascinating insights into the amount of baggage brought by newcomers. By virtue of their scope, the records offer a chance to evaluate the extent to which the Famine years affected the demography of assisted emigrants, as well as migration and settlement patterns in the Canadas. To what extent did the Famine disrupt the well-documented chain migration patterns among the Irish in Canada?[104] Do the records support Hawke's belief that by mid-decade, friends and relatives of newly arrived emigrants were less willing (and able) to help them travel inland?[105] Further study will enable Irish migrants in the 1840s to be identified and their dispersal from port cities throughout the province to be mapped. When cross-referenced with records from emigrant hospitals and sheds, routinely generated records such as census and parish registers, and with documents generated by provincial public works, a clearer picture of Irish emigrant trajectories and their new Canadian lives will emerge.

NOTES

1. Arthur G. Doughty (ed.), *The Elgin-Grey Papers, 1846–1852* (Ottawa: J.O. Patenaude, Printer to the King's Most Excellent Majesty, 1937), 12 Nov. 1847, pp 83–84.
2. The issue of the *Hamilton Gazette* is no longer extant, but preserved in the Elgin-Grey correspondence and the *British Whig*, 13 Nov. 1847 and *The Berean*, 18 Nov. 1847.
3. I have chosen the word emigrant or migrant to describe the newcomers assisted. Emigrant was used most often by agents of the Emigration Office.
4. Reprinted in *Chronicle and Gazette*, 11 July 1840.
5. Lisa Chilton's, "Managing Migrants: Toronto, 1820–1880," *The Canadian Historical Review*, vol. 92, no. 2 (June 2011), pp 231–262, outlines the structures in place to receive transatlantic migrants.
6. Library and Archives Canada (hereafter LAC) Department of Finance, Emigration Service Fund records, R200-161-0-E, 1843–1847 (Hereafter Emigration Service Fund). These records have yet to be studied.
7. Donald Akenson, *The Irish in Ontario* (Montreal: McGill-Queen's University Press, 1984); Bruce Elliott, *Irish Migrants in the Canadas: A new approach* (Montreal: McGill-Queen's University Press, 1988); Cecil J. Houston and William Smyth, *Irish emigration and Canadian settlement: Patterns, links, and letters* (University of Toronto Press, 1990); Catharine Wilson, *Tenants in Time: Family strategies, land, and liberalism in Upper Canada, 1799–1871* (Montreal: McGill-Queen's University Press, 2009), amongst others.
8. Joy Parr, "The Welcome and the Wake: Attitudes in Canada West Toward the Irish Famine Migration," *Ontario History* 65 (June 1974), pp 105, 109, 113.
9. For example, Archives of Ontario, Records of the Department of Immigration, RG 11–1, Chief Emigrant Agent's Letterbooks, MS 6910 (hereafter Hawke papers) Hawke to J.E. Campbell, Civil Secretary, 26 Oct. 1847 in which Hawke calculated that there were still "between 5 and 600 lazy idle people about these stations who must be scattered."
10. Quoted in Rebecca O'Reilly, "In a situation of great distress: The Emigrant Agency, Poverty, and the Irish in Nineteenth-Century Upper Canada," MA thesis, University of Guelph, 2006, p. 93.
11. Archives of Ontario (hereafter AO), Hawke papers, Hawke to Campbell, 29 June 1847.

12. Ibid., Hawke to Campbell, 16 Oct. 1847.
13. *Examiner*, 18 Aug. 1847.
14. *Mirror*, 20 Aug. 1847.
15. Mary Larratt Smith (ed.), Young Mr. Smith in Upper Canada (University of Toronto Press, 1980), p. 111.
16. Parr, "Welcome and the Wake," p. 108.
17. Following the repatriation of Hawke's extensive correspondence from Columbia University to the Archives of Ontario, Toronto in the early 2000s, historians have been examining the system to receive immigrants to Canada. See, Jane Errington, *Emigrant Worlds and Transatlantic Communities: Migration to Upper Canada in the First Half of the Nineteenth Century* (Montreal: McGill-Queen's University Press, 2007); Chilton, "Managing Migrants"; Mark G. McGowan, *Death or Canada* (Toronto: Novalis, 2009); Wendy Cameron's work is a macro overview of emigration management in the 19th century. See theses by Rebecca O'Reilly (University of Guelph, 2006) and Colleen Towns, "Relief and Order: the public response to the 1847 Irish Famine Migration to Upper Canada," MA thesis, Queen's University, 1990.
18. See Chilton, "Managing Migrants" for an overview of the evolution of state policy in what would become the province of Ontario. Colleen Towns' MA thesis is excellent on the journey from Quebec to Canada West.
19. Towns, p. 61.
20. McGowan, *Death or Canada*.
21. Towns, p. 61.
22. Chilton, p. 255.
23. For example, "Emigration," *Chronicle and Gazette*, 9 June 1841. Errington, *Emigrant Worlds*, discusses how emigrants used assistance to further their journeys.
24. AO, Hawke papers, Hawke to Buchanan, 11 June 1841.
25. Ibid., Hawke to Palmer, 12 May 1843.
26. O'Reilly, p. 91.
27. LAC, Hamilton Emigrant Ledger, 1847.
28. Funding was a perpetual source of debate between government bodies. See Chilton, "Managing Migrants," and Rainer Baehre, "Pauper Emigration to Upper Canada in the 1830s" *Histoire Sociale/Social History*, vol. 14, no. 28 (1981) 339–367.
29. Grey to Elgin, 19 July 1847 in Doughty, p. 57. Later Grey admitted there was "less danger" that the sick and infirm might seek more than their due, but cautioned, "it must never be forgot that it is the nature of these people to endeavour by every imaginable art to throw themselves for support upon others." Ibid., Grey to Elgin, 3 Aug. 1847, p. 62.
30. Ibid., Elgin to Grey, 13 Aug. 1847, p. 63.
31. Chilton, p. 251.
32. AO, Hawke Papers, Hawke to E. McElderry, 7 May 1847.
33. Agents recorded the number of additional wagons emigrant baggage required or the cubic weight of baggage carried by a group. Contrary to contemporary depictions of destitute Irish fleeing famine with little more than the rags on their backs, an initial

analysis of baggage records reveals that migrants arriving in Canada West between 1843 and 1847 brought a considerable amount of baggage.

34. Those under 14 were often counted as children in colonial and imperial emigration policy, but it is unclear if those criteria were applied in Canada.
35. Records for Hamilton in 1847 have not been located to date. In 1846, the local agent recorded the number of adults and children in a party but not their relationships to each other.
36. The initial analysis focused on women identified as the head of an emigrant group. The considerably larger group of unnamed wives, sisters, and daughters who travelled with their relatives was overlooked.
37. The number of passages allocated for "daughters" indicates they were not small children.
38. It is unclear whether these women had left Ireland together or whether they had met on the voyage or in the Canadian emigration system and had decided to join forces. The teamster's notes indicate that McBride's children were very young and Harrington may have had an adolescent child able to help.
39. Women's migration was a fixture of Irish migration to the United States after the Famine. Hasia Diner's *Erin's Daughters in America* (Baltimore: John's Hopkins, 1986) is the seminal work, but new projects such as the "Bad Bridget" project led by Leanne Calvert and Elaine Farrell promises exciting insights.
40. Occasionally, women traveling without adult men were identified as "Mrs." distinguishing them from widows and unmarried women. This convention was inconsistently applied, making conclusions difficult regarding a woman's marital status.
41. Women's migration is particularly significant in the 1846 records for the Port Hope/ Cobourg agency. In that year, agent William McKay appears to have prioritized helping women traveling without men—a remarkable 80 percent of the named emigrants were women, 94 percent travelling with dependents.
42. Mark McGowan's work has shed considerable light on the migration experiences of children. See, "Rethinking the Irish Famine Orphans of Quebec, 1847–1848," in Christine Kinealy et al. ed. *Children and the Great Hunger in Ireland* (Hamden: Quinnipiac University Press, 2018).
43. AO, Hawke papers, Hawke to Campbell, 16 Oct. 1847.
44. *British Whig*, 11 Sept. 1847.
45. "Emigrant Widows and Orphans Asylum Toronto" *British Whig*, 22 Sept. 1847. The discharge register for the Widows and Orphans home which was published in 1848, can be found at: http://www.canadiana.ca/view/oocihm.61829/3?r=0&s=1. It indicates that most widows used the institution briefly, many leaving, "at their own request, in some cases with their children having found work, friends &c."
46. In Toronto in 1847, 19 widows (16 with children, 3 without) were assisted in comparison to only 9 women with children.
47. Interestingly, widows often traveled with "daughters" rather than "children," a distinction that likely indicated the advanced age of both the offspring and mother.
48. AO, Hawke papers, Hawke to Campbell, 16 Oct. 1847.

49. LAC, Emigration Service Fund records, reel e011062893, 23 Aug. 1847, p. 406.
50. Ibid., reel e011062913, 7 June 1846, p. 1174.
51. Children's migration is an emerging area of study particularly for the Irish Famine period. See Kinealy et. al, *Children and the Great Hunger in Ireland*, for recent examples of scholarship in that area.
52. Buchanan, *Report of the Chief Emigrant Agent for 1847*, cited in Towns, p. 10.
53. Adults counted for a full passage, small children counted as a half. A family of six, consisting of a named male, an unnamed wife and four children requiring four passages can be assumed to include young children.
54. LAC, Canada West Provincial Secretary, numbered correspondence files, 1844 to 1867, Reel H–2375, Dr. Lee to D. Daly, 13 July 1847.
55. LAC, Emigration Service Fund records, Reel e011062907, Buchanan to P.D. O'Brien, 1846, p. 952.
56. Ibid., 1 May 1847, p. 953.
57. Ibid., pp 1090–1091. Homes were eventually found for Patrick and Mary. She was put into service in Quebec; her brother was sent to relatives on the Huron Tract.
58. See: Doughty ed., Grey to Elgin, 22 March 1848, pp 125–126. For example, "the wild western Irishman now goes out to Canada utterly ignorant of every useful kind of labour, & till he gets gradually instructed, is fit for no employment requiring more than brute strength. But he is a singularly teachable animal & one very easily brought under discipline if well managed."
59. Ruth Bleasdale, *Rough Work: Labourers on the Public Works of British North America and Canada, 1841–1882* (University of Toronto Press, 2018).
60. *Chronicle and Gazette*, 11 July 1840.
61. Ibid. In 1840, the paper noted the demand for laborers around the Bay of Quinte could not be supplied as emigrants who "entertain such extravagant notions" about their worth that they frequently refused employment. See, "The American Steamers and Emigrants," *Chronicle and Gazette*, 5 August 1840. Hawke similarly complained in 1847, that emigrants were "unreasonable in their expectations as to wages. They appear to possess but little ambition or desire to adapt themselves to the new state of things" (AO, Hawke papers, Hawke to Campbell, 16 Oct. 1847).
62. AO, Hawke papers, 19 Nov. 1840, 28 Dec. 1840.
63. Smith, *Young Mr. Smith*, 112.
64. AO, Hawke papers, 8 Dec. 1840.
65. See, Errington, *Emigrant Worlds*, for cases in which emigrants of all classes used government assisted travel or accommodation as part of their migration.
66. "Emigration," *Chronicle and Gazette*, 9 June 1841.
67. AO, Hawke papers, Hawke to Rawson, 12 July 1843; Hawke to Buchanan, 20 July 1847; Hawke to the Boards of Health, 25 Oct. 847.
68. Ibid., Hawke to McElderry, 7 May 1847.
69. McTaggart provided her own provisions for the journey.
70. LAC, Emigration Service Fund records, Reel e011062911, 21 Aug. 1844, p. 1097.

71. Summer travel was slow; a trip that took 1–2 miles an hour in summer might be completed at 7–9 miles an hour by sleigh over snow. J. Wood, *Making Ontario: agricultural colonization and landscape recreation before the railway* (Montreal: McGill-Queen's University Press, 2000), p. 121. Hawke urged the boards of health to disperse the emigrants still remaining in their care: "They must leave at once as the season is too far advanced to admit delay and the roads will soon become impassable." AO, Hawke papers, Hawke to the Boards of Health, 25 Oct. 1847.
72. William Henry Smith, *Canada: Past, Present, and Future: Being a Historical Geographical, Geological and Statistical Account of Canada West,* vol. 2 (Toronto: Thomas Maclear, 1851), p. 234.
73. Smith, *Canada past present and future*, pp 119, 238.
74. AO, Hawke papers, Hawke to Rawson, 12 July 1843.
75. Provincial Secretary Correspondence, Reel H–2374, G.B. Wall to Daly, 2 July 1847.
76. Oakland Township: Two hundred years, https://books.google.ca/books?id=sCP1GN-5p3EAC&lpg=PA725&pg=PA725#v=onepage&q&f=false, vol. 4, part 1, p. 797.
77. AO, Hawke papers, Hawke to unknown, 27 Oct. 1847.
78. Provincial Secretary Correspondence, Reel H–2374, Executive Council report, to W.B. Robinson MPP, 5 July 1847.
79. Ibid., Reel H–2374, J. Ham to D. Daly, 25 June 1847.
80. Ibid., Reel H–2375, Dr. Lee to D. Daly, 5 July 1847.
81. Ibid., Reel H–2375, Records 90–105, relates to Chatham, 1847.
82. "The Health of the City," *British Whig*, 1 Sept. 1847.
83. *Examiner*, 18 Aug. 1847.
84. The *Toronto Colonist* reported that though the emigrants were of a "better class, and paid their own expenses," they were resisting the authorities' efforts to "scatter" them into the country, but returning to Toronto, some via the U. S., *Chronicle and Gazette*, 11 July 1840. Using similar language seven years later, the *Colonist* noted that efforts to "scatter" emigrants had been "to little effect" with emigrants returning to Toronto from other Canadian ports and the U. S. *British Whig*, 22 Sept. 1847.
85. AO, Hawke papers, Hawke to Buchanan 15 July 1847.
86. Doughty, ed., Elgin to Grey, 13 June 1847, p. 50; AO, Hawke papers, Hawke to Campbell, 20 Sept. 1847.
87. AO, Hawke papers, Hawke to Buchanan, 3 July 1847.
88. Ibid., Hawke to Buchanan, 3 July 1847; McGowan, *Death or Canada*, pp 72–73. "Introduction of disease into the Country" *British Whig*, 3 July 1847; AO, Hawke papers, Hawke to Campbell, 20 Sept. 1847. The report of the death from typhus of an Irish farmer in Chinguacousy Township after the arrival of his typhus-infected emigrant brother was only one of many cases of farmers inadvertently inviting typhus into their homesteads. "Introduction of disease into the Country" *British Whig*, 3 July 1847. Another account from Lower Canada, of a mother of eight who had nursed an Irish orphan with typhus, contracting a fatal case of the disease herself, warned of the dangers of compassion and "imprudent benevolence." "Imprudent Benevolence" *British Whig*, 24 July 1847.
89. AO, Hawke papers, Hawke to Campbell, 20 Sept. 1847.

90. McGowan, *Death or Canada*, pp 72–73, 84. *British Colonist*, 27 Aug. 1847; Doughty ed., Elgin to Grey, 24 Dec. 1847.
91. *British Whig*, 6 Oct. 1847.
92. "Hamilton" *British Whig*, 13 Nov. 1847.
93. McGowan, *Death or Canada*, pp 72–73; AO, Hawke Papers, Davis to Mayor Boulton, 28 Aug. 1847; Hawke to Boulton, 10 Nov. 1847; *British Whig*, 22 Sept. 1847.
94. AO, Hawke papers, Hawke to unknown, 27 Oct. 1847.
95. Ibid., Hawke to Campbell, 20 Sept. 1847.
96. Ibid.
97. *Mirror*, 20 Aug. 1847.
98. *Examiner*, 18 Aug. 1847.
99. Ibid.
100. Doughty, ed. Elgin to Grey, 24 Dec. 1847
101. AO, Hawke papers, Hawke to Palmer, 27 Nov. 1847. Hamilton's sole charitable organization, the Ladies' Benevolent Society, did not aid those receiving support from other sources. emigrants who had received support from the emigrant agent were denied assistance.
102. Ibid., Hawke to Campbell 16 Oct. 1847.
103. Ibid., Hawke to Palmer and Hayes, 12 May 1848.
104. Historians have speculated that migrants arriving in the mid-1840s had fewer kinship ties to draw upon. Houston and Smyth, pp 86–87; O'Reilly, p. 93. Fear of disease may have prevented relatives from helping. Elliott, *Irish Migrants in the Canadas*, is the authority on chain migration.
105. "A few years ago, almost every emigrant managed to reach his friends and relations upon reaching the port nearest their residence, but last year, and indeed the year previous, neither they nor their friends would make the least effort of sacrifice to enable them to do so " (1848), quoted in O'Reilly, p. 92.

CHAPTER SEVEN

WHEN FAMINE "VICTIMS" CHALLENGE HISTORIANS

The Case of the Strokestown "1,490" and the Assisted Migration of 1847

Mark G. McGowan

Most historians do not appreciate being told they are wrong. Writing and researching the migrations that came to North America as a result of the Great Irish Famine are difficult enough, as one navigates through generations of nationalist, populist, revisionist and neo-revisionist interpretations.[1] More than once, historians interpreting evidence from the period in a non-nationalist way have been assaulted in print and in person by the confident masses that hold firmly to the "genocide" theories of writers such as Tim Pat Coogan.[2] Such attacks and counter attacks, as have been witnessed in the case of the Coogan-Liam Kennedy debates, are easily deflected by the hard evidence offered by routinely-generated records, manuscript sources, and local case studies.[3] It is less easy when the voices from the past speak, mostly indirectly through manuscript, print, and numerical sources, forcing scholars to rethink their tightly held certitudes. In such cases, the historian is reminded that honesty and humility are the best medicine, even if it means re-routing the course of one's research and question framing.

The current dose of humility has been thrust on this historian by his ongoing research on the migration of 1,490 tenants of Major Denis Mahon, who were assisted off their lands in Strokestown, County Roscommon, in May and June 1847. The case of Mahon's tenants has become somewhat of a cause célèbre in the Irish famine historiography, perhaps because in the wake of learning that many of his tenants perished on route to Quebec, Mahon was assassinated, the first landlord to die at the hands of tenants during *An Gorta Mór*. Unfortunately, journalists and historians have heaped too much attention on the murder, with its salacious "who dunnit?" qualities, than have examined the evidence regarding what actually happened to the people Mahon helped to leave his estate.[4] For some writers, the murder was an expression of general unrest on the estate, created by the mass migration and further evictions approved by Mahon and executed by his agent, John Ross Mahon.[5] Padraig Vesey has been more pointed in the allocation of responsibility: "Mahon's assassination was a protest not against landlordism as such but against his land agent's management process."[6] Other writers take a less harsh view of Mahon, seeing him as being overwhelmed by circumstances beyond his control: the inheritance of a highly indebted estate of the eve of the Famine;[7] the Famine itself; and rent strikes in adjacent townlands to Strokestown.[8] In managing these affairs, Mahon failed, enraged many tenants, and created the opportunity for two tenants, supported by the local Molly Maguires, to kill him as an example to other members of his class.[9] Mahon is also vilified by those writers taking the side of local parish priest Father Michael McDermott, who denounced the landlord from the pulpit, claiming that "so many died while he lives."[10] The scene in Strokestown was allegedly akin to Henry II's calling out of Thomas Becket—"will no one rid me of this meddlesome priest?"—except in this case, it was the clergy lamenting the alleged malevolence of the landlord. Mahon's reputation is a subject of continuing speculation—some see him as victimizer, others as victim, and others are just ambivalent. In contemporary memory in Roscommon, it is the assisted migrants of 1847—colloquially known as the "1,490"—that have been identified as victims—shipped off to Canada, to die on board coffin ships, or in the lazarettos of Grosse Île, the quarantine station in the St. Lawrence River, often referred to as Quebec's charnel house.[11]

When the manuscript evidence is re-examined and new evidence comes to light from unlikely sources, one is forced to pause, reflect, and reassess. Perhaps the murder of Mahon has obscured the way that some historians have looked at life on his estate, prior to November 1847, through the lens of the murder. Is it wise to analyze the events preceding the dastardly deed as a natural trajectory to that fateful event on the evening of 2 November 1847? Mahon's own correspondence, in the Strokestown Park Archives and in the National Library of Ireland, suggests that the events on the Strokestown estate from 1845 to 1847 can be read differently, without a subliminal reference point to Mahon's murder and the bias that all events led to it. Perhaps it is important to step back, examine the events for their own merit and what they might relate to us, without recourse to the filters provided by the murder that can tempt the mind to read events backward forming a natural trajectory to the killing. In addition, an obscure Anglican weekly paper in Quebec, *The Berean*, may force a complete scholarly re-thinking of the migration itself and the agency possessed by the 271 families that took up Mahon's offer to leave in the spring of 1847. What follows is a reflection on the new questions raised by these sources, and ultimately the manner in which scholars and local collective memory have considered the dramatic events on Mahon's estate in 1847.

Mahon and the Emigration Scheme

Had his cousin, Maurice Mahon, had a male heir, Major Denis Mahon may never have been involved in trying to salvage the estate that the restored King Charles II awarded to the Mahon family during the post-Cromwellian Restoration of the 1660s and 1670s.[12] Nicholas Mahon received 2,000 acres in the Ballynamully area of Roscommon, known now as Strokestown, an anglicized name harkening to the historical weapons of the O'Connors and Mitchells near the ford of the stream that still runs through the town. In 1696, the family commenced building a large estate house on the old O'Connor seat, and eventually, over the next few decades completed a large manor home in the Palladian style.[13] By 1845, when Denis Mahon finally inherited the estate after the death of his cousin "mad" Maurice, the third and last Baron Hartland, the Mahon estate exceeded 11,000 acres and included 11,958 people living on 68 townlands.[14] The estate was also insolvent. Denis Mahon faced a whopping debt of over £30,000, accumulated over several decades through land purchases, estate improvements, endowments to widows and children, and some eccentric investments on the estate.[15] Worse still, many tenants had been truant in the paying of their annual rents. Some tenants simply could not afford the rents given their limited yields on their tiny plots of often less than five acres.[16] Others, following the lead of tenants in the nearby Crown-controlled townland of Ballykilcline, Kilglass parish, simply went on strike, refusing to pay rent for their marginal holdings. Tenant resentment towards policies of lease-shortening and eviction, as invoked by landlords' agents, and grinding rural poverty in many townlands, spawned episodes of violence in the area.[17] Nocturnal raids of retribution against those who violated "rural codes of behaviour" or against those who served the landlord, became more frequent in Roscommon.[18] The secret society, the "Molly Maguires," was often thought to be at the heart of this exercise of vigilante justice. Mahon faced an increasing violent state of affairs on his estate compounded in the autumn of 1845, by the partial failure of the potato crop upon which most of his tenants depended.

In 1846, in an effort to reorganize and strengthen the estate's finances, Denis Mahon hired the services of John Ross Mahon, a distant relative and a partner in the Dublin firm of Guinness & Mahon. John Ross would come to the estate armed with a businesslike attitude towards all aspects of life at Strokestown, demonstrating a management style that left little room for emotional attachment to the people for whom he was responsible.[19] Denis Mahon, although often absent from the estate, served as a member of the local relief committee, a burden that became more onerous when the entire potato crop of 1846 failed and his tenants were left at the brink of starvation. Denis Mahon had been responsible for suspending the rents of many tenants whom he knew were unable to pay, which seemed consistent with his earlier efforts to provide a loan fund for tenants in need,[20] but now even they were unable to repay the earlier loans at the agreed rate. Major Mahon also provided for the distribution of food relief in the form of "American maize" in two ways—the first required a modest payment for those who could pay the penny per pound of corn, and the second, for those who were destitute, no payment was required.[21] Clearly, this relief effort was significant but hardly enough to sustain the life and health of tenants on his crowded estate.

Major Mahon then decided that the distribution of seed might assist tenant farmers directly—in a sense having farm laborers and cottiers help themselves.[22] John Ross Mahon, however, was opposed to maintaining tenants on their lands while still paying the poor rate for the growing numbers of tenants relying on Poor Law relief, so he proposed a less expensive solution. Migration, claimed the agent, would be cheaper than supporting the tenants in Strokestown or on the relief works; migration also would provide the Major with an opportunity to consolidate vacated lands for grazing or for other more profitable purposes. The agent and his landlord disagreed to the point where John Ross threatened to resign.[23] In early 1847, Major Mahon relented and suggested that the assisted tenants travel to the closest port, which was in Sligo town, where their passage to America could be subsidized, akin to what the Major considered the successful precedents set by Lord Palmerston on his Sligo estates.[24] Once again, John Ross had other plans. Through his firm, his agents could book passage through Liverpool on ships bound for Quebec, on which fares were substantially cheaper than those ships travelling to ports in the United States. The Major relented and tenants were invited to participate in the migration scheme.[25] In exchange for passage and supplies from Roscommon to Liverpool, and then to British North America, subscribers would abandon their cabins, terminate their leases, and be compensated for crops and animals relinquished. They were not permitted to return to their former holdings once the deal had been consummated.

In any event, they would have known their cabins would be tumbled by John Ross' men upon their departure. While the figure has been disputed, about 271 families representing 32 townlands, agreed to sign on to the plan.[26]

The tenants who opted for the emigration scheme were not the poorest of the poor. Evidence from the estate papers demonstrates that none of these families had previously applied for the "maize" gratuity, and many had come from townlands where some rents had been paid. The routinely generated records from the estate archives suggest that these prospective emigrants may have been the least impoverished of Mahon's tenants. In fact, in their correspondence, during the application process, in April 1847, the Major lamented to John Ross:

> I have been considering the numerous applications we have had for assistance on the score of Emigration, and it strikes me that many of those applying are of the better sort of tenant and if possible should be kept home, but at all events if determined to go they should do so at their own expense. I think the first class for us to send is those of the poorest and the worst description.[27]

The letter should not be interpreted with too much malice of intent. Mahon was suspicious that tenants may have been holding back rent and, if such was the case, they should pay their own passage. From a business standpoint, and with the original intentions of the emigration scheme in mind, if Mahon lost his most productive tenants, he would be no farther ahead because he would be liable to the poor tax for the poor who wished to stay. In one sense, John Ross Mahon's plan would have been completely undercut, but the fact remains that in the official documents of the "assisted" many of the "better" tenants left. Finally, one interesting detail that might be overlooked is that there were "numerous" applications—many tenants simply wanted to leave the estate.

Initially, what one is left with from a close reading of the estate papers is that Mahon was less the tyrannical and heartless stereotype of the Famine landlord, as might first appear, and that the tenants who opted for the migration scheme may have been far better off than their peers who stayed behind. The estate papers also confirm that the alleged 1,490 people who constituted these 271 migrating families did not leave en masse, but departed Strokestown in two waves, travelling along the banks of the Royal Canal, and then proceeding by steamship from Dublin to Liverpool about a week apart.[28] Because knowledge of what happened to the 1,490 is graphically tragic, and is the best known part of their migration story, the tendency of researchers and other interested parties, might be to read the narrative backward from the "coffin ships" and assume the worst on the estate. The Mahon family papers in the National Library and in the Strokestown Park Archives speak to a more complicated story of the lives of tenants on the estate in the years leading up to John Ross's emigration scheme. Since they shared nothing on paper with contemporaries, nor, by implication, with scholars in our own time, one can only rely on what has been said about them by others, mostly elites, or by what the numbers tell us in the estate records, routinely generated and concerned with the financial and economic health of the estate. When this evidence is combined with that gleaned from *The Berean*, the scholar is forced to challenge previously held certitudes about these hopeful travellers from Strokestown to Canada.

The Berean and its Claims

In June 1847, *The Berean* printed a short article from a Dublin newspaper reporting the arrival, on 24 May 1847, of Major Mahon's assisted migrants at Dublin. It confirmed a previously known newspaper report that they had left for Liverpool, provisioned by the landlord, on 27 May 1847.[29] *The Berean* article, however, included other startling details:

> This afternoon an unusual long train of emigrants, evidently from the same townland, and presenting marks of comfort recognizable in the bulk of people fleeing from the famine, passed along our quays to the emigrant offices, near the Customs House. There were fifteen cars, well laden with baggage, and a party of about 130 persons followed them. One of the leaders stated that they had come from the lands of Kilglass, part of the estate of Major Denis Mahon, the successor of the late Lord Hartland in the county of Roscommon, and that their destination was Upper Canada. He admitted that they had formed a community of about 2000 persons, the tenants of Major Mahon, and that all owed him rent. He had obtained venires against them, and when nothing remained to be done but to send the sheriff to take possession of their holdings, the gallant Major sent for several of them, and proposed to forgive them all of their rents, pay their passage to America, and supply them with provisions to the end of their voyage, and on condition of their levelling of their cabins and giving up quit possession. The proposition was deemed advantageous, hardly any opposition was offered, the majority of the cabins levelled, and nearly 2000 poor persons, who should have been supported by the ratepayers, are now on their way to America.[30]

The Berean's account is one of the few newspaper sources known that account for the arrival of Mahon's assisted at the Dublin quay.

The Berean claimed that the item was reprinted from the *Dublin Paper*, 24 May 1847, but no such publication is listed in the catalogues of either the National Archives of Ireland or the National Library of Ireland. This does not necessarily mean that the paper did not exist nor was the excerpt invented by the editors in Quebec. Small weekly newspapers in British North America depended on other papers for "filler" in their columns and they anxiously awaited the latest steamships to land at New York or Boston and then have the latest European news cabled to them. *The Berean* would be little different from other dailies of its day. Founded in 1844 as an unofficial weekly publication of the Church of England in Quebec, the paper was published each Thursday by Charles L.F. Hearsel, an Anglican minister of German origin. The paper itself was produced on Rue Ste-Anne in Quebec City, by Stanley Printer & Bookseller, for a subscription price of 12 shillings 6 pence, or $3.50 (American) per year.[31] It had distributers in New York, Brooklyn, and Boston, in addition to its Canadian circulation. Named after the Christian community visited by Silas and Paul in northern Greece, as recorded in the book of Acts (17: 10–15), *The Berean's* four pages were filled with Protestant theological writing, anti-Catholic diatribes and critiques, and generous news on the conversions being made by Protestant ministers among the starving Catholics of Achill and Dingle in Ireland.[32] It comes as no surprise, therefore, that this story on assisted Famine migrants caught Hearsel's eye. As for the origin of the story, it may very well have been plucked from the *Dublin Evening Mail*, one of the few papers that published on 24 May 1847.[33]

Initially, the clipping confirms some of the basic information already known to researchers. These were migrants who had travelled along the Royal Canal from the Shannon River at Clondara to Dublin, a distance of over 150 kilometers (or nearly 100 miles). The group was also reported to be of an "unusual" size, which confirms that the group was indeed a unit travelling together, "evidently from the same townland" as distinguished from the stream of individual families using the banks of the canal as their access to the port of Dublin. The reporter must have engaged them directly because he learned that they were a party of approximately 130 persons from the Kilglass civil parish.[34] This estimate is in keeping with the records of the estate, which indicate that two of Mahon's townlands—Tully and Kilgraffy—both from Kilglass, were included in the assisted migration scheme. The Strokestown Park records also indicate there were approximately 23 families or 116 persons who consented to leave, a figure not far from what the Dublin paper reported.[35]

A few of these facts suggest several other characteristics about this assisted migration. First, Mahon's tenants may have left in townland groups, which might make it possible to find clusters from the same townlands in the records of Grosse Île, or even farther into British North America where they elected to settle with friends and relatives with whom they had lived and migrated. Secondly, the fact that Kilglass migrants were among the first, makes sense, since they inhabited the most easterly townlands of the estate, were closer to the River Shannon, and evidently were the easiest to send on their way (without having to double back to the estate town to leave with migrants from other townlands). From here, the evidence presented by the reporter is even more intriguing. He indicated that this particular group of Famine migrants appeared different from those persons usually seen travelling along the canal, in hopes of reaching Dublin and beyond; these people, he described, presented "marks of comfort." What the reporter meant by "comfort" is open to debate. Was he implying that they appeared better fed? Better clothed? Or in better health? The reporter simply does not provide any other detail than they were accompanied by 15 "cars" "laden" with baggage. The importance of this detail cannot be overlooked. It suggests that the assisted migrants had the opportunity to bring their belongings with them and the 23 families from Kilglass had enough personal items to fill 15 cars or carts. It also suggests that while some families may have shared carts, others may have required their own cart, given their amount of baggage. Similarly, the number of carts, even if several families shared one, confirms, perhaps, that Major Mahon had included supplies and provisions to nourish the migrants before they arrived in Liverpool and until such time as they had boarded the ships that had been provided for them.[36] Given Mahon's past generosity as evidenced in allocating free "maize" to his most impoverished tenants, such a gesture to the assisted migrants is not impossible. The presence of numerous carts not only may attest to the "comfort" of the travellers, but of Mahon's own determination to provision them sufficiently so that they might have a fighting chance to begin anew in the colonies and not return to Strokestown. The estate papers and the correspondence between the Major and his agent clearly show that Denis Mahon was billed both for the tickets of passage and at least £9 for the baggage.[37] Travel vouchers in Upper Canada, confirm that many Famine migrants arrived in Canada with baggage.[38]

Much of what the reporter gleaned of what had transpired on the estate was extracted from the testimony of a "leader" who remained nameless in the article. One possible identification might be that the leader may have been Bailiff John Robinson, who was responsible for herding the former tenants along the canal and supervised their transfer through Dublin to Liverpool and then on to North America.[39] This might account for the positive spin placed on the report given to the journalist. The fact that the reporter does not name Robinson, nor does he identify the interlocutor as a bailiff, leaves open the possibility that the "leader" may very well be one of the heads of the households. The description of the events at Strokestown, as related to the reporter, appear framed in a manner that suggests that the "leader" could very well have been one of the household's heads, as much as it could have been Robinson. Unfortunately, one cannot identify the "leader" definitively. Yet, if the latter identification, that of a household head, is taken into consideration, it appears that there was some measure of gratitude expressed in so far as the "assisted" were not evicted to fend for themselves, but quit the estate permanently in order to begin their lives anew in the colonies.

It is the suggestion by the "leader," however, regardless of his/her identity, that raises another critical piece of information—their intended place of settlement. The mention of "Upper Canada," now the Canadian province of Ontario, is new to the story of the migration of the 1,490. No secondary source on the episode has ever identified anything but a generic "American" destination for the assisted migrants, nor has any record catalogued in the estate papers mentioned this specific colony. In the 1840s, Upper Canada had become the fastest growing of Britain's North American colonies, particularly for Irish migration.[40] The colony was quickly becoming recognized by prospective migrants in Great Britain and Ireland as a place of abundant cheap land, excellent water resources through the St. Lawrence and Ottawa River Valleys and the watershed of the Great Lakes, and a source of potential employment on state-funded canal and road projects. Since Quebec was the *entrepôt* for the central colonies in British North America, that provided the cheapest fares, it made perfect sense for agents and landlords to target Upper Canada as a choice destination in which one might build a new life. It was also far enough away that no one assisted off an estate would return to Ireland. The Canada Company had opened over a million acres of cheap land in the Huron Tract, of which 100 acres could be procured as freehold with the fees for each tract amortized over a 10-year period.[41] It was an attractive deal and well advertised in most colonial newspapers.[42] Similarly, the Welland Canal at Niagara was a hive for Irish workers, some of which had left Mahon's estate prior to the assistance scheme.[43] As far as the leaders' testimony was concerned, there was more hope reported here than despair.

Finally, the "leader" makes a statement about Denis Mahon personally, that is cause for further thought and discussion. The "leader" describes Mahon as "gallant." This was certainly not an adjective that would be used to describe him by either the tenants who plotted his murder, or by many historians and journalists thereafter, depending on their nationalist stripe. If taken at face value, the use of this word to describe the Major, suggests that those who participated in the emigration scheme may very well have regarded Mahon's actions as charitable and generous, particularly given that the "leader" admitted that most of the travellers could not pay rent and could have been legally evicted from their holdings. When compared to the dire consequences of fending for themselves along the highways and byways of a famine-ravaged country, emigration did not appear to be a bad option. In fact, in the minds of some of his tenants, Mahon's intervention appeared to be received with a degree of gratitude. The reporter cited in *The Berean* suggests that among the Strokestown tenants, there was little resistance to the emigration scheme. The estate documents do indicate minor resistance in the Cregga Park townland where the families of John Egan, James Duffy, and Michael Byrne, initially applied but then "requested to stay."[44] In Tully, the widow Stewart was registered but remained, and in Kilgraffy, after some waffling, Patrick Leonard proceeded with the first group. Of the 274 families initially subscribed, 271 made the voyage. On the whole, if such testimony of a broad acceptance of the plan by the tenants is to be trusted, the article bears a hopeful tone that would soon be extinguished by the realities of the trans-Atlantic crossing.

The Voyages, by the Numbers

If reading daily life on the Strokestown estate in 1846–47 through the lenses of the murder of Major Mahon is methodologically problematic, so is reading the nature of the migration scheme through the lens of the trans-Atlantic passage itself. Denis Mahon was in England at the time the first group of migrants departed, busy making sure that he borrowed sufficient money for the scheme and that this money was spent properly, while John Ross Mahon and his bailiffs ensured that the boarding and departure of the assisted migrants were executed smoothly.[45] There is nothing in the archival records to suggest that Denis Mahon deliberately cut corners, or that he was only half-hearted in his support of the tenants. The fact that, without sufficient capital or savings, he forced himself to approach lenders and bankers to underwrite the entire scheme, thereby placing the Strokestown estate in deeper debt, attests to his determination to see that the migration scheme worked. What he may not have known was that the Robinson firm, retained by John Ross, through his own business ties, had a poor reputation in Liverpool.[46] Robinson's attractive price point may have veiled the fact that the ships they retained were negligent in taking proper health regulations seriously and the provisions on board were substandard. Had John Ross known the shady business that was the Robinson firm? He was never formally held to account for what happened on the voyages. In fact, in the wake of the emigration tragedy and mass evictions on the estate thereafter, in 1851, he was celebrated at the Strokestown Fair as having been a kind and just land agent.[47] Major Mahon, since he was ultimately in charge of the scheme, would be held responsible for what happened to the 1,490 assisted tenants.

There is no doubt that crossing the Atlantic for Mahon's 1,490 was not easy. The first group of migrants left on board two ships departing Liverpool—the *Virginius* and the *Erin's Queen*. The former allegedly was boarded exclusively by Mahon passengers, with the overflow boarding the *Erin's Queen*. The evidence from the quarantine station at Grosse Île does not support this long-held assumption. Lists of the dead, credited to the *Virginius*, contain the names of passengers who bear surnames that are not on John Ross's list of passengers from estates who agreed to the emigration scheme.[48]

Table 1: Deaths of Household Heads by Ship Recorded for the Mahon Estate, 1847

Ship	Estimated Passengers	Strokestown Assisted	Estimated Total Deaths	Strokestown Deaths, Verified	Strokestown Household Head Deaths
Virginius	476	476	267 (56.1%)	221 (46.4%)	31
Naomi	421	350.5	196 (46.6%)	126 (35.9%)	16
Erin's Queen	493	100	136 (27.6%)	14 (14.0%)	2
John Munn	452	55	187 (41.4%)	26 (47.3%)	7
At Sea Not defined					2
Total	1,842	981.5	786 (42.7%)	387 (39.4%)	58 of 274 (21.2%)
Total if 1,490		1,490 Includes children under 14		387 (26.0%)	

Source: Strokestown List prepared from the Strokestown Park Archives and put in a database by Dr. Ciaran Reilly of Maynooth University. The 274 families appear on the glass memorial in front of the Strokestown Park Museum; Canadian data is from Marianna O'Gallagher and Rose Dompierre, *Eyewitness: Grosse Isle 1847* (Ste-Foy, Quebec: Livres Carraig Books, 1995), appendices; André Charbonneau and Doris Drolet-Dubé, eds., *A Register of Deceased Persons at Sea and on Grosse Île in 1847* (Ottawa: Canadian Heritage, Parks Canada, 1997).

A close examination of Table 1 can lead to several hypotheses. First, contemporary accounts of the individuals who boarded these ships are simply wrong. While Mahon's bailiffs under the leadership of John Robinson (no relation to the Robinson firm) may have reported that all emigrants boarded the two ships according to plan, it is entirely possible that some traded their tickets to other Irish refugees, and simply slipped into Liverpool hoping for employment closer to Ireland. It is also possible that Mahon's people were joined by others in an effort by the ship's owners and the booking agents to maximize their profits. This crowding had disastrous effects. The *Virginius* did not sink as was assumed by some locals in Roscommon, although it did sail off course and its complement of dead was as high as reported later by both Canadian and British newspapers.[49] Data from the death registers reveal that of the 476 passengers recorded on the ship, of which children under 14 were counted as half a person, there were 267 (56.1%) deaths. Of the known 271 household heads that represented the entire 1,490, 31 either died at sea on the *Virginius*, or once the ship disembarked its sick at Grosse Île.

Table 2: Status of Mahon Households in British North America, 1847

Status of the Household Head	Number	Percent
Died at Sea or in Quarantine	58	21.2
Confirmed Not Travelling	1	0.4
Located in Canada	71	25.9
Located in the United States	29	10.6
Location/Status Unknown	115	42.0
Total Located or Identified	159	58.0
Total from Estate	274	100

Source: *Census of Canada*, 1851–52; Registers of Catholic Parishes in Canada East and Canada West (online Familysearch.com); Library and Archives Canada; RG 19 D-5, v.2532, Department of Finance, Travel Vouchers and Expenses, 1843–54; André Charbonneau and Doris Drule-Dubé, *A Register of Deceased Persons at Sea and on Grosse Île in 1847* (Ottawa: Canadian Heritage, Parks Canada, 1997).

On the other hand, the overflow on the *Erin's Queen* fared somewhat better: 100 of its 493 registered passengers were from Mahon's 1,490. Of these, only 14 appear in the death registers at Grosse Île, included therein are only two household heads from the original 271 assisted families. The death rate on the *Erin's Queen*, when all passengers are taken into account, was 136 or 27.6 percent, still startling, but half of the deaths on the *Virginius*. If you had been in Mahon's overflow group, you counted yourself lucky. The second wave of migrants left Liverpool in June on the *Naomi*, with the overflow on the *John Munn*. On the *Naomi*, 350.5 of the 421 registered passengers were from the Mahon estate, while an overflow of 55 sailed on the *John Munn* as part of its complement of 452 passengers. Of the 196 dead on the *Naomi*, 126, or 35.9 percent of the ships' passenger list, were from the Mahon estate—a shocking statistic, but nevertheless, not the numbers that were reported back to the estate in the fall of 1847. On the *John Munn*, 26, or just under half of the Mahon passengers either died at sea or at Grosse Île. About 41 percent of the *John Munn's* passengers perished. When the dead on-board these two ships are added to the dead among the first wave of migrants who left in May, about 387 migrants of the 1,490 perished, or just over one in every four. Similarly, 58 of the 271 household heads, or just over one in five heads of families, never realized the "new start" that was promised them in Upper Canada. (See Table 2) While it is clear that the numbers of dead do not jibe with the dead of popular memory, the death toll is still a testament to horrific conditions on-board the four ships.[50]

The question remains whether Mahon is culpable for this catastrophe at sea and in the quarantine station. The booking agents certainly made the cheapest arrangements possible, cutting corners, which seemed to be part of John Ross's economizing on behalf of the estate. Clearly, the passengers were not inspected carefully when boarding the ships; there were not sufficient supplies of fresh water and edible food for the passengers registered, and, in the case of the *Virginius*, the navigators were handicapped by weather and currents and ended up off course. If the report in *The Berean* is to be treated with any weight, and I think it should be, it appears that in regard to at least the first wave of migrants from the townlands including Kilgraffy, Tully, and Kilmackenny, the Major had done his due diligence in supplying them with food and providing wagons for the cartage of their personal belongings. Invoices in Mahon's papers indicate that he was liable for not only the fares for each passenger, but also for considerable baggage, thus confirming the observations made by the reporter investigating the first wave of the 1,490 on Dublin's Custom House Quay.

In fact, the article from *The Berean* may be one of the most significant documents in the saga to reconstruct what happened on the Mahon estate in the spring of 1847. It helps to refocus the events of the passage of the 1,490 away from the subsequent murder of Mahon and place it on the events leading up to the emigration scheme and the departure of the first wave of assisted families. *The Berean* reprint helps the researcher to recalibrate and focus on the correspondence between Mahon, his agent, and the associates connected with the migration scheme. If anything, it forces the researcher to work forward through the ebb and flow of life on the Strokestown estate, instead of reading events backwards through the lens of the tragedy on 2 November 1847. If *The Berean* article is to been seen as a true representation of events, four major revisions of the tragic events surrounding the migration of the 1,490 may have to be revised: first, it is clear that the migrants may have been in better condition physically and materially as they made their way to Liverpool; secondly, the actions of Major Mahon were looked upon favorably by those who took up his offer of assisted migration; thirdly, resistance to the scheme may have been minimal, with only three families of the original 274 pulling out of the operation in its initial phase; and, finally, that emigrants themselves appeared buoyed by the fact that there was an actual destination in mind—Upper Canada. As has been suggested, the comments in *The Berean* article, although substantiated in part by the estate papers, are not without questions, the story of the 1,490, as it has been told, may be in need of revision. In the craft of history, periodic bouts of humility and rethinking, though sometimes unwelcome, are necessary avenues to the truth.

NOTES

1. Cormac Ó Gráda, Mary Daly, Cecil Woodham Smith, Christine Kinealy, Peter Gray, Ciarán Ó Murchadha, Michael Quigley et. al.
2. Tim Pat Coogan, *The Famine Plot: England's Role in Ireland's Greatest Tragedy* (New York: Palgrave and Macmillan, 2012); Mark G. McGowan, "The Famine Plot Revisited: A Reassessment of the Great Irish Famine as a Genocide," *Genocide Studies International*, 11, no. 1 (2017), 87–104.
3. Liam Kennedy, *Unhappy the Land: The Most Oppressed People Ever, the Irish?* (Sallins, Ire., Merrion Press, 2016). For the debate between Tim Pat Coogan and Liam Kennedy, BBC Radio Ulster, Sunday Sequence, 20 Dec. 2012: www.bbc.co.uk/programmes/b01p4s6w.
4. Peter Duffy, *The Killing of Major Denis Mahon: A Mystery of Old Ireland* (New York: Harper, 2007).
5. Anne Coleman, *Riotous Roscommon: Social Unrest in the 1840s* (Dublin: Irish Academic Press, 1999); Charles E. Orser Jr., "An Archaeology of Famine-Era Eviction," *New Hibernia Review* 9, no. 1 (Spring, 2005), p. 52.
6. Padraig Vesey, *The Murder of Major Mahon, Strokestown, County Roscommon, 1847* (Dublin: Four Courts, 2008), p. 13; a similar link between Mahon's actions in the migration scheme and his murder is offered in John Kelly, *The Graves are Walking: A History of the Great Irish Famine* (New York: Henry Holt and Co., 2012), pp 284–5.
7. Duffy, *The Killing*, pp x-xi.
8. Robert James Scally, *The End of Hidden Ireland: Rebellion, Famine & Emigration* (Oxford University Press, 2005); Mary Lee Dunn, *Ballykilcline Rising: From Famine Ireland to Immigrant America* (Amherst: University of Massachusetts Press, 2008).
9. Michael Huggins, *Social Conflict in Pre-Famine Ireland: The Case of County Roscommon* (Dublin: Four Courts, 2007), pp 156–61.
10. Enda Delaney, *The Great Irish Famine: A History in Four Lives* (Dublin: Gill & Macmillan, 2014), pp 195–6; Stephen J. Campbell, *The Great Irish Famine: Words and Images from the*

Famine Museum, Strokestown Park, County Roscommon (Strokestown: The Famine Museum, 1994), pp 47–8.

11. Ciarán Reilly, *Strokestown and the Great Irish Famine* (Dublin: Four Courts Press, 2014), p. 57. Reilly reports: "he has traditionally been portrayed as the villain in the Strokestown famine narrative." In March 2018, at a reception in Toronto, Irish TD McNaughton, the Minister of Communications, remarked about the draconian actions of Mahon to his tenants forcing them to migrate. Local dramatizations in Strokestown, in 2019, in conjunction with the inaugural National Famine Way commemorative walk along the Royal Canal to Dublin, highlighted the victimization of the tenants by Mahon and his agent, John Ross Mahon. The panels in the nearby National Famine Museum are more neutral about his actions. Local opinion is captured in Cecil Woodham-Smith, *The Great Hunger, 1845–1849* (New York: Old Town Books, 1962). Her reflections on local attitudes cannot be taken lightly since she spent considerable time on the Strokestown Estate doing research. It is likely that she picked up local opinion during her sojourn there.
12. Susan Hood, "The Strokestown Park House Archive," *History Ireland*, 3, no. 4 (Winter, 1995), p. 11. Although the family papers at Strokestown Park House Archives indicate that Charles II granted the lands of Ballynamully to Nicholas Mahon 26 March 1676. Strokestown Park Archive [hereafter SPA], PP/STR/3c.
13. Susan Hood, "The Landlord Influence in the Development of an Irish Estate Town: Strokestown, County Roscommon," *Irish Geography*, 28, no. 2 (1995), pp 119–21.
14. Susan Hood, "The Famine in the Strokestown Park House Archive," *The Irish Review*, no. 17/18 (Winter, 1995), pp 110–12. SPA, Box STR 88, Census of 21 March 1847. This local census counted 68 townlands with 2,237 families constituting 11,958 persons.
15. Vesey, *The Murder*, p. 13.
16. Mary Kelly, "The Great Famine in County Roscommon," in Richie Farrell, Kieran O'Conor and Matthew Potter (eds), *Roscommon: History and Society* (Dublin: Geography Publications, 2018), p. 389. Kelly estimates that the average amount of land held by tenants and sub-tenants was between one and five acres, amounting to between one-half and one-third of average holdings in Kerry (five to 15 acres).
17. Reilly, *Strokestown*.
18. Huggins, *Social Conflict*, pp 13–16, 113–4.
19. Vesey, pp 13–14.
20. Reilly, *Strokestown*, 26–7. SPA, Box STR 88, Charitable Loan Fund, 31 Dec. 1838 to 31 Dec. 1839.
21. SPA, STR 88, Book #8, Indian Meal Given Gratuitously, 6 Aug. 1846. On that day, 195 individuals received free meal. The "Yellowstone: File" lists those given free maize meal on Monday, 22 June 1846.
22. National Library of Ireland [hereafter NLI], Mahon Estate Papers, MS 10,102 (1), Major Denis Mahon to John Ross Mahon, 28 March 1847.
23. Ibid., Major Mahon to John Ross Mahon, 7 March 1847; Major Mahon to John Ross Mahon, 30 March 1847; John Ross Mahon to Major Mahon, April 1847. In the latter letter, the agent indicates that he can get a rate per person to Quebec from Liverpool for

between £3 10*s* and £4 10*s*, a substantial saving from having to support the tenants and the Poor Law at home. NLI, MS 10, 138, Denis Mahon Emigration File, no date, indicates that the passage of the first 405 statute passengers came in at £1,400 1*s* 6*d* or roughly £3 13*s* per person.

24. Ibid., Major Mahon to John Ross Mahon, 2 April 1847 and NLI, MS 10, 102 (2), Major Mahon to John Ross Mahon, 13 April 1847. The Major claimed he might get a rate of £2 10*s* per person at Sligo.
25. NLI, MS 10, 102 (2), Major Mahon to John Ross Mahon, 12 May and 25 May 1847; MS 10,102 (1), Major Mahon to Mr. Gale, 8 April 1847.
26. Three families chose not to leave: William Dalton of Mullevetron remained because his wife was ill. James Egan and James Duffy of the more troubled Cregga House townland elected to stay, as did Widow Stuart of Tully. Patrick Leonard of Kilgraffy was going to stay but then elected to go, only to die on the *Virginius*. The names are on the draft and duplicate copies of the Lists of Tenants from the 32 townlands at SPA, STR/74, 1847.
27. NLI, MS 10,102 (2), Major Mahon to John Ross Mahon, 14 April 1847.
28. NLI, MS 10, 138, Denis Mahon's Emigration, confirms that the assisted tenants were sent to Liverpool from Dublin via "steam packet," at a cost to Mahon of 5 shillings each. The first group of 467 people cost him £116 15*s*.
29. *The Pilot*, 28 May 1847. The article claims 300 to 400 families from "Colonel" Mahon's estate left Dublin on the 27 for Liverpool. He had supplied them with provisions.
30. *The Berean*, 24 June 1847 (vol. 4, no. 13).
31. Ibid., 7 Jan. 1847.
32. Ibid., 6 and 13 May 1847. The latter issue reported that the missionary effort in Achill was going well despite the efforts of "Romish priests."
33. The National Library holds the *Dublin Evening Mail* from 1840 to 1880 and it did publish on 24 May 1847, the only paper to do so in the NLI holdings for the period.
34. SPA, STR/74, Assisted Lists from the Townlands of Kilgraffy and Tully.
35. Ibid.
36. *The Pilot*, 28 May 1847.
37. NLI, MS 10, 138, Denis Mahon's Emigration, 1847.
38. Library and Archives Canada, [hereafter LAC] RG 19-D-5, Emigrant Services Fonds (Canada West), vol. 2532. See chapter by Laura Smith.
39. Reilly, *Strokestown,* 70.
40. Cecil J. Houston & William J. Smyth, *Irish Emigration and Canadian Settlement: Patterns, Links, and Letters* (University of Toronto Press, 1990), pp 3–9, 43–74.
41. Robert C. Lee, *The Canada Company and the Huron Tract 1826–1853: Personalities, Profits and Politics* (Toronto: Natural Heritage Books, 2004).
42. *British Colonist*, 14 and 28 May 1847; *St. Catharine's Journal*, 26 Aug. 1847; and *The Mirror*, 28 July 1843 and 2 Aug. 1844 are just three of many examples.
43. Ruth Bleasdale, *Rough Work: Labourers on the Public Works of British North America and Canada, 1841–1882* (University of Toronto Press, 2018), pp 64–6, 169–79; Paul Hutchison and Michael Power, *Goaded To Madness: The Battle of Slabtown* (St. Catharines: Slabtown

Press, 1999). See also Mark G. McGowan, "Old Sources, new discoveries: in search of the 1,490 assisted immigrants from Strokestown to Canada, 1847," *Archivium Hibernicum*, 72 (2019), 374–96.

44. SPA, STR/74. Lists and duplicates produced of the 32 townlands, the heads of households and the numbers per family group assisted. These individuals were placed in the final tally of 274 migrants in 2015, when compiling names for the commemorative wall at Strokestown Park, because the two sets of lists were not compared for omissions and additions.
45. NLI, MS 10,102 (4), Major Mahon to John Ross Mahon, 18 and 28 April 1847 and MS 10,102 (3) Major Mahon to John Ross Mahon, 20 and 27 May 1847.
46. Duffy, p. 110.
47. Ciaran Reilly, "Strokestown and the Pakenham Mahon Estate," in Farrell, O'Connor, and Potter, eds., *Roscommon*, p. 367. Reilly is citing the *Roscommon Messenger*, 19 July 1851.
48. Here the registers of the assisted immigrants of Mahon's 32 townlands filed in SPA, ST/70 are cross-referenced with André Charbonneau and Doris-Drolet Dubé, *A Register of Deceased Persons at Grosse Île in 1847* (Ottawa: Canadian Heritage, Parks Canada, 1997).
49. Duffy, pp 129–30.
50. There is the possibility of a fifth ship having been sent with more of Mahon's assisted tenants. On 13 July 1847, the *Champion* left Liverpool on what would be a 42-day journey to Quebec. The Major's correspondence with John Ross Mahon had indicated that he wished to send some of the tenants of the Castlenode townland to Canada, but there was concern about the timeline in getting them to Dublin and the preparedness of the designated families to leave. The *Champion* arrived at Grosse Île on either the 23 or 24 August and 94 of its 422 passengers died at sea or in quarantine. Some of the names of the dead match family names from Castlenode, although further investigation is required as to who actually left the Mahon estate on this journey, if anyone. Nevertheless, the Quebec papers recognized the *Champion* as the bearer of more of Mahon's unfortunate people: "The passengers of the Champion are more of the wretched, miserable tenantry of Major Mahon and are equally squalid and filthy as those who came out on the Virginius and Naomi," *Quebec Chronicle*, 24 Aug.1847; see also NLI, MS 10, 102 (2), Major Mahon to John Ross Mahon, 8 and 13 June, 1847, and 6 July 1847; O'Gallagher and Dompierre, *Eyewitness: Grosse Isle*, p. 353.

CHAPTER EIGHT

IN THE FOOTSTEPS OF STROKESTOWN'S FAMINE EMIGRANTS TO NIAGARA

Transatlantic Press Coverage and Retribution for Major Denis Mahon's Coffin Ships

Jason King

On 2 November 1847, Major Denis Mahon, the landlord of Strokestown Park, County Roscommon, was assassinated. Two days later, the *Freeman's Journal* reported that:

> The people were said to be displeased for two reasons. The first was his refusal to continue the conacre system, the second was his clearing away of what he deemed the surplus population. He chartered two vessels and freighted them away with his evicted tenantry.[1]

In the House of Commons on 23 November, Henry Grattan Jr. exclaimed:

> He had freighted two ships in which he sent out those tenants cleared from his estate, to America. But one of those ships was unfortunately lost, and the survivors having some of them returned and told their sad story, nothing could persuade the people that emigration was not a plot against their lives.[2]

In fact, Major Mahon and his agent John Ross Mahon had chartered five ships—the *Virginius*, *Naomi*, *Erin's Queen*, *John Munn,* and *Champion*—to transport former tenants from his estate across the Atlantic during the spring and summer of 1847. None of these ships were lost, but the death toll on board the *Virginius* (267 of 467 passengers) and *Naomi* (196 of 421 passengers) was especially horrific.[3] "It had been rumoured among the remaining tenants" in Strokestown, notes Robert Scally:

> that hundreds of their kin and neighbours had perished by shipwreck owing to Mahon's miserly arrangements for the voyage ... The *Virginius* became the emblematic image of the 'coffin ship' as it took shape in the first years of the famine.[4]

"When the fatalities onboard the Quebec-bound ships became known," claims Ciarán Reilly, "Major Mahon's fate was effectively sealed."[5] Yet the provenance of the rumors that sealed his fate remains unclear.

This chapter traces the source of the rumors to Canadian press coverage of the arrival of Mahon's chartered vessels at the Grosse *Île* quarantine station in Quebec in late July 1847, which were reprinted in Irish newspapers in early September. The initial Canadian accounts overstated the death toll on the *Virginius* as "leaving few passengers able to totter,"[6] who were "ghastly, yellow looking, spectres."[7] These descriptions, in turn, informed Roscommon newspaper claims that "almost every soul of the survivors was hopelessly ill."[8] More specifically, Canadian press coverage prompted a scathing indictment of the *Virginius* in the London *Times* for endangering its "feeble and tottering" passengers, which was widely reprinted in Irish newspapers.[9] "The Black Hole of Calcutta was a mercy compared to the holds of these vessels," it exclaimed. These newspaper accounts provide the only source of information about the plight of Mahon's assisted emigrants and the conduit for rumors that sealed his fate.

The same transatlantic migration and information flows that helped prompt Mahon's assassination also enabled its ringleader, Andrew Connor, to escape his would-be captors and follow Strokestown's surviving emigrants to the Niagara region of Canada West, where he blended in with labourers on the Welland Canal. This chapter builds on Mark McGowan and Laura Smith's ground-breaking research in this volume that tracks Mahon's assisted emigrants to specific destinations in Canada West, along migratory pathways that were documented by Canadian officials in Emigrant Service Fund records. In his chapter, McGowan notes his discovery in a Quebec City Anglican newspaper, *The Berean*, of a brief reprinted account of Mahon's former tenants' arrival in Dublin on 24 May 1847. The article records that:

> this afternoon an unusual long train of emigrants, evidently from the same townland, and presenting marks of comfort recognizable in the bulk of people fleeing from the famine, passed along our quays to the emigrant offices, near the Customs House ... One of the leaders stated ... that their destination was Upper Canada.[10]

As McGowan notes, the article provides the only evidence that Mahon's former tenants were not only "fleeing from the famine" but also travelling to a specific destination in Canada West. It also corroborates his previous research which has tracked many of them to the Niagara region.[11] Indeed, McGowan notes that, "the Welland Canal at Niagara was a hive for Irish workers, some of which had left Mahon's estate prior to the assistance scheme."[12] He further observes, "the article bears a hopeful tone that would soon be extinguished by the realities of the trans-Atlantic crossing".[13] More to the point, John Ross Mahon was probably more culpable than Major Mahon for the horrific fate suffered by his assisted emigrants at sea, though ultimately the landlord "would be held responsible."[14] Indeed, within two days of his assassination, the *Freeman's Journal* attributed the motive to his "clearing away" of "the surplus population."[15]

The assassination of Major Mahon on 2 November 1847, caused international headlines and led to reprisals on his estate. Numerous tenants were evicted in its immediate aftermath.[16] Several people were charged, tried, and three were hanged for the murder.[17] Yet the suspected ringleader, Andrew Connor, was not apprehended. By 1849, he had become a fugitive and was tracked to Canada. As Padraig Vesey notes, "the evidence generated at the trials showed that a man who resided on the Sliabh Bawn mountain, named Andrew Connor, was the real leader of the murder gang ... Despite the intense police activity in Strokestown Andrew Connor evaded arrest."[18] Vesey's research is based on a dossier of letters that he discovered between Dublin Castle and Government House in Montreal, including reports by Canadian superintendents and police inspectors, and held in the National Archives of Ireland. In his analysis, Vesey repeatedly claims that they trace the movements of Andrew Connor from Strokestown to Montreal. In his words:

> Mr John Kearney wrote to the lord lieutenant in August 1849 claiming that he had met Andrew Connor in Canada at Port Robinson in Montreal, where Connor resided in a house with his two brothers, Martin and John, and that he was posing as a deserting soldier, and appeared to have plenty of money to spend.[19]

Vesey added:

> In a letter dated 10 August 1849, the chief of police of Port Robinson, Montreal, wrote 'Andrew Connor a labourer of this place ... left Port Robinson about six weeks since, he is supposed to be somewhere in the neighbourhood of New York. His two brothers Martin and John Connor still reside in Port Robinson.'[20]

Yet Vesey makes a basic geographical error in his analysis: there is no Port Robinson neighbourhood in Montreal. In fact, Port Robinson in Canada West (now Ontario) and Montreal in Canada East (now Quebec) are approximately 670 kilometres apart. More importantly, Port Robinson is on the Welland Canal at Niagara which McGowan had demonstrated, "was a hive for Irish workers" who migrated from

Mahon's estate in 1847 and earlier. Vesey misunderstood that the letters in the police dossier were, in fact, tracking Andrew Connor's locations in 1849 while he was still on the move from Montreal to the same destination in Niagara as Mahon's assisted emigrants two years earlier. This chapter argues that he followed precisely in their footsteps to find refuge amongst his kindred on the Welland Canal.

"Ghastly, yellow looking, spectres"

Major Denis Mahon knew that his life was in danger even before the rumors of *Virginius's* calamity had reached Strokestown. A letter in the Strokestown Park House Archive written by John Ross Mahon on 23 July 1847 warned Major Mahon of an assassination plot "by persons in comfortable circumstances" and that, "emigrants in America had provided the money to do so."[21] The threat significantly escalated when news of the *Virginius's* death toll reached Roscommon in early September. The catastrophic conditions below deck were emphasized in newspaper coverage from the moment of its arrival at the Grosse *Île* quarantine station in Quebec on 28 July 1847. The next day, the *Quebec Mercury* reported "from Grosse *Isle* our latest information is given ... The mortality on board the ... *Virginius* is fearful to think of ... 495 passengers—186 sick, 158 deaths—The master, mate and crew, except six, are ill—and few passengers able to totter—out 9 weeks."[22] On 31 July, the *Quebec Mercury* documented the horrific conditions on board both the *Virginius* and the *Naomi* in more detail. The newspaper recounted that:

> The last accounts from Grosse Isle are most harrowing, and forebode gloomily. We have received the latest information from the Quarantine Station, which states the late arrivals to present an equal condition of squalor, misery, mortality, and disease, to that which existed on the *Virginius* ... The barque *Naomi*, from Liverpool, with 331 passengers, lost 78, and had upwards of 100 sick on her arrival at Grosse Isle. The master of the *Virginius* was dying or dead when the steamer left the island last evening, and there remained but three hands of the ship's company fit for duty. The mate is dead, and the balance are said to be ghastly, yellow looking spectres, of whom not more than six or eight are able to exert themselves:—they are all long bearded and hollow cheeked.[23]

On 10 August 1847, the *Quebec Mercury* confirmed that, "the captain of the *Virginius* died the day after his arrival at Grosse Isle."[24]

These accounts of the *Virginius* in the *Quebec Mercury* informed Canadian press coverage that was subsequently reprinted in Ireland. The death toll of 158 from the trans-Atlantic crossing had been accurately reported, but not the dire conditions of the surviving passengers, which was overstated. Even so, another 19 steerage passengers died while the ship was anchored at Grosse *Île*, and 90 more while in quarantine, bringing the total death toll on the *Virginius* to 267 out of 476 passengers. The ship was detained for 13 days at Grosse *Île*, arriving in the port of Quebec City on 12 August 1847.[25] On 4 August 1847, the Toronto *Globe* reported under the headline "Mortality Among the Immigrants" that, "the Virginius from Liverpool, with 496 passengers, had lost 158 by death; nearly one third of the whole; and she had 180 sick; above one half of the whole will never see their own house in the New World."[26] The article was reprinted under the headline "The Emigrant Fever in Canada" in the *Roscommon and Leitrim Gazette* on 18 September 1847.[27] A second article entitled "Ship Fever in Canada," with the byline, "Kingston, Canada West, Aug. 10,"[28] stated:

> *Virginius* and *John Munn*, which left Liverpool with 496 and 425 passengers respectively, the one with 158 and the other with 52 dead, while almost every soul of the survivors was hopelessly ill—of the crew of the *Virginius* but three are left, the captain and officers having died with the rest, and it was seriously contemplated to scuttle the ship and sink her for a while, as the only means of purifying her from the infection she has absorbed—it is said that everyone has abandoned her at Grosse Isle.[29]

This article was widely reprinted in Irish newspapers in early September, including in the *King's County Chronicle* (8 September), *The Vindicator, Belfast* (4 September), the *Dublin Evening Post* (2 September), and the *Roscommon and Leitrim Gazette* (4 September). The *Cork Examiner* (3 September) featured a slight variation on the *Virginius's* calamitous arrival at Grosse *Île*, noting that:

> but two seamen [were] left to work the ship. Of the wretched remnant of 150 survivors, only forty have since been taken down, and it is not expected that more than a tithe of the whole number will ever live to settle in America. *Ex Uno Disce Omnes.* The dread record of one is that of all.[30]

These press accounts accurately reported the *Virginius's* death toll at sea but overstated the suffering of its passengers and crew. The ship was never abandoned. Rumors of the *Virginius* shipwreck emanated from press claims that it was scuttled.

"The Black Hole of Calcutta was a mercy compared to the holds of these vessels"

By early September, the fate of Mahon's assisted emigrants was being widely reported in Ireland, specifically in Roscommon. The negative press coverage of the *Virginius* was compounded by a scathing editorial in the *Times* on 17 September, which was also extensively reprinted in Ireland. It was both strident and strikingly atypical in its denunciation of the horrific conditions of the Irish Famine migration. The paper editorialized at length:

> Did Ireland possess a writer endued with the laborious truth of Thucydides, the graceful felicity of Virgil, or the happy invention of De Foe, the events of this miserable year might be quoted by the scholar for ages to come, together with the sufferings of the pent-up multitudes of Athens, the distempered plains of northern Italy, or the hideous ravages of our great plague ... The fact of more than a hundred thousand souls flying from the very midst of the great calamity, across a great ocean, to a new world, crowding into insufficient vessels, scrambling for a footing on a deck and a berth in a hold, committing themselves to these worse than prisons, while their frames were wasted with ill fare and blood infested with disease, fighting for months of unutterable wretchedness against the elements without and pestilence within, giving almost hourly victims to the deep, landing at lengths on shores already terrified and diseased, consigned to encampments of the dying and of the dead, spreading death wherever they roam, and having no other prospect before them than a long continuance of these horrors in a still farther flight across forests and lakes under a Canadian sun and a Canadian frost—all these are the circumstances beyond the Greek historian or Latin poet, and such as an Irish pestilence alone could produce.
>
> By the end of the season there is little doubt that the immigration into Canada will have amounted to 100,000; nearly all from Ireland. We know the condition in which these poor creatures embarked on this perilous adventure. They were only flying from one form of death. On the authority of the Montreal Board of Health we are enabled to state that they were allowed to ship in numbers two or three times greater than the same vessels would have presumed to carry to a United States port.
>
> The worst horrors of the slave trade which it is a boast of this empire to suppress, at any cost, have been reenacted in the flight of British subjects from their native shores.[31]

In equating the "worst horrors of the slave trade" with the Irish Famine migration, the *Times* exposed the deplorable conditions on the transatlantic crossing as an epochal failure of empire. The magnitude of suffering on these emigrant vessels required an author of the stature Thucydides, Virgil, or De Foe to register the scale of calamity and bear witness to the emigrants' plight. Indeed, the unfolding "Irish pestilence" at sea only augurs further misery and "a long continuance of these horrors in a still farther flight across forests and lakes under a Canadian sun and a Canadian frost."

This strident editorial in the *Times* was prompted by the spectacle of the *Virginius's* arrival at Grosse *Île*. Two days earlier, on 15 September, the paper published an article entitled "Immigration of 1847," taken from the "*Toronto Globe* of Aug. 14" that contained "an extract from the report of the Montreal Board of Health, dated 12th of August."[32] This extract stated (as reported in the *Quebec Mercury* on 31 July) that:

> The Virginius sailed with 496—158 died on the passage, 186 were sick, and the remainder landed feeble and tottering—the captain, masters, and crew were all sick. The Black Hole of Calcutta was a mercy compared to the holds of those vessels.

The same extract was then repeated verbatim in the *Times* editorial on 17 September. Yet, in invoking the authority of the Montreal's Board of Health, the paper was inadvertently reproducing a polemic that had little to do with the *Virginius*. In fact, a prolonged dispute had arisen in July 1847 about where the city's fever sheds should be relocated that pitted Montreal's municipal Board of Health, a body "composed of men from both sides of Montreal's ethnic and political divide," against the less representative colonial administration's Emigrant Committee, which comprised "members from the city's British Protestant élite, the majority of whom were supporters of the current Tory administration."[33] The mayor of Montreal, John Easton Mills, was represented on both groups until he succumbed to typhus on 12 November 1847. Dan Horner observed:

> While the Board of Health, the majority of civic élites, and what appears to be a sizable swath of public opinion, saw the desperation and misery of Irish emigrants landing in the vicinity of the city as a threat to public order, the Emigrant Committee saw the same scene as a necessary by-product of economic growth and a symbol of a particularly British drive towards self-improvement in the face of crisis."[34]

The Board of Health's report on 12 August expressed frustration that it "could be of no avail in warding off very serious consequences to the inhabitants, which are still to be apprehended, from the unnatural immigration of this year."[35] Its denunciation of the *Virginius's* steerage as being akin to "the Black Hole of Calcutta" arose from this localized dispute with the Emigrant Committee rather than the arrivals to the city. The *Times* reproduced this graphic image of the *Virginius*, which was extensively reprinted in Irish newspapers such as the *Limerick and Clare Examiner* (22 September), the *Kings County Chronicle* (29 September) and the *Southern Reporter* (29 September). There is some dispute between Robert Scally and Mary Lee Dunn about how quickly news travelled in rural Roscommon in the late 1840s.[36] Yet, by September, rumors of Mahon's migrants were in wide circulation and had reached Strokestown.

Chasing an Assassin

The *Virginius* became the emblematic coffin ship because of Canadian press coverage likening its hold to the "Black Hole of Calcutta," which was amplified by the *Times*. Initial accounts of its death toll at sea were accurate, but not subsequent claims that the ship was scuttled and abandoned. Rumors of shipwreck originated in these reports. They provided a motive for the assassination of Major Mahon. He was shot in his carriage returning from a Famine relief meeting in the company of his physician, Dr Terence Shanley. The news of his death quickly spread across Roscommon and was widely celebrated: "bonfires were seen to be on the hills for many miles extent," notes Reilly.[37] Major Mahon was buried in the ruined mausoleum near Strokestown Park House. He was the first and most high-profile Irish landlord to be murdered during the Great Hunger. Nearly a century later, he was still recalled in the National Folklore Commission's Schools' Collection as a ghostly figure riding "in a coach drawn by four headless horses."[38]

In the months following Mahon's killing, numerous suspects were apprehended and three people were tried and hanged. The most likely mastermind behind the assassination, however, was Andrew Connor, whom Reilly described as the leader of "a notorious agrarian conspiracy from Graffogue at the foot of Sliabh Bawn mountain."[39] As Vesey noted:

> The Connor brothers, Andrew, Martin and John, lived in the townland of Mahon's Yard, a distance of some miles from where the other accomplices lived. Andrew Connor features regularly in the surviving correspondence from the Famine years in Strokestown Park House. Tenants complained often to their landlord that they were being robbed of the money they received after selling their farm produce by a gang led by Andrew Connor.[40]

Andrew Connor did not pull the trigger, but was implicated in playing "a leading part in planning and financing the conspiracy."[41] At his accomplices' trials, it was revealed that Connor had been seen on Christmas Eve 1847 distributing funds to the perpetrators. All three Connor brothers were subsequently evicted from their homes in Mahon's Yard townland during the sweeping clearances that took place in the assassination's aftermath. Their names were published in April 1848 by Bishop George Browne of Elphin, County Roscommon, on "a list of tenants evicted from the Mahon estate." According to Bishop Browne, "the evictions on the estate since Major Mahon had taken over amounted to 3,006 people."[42] His list was published in the *Freeman's Journal* on 29 April 1848, and included, "Martin Connor... [family of] 2, John Connor... 4, Andrew Connor... 3."[43]

The Connor brothers soon thereafter fled from Ireland to Canada but left their dependents behind. A letter in the Strokestown Park Archive reveals that even from overseas Andrew Connor instilled a sense of terror amongst his neighbours. On 15 May 1849, James Nerheny wrote to John Ross Mahon about the threat Connor represented:

> Sir, pardon me to say that within those years past I have lived in the utmost danger of my life in consequence of my neighbour Michael Nerhenry who is Brother in law to Andrew Connor whose character I need not describe. This Michael Nerhenry has now in his house Connor's wife + children as a terror to all his neighbours and has received from Connor a considerable portion of the money collected for the conspiring of the Major's life. 'Tis evident too that he has Connor's arms together with letters of communication from him where ever he is beside.
>
> Michael kept a shebeen house previous to the Major's death wherein Connor + his associates often drank together and after the perpetration of the barbarous deed shewed the greatest symptoms of joy which many can testify.[44]

Nerheny's letter reveals that Andrew Connor left his wife and children in the care of his brother-in-law, Michael Nerhenry, and continued to support them from abroad. He also attests to Connor's "letters of communication from wherever he is" that linked him with his home and family. Furthermore, he still represented "a terror to all his neighbours" in spite of fleeing Ireland. The final record of Andrew Connor in the Strokestown Park Archive is a letter from Luke Murray to John Ross Mahon on 21 December 1849. It states that after the Connor brothers' evictions they had attempted to lease land from Nicholas Balfe, who told Andrew "to be off to America as he would give him no land and no other landlord would either."[45] Indeed, the Connor brothers had already fled long before Luke Murray's letter was written. "It is amazing," concludes Vesey, that Connor "escaped the police dragnet in the almost martial law conditions which prevailed in Strokestown after the murder and more amazing still that when the Canadian authorities were ready to arrest him he was gone."[46]

Yet Vesey does not appreciate how close they came to apprehending Connor, based on his misinterpretation of the police dossier of letters written from Ireland and British North America in pursuit of Connor as he moved from Canada East to Canada West. Vesey's failure to distinguish between Montreal in Canada East and Port Robinson in Canada West as distinct locations, hundreds of kilometres apart, made him oblivious to Connor's direction of travel. More to the point, Connor eluded his pursuers as they sought to document his movements from Ireland following in the footsteps of Mahon's assisted emigrants to the Niagara region and Welland Canal. The charge sheet signed by Sub-Inspector Makeney on 10 August 1849, notes that in October 1847, Connor "with others did feloniously conspire, confederate, and agree together to murder the late Major Denis Mahon of Strokestown House."[47] It describes him as "a wild and strong person in appearance, speaks mild and easy, is very shrewd and cunning, can read and write and rather intelligent." Connor was listed as "5 feet nine inches in height, stout build, dark complexion, dark to grey hair, stooped and round shouldered, wears a hat or sometimes a cap, cord breeches and leggings, and a dark coat."[48] By the time the charge sheet was created, Connor had already fled Ireland for Canada.

The charge sheet's police dossier also contains letters from Dublin Castle, Government House in Montreal, the Sheriff's Office, Niagara, and Port Robinson on the Welland Canal. Connor's evasion of Canadian authorities amazed Vesey, yet he showed little understanding of how far the fugitive travelled. The first letter in the dossier written by John Kearney in Montreal on 18 July 1849, does indicate that Connor was within their grasp.[49] Kearney's letter states:

> Sir, This is to inform you that about 14 days after my arrival in Canada I fell in with Andrew Connor in Montreal—he has a house taken here and appears to be settled—he is spending a great deal of money—he is a low sized stout man.
>
> I now request an order from you as soon as possible to let me know how to act. I have spent a great deal of money in looking after him and keeping him in view—I was speaking to Mr Flynn about it and he told me that if you send an order he would have him arrested instantly. He is busy living in Burlington and hear [sic] better than two years.
>
> I have refused the offer of 11 dollars ... for the purpose of looking after him and that I hope you will not see me at a loss.
>
> I remain your humble servant.
>
> John Kearney
>
> P.S. Please send your order to Chief of Police Mr Flynn, with all speed as I do not know how long this man will remain hear [sic]. I attend the police station every day myself and will continue to do so till your order comes. He gave himself out as a soldier who had service 12 or 13 years in the army deserted but I am quite sure of who he is.[50]

Kearney's letter indicates that Connor had been resident in Montreal and Burlington, Vermont, for an extended period before July 1849. The fact that, "he has a house taken here and appears to be settled [and] is spending a great deal of money" suggests that Connor felt comfortable and inconspicuous in Montreal's Irish community. The Sliabh Bawn assassin had escaped from Strokestown to Montreal, where he found congenial surroundings. Indeed, his disguise "as a soldier who had service 12 or 13 years in the army deserted" implies that he lived amongst disaffected Irish migrants with little sympathy for British rule.[51] Kearney himself appears to be a paid informant who was observing Connor but not authorized to apprehend him. He negotiates his fee for "looking after him and keeping him in view." Kearney's daily visits to Chief of Police, Mr Flynn, also suggest that an arrest was imminent.

Clearly, something spooked Connor to move on. The next letter in the dossier is addressed to John Reddington, Esq., in Dublin Castle, from Government House in Montreal, dated 18 August 1849. It reveals that the Canadian authorities had missed their opportunity to capture Connor. The letter states:

> Sir, I am commanded by the Governor General to acquaint you with the result of the enquiries which have been made for the discovery of one Andrew Connor described in your communication of the 29 March last, as charged with being implicated in the conspiracy to murder Major Denis Mahon who was assassinated in the County of Roscommon in the month of October 1847 [sic], and to state that the delay which has taken place in communicating this information to you has arisen in consequence of the orders at first issued by the Governor General having, it appears, miscarried.
>
> I have now the honour to enclose a copy of a letter from the Deputy Sheriff of the Niagara District stating that Connor is supposed to be in the neighbourhood of New York, but that he is expected to return to Port Robinson.[52]

The letter reveals that delayed communications between Montreal and Dublin gave Connor the opportunity to escape and move on to Port Robinson in Canada West. It also notes that Dublin Castle had first sought assistance in apprehending Connor on 29 March 1849. By 18 July, he was in John Kearney's sights and Chief of Police Flynn was awaiting the order to arrest him. But the order never came. "Miscarried" information from Government House enabled Connor to elude his pursuers.

More to the point, Connor had his own "letters of communication" and network of fellow travellers, which led him to seek refuge amongst Irish labourers on the Welland Canal. The aforementioned enclosed letter, "from the Deputy Sheriff of the Niagara District," is also in the same police dossier. It was written by Deputy Sheriff L.W. Mercer from the Sheriff's Office in Niagara on 13 August 1849. Mercer wrote:

> In the absence of the Sheriff I beg leave to acknowledge the receipt of your letter of the 29 ... and to inform you that it is the only communication we have received upon the subject. Immediately on receipt we took the necessary steps to procure information without appearing particular in our inquiries, the result you will be better able to see by the enclosed letter of the superintendent of Police, who resides at Port Robinson.
>
> By a conversation with him, he expressed no doubt of his coming back again soon. If he does come, are we to arrest him?[53]

The letter Mercer alludes to was written by Police Superintendent Edward Wheeler from Port Robinson on the Welland Canal on 10 August 1849. Wheeler's letter states in full:

> My dear sir, Andrew Connor a labourer at this place, answering the name and description handed me by Copeland a few days ago, left Port Robinson about six weeks since this happened—he is now somewhere in the neighbourhood of New York.
>
> His two brothers Martin & John Connor still reside at Port Robinson.
>
> I shall keep a sharp look out, in case of his return, and let you hear instantly if I should get any information that will lead to his apprehension—I wish I had known it six weeks earlier.[54]

Wheeler's letter makes clear that Connor's information network and letters of communication were better than his pursuers. He had followed in the footsteps of Mahon's assisted emigrants to become a laborer with his brothers in Port Robinson, Canada West, on the "Deep Cut" for the second Welland Canal. The village of Port Robinson had only been founded in 1829 and was inhabited mainly by Irish canal workers in the late 1840s. Superintendent Wheeler was stationed there because of its transient and potentially violent population. He recognized Andrew Connor as "a labourer at this place" and that "his two brothers Martin & John Connor still reside at Port Robinson." "I shall keep a sharp look out, in case of his return," Wheeler added, "and let you hear instantly if I should get any information that will lead to his apprehension." Yet by the time Connor was tracked to Port Robinson, he had already moved on to New York. Indeed, he probably sought to blend in with the cluster of Mahon's former tenants settled nearby in Lockport, Niagara Country, New York. According to McGowan:

> Despite the harsh circumstances of their assistance, once off the Mahon estate, and their harrowing journey to America, the Strokestown survivors appear to have demonstrated remarkable agency in selecting potential settlement areas where their agricultural skills and experience in manual labour could be to put to good use.[55]

Both in Port Robinson, Canada West, and Lockport, New York, they found employment and recreated communities that had been scattered by the Irish Famine migration of 1847. They also provided refuge for fugitives from Ireland.

Why would Andrew Connor flee to Port Robinson to become a laborer with his brothers on the Welland Canal? Because it was the destination of his fellow Strokestown emigrants amongst whom he could find shelter and support. As McGowan notes, it was "a hive of Irish workers." The enlargement of the second Welland Canal attracted many Irish laborers, especially from Connacht and Cork, who often fought each other in the early 1840s.[56] It was also a site of sectarian clashes when Irish Catholics and Protestants came to blows, such as during the Battle of

Slabtown on 12 July 1849, that left at least two dead.[57] In this lawless environment with Irish laborers on the move, Connor could easily blend in. Between Montreal and Port Robinson, he eluded his captors and found refuge among his kindred. Missives from Dublin Castle, Government House in Montreal, the Niagara Sheriff's Office and Port Robinson proved futile in tracking him down. Connor had a superior network of information and letters of communication to his pursuers in Ireland and Canada. Ultimately, the Strokestown assassin remained one step ahead of the law. From Port Robinson, he disappeared without a trace. He was never caught.

Awakening from a Nightmare

In conclusion, the assassination of Major Mahon was initially perceived as retribution for the death and suffering of his assisted migrants on the *Virginius* and other chartered vessels. Canadian newspaper coverage of "feeble and tottering passengers" being reduced to "ghastly, yellow looking, spectres," on a ship that was scuttled, was widely reprinted in Ireland from early September 1847. These accounts prompted a scathing editorial in the *Times* that likened the *Virginius's* hold to "the Black Hole of Calcutta," which was also widely republished in Irish newspapers. Rumors of shipwreck and hopelessly ill survivors emanated from these accounts and provided a motive for Mahon's killing. In her classic study *The Great Hunger* (1962), Cecil Woodham-Smith contends that "the legend in the west of Ireland is that 'coffin ships' were chartered, when one foundered, and all aboard were lost, Major Mahon was shot by the lover of a girl who had been drowned."[58] Similar rumors had informed Henry Grattan II's claim in the House of Commons on 23 November 1847 that "nothing could persuade the people that emigration was not a plot against their lives."[59] Yet the actual mastermind behind the assassination of Major Denis Mahon, Andrew Connor, fled from Ireland never to return. He followed in the footsteps of Mahon's assisted emigrants and found shelter amongst their clusters in Montreal, Port Robinson and New York. McGowan's research on the formation of these clusters and settlement patterns of Strokestown's surviving emigrants further illuminates Connor's escape route from Ireland. His communication networks with fellow travellers proved superior to those of his would-be captors.

Ultimately, the only survivors from Mahon's assisted emigrants who ever returned to Strokestown were not assassins but priests: the brothers, Patrick (10) and Thomas (5) Quinn, who were left orphaned on Grosse *Île* in 1847, yet made a homecoming visit to their birthplace long after their ordinations in 1889.[60] Decades after leaving, Thomas Quinn provided the only eyewitness account of the traumatic experiences of Mahon's assisted migrants on the transatlantic voyage and arrival at Grosse *Île*. He recalled being summoned to his father's deathbed on the island, who enjoined him to "remember your soul and your liberty."[61] He also recounted lying delirious afterwards and falling "into a deep sleep: when I awoke, all my compatriots were gone."[62] Soon thereafter, he was reunited with Patrick in the home of his adoptive father, but recoiled in terror: "I did not recognize him at first," Thomas recalled, "but then I loudly expressed my fear, thinking that he was coming back to find me to share again the dark days that we had just gone through."[63] Yet his brother was no revenant reliving the horrors of the ocean voyage. Rather, Patrick had come to express a "legitimate desire" to be adopted into the same household, and "what a joy" it was "for the two brothers to live together."[64] More to the point, Thomas Quinn had no memory of Major Mahon or the nefarious Andrew Connor. They were consigned to his nightmare and left no trace in the legacy he shaped.[65]

NOTES

1. *The Freeman's Journal*, 4 Nov. 1847.
2. *Hansard's Parliamentary Debates*, vol. 95, series 3, 23 Nov. 1847, 2.
3. Marianna O'Gallagher and Rose Dompierre, *Eyewitness: Grosse Isle 1847* (Ste-Foy, Quebec: Livres Carraig Books, 1995), p. 352.
4. Robert James Scally. *The End of Hidden Ireland: Rebellion, Famine & Emigration* (Oxford University Press, 1995), p. 39.
5. Ciarán Reilly, *Strokestown and the Great Irish Famine* (Dublin: Four Courts Press, 2014), p. 84.
6. *Quebec Mercury,* 29 July 1847.
7. Ibid., 31 July 1847.
8. *Roscommon and Leitrim* Gazette, 4 Sept. 1847.
9. *Times*, 17 Sept. 1847.
10. *The Berean*, vol. 4, no. 13, 24 June 1847.
11. Mark McGowan, "Migration, Mobility, and Murder: The Story of the 1,490 Assisted Immigrants, from the Mahon Estate, Strokestown, County Roscommon, 1847,"*Breac: A Digital Journal of Irish Studies* (2018); https://breac.nd.edu/articles/migration-mobility-and-murder-the-story-of-the-1-490-assisted-immigrants-from-the-mahon-estate-strokestown-county-roscommon-1847/; Mark McGowan, "Old Sources, new discoveries: in search of the 1,490 assisted immigrants from Strokestown to Canada, 1847," *Archivium Hibernicum*, 72 (2019), 374–96.
12. See chapter by Mark McGowan.
13. Ibid.
14. Ibid.
15. *The Freeman's Journal,* 4 Nov. 1847.
16. Reilly, pp 111–132.
17. For detailed accounts, see Padraig Vesey, *The Murder of Major Mahon, Strokestown, County Roscommon, 1847* (Dublin: Four Courts, 2008); Peter Duffy, *The Killing of Major Denis Mahon: A Mystery of Old Ireland* (New York: Harper, 2007), pp 165–311.

18. Vesey, pp 5–36, 37.
19. Ibid., p. 37.
20. Ibid.
21. Cited in Reilly, p. 84.
22. *Quebec Mercury,* 29 July 1847.
23. Ibid., 31 July 1847.
24. Ibid., 30 Aug. 1847.
25. O'Gallagher and Dompierre, *Eyewitness: Gross Isle,* p. 352.
26. *The Globe*, 4 Aug. 1847.
27. *Roscommon and Leitrim* Gazette, 8 Sept. 1847.
28. The source of this article remains unclear. None of Kingston's periodicals, the *British Whig,* the *Upper Canada Herald,* and the *Kingston Chronicle and Gazette*, were published on 10 Aug. 1847.
29. *Roscommon and Leitrim Gazette*, 4 Sept. 1847.
30. *Cork Examiner*, 3 Sept. 1847.
31. *Times*, 7 Sept. 1847.
32. Ibid., 5 Sept. 1847.
33. Dan Horner, "'The Public has the Right to be Protected from A Deadly Scourge': Debating Quarantine, Migration and Liberal Governance during the 1847 Typhus Outbreak in Montreal," *Journal of the Canadian Historical Association / Revue de la Societé historique du Canada* (2012 23 [1]), 65–100, 76. See also, Jason King, "'The Atrocious Avarice of the Irish Landlords': Canadian Public Sentiment and the Irish Famine Migration of 1847," in Marguérite Corporaal, Peter Gray (eds), *The Great Irish Famine and Social Class: Conflicts, Responsibilities, Representations* (New York: Peter Lang, 2019), pp 237–256.
34. Horner, pp 84–85.
35. *Quebec Mercury*, 17 Aug. 1847.
36. In *The End of Hidden Ireland* (pp 133–158), Scally argues that the cottiers on the rural and remote townlands of Denis Mahon's estate and the Crown Estate at Ballykilcline were mostly illiterate and only partially exposed to the forces of modernization, that is, a market-oriented monetary economy, commercialized agriculture, standardized compulsory education, the diffusion of print technology, and the prevailing institutions and ethos of Irish civil society prior to 1847. "The mental isolation of the townland had to be penetrated from outside" and was largely impervious to events beyond the parish (p. 136). By contrast, Mary Lee Dunn argues in *Ballykilcline Rising: From Famine Ireland to Immigrant America* (Amherst: University of Massachusetts Press, 2008) that rural Roscommon "was not as cut off as it might have appeared [as] can be shown in a calculation of the number of seasonal migrant laborers who set off annually from the parish; considerations of communications, transportation, and economic infrastructure; a survey of the content of a country newspaper available to the people ... Indeed, the Irish had a widening world view," p. 5.
37. Reilly, p. 97.
38. National Folklore Collection, UCD, The Schools' Collection, vol. 0253, 300. At: www.duchas.ie/en/cbes/4798702/4791746.
39. Reilly, p. 97.
40. Vesey, p. 36.
41. Ibid.

42. Reilly, p. 103.
43. *Freeman's Journal*, 29 April 1847.
44. Strokestown Park Archives (hereafter SPA), uncatalogued letter from James Nerheny to John Ross Mahon, 15 May 1849.
45. SPA, uncatalogued letter from Luke Murray to John Ross Mahon, 21 Dec. 1849. Cited in Vesey, p. 36.
46. Ibid., p. 37.
47. Outrage Papers, Roscommon (OPR), 1849, National Archives of Ireland (NAI).
48. Cited in Vesey, p. 37.
49. Vesey mistakes the date of the letter sent presumably "to the lord lieutenant in August 1849" (36) though the recipient is not indicated.
50. John Kearney, Montreal to lord lieutenant, 18 July 1849, OPR, 1849, NAI.
51. For a broader discussion of the political radicalization of Famine emigrants in British North America. see Jason King, "'The Noble, Deluded People': Stephen De Vere and Famine Irish Emigrant Political Sentiment," in William Jenkins (ed.) "*Canada and the Great Irish Famine* (Montreal & Kingston: McGill-Queens University Press, forthcoming).
52. Letter from Government House, Montreal to John Reddington, Esq, Dublin Castle, 18 Aug. 1849, OPR, 1849 (NAI).
53. Ibid., Letter from Deputy Sheriff L.W. Mercer, Sheriff's Office in Niagara, to Government House, Montreal, 13 Aug. 1849.
54. Ibid., Letter from Superintendent of Police Edward Wheeler, Port Robinson, Welland Canal, 10 Aug. 1849.
55. See Mark McGowan, "Migration, Mobility, and Murder: The Story of the 1,490 Assisted Immigrants, from the Mahon Estate, Strokestown, County Roscommon, 1847," *Breac: A Digital Journal of Irish Studies* (2018). https://breac.nd.edu/articles/migration-mobility-and-murder-the-story-of-the-1-490-assisted-immigrants-from-the-mahon-estate-strokestown-county-roscommon-1847/.
56. J. Lawrence Runnals, *The Irish on the Welland Canal* (St Catharines: St Catharines Public Library, 1973), pp 36–56.
57. Ibid., pp 39–53.
58. Cecil Woodham-Smith, *The Great Hunger, Ireland 1845–1849* (London: Hamish Hamilton, 1962), p. 225.
59. *Hansard's Parliamentary Debates*, vol. 95, series 3, 23 Nov. 1847.
60. See Jason King, "Une Voix d'Irlande: Integration, Migration, and Travelling Nationalism Between Famine Ireland and Quebec in the Long Nineteenth Century," in Ciaran Reilly (ed.) *The Famine Irish: Emigration and the Great Hunger* (Dublin: History Press, 2016), 193–208, 207–208.
61. Ibid., p. 191. Also see, Thomas Quinn, "Une Voix d'Irlande," in *Premier Congrès de La Langue Français au Canada* (Québec: Imprimerie de l'Action Sociale Limitée, 1913), pp 227–232.
62. "Monsieur l'abbé Thomas Quinn, 1841–1923. Souvenirs D'Enfance (Arrivée au Canada)," in *Metáire St-Joseph, Nicolet (Chronique). 1895–1935*, vol. 1, 58–60, 59. Archives du Séminaire de Nicolet. Fonds Thomas Quinn Annexe. Translated by Simon Jolivet.
63. Ibid.
64. Ibid.
65. The Quinn brothers' legacy is explored in Jason King, "Une Voix d'Irlande," pp 193–208.

CHAPTER NINE

"CONNAUGHT OR HELL"

The Rise and Fall of a Proposed New Ireland in the Canadian West, 1880–1882

Timothy S. Forest

The winter of 1879–80 was disastrous for the west of Ireland. The potato blight returned in its worst form since the Great Famine, with the yield falling from an average of 3.3 tons per acre in 1876 to 1.3 tons in 1879.[1] The official Preliminary Report on Agricultural Produce declared the entire 1879 crop "a complete failure."[2] Heavy rains also ruined the oat, barley and hay harvests. Complicating matters, the price of wool plummeted by 47 percent. Traditionally, these calamities would have been offset by demand for Irish seasonal farm labor in Britain. Yet this, too, dropped, due to the similarly cold and damp weather there, new competition from cheaper and more efficient North and South American and Australasian producers, and widespread economic depression in the United Kingdom.[3] Consequently, economic, social and political conditions in the west of Ireland destabilized. Farmers, the vast majority of whom rented their holdings, were unable to make payments and many were evicted. Landowners, in turn, went bankrupt. Rent strikes, boycotts, land squatting, estate raids and riots swept across the region, on a scale unseen since the 1840s. Between 1879 and 1880, the number of evictions jumped from 1,238 to 2,110, and the number of listed outrages almost quadrupled, from 863 to 2,590.[4] Unlike in the 1840s, by the 1880s the Irish people had mobilized, refusing to allow any repeat of the Great Famine, leading to a conflict that commentators would brand as the Land War. The Land League and the Irish Parliamentary Party, the two leading voices of Irish nationalism, demanded that William Gladstone's new Liberal administration take action.[5] Over the next two years, the British government offered several solutions to the unrest spreading across Ireland. One was state-aided emigration. Gladstone promised over £150,000 in direct support for the emigration of families from the "distressed parishes" of Connacht and western districts in Munster and Ulster. His government also allowed local Poor Law Unions to use their resources for this purpose. These monies were supplemented by funds from philanthropic bodies like the Mansion House Committee, Mr. Tuke's Fund (named after Quaker philanthropist, James Hack Tuke) and the Duchess of Marlborough's Relief Fund.[6]

Across the Atlantic, the Canadian government seized on the idea of subsidized, state-funded Irish immigration, releasing funds to pay for it. On 30 October 1880, the federal Minister of Agriculture, J.H. Pope, and the Canadian High Commissioner in London, Sir Alexander Galt, presented a plan to establish a "New Ireland" in Manitoba. A consortium consisting of the Canadian Pacific Railway (CPR) and the Canada North West Land Company (CNWLC), would provide £4 per family to transport them from Ireland to Winnipeg, with the British government advancing the rest of their passage costs.[7] The immigrants would then be transported by wagon to lands in southwestern Manitoba. There, each family would receive a 160-acre homestead, with the option to purchase an adjoining 160-acre plot. Houses would await them, along with six acres already cleared and planted with grain and potatoes. They would receive £17 worth of tools, "other necessities, and contingencies." In total, the scheme would loan up to £100 per family. This amount, the maximum allowed per homestead by the Dominion Lands Act of 1872, would be repaid at a rate of six percent interest.[8] At first, some 250 families would take part. If they succeeded, it was hoped that several thousand more would follow.[9]

On 9 November, the Governor-General of Canada, the Marquis of Lorne, forwarded the plan to the Earl of Kimberley, the Secretary of State for the Colonies. Kimberley enthusiastically endorsed it. Lord Dufferin, Lorne's predecessor, came on board.[10] Lord Stanley, Viscount Monck, and Lord Cranmore, also offered support for an Irish colony in the Canadian West.[11] They believed that the removal of the "surplus" population of Ireland would benefit those who stayed by increasing their holdings, while giving those who emigrated fresh starts. Moreover, the proposal solved several difficulties, for Britain, for Canada, and for Ireland, in one fell swoop. The first goal was the rehabilitation of the Irish themselves. Supporters pointed to the unhealthiness of the damp climate, the infertility of the soil, and the legacy of clearances and landlordism, concluding that the physical, economic and social climate of the west of Ireland was responsible for the persistency of the "Irish problem." They contrasted this with the opportunities that the new frontiers of Canada offered. There, they could gain fresh starts that were impossible at home. They also cited Irish over-population versus the wide, open spaces of Manitoba.[12] By removing a section of the population, competition for scant resources in Ireland would be lessened, freeing up land for those who remained, whose plots would be increased to viable sizes. Additionally, those who left would remit some of their newfound prosperity to friends and family back home.[13] In eastern Canada, the soil was fertile, the air bracing. Here, an Irish "'peasant proprietary' on a grand scale" could be achieved. This theme was picked up by Lord Dufferin, who believed that once the Irish were placed on "the richest soil that is to be found upon the face of the globe," men would be "in better heart, the women healthier, and the children rosier than ever they have been for generations."[14] Furthermore, Galt promised that the Irish in Canada suffered no discrimination and their religion was "respected." He even claimed that "the Irish in Canada are better off, and are better citizens, than their compatriots in the United States."[15]

There was, at first, significant support from the Irish-Catholic community in Canada, especially its hierarchy. By the early 1880s, Irish Catholics had acquired a significant position within society, which they used to demand that Canada do something to alleviate Irish suffering.[16] The Archdiocese of Toronto alone had raised a significant amount of donations, which it provided to the Duchess of Marlborough to dispense to the needy in the west of Ireland.[17] They saw Canada as rehabilitating their brothers and sisters, just as they had been over the previous decades. The scheme attracted the support of the influential Archbishop of Toronto, John Lynch. Lynch, in 1881, saw a solution for the suffering Irish was to "let them be taken out of Ireland. Let them go to the Red River."[18] Furthermore, the scheme was a means to an end for Irish and Irish-Canadian Catholics. The Catholic Church in Canada had long been dominated by French Canadians and francophones. Many Irish resented this, especially as their numbers grew. The Diocese of St. Albert, near Edmonton, protested that the Catholic hierarchy in western Canada was all French. To correct this, it publicly urged the introduction of "a certain class of Irish people to settle in Canada."[19] They increasingly demanded schools and English rather than French ministers. By the late 19th century, most Irish were anglophone, or assumed to be English-speaking. Therefore, the infusion of Irish immigrants would lead to a power shift in the Church, in favour of the Irish.[20]

Supporters also cited glowing reports from the Irish colonies in the adjoining Great Plains in the United States in the late 1870s and in 1880. In 1874 and 1875, General John O'Neill, a noted Irish-born American Fenian who had unsuccessfully attacked Manitoba in 1870, established a settlement of Irish settlers in Holt County, Nebraska, known as "O'Neill City." Later that decade, the Irish Catholic Colonization Association (ICCA) resettled Irish Americans on farms in Greeley County,

Nebraska.[21] In spring 1878, Bishop John Ireland of St. Paul, through the ICCA, resettled 175 Irish families from Connacht in Graceville, in western Minnesota.[22] In 1879, 800 more Irish joined them. *The New York Times* reported that women who had been "shoeless, ragged and starving" in Ireland were now "plump, handsome girls in fashionable attire."[23] In Toronto, *The Irish Canadian* reprinted news that Graceville, along with the colonies in Nebraska and in Arkansas (St. Patrick's), were "flourishing," with the Irish having "attained comfortable and independent positions which they could never have hoped to occupy at home or in the eastern cities of America."[24] James Hack Tuke, the philanthropist behind his eponymous fund, visited the Graceville colony. This inspection convinced him that once the Irish became landowners, they became "a thrifty and industrious race, contented and well-to-do," convincing him to send as many from the west of Ireland to New Ireland as he could muster.[25]

With no irony, some believed that the Irish presence would rejuvenate the anglophone, "British" nature of Canada. This was a time when, according to historian Paula Hastings, many British Canadians saw Canada's very survival as a "British" nation requiring "a singularity of race, religion and language."[26] Regarding the French, Toronto's *Mail* warned that the francophone population had risen twice as fast as anglophones between 1851 and 1881. It asked that "the question of the day is ... whether this British Dominion shall remain British."[27] Irish immigrants were a solution to this. The architects of the scheme and its supporters argued that the Irish were bona fide Britons and that this scheme would contribute to getting more people "from the Old Country."[28] This was accompanied by a fear that too many European and American immigrants were arriving in the prairies. People accepted attitudes such as those of Rev. M. Baird who, when lecturing in Edmonton in late 1882, asserted that the Germans had "an intense hatred of everything Britian [sic]," a sentiment that was anathema in many circles.[29] In November 1880, Toronto's *Globe* quoted S. Byers, the American Consul in Zurich, who claimed that European governments were subsidizing the immigration of "scores of paupers, criminals, and recognized failures" to North America. He emphasized the growing Russian, Polish and Slavic contingents. The newspaper supported Byers' assertions, agreeing that, "measures must be taken to neutralize all the efforts of foreign states to get rid of their 'hard cases' at our expense."[30] In 1882, 10,000 Americans crossed the border to establish homesteads in the province, and 9,000 Europeans did the same.[31] American immigrants, American culture and American industry were seen by many Canadians as threatening, especially in its west. American popular culture was permeating Canada and the Canadian West in the 1880s and the 1890s as never before. American newspapers and magazines flooded the market.[32] American implements from John Deere to the McCormick

Harvesting Machine Company tilled western farms, brought direct to Manitoba by the rail link to Minneapolis. American farmers followed American manufacturers. By making the Irish such a generous offer, the British and the Canadians believed that the Irish would remain, or become, loyal to British norms, to British businesses, and thus resist the siren songs of Canada's southern neighbor.[33]

The Irish were also viewed as a means of countering a perceived threat posed by the First Nations and the Mêtis. In the early 1880s, Big Bear, a Cree chief, hoped to build a pan-First Nations alliance to protect their standing. Rumors circulated that none other than Louis Riel, the Mêtis leader of the 1869–70 Red River Uprising against British-Canadian rule in the prairies, might return to Manitoba from exile in the United States.[34] First Nations were sabotaging the extension of the CPR and stealing from homesteaders. Fears circulated that First Nations were swarming police stations and settlements under the guise of starvation, but with an ulterior aim of "tak[ing] them by force."[35] Anglophones openly called for a bulwark, a ready-made militia, against this. Months before the scheme was proposed, Prime Minister Sir John A. Macdonald had recommended state-directed colonization in the prairies as "the best means of dealing speedily and effectually, if necessary, with the Indians inhabiting that region."[36] Likewise, the Marquis of Lorne suggested countering any threat with the establishment of "embodied Reserve[s] in Canada" of men with military training that would be "efficient in all the branches of its interior economy," while providing "an infusion of more military training throughout the country at no fresh expense."[37] The Irish, with their long record of service in the British army and navy (and, earlier, as mercenaries in armies throughout Europe), would fulfil this role in Canada. There were precedents for the Irish providing this reserve, based on their reputation as loyal, fierce warriors. In 1818, Richard Talbot had sent 237 Irish colonists to Upper Canada, to create a frontier settlement to defend against Americans and First Nations.[38] The British Colonial Office gave each male migrant £10 upfront.[39] Most of the settlers remained, with 19 families establishing a colony near London, in the southwest.[40] In 1823, and again in 1825, the British government funded Peter Robinson's Irish settlements in eastern Ontario, in the western Ottawa Valley and near Peterborough, as much to defend against the United States as to rehabilitate the Irish.[41] These schemes were viewed as successful instances where the "wild Irish" could be used for the Empire's advantage.[42]

In the 1870s, the Canadian Government had sponsored colonies of Icelanders and German Mennonites from Russia in Manitoba, and these communities were thriving. In December 1880, the *Mail* boasted that the Mennonite colony had increased its production of grain from the previous year, almost tripling its wealth in "stock and implements" in the process from $140,000 to $383,417.[43] Mary FitzGibbon observed that the Icelanders "learn English rapidly, and are teachable servants, neat, clean and careful," and that "in time" the women "often make exceptional servants, and many people prefer them to Ontario or English servants."[44] The success of the Mennonites and Icelanders in adapting to their new homelands, assimilating into the majority culture, and overcoming poverty and despair at home to achieve health and prosperity in Canada, did not escape men like Pope, Galt and CPR President George Stephen. They reasoned that if these groups could achieve such results, then certainly the Irish could. *The Mail* asked in 1881, "if the Mennonites and Icelanders were aided liberally, why not the Irish also?"[45] Colonization was also beneficial for the Irish. At its center was the transportation of preexisting communities, from the west of Ireland to western Canada, keeping the ties of family and friendship intact, and alleviating the anomie and the fear of the unknown that might deter the Irish from emigrating. For those who spoke mostly Irish and were Roman Catholic, they could maintain their language and their faith largely unimpeded, as they assimilated into Canadian life. Lord Fortescue, in an 1880 debate on colonization, supported schemes like New Ireland on these grounds. In allowing them to retain aspects of their culture, "they would be a source of strength and wealth to the Dominion."[46] Yet this rationale of the Irish needing special protections and accommodations likened them more to the Icelanders, the Mennonites, and even the First Nations on their reserves, than to their fellow British subjects.

The lure of prairie living was bolstered by comparisons between Ireland and Canada. While conditions in the former remained dire, the opposite was true for Manitoba. Unlike many Britons, who had become degraded by factory work and city living, the Irish were viewed as "natural" agriculturalists who pursued virtuous, if poor, livelihoods. Yet, there was not enough affordable, available arable land in Ireland, while redistribution would be unfair to those who had acquired their estates legally. *The Globe* reminded its readers that even with the reclamation of waste lands in Ireland and some land redistribution, it was unlikely that "the surplus population can be comfortably accommodated in the island," and so, "liberal provision for assisting emigrants must be made."[47] Conversely, Manitoba possessed vast stretches of fertile land with few to farm it. Canada could acquire a class of ready-made "British" agriculturalists, who were used to the privations of pioneer living and eking out rough yet humble existences, surviving on hardscrabble terrains in difficult climes. With the arrival of the railways in 1878 (connecting Winnipeg to the United States) and 1882 (with the CPR linking that city to the rest of Canada), a land speculation and construction boom erupted. In 1881, property lots in Winnipeg fetched higher prices than those on Michigan Avenue in Chicago, selling for "$1,000 per foot frontage".[48] Opportunities abounded, with lands opening for settlement almost daily. *The Globe* believed that throughout Canada West, "there are still homes...for millions of people."[49] Lynch touted that in Manitoba, wages were "enormous, but living is cheaper in Canada than in the United States."[50] The boom also led to a severe labour shortage in the prairies, especially in agriculture. A government agent reported that "I would have no difficulty today placing a large number of immigrants in good situations if I had them."[51]

Letters from the Irish themselves, from all socioeconomic classes, indicated that they wanted to go to Manitoba. In January 1880, two petitions were sent from William Mercer of County Down to Pope, stating that the crofters were aware of "the railway scheme" and they requested further information.[52] Thomas Connolly, the Canadian government agent for Ireland, informed the acting High Commissioner in Britain that should a decent offer be made, a "much larger immigration" would result, as soon as 1881.[53] The Catholic Churches in Canada and Ireland also supported the scheme. Besides Lynch's advocacy, the archbishop of St. Boniface, Alexandre Taché, the most senior Catholic official in western Canada, along with the other bishops, endorsed the scheme, on the grounds that state-directed colonization would create communities where the faith could be maintained, if not spread.[54] Across the Atlantic, in April 1882, Archbishop Lynch wrote to Prime Minister Macdonald, informing him that "many of the Bishops of Ireland" backed it.[55]

The rehabilitation of the western Irish would not just be physical. Supporters also believed that they could be rewired psychologically. The British wanted to steer discontented Irish peasants to Canada, instead of to the potentially seditious cities of the United States. Many blamed Irish-Americans for inciting and funding the Land War in Ireland and Fenianism in Canada, arguing that America embittered and radicalized the Irish.[56] In contrast, Canada was loyal to Britain and the Empire. They often cited Thomas Darcy McGee, an Irish nationalist immigrant-turned-steadfast loyalist champion of a British Canada, to argue for the possibilities of such a project.[57] If he could be turned, even the most disaffected Irish could. *The Winnipeg Daily Sun* opined that "we have the most profound admiration for the Irish patriot who, far removed from the oppression of his countrymen, finds congenial employment ... He enjoys at once the most perfect security as a citizen."[58] This was important in the 1880s because many feared that an increasingly assertive Irish nationalism, combined with famine, might turn agitation into rebellion. A confidential report by the Royal Irish Constabulary in 1880 revealed the extent of the distress and disaffection in the "Congested Districts" of western Ireland. In the west of County Galway, "the temper of the people, and their disposition towards the landlords and the Government is bad, and the prospects of the coming winter are not reassuring." Even in its more prosperous eastern half, "Fenian agents" were whipping up discontent and lawlessness, to the point that, "assassination can be committed with perfect impunity, owing to the general sympathy of the people." In west County Cork, "the minds of the tenants are filled with absurd expectations," with "their disposition towards landlords and Government unsatisfactory."[59] Worryingly for British officials and politicians, the number of "agrarian" outrages spiked, from 301 in 1878, to 863 in 1879, to 1,158 in 1880.[60] The *Leeds Mercury* warned that, "a general state of disaffection" remained throughout the west of Ireland.[61]

Just as in the days of transportation, exporting the rebellious and the seditious was seen as a quick, cheap and permanent solution. The scheme would remove the innocent Irish from pernicious nationalists and radicals, who were believed to be inciting the normally docile Irish into rebellion. The "Fenians" were taking advantage of their "generous impulsiveness" and naiveté to lead them to rebel against the social order.[62] One article in *The Mail* blamed the unrest on "Irish-Americans" like Michael Walsh and John Dillon, claiming that the boycotts, strikes, land raids, etc. were "inspired by the spirit of the Bowery rather than by the misguided genius of the Irish people."[63] Removing them from these influences and placing them under the supervision of approved priests, government bureaucrats, and their British and Canadian neighbors, would purge them of their violent impulses.

Less publicized was the belief that profits would not merely accrue to the Irish. As they became independent, stalwart producers, and repaid their advances, the CPR, and the Canadian and British governments would profit, with the 6 percent interest being divided evenly between those three bodies.[64] Galt himself boasted that he had made C$15,000 (£3,082) profit on lands he owned in Winnipeg, based solely on the recent settlement and development of that city. Furthermore, he and his son owned coalfields in southern Alberta, lands which the railway had yet to extend to. The Irish could help connect his proposed collieries by extending the CPR, while he made millions in the process.[65] The CNWLC, for its part, hoped to earn a profit of £25 interest on the £100 advanced per family. This represented a rate of interest far higher than what could have been negotiated directly with banks with the same £100 collateral.[66]

This rehabilitation was not limited to the Irish. One of the scheme's aims was to rejuvenate the ties that bound Canada to Britain and the wider empire. The 1880s marked dramatic challenges to both Canada's relationship with Britain, and to Britain's domination of the world. Galt, when lobbying the British government, promised that it was a means of promoting the food security of the mother country. The Canadian prairies were destined to become its granary, but to do that it needed farmers. This was of vital importance, as Britain, he argued, was becoming dangerously dependent on non-imperial sources to meet its food needs.[67] Furthermore, this flow of migrants would ensure its success.[68] Because of this, the "New Ireland" scheme remained alluring, well into 1881 and 1882. On 2 June 1881, Galt let Dufferin know that the Canadian Prime Minister had officially endorsed the scheme.[69] Macdonald's support was essential in the formal submission by the Canadian Privy Council in November 1881 to the Colonial Office in London.[70] In the summer of 1882, the Under Secretary for the Colonies, Robert Herbert, travelled to Manitoba to assess the feasibility of the land.[71] This combination of perceived benefits led the scheme to gain key public endorsements. *The Mail* hoped it would be the harbinger of "a tide of English emigration (that) will be concentrated on our North-Western prairies."[72] *The Edmonton Journal* believed that "if room can be found for them, it is to be hoped that they will come in thousands and tens of thousands ... there are no men who will do better service in the good cause than these same wild Irishmen from the county [sic] Galway.[73]

The scheme dies, 1882

This "New Ireland" in Manitoba never materialized. The official reason was a disagreement over who would be responsible if the scheme should fail. The CPR pointed to the "difficulty which will inevitably be experienced in the collection of the money advanced" to the Irish. It wanted the Canadian government to guarantee any losses resulting from the inability or the unwillingness of the Irish to repay their advances, arguing, "a reasonably good margin of profit" was necessary for it to get involved.[74] The British insisted that Ottawa repay should the Irish default on their loans. Lynch told Macdonald that the British wanted to see this scheme realized, and were even ready to provide money at a low rate of interest—3.5 percent—if the Canadian government "would give sole guarantee for the repayment."[75] Macdonald insisted that if any guarantee were made, it should be by the British.[76] They refused. The British government had other reservations. Gladstone worried that state-sponsored emigration would be attacked as a substitute for land reforms and reopen historic charges of British indifference toward Ireland.[77] This explained why Sir John Rose, a former Canadian minister of finance, lamented the "luke-warmness" of British officials, and encouraged whipping up British public opinion to force their hand.[78] One Colonial Office official observed that "the whole scheme partakes of the nature of a commercial speculation nor would it be desirable to set such a precedent."[79] Even Galt privately believed that the British government would not lend "a copper of public funds" to this scheme, due to Gladstone's opposition.[80] The Canadian government was afraid that the profits, while fiscally positive, could be disastrous from a public relations' perspective, if it were too publicly associated with this scheme. It was facing criticism for giving a C$25,000,000 (£5,137,057) bailout to the CPR in December 1880, and fretted that this would be seen as yet another insider deal aiding one company, to the exclusion of others. Some wondered why the state should assist the Irish; others worried that if it profited, it could be criticized for exploiting an already impoverished and oppressed people. George Stephen, President of the CPR, who in 1883 proposed a different New Ireland scheme, warned Macdonald that Galt's real motivations were to "strike something that will have the effect of opening the N.W. and at the same time do something for its investors and promoters."[81]

Concerns over the Catholicity of the western Irish also played a role. In November 1880, Charles Foy, the Canadian recruitment agent in Belfast, argued that "Southerners" would be bad settlers, averring, "what the Southerners talk about the Northerners do."[82] The Orange Order, which in the 1880s was rapidly growing in strength on both sides of the Atlantic, accused Irish Catholics of suffering from "Anglophobism," and being insufficiently loyal to the Imperial cause.[83] Orange lodges who promoted emigration to Manitoba to ensure that it became a Protestant province, vociferously opposed the scheme.[84] *The Irish Canadian*, however, chastised the government for targeting Protestant continental Europeans over Irish Catholics.[85] This anti-Irish and anti-Catholic sentiment in the Canadian West swelled in the mid-1880s, as tensions between Catholics and Protestants rose in advance of the Riel Rebellion in 1885. In 1882, *The Irish Canadian,* reported on an unspecified "gross injustice" done to an Irish Catholic immigrant, Thomas Ryan, by Police Officer Herchmer, as well as his attempts to "oust and injure" another, unnamed, settler. It asked why Herchmer was "tolerated, even encouraged," in his bigotry.[86] Added to this was the longstanding fear among British-Canadians that the western Irish would prioritize their faith, and align with their fellow Catholics, the Métis, the First Nations, and the francophones, at a time when the relationship between them and the anglophone community was souring.[87] Catholicism doomed this scheme in another way. One of its selling points had been that the immigrants could keep their faith alive in Manitoba, by providing them with an Irish-speaking priest and a Catholic school for the children. This raised problems that were never fully resolved. Under the terms of the Dominions Land Act of 1872, half of the lands of each township could be released by the CPR and the CNWLC for settlement—the even-numbered sections. If each family took its 160-acre farm, and used its option to preempt an adjoining homestead, only two families per section would be established. This meant there would be no cost-efficient, let alone practical, way to establish a discrete colony. The Irish would be "interspersed by a Protestant population," which, as Catholic leaders on both sides of the Atlantic admitted, "all the objects sought by the colony will be lost." It was suggested that a special act of Parliament be passed to allow the consortium to provide the odd, as well as the even-numbered, sections for this scheme. However, this opened the consortium to charges of favoritism. Even the scheme's proponents worried that other companies would demand similar concessions.[88]

These debates coincided with attacks on colonization in general. By late 1882, many of the perceived benefits of settling the prairies quickly and cheaply, while easing the process of assimilation, had lost their luster. Within a year, only 24 out of the 300 companies granted land in 1881 were still extant, and they had attracted a mere fraction of colonists, who were struggling to establish themselves. This record fueled suspicions that the real aims of schemes like "New Ireland" was to line the pockets of a select few. *The Globe* claimed that elites proposed colonization with "no idea of undertaking the work of colonization. They hoped to sell their interest in each one of these reservations for hundreds of thousands of dollars within a few days," at an "incalculable" loss to Canada and the settlers themselves.[89] This was exacerbated by charges by an anonymous "Irish Immigrant" in 1881 that the Ministry of Agriculture, then responsible for immigration, was being "mismanage[ed]" by Pope, with "the people's money … squandered."[90]

Sympathy for the Irish quickly eroded. As violence in Ireland escalated and distress continued, regardless of reforms and aid, public opinion switched to contempt. Their poverty and violence were no longer circumstantial; they were inherent.[91] A reporter for *The Mail* summarized, "if the Land bill, which is, whatever may be said in its behalf, a partial measure of confiscation, does not satisfy the malcontents, there is no satisfying them."[92] The image of the suffering Irish worthy of redemption was increasingly replaced by that of the Fenian rebel, who would do anything to sever Canada's ties with the mother country. *The Mail* published an interview with John Gallagher, who boasted that he had Irish immigrants and their sons all along the border, ready to invade Canada. Furthermore, they had "fifth columns" in Canada, to "give us the aid the Government little dreams of."[93]

Tensions were exacerbated by the murder of Lord Frederick Cavendish in the Phoenix Park in Dublin on 6 May 1882. The murder damned not only the conspirators, but in the eyes of many in Canada and Britain, all Irish. Headlines such as "England's Terror: Dynamite and a Drunken Irishman Found" and "The Irish

Assassins: Fiendish Schemes of the Dynamiters: Spreading the Infection of Smallpox" populated North American newspapers.[94] The scheme was increasingly conceived as Britain's way of dumping its political problems onto an innocent Canada. *The Mail* warned in a front-page headline in 1882, "Troubles in Ireland: Irish Emigration to Canada Recommended."[95] Images of the "feckless" Irish also grew. Many believed that the Irish would say they wanted to farm in Canada, only to renege on their word and travel to the United States as soon as their advances became due, if not sooner. *The Newcastle Courant* claimed that "Paddy will take any money as a gift."[96] *The Globe* warned that they were "professing to be agriculturalists and desiring to settle in Canada, whereas their true purpose is to get passed as far westward as possible at the expense of Canada toward their real destination in the States."[97] Bad reports from the Irish colonies in the American Great Plains confirmed these assessments. In 1882, the Irish-American Colonization Society, which had established a colony of Irish Catholics in southwestern Minnesota in 1881, reported a loss of £5,104 because settlers either could not or would not repay their loans.[98] This was on top of the very public failure of Graceville. By the end of 1881, only seven families remained, the rest having moved to an impoverished section of St. Paul known disparagingly as the "Connemara Patch."[99] Even the staunchest advocates of state-aided immigration, like Dillon O'Brien of the ICCA, deemed the settlers to be "shiftless; a group composed of mendicants who knew nothing of farming, and were entirely unfit to cope with the life upon the American prairie."[100]

The negative views of the Irish coincided with the growth of Social Darwinism, which rejected the very possibility of rejuvenation. Some, like the Duke of Argyll, openly claimed that the Irish could never be redeemed, arguing, "the survival of the fittest is the rule of nature. Special and elaborate securities for the survival of the unfittest seems to be the favourite panacea for the ills of Ireland."[101] In the early 1880s, men like J.H. Froude and Herbert Spencer were influential, with ideas regarding the inherent inferiority of the Irish, with no possibility of redemption. Science reinforced the belief that the Irish were bad farmers, something that would never change, no matter how much assistance and tutelage they received.[102] Even Galt grew contemptuous of the Irish, privately telling Macdonald, "I am bound to say I am getting extremely tired of the assumption by Forster and Co. that we in Canada <u>want to get</u> the cowardly ruffians who are allowed to make a [indecipherable] of Ireland". He went on to deny the Irish were even preferable to those they were to replace, "I believe we are within 'reasonable distance' of a declaration by the Canadian people that they want none of them, no more than they do of the comparably harmless Chinese."[103] This statement explains why New Ireland never materialized. Others disagreed. They saw Britishness not as something inherent in an individual, but as something that could be imparted upon those willing to learn it. Based on this view, the Irish had been exposed to Britishness for centuries, and rejected it, or were unable to acquire it. It would be better to focus on the northern and eastern Europeans. To this end, the Canadian government in April 1882 announced a bonus of $5 to be paid to recruiters in Germany, the Netherlands, and Scandinavia for every adult immigrant they settled in Manitoba and the Northwest Territories.[104] Samuel Rollin Hesson, Conservative M.P. from Perth North in Ontario, informed his colleagues that no "better class of immigrants could not be desired" than the Germans.[105] John Lowe, the deputy minister for immigration, testified to the parliamentary committee on Immigration and Colonization in 1883 that Germans and Scandinavians were "a class which will succeed here." He noted that the assisted Irish came with little means, which was where "difficulties came." He believed, somewhat skeptically, that "they may be, nevertheless, very valuable emigrants," though, coming immediately after his glowing praise of Germans and Scandinavians, this sounded like faint, if not damning, praise.[106]

Overwhelmingly, the Irish and Irish Canadians were doubting the benefits of the Manitoba scheme. Suggestions were made that the glowing reports had been wholesale lies, based on the longstanding British remedy of transportation, dressed up in a more palatable guise. Many Irish believed what truly awaited them were "frozen graves." Toronto's *Mail* informed its readers that the Irish believed that the Canadian prairies were in the hands of unscrupulous syndicates who "were worse than the landlords in Ireland," where "settlers were robbed, ruined, and oppressed."[107] Lynch himself noted that among the Irish, "many fear that they only exchange climates and country, but not masters and landlords."[108] In 1882, the British government announced that it was closing the public works in Ireland, a move that was seen as forcing the Irish destitute to "choose" between entering the draconian workhouses at home, or moving to "New Ireland."[109] The *Belfast News-Letter* warned its readers that they were being "deluded" into being "deported on tickets-of-leave to British Siberia."[110]

There apparently was some truth to this. A confidential 1881 memorandum spelled out another purpose for the scheme. It stated that the "able-bodied" of each family would be immediately available "to obtain employment on arrival." They were to be set to work building "the railways in progress," and "generally amongst the community, especially during the harvest season."[111] Another memorandum argued that because the Irish would have paying jobs, they could immediately pay back their advances, thus "greatly reducing the cost of the undertaking."[112] Critics pointed out, however, that this would retard the ability of the Irish to improve their own homesteads, and make them just as beholden to the consortium as they had been to their landlords in Ireland. Others cautioned about working conditions. A letter to the editor of *The Irish Canadian* believed that the settlers would be forced to work for "the Railway Syndicate" to make ends meet at starvation wages, and they would experience "a never-ending life of slavery if they outlive it, and in the end ... die like sheep by thousands."[113]

Many Irish rejected the belief that Ireland was overpopulated, and that there was not enough viable land there. Others argued that at a time of imperial crisis, as some believed Britain to be in, it would be folly to remove its largest class of agriculturalists and military reservists. Dublin's *Freeman's Journal* attacked the scheme, saying that it "could not lend [its] voice to the recommendation of any scheme for further depletion, or, as it is called, 'relief of the congestion of population.'" It went on to say, "Ireland was meant for men, not merely for sheep or cattle."[114] Charles Stewart Parnell consistently attacked the scheme, arguing that state-directed colonization should not replace land redistribution in Ireland as the primary remedy for its socioeconomic woes. He consistently suggested that there was "an abundance of land," which, if redistributed, would provide enough acreage for every family, at an affordable cost.[115] He claimed that "it is, in fact, not an emigration from Ireland to America but a migration from the barren hills of Connaught to the fertile lands of Leinster and Munster that we want," preferring internal migration to emigration or colonization.[116] The Catholic Church hierarchy took a similar position as Parnell, but arrived there from a slightly different perspective. It attacked any plans for a "New Ireland" on the grounds that the lands vacated by the Irish would ultimately be acquired by Protestants, instead of being freed up for redistribution to the Catholic poor. The Church also believed that despite promises, the Irish colonists in Canada would, outside of its watchful eye, be ultimately lost to the dominant Protestant culture in North America.[117]

In Canada, many Irish Canadians, both first and second generation, started to have reservations about "New Ireland." Throughout the 1860s and the 1870s, Irish settlers in Canada and in the United States had generally seen an elevation in their status. While there was sympathy toward the plight of the Irish, and many contributed their time, their effort, and their funds toward relieving them in Ireland, they were apprehensive that the influx of several thousand poor Irish would undermine recent gains in "respectability." Should the scheme fail, then their newfound reputations might end up in tatters.[118] This was exacerbated by a fear that the economic boom that Manitoba had been experiencing since 1878 was about to come to a rapid end. Nicholas Flood Davin warned in 1882 that, "there is a point beyond which the force of 'booming' can no longer go." He forecast that speculators would move to

Regina, where the next boom would occur, leaving Winnipeg and Manitoba quite literally in the dust.[119]

There was also a problem regarding the Canadian government. Precisely when John Lynch was meeting with various British officials, singing the praises of both the scheme and Canada, the Canadian Parliament adopted a resolution, introduced by M.P. John Costigan, supporting Home Rule for Ireland. Almost immediately there was blowback in Britain. Macdonald wrote to the Governor-General, the Marquis of Lorne, apologizing for the vote. He emphasized both Ottawa's and Costigan's usual deference to Britain, saying the latter was "a man of good judgement and moderation, except when 'the wrongs of Ireland' are discussed." He stressed that the resolution was "profuse in its expressions of loyalty to the Queen, and of the contentment of the Irish in Canada with their position here." Lastly, he claimed he personally intervened with Costigan to temper the resolution, removing inflammatory language demanding the release of political prisoners and immediate Home Rule for Ireland.[120] Nonetheless, it was apparent that the British were upset that a "colony" had inserted itself into Irish affairs. It also cast doubt on the notion that the Irish in Canada, whether first or second generation, would eschew their animus toward Britain, and become patriotic, pliant, British subjects. Kimberley told Galt that his fellow cabinet members resented such interference, and that this would have a negative impact on the proposed scheme.[121]

This dispute reached the heart of another accusation directed at Irish immigrants to Canada. Many believed that they possessed anti-British, pro-Republican and pro-American sentiments. If these immigrants were admitted into the Dominion in significant numbers, then they would work to dilute the British connection or, even worse, enable the American cultural or political annexation of Canada. An editorial in *The Mail* warned that the only true believers of annexationism in Canada were "Americans with an overweening conceit of their country or by some second-rate or third-rate denizen of the Green Isle."[122] Macdonald himself believed this, telling Sir Charles Tupper, M.P. and future High Commissioner, in 1883, that:

> *Entre nous,* we don't want the Western Irish emigration. They are bad settlers and thoroughly disloyal. It won't do to have a little Ireland in the North West. I look forward with considerable apprehension to Fenian intrigues between our Irish and Yankee Irish.[123]

The *Belfast News-Letter* categorized the British and the Canadians as "imbeciles" if they believed that if "a large number" of Irish were "colonized in Manitoba," they would not "revolt against Canada and England." Furthermore, they would "receive active and material sympathy from their brothers in the United States," with the ultimate result being "an unbroken Republic from Florida to Alaska."[124] For these reasons, by August 1882, the scheme was effectively dead. Gladstone, living up to Kimberley's warning, never met with Lynch. J.G. Colmer, Galt's assistant, informed Lynch that, "just at present," the British government was unwilling to proceed.[125] Without the prospect of British backing, official support in Canada almost instantly evaporated.

Governments on both sides of the Atlantic seized upon a program of state-aided colonization of the Irish from the west of Ireland in the early 1880s as a simple solution to multiple problems each was facing. However, lack of consensus regarding what the scheme was to accomplish, who it would benefit, who would pay for it, and whether the Irish could fulfill the tasks assigned to them, explains why their resettlement in the open plains of the United States and Canada was so stridently championed by all parties concerned at first, and why all of these schemes were abandoned less than two years later.

NOTES

1. Samuel Clark, *Social Origins of the Irish Land War* (Princeton University Press, 1979), p. 227.
2. Ibid., p. 227.
3. Kerby Miller, *Emigrants and Exiles: Ireland and the Irish Exodus to North America* (Oxford University Press, 1985), pp 227, 228, 399; Gerard Moran, *Sending Out Ireland's Poor: Assisted Emigration to North America in the Nineteenth Century* (Dublin: Four Courts Press, 2004), p. 162; Michael Turner, *After the Famine: Irish Agriculture, 1850–1914* (Cambridge University Press, 1996), pp 72–75; Bernard Porter, *The Lion's Share: A Short History of British Imperialism, 1850–1970* (London and New York; Longman, 1975); P.J. Cain and Anthony Hopkins, *British Imperialism, 1688–2000* (New York: Longman, 2002).
4. *Returns of Outrages Reported to the Royal Irish Constabulary from 1844 to 1880,* 21–3, House of Commons, 1881 (c. 2756), LXXVII, pp 907–909; *Returns of Cases of Evictions in Ireland in Each Quarter of Each Year... for 1880,* 3, H.C. 1881, (2), LXXVII, p. 727. Cit. Paul Bew, *Land and the National Question in Ireland, 1858–82* (Atlantic Highlands, NJ: Humanities Press, 1979), p. 36.
5. Eoin McLaughlin, "Competing Forms of Cooperation? Land League, Land War and Cooperation in Ireland, 1879 to 1914," *Agricultural History Review,* vol. 63, no. 1 (June 2015), pp 81–112; Andrew Newby, *Ireland, Radicalism, and the Scottish Highlands, c. 1870–1912* (Edinburgh University Press, 2007).
6. R.F. Foster, *Paddy and Mr Punch: Connections in Irish and English History* (New York: The Penguin Press, 1993), p. 239; Virginia Crossman, "Writing for Relief in Late Nineteenth-Century Dublin: Personal Applications to the Mansion House Fund in 1880," *Cultural and Social History,* vol. 14, issue 5 (2017), pp 583–598.

7. "Despatch from the Governor General of Canada, Forwarding the Report of the Committee of the Privy Council on a Proposal for the Organization of Irish Immigration to Manitoba and the North-West," CMD Paper No. 2835, from the Enhanced Parliamentary Papers on Ireland, at http://eppi.dippam.ac.uk/eppi_documents/16881.
8. Libraries and Archives, Canada (LAC), MG–26-A, v. 323, "Memorandum" of scheme, 1881 (n.d.).
9. Archdiocese of Toronto Archives (ATA), Fonds Series L AE, File 7, Item 11a, "Memorandum Explaining the Outline of the Scheme Proposed by the North West Colonisation Company," 1881 (n.d.).
10. Public Record Office of Northern Ireland (PRONI), File D/1071/H/B/G/26/3, Galt to Dufferin, 3 Dec. 1880.
11. "Irish Emigration Schemes," *Baltimore Sun,* 27 Aug. 1880.
12. Ralph Mann, "Frontier Opportunity and the New Social History," *Pacific Historical Review,* v. 53, no. 4 (Nov. 1984), pp 463–491; See, Frederick Jackson Turner, *The Frontier in American History* (Malabar, FL: Robert E. Krieger Publishing Co., 1985).
13. "The Land Question: Supply and Demand," *Dublin Daily News,* 2 Dec. 1880.
14. Cit. Andrew Crawford, "Emigration as a Cure for Irish Destitution," *The Catholic Presbyterian,* vol. VI (July-Dec. 1881), p. 31.
15. A.T. Galt, "The Future of the Dominion of Canada: A Paper Read before the Royal Colonial Institute," 25 January 1881, p. 15.
16. Donald H. Akenson, *Being Had: Historians, Evidence, and the Irish in North America* (Port Credit, Canada: P.D. Meany, 1985); David A. Wilson, ed., *Irish Nationalism in Canada* (Montreal and Kingston: McGill-Queen's University Press, 2009); Michael Cantrell, "The Irish in Saskatchewan, 1850–1930: A Study in Intergenerational Ethnicity," Gregory Marchildon, ed., *Immigration and Settlement, 1870–1939* (Regina: Canadian Plains Research Center, 2009); Gerald J. Stortz, "Archbishop Lynch and New Ireland. An Unfulfilled Dream for Canada's Northwest," *The Catholic Historical Review,* v. 68, no. 4 (Oct. 1982), pp 612–624.
17. ATA, Fonds L, Series AE, File 06, Item 47, Lynch to the Duchess of Marlborough, 18 Jan. 1880.
18. "The Churches: Dr. Wild on Irishmen and the Rev. Pelham Dale," *Toronto Daily Mail,* 17 Jan. 1881.
19. "The Church in the North-West," in *Irish Canadian,* 1 Sept. 1881.
20. Cattrell, "The Irish in Saskatchewan," pp 515, 525.
21. "The Catholic Movement in Western Colonization: Colonization in Nebraska," in *The American Catholic Quarterly Review*, vol. VI, July 1881, pp 434–445.
22. "Catholic Colonization," in *The Catholic World: A Monthly Magazine of General Literature and Science,* vol. XXXI, no. 18 (May 1880).
23. "Father Nugent's Good Work," 9 Oct. 1880, p. 3.
24. "Catholic Colonization," 25 May 1882, p. 1.
25. Tuke, "Irish Immigration," *Nineteenth Century,* vol. 9 (1881), p. 369.
26. Phillip Buckner and R. Douglas Francis (eds), *Canada and the British World: Culture, Migration and Identity* (University of British Columbia Press, 2006), p. 92.

27. "The French Advance," 11 Nov. 1891.
28. "Irish Emigration," *Irish Canadian,* 20 July 1882.
29. "Lecture," in *Edmonton Bulletin,* 23 Dec. 1882.
30. "Dangers in Immigration," 17 Nov. 1880.
31. John Langton Tyman, *By Section, Township, and Range: Studies in Prairie Settlement,* (Brandon, MB: Assiniboine Historical Society, 1995), p. 45.
32. Paul Litt, "Canada Invaded! The Great War, Mass Culture, and Canadian Cultural Nationalism," in David MacKenzie (ed.), *Canada and the First World War: Essays in Honour of Robert Craig Brown* (University of Toronto Press, 2005), p. 341.
33. Ged Martin, *John A. Macdonald: Canada's First Prime Minister* (Toronto: Dundurn, 2013), p. 150.
34. George F.C. Stanley, *Louis Riel* (Toronto: Ryerson, 1972), pp 256, 257.
35. "Canadian Savages," *The North-Western Chronicle,* 18 June 1879; Michael Hogue, "Disputing the Medicine Line: The Plains Cree and the Canadian-American Border, 1876–85;" Carol Higham and Robert Thacker (eds), *One West, Two Myths: A Comparative Reader* (University of Calgary Press, 2004), pp 92, 93; Thomas Flanagan, *Riel and the Rebellion: 1885 Reconsidered, Second Edition* (University of Toronto Press, 2000).
36. National Archives (NA), CO 880/9, North America 106, "Memorandum Respecting the Pacific Railway," 1879 (n.d.).
37. NA, CO 885/5/5, N. 12, "Confidential Memorandum to Privy Council," 21 Oct. 1879.
38. B.S. Elliott, *Irish Migrants in the Canadas: A New Approach* (McGill-Queen's University Press, 2014), p. 65.
39. Ibid.
40. Ibid., pp 66, 67.
41. Wendy Cameron and Mary McDougall Maude, *Assisting Emigration to Upper Canada: The Petworth Project 1832–1837* (McGill-Queens University Press, 2000), pp 145, 146; Donald Akenson, *The Irish in Ontario: A Study in Rural History* (McGill-Queen's University Press, 1984).
42. Heather Streets, *Martial Races: The Military, Race, and Masculinity in British Imperial Culture, 1857–1914* (Manchester University Press, 2004); Alexander Bubb, "The Life of the Irish Soldier in India: Representations and Self-Representations, 1857–1922," *Modern Asian Studies,* vol. 46, issue 4 (July 2012), pp 769–813; Terence Denman, "'Ethnic Soldiers Pure and Simple?' The Irish in the Late Victorian Army," *War in History,* vol. 3, issue 3 (1996), pp 253–273.
43. "Editorial Notes," 2 Dec. 1880, p. 4. See, Marchildon (ed.) *Immigration*, pp 457–482; Laurie L. Bertram, "Eskimo Immigrants and Colonial Soldiers: Icelandic Immigrants and the North-West Resistance, 1885," *Canadian Historical Review,* vol. 99, no. 1 (Match 2018), pp 63–97; Royden Loewen, "New Themes in an Old Story: Transplanted Mennonites as Group Settlers in North America, 1874–1879," in *Journal of American Ethnic History,* vol. 11, no. 2 (Winter 1992), p. 5; John Warkentin, "Mennonite Agricultural Settlements of Southern Manitoba," in *Geographical Review,* vol. 49, no. 3 (July 1959), p. 342; C.C. Eldridge (ed.), *Kith and Kin: Canada, Britain and the United States from the Revolution to the Cold War* (University of Wales Press, 1997), p. 106.

44. From *A Trip to Manitoba* (London: R. Bentley and Son, 1880), at www.gutenberg.org/cache/epub/7099/pg7099/html.
45. "Irish Emigration," 22 Nov. 1880.
46. "The Emigration Question," *The Globe,* 24 Aug. 1880.
47. "The Irish Land Bill," 9 April 1881.
48. Raymond J.A. Huel, *Archbishop A.A. Taché of St. Boniface: The "Good Fight" and the Illusive Vision* (University of Alberta Press, 2003), p. 213.
49. "Manitoba Affairs," 1 Dec. 1880.
50. "Letter from Archbishop Lynch," 29 June 1882, p. 1.
51. "Treatment of Immigrants," *Mail,* 13 May 1881.
52. LAC, RG–17, I–1, Box 302, petitions received 13 Jan. and 2 Feb. 1881.
53. Ibid., v. 297, file 30634, Connolly to H. Bernard, 6 Nov. 1880.
54. Cecil J. Houston and William J. Smyth, *Irish Emigration and Canadian Settlement: Patterns, Links, and Letters* (University of Toronto Press, 1990), p. 223.
55. LAC, MG–26-A, v. 228, Item No. 98057, Lynch to Macdonald, April 1882 (n.d.).
56. Dierdre M. Moloney, "Land League Nationalism in Transnational Perspective," *U.S. Catholic Historian,* vol. 22, no. 3 (Summer 2004), pp 61–74.
57. Gerard Moran, "State Aided Emigration from Ireland to Canada in the 1880s," in *The Canadian Journal of Irish Studies,* vol. 20, no. 2 (Dec. 1994), 1–19; David A. Wilson, *Thomas D'Arcy McGee, Volume II: The Extreme Moderate 1857–1868* (McGill-Queen's University Press, 2011).
58. "It Was a Great Day for the Land," 31 Oct. 1881.
59. British Library (BL), MSS Eur. D 604/46, "Condition of Ireland: Reports of County Inspectors of Royal Irish Constabulary, Arranged by Provinces," pp 15, 17, 29.
60. Ibid., "Return of Outrages Specially Reported to the Constabulary Office from the 1 Jan. 1844 to 31 Oct. 1880, Pursuant to Minute of the Chief Secretary, 28 Oct. 1880."
61. "The Distress in Ireland," 26 Nov. 1879.
62. "Mr. Parnell Backing Down," *Mail,* 24 June 1881.
63. "The Arrests in Ireland," *Mail,* 5 Nov. 1880. Dillon and Walsh were part of the Land League's fundraising tour of the U.S. in 1880. The claim that they were Irish American was hyperbole. Both men were born and raised in Ireland.
64. LAC, MG–26-A, v. 323, "Memorandum," 1881.
65. A.A. den Otter, *Civilizing the West: The Galts and the Development of Western Canada* (University of Alberta Press, 1986), p. 81.
66. *Report from the Select Committee on Colonisation, Together with the Proceedings of the Committee, Minutes of Evidence, Appendix, and Index* (London: HMSO, 1891) p. 45.
67. Galt, "The Future of the Dominion of Canada: A Paper Read by Sir A.T. Galt, G.C.M.C., Before the Royal Colonial Institute, 25 Jan. 1881," pp 4, 16.
68. Ged Martin, *John A. Macdonald: Canada's First Prime Minister* (Toronto: Dundurn, 2013), p. 150.
69. PRONI, D/1071/H/B/G/26.
70. George Sheppard, "Starvation, Moral Ruin and a Frozen Grave: An Irish view of Victorian Canada," in *Beaver*, vol. 70, no. 5, pp 7, 8.

71. "Irish Emigration to Canada," *Belfast News-Letter,* 16 Aug. 1882.
72. "Canada and the Empire," 2 Aug. 1881.
73. "Colonists," 24 Jan. 1881.
74. LAC, MG–26-A, v. 323, Dennis to Macdonald, Item Nos. 145766–145770, 30 April 1881.
75. Ibid., Macdonald Papers, v. 219, Item No. 93438, Galt to Macdonald, 12 April 1882.
76. Ibid., Macdonald to Galt, no. 93447, 15 April 1882.
77. Oscar D. Skelton, *Life and Times of Sir Alexander Tilloch Galt* (Toronto: McClelland and Stewart, 1966), p. 268.
78. LAC, MG–16-A, v. 259, Rose to Macdonald, 24 March 1881.
79. NA, CO 42/763, memorandum by (?) Bramston, 9 Nov. 1880. Cit. den Otter, *Civilizing...,* p. 51.
80. Ibid., p. 52.
81. Ibid., p. 53; LAC, MG–25-A, v. 267, Stephen to Macdonald, 8 May 1881.
82. LAC, RG–17, I–1, Box 354, Foy to Galt, 4 Nov. 1880.
83. Quoted in "A Wayward 'Brother,'" *Irish Canadian,* 3 Aug. 1882. See also George Sheppard, *Canada's Forgotten Irish: The Assisted Tuke and Union Migrations of the Early 1880s,* unpub. MA thesis, Laurentian University, 1984, p. 2.
84. Houston and Smyth, p. 222.
85. "The Immigration Question," 11 May 1882, p. 4.
86. "A North-West Grievance," 7 Sept. 1882.
87. Rosalyn Trigger, "Classical Containment of Diasporic Irish Nationalism: A Canadian Example from the Parnell Era," in David A. Wilson, ed., *Irish Nationalism in Canada* (McGill-Queen's University Press, 2009), p. 162.
88. "The Irish Colonization Scheme," *Manitoba Free Press,* 8 Dec. 1880.
89. "Colonization Companies," 18 Sept. 1883.
90. "An 'Irish Immigrant' Again," *Mail,* 12 July 1881.
91. *The Eternal Paddy: Irish Identity and the British Press, 1798–1882* (University of Wisconsin Press, 2004), p. 209.
92. "The Irish Troubles," 9 June 1881. The Land Act (Ireland) of 1881 largely granted the Three Fs— fixity of tenure, fair rents and free sale of their interest.
93. "The Movement on Canada," 25 Jan. 1881.
94. *Boston Daily Globe*, 2 April 1883; *The Brandon (MB) Daily Mail,* 4 April 1883.
95. "Troubles in Ireland," *Mail*, 4 Dec. 1882.
96. "Echoes of the Week," 15 Dec. 1882.
97. "An Immigration Squabble," 16 June 1881.
98. Irish-American Colonization Company Papers, Minnesota Historical Society (MHS), BB2 I68, Box 1, F4; Malcolm Campbell, "Immigrants on the Land: Irish Rural Settlement in Minnesota and New South Wales, 1830–1890," in *New Hibernia Review,* vol. 2, issue 1 (Spring 1998), p. 43.
99. "Irish Emigration," 14 July 1881.
100. Gerard Moran, "'In Search of the Promised Land': The Connemara Colonization Scheme to Minnesota, 1880," in *Éire/Ireland: An Interdisciplinary Journal of Irish Studies,* vol. xxxi (Autumn/Winter 1996), p. 143. See also Jane Kennedy's chapter.

101. "Editorial Notes," *Mail,* 17 May 1881.
102. Ibid.
103. LAC, MG–26-A, v. 219, Item 93438, Galt to Macdonald, 12 April 1882.
104. LAC, RG–17, v. 339, File 36033, Galt to Colmer, 27 April 1882.
105. "House of Commons," *Mail,* 2 March 1883.
106. *Report of the Select Standing Committee of Immigration and Colonization* (Ottawa: MacLean, Huber and Co., 1883), pp 23, 24.
107. "Immigration," 20 July 1881, p. 4; "Immigration," *Mail,* 9 April 1881.
108. LAC, MG–26-A, v. 228, no. 98044, Lynch to Macdonald, 20 Feb. 1882.
109. "Distress in Ireland," *Mail,* 30 Dec. 1882.
110. "Canada," 7 Sept. 1881.
111. LAC, MG–26-A, v. 323, "Memorandum," 1881 (n.d.).
112. BL, MSS Eur. D 604/46, "Emigration to Canada," 26 Dec. 1880.
113. "Irish Emigration," 28 April 1881.
114. "Our Second Edition," 26 March 1882.
115. "The Irish?" *Mail,* 11 April 1881.
116. *Freeman's Journal,* 22 April 1880; Bew, p. 83.
117. LAC, MG–26-A, 98026, Lynch to Macdonald, 11 May 1881.
118. Sheppard, *Canada's Forgotten Irish,* p. 30; Foster, *Paddy*, p. 285; Stephen Howe, *Ireland and Empire: Colonial Legacies in Irish History and Culture* (Oxford University Press, 2000), p. 39; Noel Ignatiev, *How the Irish Became White* (New York: Routledge, 2009); Matthew Frye Jacobson, *Whiteness of a Different Color: European Immigrants and the Alchemy of Race* (Harvard University Press, 1999); David Roediger, *The Wages of Whiteness: Race and the Making of the American Working Class* (London: Verso, 2007).
119. "Glorious Outlook," *Mail,* 2 Dec. 1882.
120. Macdonald to Lorne, 2 May 1882, in Sir Joseph Pope, *Correspondence of Sir John Macdonald: Selections from the Correspondence of the Right Honourable Sir John Alexander Macdonald, G.C.B., First Prime Minister of Canada* (Oxford University Press, 1921), pp 287–289.
121. LAC, MG–25-A, v. 219, Galt to Macdonald, 27 April 1882; den Otter, *Civilizing,* p. 58.
122. "The Future of Canada," 2 July 1881.
123. LAC, MG–25-A, Macdonald to Tupper, 25 July 1883; Lamb, *History*, p. 219.
124. "Canada," 7 Sept. 1881.
125. LAC, MG–26-A, v. 219, Colmer to Lynch, Item 93545, 8 July 1882.

Post 1852: forgotten famines

CHAPTER TEN

A PHILANTHROPIST'S RESPONSE TO THE FAMINE OF 1879–82

James Hack Tuke and his Assisted Emigration Scheme

Gerard Moran

The crisis of 1879–82, when at least one million people faced famine and destitution, was largely averted through foreign intervention and private relief. The prompt manner in which the outside world was informed by the Catholic clergy and newspaper reports of an impending catastrophe on the scale of the late 1840s led to a swift international response.[1] The crisis, however, has been largely overshadowed by the political and agrarian events taking place in the country at the same time, and by the catastrophe that took place in Ireland in the 1840s. As a consequence, this later subsistence crisis has been called "the Forgotten Famine" or "Little Famine." The history of this famine has been largely ignored with only N.D. Palmer's, *The Irish Land League Crisis*, first published in 1940, and Donald E. Jordan's, *Land and Popular Politics in Ireland*, published in 1994, providing detailed accounts and analysis.[2] While there was not the same reliance on the potato nationally in the late 1870s compared to the Great Famine period, in large parts of the country, particularly along the western seaboard, it still remained the principal food source of the people. The decimation of the potato crop after 1879, with the average potato yield falling to 1.4 tons per acre, was the worst since 1847. Moreover, other factors exacerbated the crisis of 1879–82, including the decline in seasonal migration earnings, the collapse in the kelp industry and the failure to source credit. The result was that 40 percent of the population along the west coast faced famine, while in places like Connemara, the figure was as high as 80 percent.

The prevailing pre-Famine structures of large parts of Connacht, Donegal and Kerry meant there was a heavy reliance on the potato, a fact that was evident in places like the Clifden Poor Law Union where half of the tillage crop was under the potato. What was significant about "the Forgotten Famine" crisis was the realization that many parts of the country had not progressed since the 1840s, and a new and more radical approach was required to ward off the perennial famines and destitution that affected these regions. Even government officials questioned the feasibility of providing large sums of money for relief operations during times of crisis that brought no long-term benefits.[3] While the government was not directly involved in relief operations, leaving this to private relief organizations such as the Mansion House Relief Committee and the Duchess of Marlborough Relief Committee, it indirectly provided up to £2 million in funds through grants and loans. This money was used primarily for the purchase of seed potatoes and to help finance poor law unions. Much of the money that came back to Ireland during this period was contributed by Irish emigrants who left as a result of the Great Famine and now responded to the crisis with more than £1.7 million being remitted in 1880, most coming from the United States.[4] However, it was argued that this approach had no long-term benefit, and famine and destitution remained a constant threat to the people in the most destitute parts of the country. The crises of the early 1860s and again in 1879–81 had been overcome through the intervention of foreign contributions and some government aid but had made little permanent material impact. The donation by the Canadian government in 1881 of $100,000 toward the construction of harbors along the western seaboard and the development of the fishing industry was the only progressive initiative, but this money had to be matched by British government funding, which was begrudgingly provided only following pressure from the former Governor General of Canada, Lord Monck, a native of Dublin.[5] It was left to outsiders, and in particular those who had witnessed the horrors of the Great Famine, to provide radical suggestions to counteract the perennial famines and crises that hit the most vulnerable parts of the country. Among those who advocated a different approach was the English Quaker and philanthropist, James Hack Tuke.

Philanthropy can be divided into a number of categories, including direct engagement during periods of famine and natural disasters, providing direct help for the poor over a long period of time to improve their economic position and indirect intervention to better the lives of people through educational and health provisions. Tuke's role in these three areas was evident in the 1880s and 1890s. In 1882, he provided £100 for the purchase of food in Carna when the potato once again failed and the Irish Chief Secretary, Sir George Trevelyan, had refused to send aid.[6] In the case of long-term aid to benefit the people, this can be seen through his assisted emigration scheme between 1882 and 1884, which was introduced to benefit both those who emigrated to North America and those who remained in the west of Ireland. His contribution toward improving people's lives through education and economic development can be noted through his role in the establishment of the Congested Districts Board, which had a major impact in improving the lives of the people along the western seaboard. When asked at the Select Committee of the House of Lords on Land Law (Ireland) in July 1882 why he was involved with "pauper emigrants," he replied, "I hardly like to use the word 'paupers,' because these people are the rank and file of the poorer classes of the district ."[7] This shows the Quaker philosophy about community, built around the idea that no one individual should be prized over another. In June 1883, when the last of the emigrants had left Clifden for that year, Tuke wrote, "the normal misery and discontent springing therefrom, are ever behind all other things in my mind and form the strongest incentive to continue work in a field which most retire from in disgust or look and pass on the other side."[8] Yet it was his work on assisted emigration from Connemara and Mayo that Tuke's philanthropy had the most impact. His visit to the west of Ireland during the Forgotten Famine led him to play a major role and, as he confessed to his daughters, it changed his life and "began the chapter of my Irish work of which this journey will be a continuation."[9]

Tuke arrived in Ireland in February 1880, at the height of the famine crisis and at a time when the private relief organizations were under great pressure with growing demands for their limited resources. He had been asked by the Society of Friends in England to travel there and report on the distress, thus providing reliable information as to the extent of the crisis. He was also to work with the two major relief organisations, the Duchess of Marlborough and Mansion House Relief committees. Tuke brought £1,600 to be distributed among the communities where the distress was greatest such as Tourmakeady in County Mayo. Over a six-week period, Tuke revisited those areas in Connaught and Donegal which he had first reported from in 1847 and was appalled by the levels of poverty and destitution that he witnessed. He concluded that no material improvement had taken place in these areas in the intervening period with the population still living on a knife-edge for survival. From Camus he reported on 2 April:

> I wish I could produce that rocky coast and wild miserable village, or rather introduce it into England for a while, so that English might realise how, in these remote places, so many thousands of people are living.[10]

It was to be the first of seven visits to the west of Ireland between 1880 and May 1882.

Tuke realized that a dual economy existed in the country: while parts of the country had progressed since the Great Famine and had become commercialized, this was not the case along the western seaboard with many people remaining at a subsistence level of existence. What angered him was that the plight of these people was being overlooked by the agrarian agitation. While he was sympathetic to the need for tenant rights, and he published articles on the land question and was clearly supportive of the tenants' demands, Tuke realized that a more radical measure was needed to counteract the problems of over-population, famine and destitution. In those areas that he visited, the holdings were too small and uneconomical:

> It is of the utmost importance to realise the fact that farms of ten, fifteen, or twenty acres of land, according to its quality, are too small to support a family. It matters not whether a man has fixity of tenure or, being a peasant proprietor, has no rent to pay, he cannot unless he has some other source of income, live and bring up a family on the small farms under ten or fifteen acres of land, which form so large a proportion of the holdings in the West of Ireland.[11]

He concluded that, "The gift of land would not, I think, enable the people to live who are attempting to live on such small holdings of land." Approximately 1,000 families, or 6,000 people, were living on holdings in Clifden with an average valuation of £2 per holding and 69 percent of the farms were under 15 acres. Out of a total of 195,000 acres in the union, only 10,000 to 11,000 acres were arable. Each farm had only an average of three-quarters of an acre of oats and one and one-quarter acres of potatoes.[12]

Tuke acted quickly. After leaving Ireland in April 1880, he made arrangements to travel to Canada and the United States to ascertain the feasibility of sending emigrants from the west of Ireland to areas where there was a demand for labor. The journey to Canada was influenced by the Canadian government's memorandum of 1880, which had proposed "a systematic immigration from Ireland" as a means of counteracting the prevailing famine crisis. He further proposed that families would be sent to the newly opened up lands in Manitoba and the North West Territories.[13] During his three months in North America during the summer of 1880, Tuke held meetings with J.A. McDonald, the Canadian Prime Minister; Bishop John Ireland of St. Paul, Minnesota; President Hayes of the United States, and the Governor-General of Canada, Lord Lorne. With each of these men, he discussed the emigration plans that he saw as the solution to the problems of the west of Ireland.

Tuke put forward his proposals in an article titled, "Irish Emigration," published in *Nineteenth Century* in February 1881, in which he stated that the only solution to the poverty, destitution and over-population along the western seaboard was through a reduction of the population and, in the short term, people should be assisted to emigrate. He urged that families and not individuals should be sent as this would have the dual advantage of improving the position of those who were left since they would receive remittances from friends and relations, while the vacated holdings could be divided up among those who remained, thus creating viable economic farms. This was followed by an article titled, "Ought emigration from Ireland be assisted?," which was published in the *Contemporary Review* in April 1882.[14]

Tuke's proposals were radical and controversial and he knew he would be denounced by nationalists who regarded assisted emigration as "a treacherous devise for weakening the country."[15] However, he regarded such criticisms as important, believing that they opened up the debate on the perennial problems experienced in the poorest parts of Ireland. Furthermore, because of his influence and position in British society, its merits were discussed and considered by political and business leaders in England. It led to a meeting in the London home of the Duke of Bedford on 31 March 1882, organized by William Rathbone and Samuel Whitbread, and the attendance included W.H. Smith, H.S. Northcote and Henry Cowper. Among those who sent a letter of support and a financial contribution was the Irish Chief Secretary, W.E. Forster, who was unable to attend.[16] The caliber of those who did attend indicated Tuke's position and influence within British society. Moreover, they contributed £8,000 toward the emigration scheme. While Tuke's proposals were radical, the convening of such an influential group at the home of the Duke of Bedford indicates there was an audience of individuals who were prepared to promote emigration as an alternative remedy to the perennial problems of famine and destitution in Ireland.

Tuke's proposals were not original for, in June 1880, Father James Nugent had sent 309 people from Connemara, many of them from Carna, to Graceville, Minnesota, where Bishop John Ireland of St. Paul had established a colonization settlement, while Vere Foster was providing vouchers for single girls to emigrate to the United States.[17] Tuke himself and the Tuke Committee each contributed £100 to the Vere Foster scheme in 1882, although Tuke felt that, by only sending young girls, the scheme had a negative demographic impact as it left those areas they vacated devoid of women for marriage.[18] Prior to embarking on his emigration scheme in Connemara in April 1882, Tuke consulted with both Nugent and Foster, as well as John Sweetman, who was also engaged in colonization to the American Mid-West, as to their experiences with their emigration programs.[19] This enabled him to address any problems he was likely to encounter with his scheme.

Tuke was aware of the magnitude of the task ahead of him and prior to leaving for Ireland, said, "A feeling akin to dread, a feeling endangered by the magnitude of the task naturally sobers my rejoicing."[20] He immediately set out for Clifden because the local Poor Law Guardians had passed a resolution the previous February to apply for a £2,000 loan toward pauper emigration. Tuke had initially intended to collaborate with the Clifden guardians to promote emigration for a number of reasons. First, the Clifden authorities and their officials could provide the necessary local expertise required in interviewing and selecting candidates for emigration, many of whom were Irish speakers. The clerk of the union and the inspecting officer for each district instructed the relieving officers to collect the names of those who wanted to emigrate.[21] Second, the combined financial resources of the guardians and the Tuke Fund would ensure the maximum number of emigrants were assisted. Third, local opposition from powerful groups such as the Catholic clergy was minimized. While many priests such as the Rev. Patrick Greally, the Administrator of Carna, had publicly called for emigration to be introduced during the famine crisis of 1879–81, at least 10 priests from Connemara, including Revs. R. McDonagh from Oughterard, Bernard McDermott from Clifden and P. Kenny from Moycullen, had applied to Foster between 1880 and 1881, to assist young girls from their parishes to emigrate to the United States, and others, like the Rev. James Stephens, had participated in the Nugent emigration scheme from Carna to Graceville, Minnesota, in 1880. Others, notably Rev. Thomas Flannery, were vehemently opposed to their parishioners leaving for North America.

Throughout the period 1882–84 when Tuke was involved with the emigration scheme, he worked closely with local groups to promote, advance and bring to fruition the program. These included local poor law union relieving officers such as Peter King from Letterfrack and John Burke from Clifden; as well as local doctors, such as Dr. Kearney of Carna and Dr. Gorham from Letterfrack, and local clergymen like Father Greally, Father McAndrew from Letterfrack and Rev. Kane from Rosmuc. This ensured the most suitable candidates were selected in addition to expediting the program. Without this local participation, Tuke would have been unable to interview, select and send 1,276 people from the Clifden union on three ships between 28 April and 18 May 1882. Within seven weeks of his arrival in Clifden, Tuke had sent three groups of emigrants to Boston and Quebec. This was achieved despite a number of setbacks. First, the Clifden Board of Guardians rescinded their loan application for emigration, fearing the removal of such large numbers of the population would lead to higher poor law rates and negatively impact the local economy, in particular their own businesses. They also were concerned that many of those wanting to leave owed the union money for the seed potatoes they had received under the 1880 Seed Supply Act, meaning that the union now had debts in excess of £2,000.[22]

Local shopkeepers proved to be the most vocal opponents to the emigration scheme, objecting to the families that were selected, maintaining they owed them money. It led Tuke to state, "The unwillingness of the shopkeeper guardians to lose their hold upon the people is so great that they will not vote for emigration."[23] Another issue that had to be addressed was what to do with the large number of families who had been evicted from the Kirwin, Blake, Eyre and other estates because they were in rent arrears and who were now destitute and living in appalling conditions. Many wanted to emigrate, but they did not have the resources. Yet, if they remained in Connemara, they would have to be maintained by the poor law thus putting further pressure on already overstretched rate-payers. While the Tuke Committee had initially envisaged that the emigrants would contribute a small amount toward their passage fares, this was not feasible from those who had been evicted. Not only were they unable to contribute, but most did not possess adequate clothing for travelling, putting an additional burden on the Tuke Fund resources.

Tuke's commitment and dedication to the emigration scheme did not waiver. Despite the obstacles, in particular the withdrawal of the loan application by the Clifden Board of Guardians, he decided to proceed after consulting with the Tuke Committee in London. It meant that most of the committee's funds had to be committed to the Clifden area and not extended to the other unions he had initially hoped to engage with, namely Belmullet, Newport and Oughterard. These were regarded as the poorest unions in the country and, as a result of the famine crisis of 1879–82, were on the verge of bankruptcy and unlikely to be able to finance a large-scale emigration scheme for the poor. When Tuke visited Mulranny in County Mayo in April 1882, he was approached by over 300 people who wanted to emigrate, but these requests had to be deferred because of the pressure from the Clifden union.[24]

Demand for emigration was even greater than Tuke had anticipated. As Foster stated, "There is at present a desire, amounting almost to a mania, among the juvenile portion of the population in the West of Ireland to emigrate to America, but they are without the means of gratifying their desire."[25] Between 1880 and 1882, Foster received 1,900 applications from young, single girls in Connemara looking for assistance to emigrate: 400 from the parish of Clifden and 360 from Ross parish.[26] Within days of his arrival in Clifden, Tuke had recorded the names of nearly 2,000 people and was overwhelmed with the response; relieving officers reported that nearly 1,000 people on the Blake estate at Renvyle and the Berridge property at Roundstone wanted to leave.[27] He realized that the demand for emigration was greater than the resources available to a private organization and his efforts in 1882 highlighted the demand of the people to leave. The failure to send out more when the project ended in 1882 can be seen in Tuke's letter to his daughter, Frances, "It is very hard to refuse thousands of people who are begging to go, when one knows that the money is there for a certain number at any rate."[28] He was convinced that between 4,000 and 5,000 people would have left from the Clifden union if the committee had the resources to send them. Such was the demand to leave that many applicants travelled 40 to 50 miles to register their names for emigration.[29] Tuke and his committee responded to this demand by using their political and business connections to further the emigration program and seeking financial aid from the government, arguing that assisted emigration should be extended to other parts of the western seaboard. In a memorandum of July 1882, the Tuke Committee stated that assisted emigration was beyond the resources of a private organization and state involvement was required.[30] Parliamentary support for assisted emigration was increasing as the effectiveness of the relief provided in the aftermath of the Forgotten Famine: was being questioned as a large amount of money had been spent, but with little impact.[31] While the Prime Minister, William Gladstone, initially opposed the proposal to provide money for emigration, he was persuaded by other political figures, including the former Irish Chief Secretary, William Forster, of the merits of the scheme. It resulted in £100,000 being made available under the 1882 Arrears of Rent Act, thus enabling the Tuke Committee to extend its operation to Belmullet, Newport and Oughterard unions who were on the edge of bankruptcy. At the same time, assistance to emigrate was provided to another 34 unions along the western seaboard, supervised by the local poor law guardians. The government provided £5 for each emigrant with the Tuke Committee covering any additional cost: more than £12,000 was provided by the committee, which came from private donations, and the remaining money came from the Duchess of Marlborough Relief Fund, which had ceased operations in April 1880.[32]

Guidelines that had been introduced in 1882 were now applied to the other unions that came under the committee's jurisdiction. Only families were to be assisted, although in exceptional circumstances individuals were included. Each family had to have a proportion of its members of a working age: this was to ensure that the emigrants would not become dependent on charity or public services in North America. As a result, families with a large number of dependent children, with four or five aged under 8 years old, were excluded. As most of the population of Connemara were Irish speakers, at least one family member had to be proficient in English. When Tuke and his wife, Georgina, who had married James the previous November and who accompanied him to the interviews, went to Letterfrack in February 1883, they had to use the local relieving officers as interpreters as nearly all of the applicants spoke no English.[33] The inclusion of an English-speaking family member ensured the emigrants were not isolated in their new surroundings in North America. While it was hoped that the emigrants would make some contribution toward their travel costs, it was soon realized that those applying were so poor they could not even make provision toward their clothing for travelling and an additional £1 per person had to be added for clothing. Under the scheme, those intending to leave had to apply before 31 January 1883. This was to ensure that unsuccessful candidates could return to their holdings and plant a crop in the spring. To expedite matters, a decision was made to separate the administration of the scheme with Tuke remaining in charge in Clifden, Major Gaskell taking over in Oughterard and Sydney Buxton appointed to oversee operations in Belmullet and Newport.

The work was onerous and time consuming. When the interviews were held at the Letterfrack dispensary on 19 February in the presence of the local relieving officer, Henry Burke, Tuke found the building full of former kelp workers who had fallen on hard times because their industry was facing intense competition from German artificial chemical fertilizers and South American guano and as a result the price of kelp had declined dramatically.[34] It took over four hours to complete the interviews as most of the applicants could not speak English and Henry Burke had to act as a translator. This led Georgina Tuke to state, "Hard, anxious work this selecting is, and we have so many applications that could be granted for the steamer on the 23rd [March]."[35]

Once again the demand for places exceeded all expectations: when Tuke arrived in Carna on 27 February 1883 he found a crowd of between 300 to 400 people waiting to be interviewed and similar crowds assembled in Cleggan, Maum, Ashleigh, Roundstone and Renvyle.[36] Crowds also gathered in Belmullet and Newport unions, and Sydney Buxton, who took charge of the operation in these unions, reported that, when he visited Achill Island, all of the applicants stated they wanted to be sent to "Americkay," but did not state where in the United States.[37] The intensity of the operation can be seen in that Tuke worked from 8 o'clock in the morning until after midnight on most days: interviewing, selecting, organizing the travel arrangements, accompanying the emigrants to Galway and seeing them off. In addition, there was the high level of bureaucracy, with up to 14 forms being filled out for each emigrant. Coordination also was required with the other areas that the Tuke Committee administered so the groups could leave on the one ship and thus reduce costs as when the *Canadian* left from Galway on 21 March 1883 with 173 passengers from Clifden, 54 from Oughterard and 144 from Belmullet who had embarked at Blacksod Bay the previous day.[38] Despite the pressure on time and resources, Tuke was not disheartened and told his daughter, Frances, "Poor things it is worth the trouble and much more to deliver them from our hard woes."[39] He encountered desperate cases of people wanting to leave, such as the instance of a widow with her four children who wished to be sent to Pittsburgh where she had relations. She had walked 40 miles to ask for help but was informed that the last boat which was to leave on 23 June, the *SS Waldesian*, was full and the committee's funds exhausted. Tuke met her again in Oughterard and when she begged him on her knees to be sent, he was so moved by her story that he paid the fare for the family himself.[40]

Not all who applied were selected: families with too many dependent children or no family member who could speak English were rejected on the grounds that they then would face hardship in North America. Some were refused for other reasons. Nearly all of those interviewed at Maum on 17 May were considered to be unsuitable. An ex-policeman employed on Mitchel Henry's estate at Kylemore and earning 3*s* 6*d* a day was refused as it was felt he could finance his own travel. Applicants were also turned down when the constabulary objected as in Letterfrack, when they provided a list of those suspected of being involved in agrarian crimes.[41] Martin Daly was not allowed to leave because he was a key witness for the Crown Prosecutor in the Letterfrack murders that had occurred on 24 April 1881.[42] These refusals led to conflicts with those local officials providing valuable assistance in the selection process as with Father McAndrew, the Parish Priest in Letterfrack, who was angry when Widow Joyce and her family were refused on the grounds that she had too many dependent children.[43]

Between 23 March and 23 June 1883, 5,327 emigrants were assisted by the Tuke Committee: 1,589 from Clifden, 1,224 from Oughterard and 2,514 from Belmullet and Newport, the first group leaving on the *Phoenician*. Among those on the first sailing were Michael Hughes and his family from Letterfrack. No sooner had one group departed than preparations were put in place for the next, with the *Nestorian* leaving on 31 March with 538 men, women and children. Between 21 and 28 April, the Tuke Committee sent 1,115 emigrants on three sailings, two to Quebec and the other to Boston. The pressure that they were under can be seen in Tuke's letter to his daughters in May, when he wrote, "This has been harrowing work and we are both ragged."[44] Events did not always run smoothly and immediate decisions had to be made. There were occasions when those selected failed to turn up, as with a group from Carna who were to sail on the *Manitobian* bound for Quebec on 5 May, when 30 of the emigrants were absent, and replacements had to be found to fill the quota.[45]

Unlike previous assisted emigration schemes from Ireland in the 19th century, in particular the landlord schemes during the Great Famine or Nugent's scheme to Minnesota in 1880, Tuke's strategy was well planned and coordinated, and not a knee jerk reaction to a famine crisis. As the selection process was rigorous, and only families with the potential to succeed were sent, it had a better chance of success. While

Tuke was prepared to send emigrants to the locations of their choice, he discouraged settlement in the industrial cities of the east unless friends and relations in those locations were prepared to look after them. Instead, the emigrants were sent to various locations throughout Canada and the United States where arrangements were made to provide assistance from the time of their arrival. The emigrants were encouraged to settle in Canada because the administration there was prepared to look after the new arrivals. At the same time, Tuke was reluctant to send emigrants to the United States where there was hostility to Irish emigrants.[46] There was, however, an initial reluctance to travel to Canada and the Mitchells who sailed on the *Austrian* in April 1882 were the first family to settle in Canada. While those selected in Clifden were initially reluctant to go there, when the last group was leaving on the *Winnipeg* on 19 May, they told Tuke, "send us wherever you like, only let us get out of our misery here."[47] Once a connection was established and families informed that Canada was the only destination available, the number going to the country increased with 1,850 travelling in 1883. The committee had more control of where the emigrants settled in Canada, which was mainly in small towns with populations of between 2,000 and 10,000.[48] The Canadian authorities were prepared to meet the emigrants when they arrived in Quebec and send them to Toronto where agents then placed them in suitable locations. Local Catholic clergy took in 650 of the emigrants, while officials in Hamilton rented houses for those sent to its jurisdiction. A further 200 were sent to Manitoba.[49] The families sent to Peterborough, Ontario, were provided with accommodation by the local community, many of whom were descendants of those assisted under the Peter Robinson scheme from the Blackwater region of north Munster between 1823–25.[50] Arrangements also were made with others such as Bishop John Ireland in Minnesota and a mill owner in Grosvenordale in Connecticut for the emigrants to be looked after. Sixty-six people from Belmullet poor law union were sent to Warren, Rhode Island, including Pat Monaghan and his family from Tallagh and the Phillips, Bourke and Doherty families. The Gaughans from Rossport were among the families who settled in Lost Creek in Pennsylvania, where there were employment opportunities in the slate and coal mines. Only two families were sent to the same location in North America on each vessel that sailed from Galway and Belmullet. Two families, the Gaughans and Duceys from Bunawilliam, Belmullet, settled in Richmond, Indiana, where the local pastor, Rev. McMullan, agreed to provide for them.[51] This was to ensure no local hostility occurred when the emigrants settled in Canada and the United States.

In order to assist the emigrants to settle in their new environment in North America, Tuke sent Howard Hodgkins and Major Richard Ruttledge-Fair to Canada and the United States in the autumn of 1883. Their report in November was positive, with those who had settled in Canada earning higher wages than those who remained in the eastern and central states of the United States. They believed that the small towns of Ontario were preferable "morally and religiously for raw Irish emigrants than the large towns of the eastern and central states of America." One family they interviewed in St. Thomas in Ontario was earning $100 a month. The report concluded that only three of the Tuke families were experiencing difficulties.[52] Others corroborated these findings, such as Bishop John Ireland of St. Paul, Father Michael O'Mahony from Preston, who had travelled with the group that sailed on the *Nepigan* on 31 March 1883 and had taken up a position in the diocese of St. Paul, where many of the emigrants settled. The coordinated and structured approach of Tuke demonstrated that assisted emigration could be beneficial and successful when properly organized and planned.

The success of the scheme in 1883 prompted the Tuke Committee to petition the government in July 1883 for further funding for emigration with Sydney Buxton estimating that 25 to 30 percent of the population in the west of Ireland still needed to be sent to North America.[53] Initially, the government agreed to provide a further £100,000 under the Tramways and Public Companies Act, but this was subsequently reduced to £50,000 due to opposition from the Irish Parliamentary Party who argued that an equal amount should be made available for internal migration within Ireland.[54] In addition to the four unions already under its administration, the Tuke Committee took charge of the scheme in Swinford union and Arranmore Island off the Donegal coast because of their perilous financial position. However, when Tuke began his tour in February 1884, he found the demand for emigration had greatly declined. A number of factors were responsible for this change. Tuke could no longer rely on the services of poor law union officials to provide lists or take part in the selection process as the boards of guardians warned their employees they could be dismissed if they engaged with the Tuke Committee. By this stage, the boards of guardians were controlled by the Irish Parliamentary Party.[55] Clerical involvement was also curtailed after the hierarchy condemned emigration and in November 1883 Archbishop John McEvilly of Tuam stated that it should be opposed by every local and constitutional method available. It led 97 priests from the archdiocese of Tuam, which covered most of Connemara and large parts of west Mayo, to follow the opposition to assisted emigration.[56] Tuke maintained that the priests favored sending out individual boys and girls to America, "but the moment it came to emigrating the family they do not like it."[57] He found that while Father McDonagh of Oughterard was receptive to the emigration scheme, his curate refused to have any contact with him. At the same time, the 1883 harvest was very good, leading to a decline in the demand for emigration. Sydney Buxton summed up this situation when he observed that the level of emigration depended on agricultural circumstances: if the harvest was poor, the numbers wanting to leave was high, but if the crops were abundant, fewer people wished to leave.[58] However, the most important factor in the Tuke Committee's decision to discontinue the emigration after 1884 was the decision by the Canadian government in March 1884 to no longer accept assisted emigrants from Ireland, angry with the way the poor law unions sent their emigrants without any engagement or contact with the North American authorities. While David Spence, Secretary of the Department of Immigration in Ontario, told the Tuke Committee that the Canadian authorities were happy with the emigrants that the committee sent out, their anger was with the poor law unions and many Canadians felt all Irish emigrants were a burden on the state and living on charity. Despite these challenges, the Tuke Committee assisted 2,802 to leave from the five unions under its charge in 1884: 347 from Clifden, 996 from Belmullet and Newport, 594 from Swinford, 769 from Oughterard and 96 from Arranmore Island. They left on 10 boats between 28 March and 13 June, 613 leaving on 14 April on the *Canadian*.

While the Tuke emigration scheme ended in 1884, the committee did not disband as Tuke believed that emigration remained an integral solution to the poverty and destitution of the west of Ireland. Even when the Congested Districts Board was established in 1891, Tuke ensured that assisted emigration was included in its remit although it was seldom used. Throughout the 1880s Tuke personally provided the funding for people to leave: 100 people from Clifden and Belmullet between 1886 and 1889, and 80 from Clifden in 1890. It led Tuke to state in 1890, "There is very clear evidence on the part of the people themselves how strong the desire to emigrate still is ... as shown by the numerous applications for assistance I receive."[59] He was unsuccessful in his many attempts to access the remaining funds for emigration from the Tramways and Public Companies Act. The importance of the emigration as a solution to the problems of the west of Ireland and Tuke's role was acknowledged in 1886 by the Duke of Bedford, a major and influential supporter of the emigration project, when he said emigration was the savior of Ireland "and it succeeds when undertaken by a man of power like yourself, animated by a sense of duty."[60] By the mid-1880s, Tuke was regarded as an expert on emigration and was appointed to the Emigrants Information Council when it was established by the Secretary of State for the Colonies in September 1886. He remained a member until he retired in December 1893.[61]

Tuke saw emigration as having two main advantages for the people of the west of Ireland. Those who remained would have access to more land as the farms of those leaving could now be redistributed. A total of 11 of the farms vacated in Clifden poor law union were reallocated to neighboring tenants, although the same was not achieved in Belmullet: of the 293 holdings vacated, only half were taken over by neighboring tenants.[62] While it improved the position of those who received additional land, congestion continued to be a major problem and a witness at the Poor Relief Inquiry in 1886 stated, "The people are dependent on land, and the land as now cultivated, will not support them."[63] However, Tuke's emigrants provided assistance to overcome this problem through remittances sent back to families and friends in the west of Ireland. In 1884, Tuke estimated that the emigrants sent between £4,000 and £5,000 over the previous two years, £2,500 coming to the Clifden area in sums ranging from £5 to £30, and in one case £40.[64] Michael F. who left Galway on the *Canadian* on 21 May sent £2 to his cousin, Tom, in Clifden from Sonk Centre in Manitoba.[65] Remittances also benefited the local community as debts to merchants and shopkeepers were paid off. Families and friends also received the passage fares to North America. It was an objective of Tuke that his scheme would initiate a chain migration process in those areas where it did not previously exist. As one emigrant from Crumpaun who had settled in Chicago told her sister, she would forward her the passage fare so "father can sit by the fire then and let the rough days pass him and us earning enough money in this country where there is plenty of it."[66] Forty people from Belmullet had their passage paid to Montana in the late 1880s by friends and relatives who settled there as a result of the assistance provided by the Tuke Committee.[67] The emigrants also acted as agents for emigration though the letters sent back highlighting how they were progressing, the wages they were earning and how well they were doing. As one emigrant from Belmullet who had settled in Toronto wrote, "I could buy more provisions here for one shilling than I could in Ireland for two shillings. If you gave me a present of a house and farm in Tip [a townland on the Mullet] I would not go back to it."[68]

The success of the scheme raises the question—why has Tuke's philanthropic work been forgotten, or at best side-lined, in Irish history as he did so much to improve the lives of the poor in the most destitute parts of Ireland. Many of his contemporaries did acknowledge his contribution with the former Governor General of Ceylon and Galway landowner, Sir William Gregory, describing him in March 1883 as "Ireland's greatest benefactor," while his old adversary, Father Thomas Flannery of Carna, stated in 1886, "I don't know what would have become of these people only for you."[69] In 1893, when Tuke came across a man called Folan in Connemara and when he heard that the Tuke Committee had helped his relation, John Folan, leave for America, he took off his hat and said, "Then it is you we ought to be cheering."[70]

The humility of the man is evident in that he never sought or wanted recognition or accolades for his work. His emigration scheme in Clifden in 1882 went largely unnoticed by the media and public because of the prevailing political and agrarian agitations, including the "No Rent Manifesto," the Phoenix Park Murders and the Kilmainham Treaty. Only in June 1882 did the Irish Parliamentary Party inquire who this Mr. Tuke was, and they were told by W.H. Smith and Samuel Whitbread that he had been "distinguished for philanthropy in all parts of the world," noting in particular his relief work in Paris in 1870 during the Franco-Prussian War. Tuke would have preferred his work had remained out of the spotlight and said, "I think a great deal too much has been said about my little bit of work and I hope it is all over now."[71] In 1886, he also refused to accept a knighthood and a seat in parliament in recognition of his work in Ireland.

Tuke's work in the west of Ireland should not be forgotten as it impacted on so many people in a positive way. He was responsible for delivering more than 9,500 people out of poverty and to a better life in North America. While emigration was never going to be accepted by the influential sections of Irish society, for Tuke it remained a cornerstone of any economic policy that was implemented along the western seaboard. As late as 1889, when plans were afoot for the construction of light railways and the fostering of fishing, Tuke also urged that family emigration be included which would be administered and coordinated by a government department.[72] The Tuke Committee assisted 17 percent of the populations of the unions that it worked with, but the resources of these unions were still not able to contend with the remaining people. Tuke's commitment and dedication to the poor of the west of Ireland eventually led to a change in government policy with the establishment of the Congested Board in 1891, which promoted economic development with government aid. As Ciara Breathnach argues, the role of Tuke in the establishment and advancement of its activities is greater than has previously been realized.[73] While emigration was only a partial solution to the problems of these areas, it took the compassion, diligence and influence of the philanthropist, James Hack Tuke, to improve the lives of so many people.

NOTES

1. See Gerard Moran, "'Near Famine': The Roman Catholic Church and the subsistence crisis of 1879–82" in *Studia Hibernica*, no. 32 (2002–3), pp 155–78; idem, "From Great Famine to Forgotten Famine: the crisis of 1879–81," in Patrick Fitzgerald, Christine Kinealy & Gerard Moran (eds), *Irish Hunger and Migration: Myth, Memory and Memorization* (Hamden, CT: Quinnipiac University Press, 2015), pp 121–32.
2. N. Palmer, *The Irish Land League Crisis* (New York: Octagon Books, 1978), pp 64–105; Donald E. Jordan, *Land and Popular Politics in Ireland: County Mayo from the Plantation to the Land War* (Cambridge University Press, 1994), pp 200–9.
3. Brendan O'Donoghue, *Activities Wise and Otherwise: the Career of Sir Henry Robinson* (Dublin: Irish Academic Press, 2015), pp 20–1.
4. Arnold Schrier, *Ireland and the American Emigration, 1850–1900* (Chester Springs, PA; rep. Dufour Editions, 1948), p. 111.
5. *Report of the Joint Committee, selected from the Committees of the Duchess of Marlborough Relief Fund and the Mansion House Fund for the Relief of Distress in Ireland, to administer the sum of 100,000 Dollars, voted by the Parliament of the Dominion of Canada towards the Relief of Distress in Ireland*, HC 1881 (326), lxxv.
6. Georgina Tuke diary, 27 February 1883 (NLI, Ms 49,529/90, John Pitt Kennedy papers).
7. *Second report from the Select Committee of the House of Lords on Land Laws (Ireland); together with the proceedings of the committee, minutes of evidence and appendix*, HC 1882 (379), xi, p. 259, q. 7667.
8. Tuke to unknown, 10 June 1883, University of Limerick (UL), Tuke papers.
9. Tuke to Frances and Meta Tuke, 22 July 1882 (UL, Tuke papers).
10. James Hack Tuke, *A Visit to Donegal and Connaught in the Spring of 1880* (London, 1880), p. 76.
11. James Hack Tuke, "Peasant proprietors at home" in the *Nineteenth Century*, viii (Aug. 1880), p. 191.
12. *Second report from the Select Committee of the House of Lords on Land Laws (Ireland)*, p. 271, q. 7778; p. 274, q. 7808; p. 273, qs 7801–2; p. 261, q. 7673.
13. Gerard Moran, *Sending Out Ireland's Poor: Assisted Emigration to North America in the Nineteenth Century* (Dublin: Four Courts Press, 2013), pp 170–1; James Hack Tuke, "Ought emigration from Ireland be assisted,' in *Contemporary Review* (April, 1882), p. 702.
14. Ibid.
15. James Hack Tuke, "Irish emigration," in the *Nineteenth Century* (Feb. 1881), pp 370–1.
16. *Reports and Papers relating to the Proceedings of the Committee of "Mr Tuke's Fund" for assisted emigration from Ireland during the years 1882, 1883 and 1884* (London, 1884), p. 25.
17. See Gerard Moran, "'In search of the promised land': the Connemara colonization scheme to Minnesota, 1880' in *Eire/Ireland*, 31:3 & 4 (Fall and Winter, 1996); Bridget Connelly, *Forgetting Ireland: Uncovering a Family's Secret History* (St. Paul: Borealis Books, 2003); Ruth-Anne Harris, "'Where the poor man is not crushed down to exact the aristocrat': Vere Foster's programmes of assisted emigration in the aftermath of the Irish

Famine" in Patrick O'Sullivan (ed.), *The Irish World Wide: History, Heritage, Identity, vol. 6; The Meaning of the Famine* (Leicester University Press, 2000), pp 172–94.

18. *Second report from the Select Committee of the House of Lords on Land Laws (Ireland)*, p. 244, q. 7529; pp 266, q. 7701.
19. Tuke to Meta Tuke, 5 April 1882 (UL, Tuke papers).
20. Sydney Buxton, "Tuke and his work," in the *Contemporary Review,* 69 (June 1896), p. 866.
21. *Second report of the Select Committee of the House of Lords on Land Law (Ireland)*, p. 270, q. 7769.
22. Gerard Moran, *Fleeing from Famine in Connemara: James Hack Tuke and his assisted emigration Scheme in the 1880s* (Dublin: Four Courts Press, 2018), p. 31.
23. *Second report of the Select Committee of the House of Lords on Land Law* (Ireland), p. 265.
24. Gerard Moran, "James Hack Tuke and assisted emigration from Galway and Mayo in the 1880s" in Mary Clancy et al (eds), *The Emigrant Experience. Papers presented at the Second Annual Mary Murray Weekend Seminar* (Galway: Galway Labour History Group, 1991), p. 77.
25. Mr. Vere Foster's second emigration female fund, 1880–3 (NLI, Ms 13,552, William O'Brien papers).
26. *Second report of the Select Committee of the House of Lords on Land Law (Ireland)*, p. 247, q. 7545.
27. Tuke to Meta Tuke, 18 April 1882 (UL, Tuke papers).
28. Ibid., Tuke to Frances Tuke, undated 1882.
29. *Second report of the Select Committee of the House of Lords on Land Law (Ireland)*, p. 258, q. 7657.
30. *Report and Papers relating to "Mr Tuke's Fund,"* p. 104.
31. Henry Robinson, *Memories, Wise and Otherwise* (Dublin: Cassell & Company, 1924), p. 42.
32. *Emigration from Ireland: being the second report of the committee of "Mr Tuke's Fund"* (London: National Press Agency, 1883), p. 6.
33. Georgina Tuke diary, 19 Feb. 1883 (NLI, Ms 49,529/90, John Pitt Kennedy papers).
34. Ibid.
35. Georgina Tuke diary, 22 Feb. 1883; Fry, *Tuke: A Memoir,* pp 170–1. It was the SS *Phoenician*.
36. Georgina Tuke diary, entry 27 Feb. 1883.
37. Sydney Buxton, "Tuke and his work."
38. *The second report of "Mr Tuke's Fund*, p. 4.
39. Tuke to Frances Tuke, undated, 1883 (UL, Tuke papers).
40. Ibid., Tuke to Meta Tuke, July 1883.
41. Georgina Tuke diary, 17 May 1883.
42. Fry, *Tuke A Memoir*, pp 171–3; Georgina Tuke diary, 27 Feb. 1883 (NLI, Ms, 49,529/90, John Pitt Kennedy papers).
43. Ibid., 19 Feb. 1883.
44. Tuke to Frances and Meta Tuke, 9 May 1883 (UL, Tuke papers).
45. Georgina Tuke Diary, 4 May 1883.
46. *Second report of the Select Committee of the House of Lords on Land Law* (Ireland), p. 259, q. 7662.
47. Ibid., p. 259, q. 7664.
48. Ibid., p. 148, qs 2517–21.
49. Moran, *Fleeing from Famine in Connemara*, p. 42.
50. For the Peter Robinson emigration scheme of 1823–5 see Moran, *Sending Out*, pp 21–8;

Wendy Cameron, "Selecting Peter Robinson's emigrants" in *Histoire Sociale/ Social History*, 9:17 (May 1976).

51. Reports and proceedings of "Mr Tuke's Fund," p. 117.
52. Ibid., pp 128–32.
53. Buxton, "A new exodus," pp 855–6.
54. See Gerard Moran, "The Land Purchase and Settlement Company and the attempted migration scheme to Kilcloony in the 1880s" in *Irish Economic and Social History*, xxxii (2015), pp 47–62. Tuke was opposed to internal migration arguing it would not deal with the issue of poverty in the west of Ireland.
55. See Moran, *Fleeing from Famine in Connemara*. p. 46.
56. *Connaught Telegraph*, 10 Nov. 1883; *Galway Vindicator,* 10 Nov. 1883.
57. *Second report from the select committee of the House of Lords on Land Laws (Ireland),* p. 270, q. 7763,
58. Buxton, "A new exodus," p. 885.
59. *Report of the Select Committee on Colonisation; together with the proceedings of the committee, minutes of evidence and appendix*, HC 1890, xii (345), p. 204, q. 3429.
60. Sir Edward Fry, *James Hack Tuke: A Memoir* (London: Macmillan, 1899), pp 220–1.
61. Ibid., p. 255.
62. *Second Report of the Committee for "Mr Tuke's Fund,"* p. 31.
63. *Poor Relief (Ireland) Inquiry,* HC 1887, xxxviii (c–5043), p. 156, q. 7484–5.
64. *Select Committee on Colonisation,* p. 203, q. 3427; Moran, *Fleeing from Famine*, p. 149.
65. *Third report of the committee of "Mr Tuke's Fund,"* p. 115.
66. Ibid., pp 25–6.
67. *Select Committee on Colonisation*, p. 204, q. 3429.
68. Ibid., p. 8.
69. Georgina Tuke's diary, 17 March 1883 (NLI, Ms49, 529/90, John Pitt Kennedy papers,); *Reports and proceedings of the committee of "Mr Tuke's Fund,"* p. 121.
70. Tuke to Meta Tuke, 13 Aug. 1883 (UL, Tuke papers)
71. Ibid., Tuke to Meta Tuke, undated, 1882.
72. Carla King, "'Our destitute countrymen on the western coast': relief and development strategies in the congested districts" in Carla King and Conor McNamara (eds), *The West of Ireland: New Perspectives on the Nineteenth Century* (Dublin: The History Press, 2011), p. 171.
73. Ciara Breathnach, *The Congested Districts Board of Ireland, 1891–1922: Poverty and Development in the west of Ireland* (Dublin: Four Courts Press, 2005), pp 21–2.

CHAPTER ELEVEN

AMERICA'S ERRAND OF MERCY TO IRELAND

Harvey Strum

Food shortages and desperation appeared in Ireland during the "Little Famine" of 1879–82. Rain and bad weather conditions in the summer of 1879 produced potato blight in the west, with crop yields dropping to half of those in the early 1870s. Falling crop prices due to international competition and declining prices for kelp as a fertilizer severely reduced the incomes of tenants and small independent farmers. Remittances from Irish seasonal workers in Scotland and England declined, further reducing the ability of people in the west to purchase alternative sources of food. Concerned about their parishioners, 200 Catholic priests warned in June about food problems on the western and southern coasts of Ireland, while "Miss Eyre of Clifden Castle stated that all over Connemara there was already scenes of harrowing distress."[1] In the succeeding months, grim reports appeared in the Irish press. Local priests reported mass starvation in communities in the western counties. Father Griffen in Parke, near Castlebar, described the desperate conditions of 500 starving families in his parish. In Ballina, laborers staged a protest and held up banners "Our wives and children are starving."[2] By January 1880, the situation had become so dire that Father Greally reported from Carna that if relief supplies failed to arrive, "I fear we will have many inquests."[3] Because two-thirds of the potato crop had rotted, 250,000 people were "without food or the means of buying it." Another 500,000 "stood on the verge of ruin."[4]

Responding to the crisis, the Duchess of Marlborough, wife of the Irish Lord Lieutenant, wrote to the London *Times* on 16 December calling for a fund to help the

Irish poor. This appeal led to the creation of the Duchess of Marlborough's Relief Fund. The committee won the support of both the English aristocracy and Irish landlords, and it succeeded in attracting international contributions. In early January, the Mansion House Committee, chaired by Edmund Gray, the Lord Mayor of Dublin, was established in Dublin to raise and distribute funds. Politicians, public figures, members of the clergy of all denominations and businessmen joined the committee, providing the prestige to make it the major Irish relief organization, which had the goal of attracting "Australian and American assistance."[5] Irish nationalists, led by Charles Stewart Parnell, organized the Irish Land League Relief Fund. It attracted donations from a large number of Americans. Parnell was helped in this endeavor by his sister, Fanny, who was based in New Jersey. Parnell visited the United States in early 1880 and traveled across the country raising funds for Irish relief and encouraging the formation of chapters of the Land League.[6]

In December 1879, the Fenian Brotherhood and several other Irish benevolent and nationalist societies in New York City approached Judge Charles Daly. They asked him to lead the campaign to "assist our starving countrymen in Ireland" and expected "the citizens of New York of every creed and nationality" to join in this worthy cause.[7] Daly had led the 1862–63 effort to raise funds for Ireland and he helped establish the New York City Irish Relief Committee on 19 December 1879. Daly recruited some of the men who had participated in the earlier effort. The New York Irish Relief Committee included many prominent people including William Grace, soon to be elected the first Irish Catholic mayor of the city. To reach a national audience, the committee sent out 40,000 copies of its appeal, stating that, "The evidence of distress of an acute and exceptional character, certain to involve actual starvation unless speedily relieved has now reached us ... A great disaster has befallen Ireland."[8] The Mansion House Committee expressed its gratitude to the New York committee and the people of the United States.[9] Once again, Americans, as they had during the Great Hunger and again in 1862–63, had started a campaign of voluntary aid to assist the starving people of Ireland.

For a brief period, it looked like the United States government might provide direct aid. Democratic Congressman Richard Graham Frost, a lawyer in St. Louis, expressing his sympathy for the Irish and their fight for self-rule, on 9 December 1879, he moved a resolution noting that, "the people of Ireland are seriously threatened with the horrors of famine." He blamed the land tenure system in Ireland and urged reform and greater "self-government."[10] On the same day, a Greenbacker, Edward Hooker Gillette from Iowa, introduced a similar joint resolution, which encouraged the British government to help the Irish. Gillette's resolution emphasized, "that we cordially sympathize with the people of Ireland in their present alarming condition from threatened famine." Gillette's resolution supported the aims of the Land League and asked the British government to create a more equitable distribution of land. Both implied American aid for the Irish.[11] More explicit congressional resolutions advocating American relief were introduced in January and February 1880 by two congressmen. Democrat John Ellis of Louisiana, a former Confederate officer, asked for an appropriation of $100,000 "for the relief of the starving people of Ireland," because there are 300,000 "Irish men, women, and children suffering for food."[12] James Phelps, a Democrat from Connecticut, on 2 February 1880, proposed, "providing national aid to the suffering poor of Ireland." The resolution stated that the Senate and House "recognized their obligations to render National assistance and relief to the unfortunate sufferers and for that purpose the sum of one hundred thousand dollars" be appropriated.[13] Members of Congress sent these two resolutions to the Committee on Appropriations and Committee on Foreign Affairs, respectively.

To encourage Congress to do the right thing, the Chamber of Commerce of St. Paul, Minnesota, sent a petition to the House and Senate on 9 February calling for "a liberal appropriation be made from the national treasury to be applied for the relief of the sufferers ... to save thousands from this starvation" and demanded, "that such aid be afforded without delay." The petitioners wanted Congress to understand that they represented "not only the business community of St. Paul, but the wishes of all the people of Minnesota without exception."[14] In late January, the citizens of Washington, D.C., held a meeting for Irish relief. Judges, senators, congressmen and other important people attended the mass meeting chaired by Chief Justice David Cartter of the District Court. In addition to raising over $3,000, the meeting expressed its desire for a federal appropriation for Irish relief. Resolutions were adopted thanking "Congress for their speedy and cordial action in rendering early relief to the suffering people of Ireland."[15] Like the businessmen in St. Paul, the citizens of Washington anticipated congressional action to aid the Irish.

While waiting to see what Congress would do, the American public donated their pennies, dimes and dollars for Irish relief. Catholic bishops in many cities asked their parishioners to donate. For example, the Bishop of Cleveland directed "that on the first Sunday in Advent a collection be taken up throughout the Diocese" for the suffering Irish.[16] William McCloskey, the Bishop of Louisville, Kentucky, sent £300 donated in his diocese to the Archbishop of Dublin, Edward McCabe, in January 1880.[17] Cities from Maine to California established Irish relief committees suggesting the widespread sympathy of the American people. Residents of St. Louis, Missouri, held a mass meeting in December 1879. It was "an immense affair attended by citizens of all nationalities," All of these activities were evidence of the widespread support Irish relief had among Americans.[18] Mayor Courtenay, Chairman of the Charleston Irish Relief Committee, reported that residents had donated $2,000 for Irish relief by early February 1880.[19] In Albany, New York, Mayor Michael Nolan, chaired the local relief committee.[20] William Rice, Mayor of Trenton, New Jersey, organized a meeting for Irish relief and issued an appeal to "the charitable of our city to respond to this call for aid."[21] The Irish Relief Committee of Milwaukee, Wisconsin, split its contributions between the Land League and Mansion House Committee, but wanted to make sure "that the fund be used exclusively in procuring the necessaries of life for the suffering people."[22] Professors and students at the University of Virginia in Charlottesville donated over $300 in early March.[23]

The arrival of Parnell in the United States in January 1880 produced an outpouring of support from Irish-Americans and American political leaders with tens of thousands of dollars being donated to the Land League Famine Relief Fund. Parnell lectured in 62 cities including addressing the Kentucky state legislature, the New York state legislature in Albany, the Virginia state legislature, and the joint Houses of Congress on 2 February 1880 in Washington.[24] Parnell spoke about the famine, urged land reform, and solicited donations for both the Land League and the Land League Relief Fund. He also raised doubts about the wisdom of donations sent to other Irish relief groups. Americans proved generous, subscribing $200,000 to the Land League Relief Fund. James Gordon Bennett Jr., editor of the *New York Herald,* stole the limelight. On 4 February 1880, he created his own *New York Herald* Irish Relief Fund and started off the campaign with a personal donation of $100,000. Bennett's magnificent gesture impressed other editors who publicized the *Herald's* fund throughout the country. Through its own circulation, the *Herald* predicted it would reach "every city and village in the United States and Canada." The newspaper accurately boasted "we expect contributions from every American city from Bangor to Galveston, from New York City to San Francisco."[25] By March, the *Herald's* fund emerged as the leading private Irish relief organization in the United States. Bennett established a committee in Ireland to distribute the funds thus raised.

Meanwhile, in early March, the House Foreign Affairs Committee declared its support of a $300,000 appropriation for Ireland. The report, largely written by Democratic Congressman Samuel Cox of New York City, but strongly supported by his Republican colleague from New York City, Levi Morton, proposed replacing the previous resolutions in favor of a joint resolution endorsing Irish relief. Members of the committee believed Congress had the constitutional authority to provide aid to the suffering Irish and cited the example of 1812, when Congress had voted $50,000 to help the victims of an earthquake in Caracas, as precedent. The House Committee also reminded its fellow representatives that, in 1847, the Senate had proposed giving $500,000 for Irish relief—another precedent for action in 1880. The 1847 bill had been quashed.[26] Yet, as the House Committee observed, "There can be no doubt that the charity and sympathy of the whole American people are deeply moved toward the unhappy people of Ireland." The committee recommended appropriating $300,000 because it represented "the best wishes of the people of the Republic."[27] As a people of plenty with "bountiful harvests," Americans had an obligation to help "the starving people of heroic and suffering Ireland."[28] The committee argued that the American "government recognizes the claim upon its humanity to render national assistance and relief to the unfortunate sufferers."[29] Unfortunately, an odd coalition of southern Democrats and Republicans with constitutional scruples about foreign aid blocked the appropriation. Republican President Rutherford B. Hayes shared the constitutional reservations about foreign aid and refused to endorse the House proposal.[30]

However, as in 1847, pressure to do something for the Irish led to another proposal to send a warship to Ireland carrying privately donated relief supplies. Several members of the Senate and House introduced bills and resolutions to allow the Navy Department to loan a vessel for relief. Congressman William Ward, Republican from Chester, Pennsylvania, proposed on 9 February 1880, to authorize "the Secretary of the Navy to designate a vessel of the United States to carry ... contributions for the relief of the suffering people of Ireland."[31] Two Republicans, Samuel McMillan of Minnesota and John Logan of Illinois, sponsored a joint resolution containing the same language as Ward's proposal. The Senate Committee on Naval Affairs quickly considered the resolution. "Ardently" supported by the Irish-born Charles William Jones of Florida, a Democrat, who chaired the Committee on Naval Affairs, the joint resolution won the support of this committee. Members of the Senate passed the joint resolution on 18 February 1880.[32] Congressman Washington Whittorne, a Democrat from Tennessee and former Adjutant General in the Confederate Army, acting for the House Committee on Naval Affairs, suggested approving the joint resolution, and the House agreed. President Hayes signed the joint resolution on 25 February 1880. Like Polk in 1847, Hayes did not object to loaning a warship to carry privately donated foodstuffs to Ireland.[33] In contrast to 1847, the congressional joint resolution of 1880 appropriated the funds necessary to pay the expenses for a naval vessel to transport the relief aid and gave the Secretary of the Navy the option to charter a privately owned vessel if using a naval vessel appeared inappropriate. This proposal won support across the political spectrum as Democrats, Republicans and Greenbackers endorsed turning a ship of war into a messenger of peace, charity and humanitarianism.

Secretary of the Navy Richard Thompson decided to use a Navy vessel, sloop of war *Constellation*, with a full complement of regular Navy officers and sailors to undertake the mission. In 1847, civilians had commanded the warships *Jamestown* and *Macedonian* and volunteers had made up the crews. Commander Edward Potter, a career naval officer, commanded *Constellation* which was docked at the Brooklyn Navy Yard. Preparations were made to fit the warship for transporting the food. Thompson ordered the removal of all the guns on the grounds it was a "mission of peace and benevolence." As Thompson told Commander Potter, "your visit will enable the people of Ireland to realize that peace hath her victories no less renowned than war." Creating amicable relations between people was a far better use of warship than service in war.[34] Unfortunately, the government failed to reach out to private citizens or to local Irish relief committees for foodstuffs needed to fill *Constellation*. A Washington newspaper criticized the Navy Department for not doing so because, "in the absence of a cargo," the proposed relief ship appeared "only ornamental."[35] In 1847, at least 118 merchant ships and two warships had carried food to Ireland and Scotland. However, in 1879–80, Americans sent cash and bank drafts to help the Irish, with relatively little food being shipped.

Quickly realizing the problem, Republican Congressman Levi Morton, representing the Murray Hill district in New York City, acted. Morton offered to pay for 25 percent of the food shipped aboard *Constellation* if others would match his offer. In fact, Morton informed Whitelaw Reid, editor of the *New-York Tribune,* "I have been quite willing to charter and furnish the cargo of a ship, and thought seriously of filling the *Constellation* myself," but after consulting with friends "feared that would have an ostentatious look" and be resented by some of his congressional colleagues who lacked the financial resources to match Morton's generosity.[36] Instead, he worked through intermediaries, like Reid, to find other contributors. When no one came forward, he anonymously solicited contributors through the New York newspapers. For example, Morton wrote to Gordon Bennett, the mercurial editor of the *Herald,* that Secretary Thompson had informed him that no one had offered to supply the cargo for *Constellation.* "You are authorized to announce that a gentleman personally, known to you, who declines to have his name made public, offers to pay for one-quarter of the cargo of the *Constellation* if others will make up the balance."[37] Responding to Morton's offer, Gordon Bennett announced: "The *Herald* offers to bear the expense of another one-fourth of a full cargo for the *Constellation* on the same condition made by this gentleman—'if parties will make up the balance.'" Bennett expressed the hope for the creation of a movement "like that of 1847 when so many shiploads of provisions were sent from this country" to Ireland.[38]

Meanwhile, a third benefactor came forward, William Grace, a successful ship-owner and native of Cork, and soon to be mayor of New York City. While Bennett and Morton were Republicans, Grace was an independent Democrat. In 1879–80, as in 1847, support for the Irish came from across the political spectrum. Grace had already contributed to Daly's New York Irish Relief Committee. Grace planned to offer his ship, *W.R. Grace*, to the New York Committee "to carry a cargo of provisions." Congress, by sending the *Constellation*, had made it unnecessary although, "it would have been a matter of very great pride and pleasure to me to have had an opportunity of sending to Ireland a cargo of provisions in a vessel bearing my own name."[39] Instead, Grace pledged one-quarter of the cargo and offered to take charge of the loading of the provisions. He loaned his staff to supervise, and stevedores to load, the *Constellation*, and the services of his shipping clerks to expedite the classifying of donations.[40]

During March 1880, the finishing touches were put on the warship for its mission. All guns, except for two signal guns, were removed to make more room for foodstuffs. The crew built additional storage space, extra sheds on deck, to carry even more supplies. Meanwhile, Grace made it clear that his support for the enterprise was partially motivated by the example set by Gordon Bennett and the *New York Herald* Irish Relief Fund, "Animated by a desire to emulate in a small degree the ... generosity of your paper in having worked up so great a result for Irish Relief." [41] Grace, Morton and Bennett agreed that the major part of the cargo would consist of potatoes, cornmeal, flour and oatmeal. They each donated 825 barrels of potatoes, 256 barrels of corn meal, 200 barrels of flour and 50 barrels of oatmeal purchased in New York City.[42] Another local shipping company, Greenpoint Lighterage Company of Brooklyn, volunteered the lighters and barges to carry the cargo to the Brooklyn Navy Yard. The Longshoreman's Union, heavily Irish, offered its services to load and unload the lighters while the Lighterage Company contributed the assistance of some of its stevedores.[43] Individuals also volunteered. John J. Roberts, for example, became the head stevedore, giving his labor because his stevedore father had helped load a ship of food sent to Ireland by department store king A.J. Stewart to his hometown, Lisburn, in 1847. Under Roberts' leadership, the stevedores did so well in stowing the barrels that the vessel had room for an additional 300 barrels of foodstuffs.[44]

Individuals, businesses, communities and churches made up the remaining quarter of cargo aboard the *Constellation*. An unnamed Irish-American delivered the first cargo to reach the warship. He delivered three barrels with the legend "Potatoes for the Irish Sufferers," and at the bottom they were marked "for the County Cavan." For the officer on duty, "it was considered a singular fact that the first 'mite' of the cargo to be put on the great ship should be from an unknown source."[45] Women contributed, like Mrs. Kate Sheehan, who donated one barrel of flour and one barrel of potatoes. Mrs. Hannah McDonough sent one barrel of seed potatoes for planting the next season since there was a shortage for the upcoming season. Mrs. George W. De Cunha visited every storekeeper on Sixth Avenue soliciting donations and encouraged the *New York Herald* to promote the idea "that other ladies will do likewise with other avenues. I think we can fill the ship."[46] Edwin Murphy, President of the Irish Famine Club in Bellow's Falls, Vermont, sent 18 dozen cans of soup. Members of the Universalist Church in Canton, St. Lawrence County, New York, near the Canadian border, forwarded seven dozen cans of soup. Residents of Winchester, Virginia, donated 61 barrels of flour and 14 barrels of potatoes. In 1847, the people of Winchester had collected $3,300 to purchase corn and flour for the starving Irish. Workers in the woolen mills of Bennington, Vermont, purchased 10 barrels of flour. One man sent 10 barrels of potatoes to his brother in Ireland. In addition to food, thousands of destitute Irish boys and girls needed clothing. When Rev. George Hepworth, a New York City minister and member of the *Herald's* Distribution Committee in Ireland, sent word of the shortage of children's clothing, New Yorkers rushed to donate clothes. Mrs. Edward Connolly, for example, gathered 18 sets of girls' clothing. These contributions all suggest American public support for the Irish in 1880.[47]

"All hands began their preparations for their voyage of mercy" on 19 March when the officers and crew were piped aboard the *Constellation*. During the refitting, the crew remained on the nearby *Colorado*. They spent the next several days removing the guns, shells and ammunition. "Visitors from the City and groups of girls walked among the pyramids of cannon balls" on the dock as they made their way for tours of the famine ship.[48] After the removal of the implements of war, barrels of potatoes, flour and cornmeal took their places. Stevedores filled every available space with foodstuffs or clothes for children. A sunny and pleasant day dawned on 27 March as the *Constellation* prepared to depart. The crew consisted of 79 sailors and apprentices and 17 officers. Rain began to fall as a group of 50 naval officers, ladies and others gathered at the Brooklyn Navy Yard to bid goodbye. Senior officers from *Constellation, Colorado* and *Tallapoosa* exchanged handshakes just prior to the *Constellation* leaving the wharf at 9:00 a.m. As the ship cast off, hundreds of sailors aboard *Colorado* and *Tallapoosa* rushed up the rigging of their vessels to cheer and shout for the crew. The Marine band on the *Colorado* played "Hail, Columbia," "Wearing of the Green," "St. Patrick's Day in the Morning," and other tunes for the departing ship. Steamboats on the East River "began to whistle and ring their bells, Ladies on the ferryboats waved their little handkerchiefs, men slashed at the air with their hats," and people in Brooklyn and New York City waved.[49] While the sailors and residents cheered, one impediment stood in the ship's way—the newly constructed Brooklyn Bridge. The bridge was not high enough for the ship to pass under so the crew of the *Constellation* "had to lower her topgallant mast, which was a troublesome and annoying task."[50] Once beyond the bridge, more ships whistled in honor of the *Constellation* or lowered and raised their colors. Similarly, the flag at Governor's Island was run up and down with the warship returning the salute. As a reporter for the *Herald* noted: "It is safe to say that such an exhibition of enthusiasm has not been witnessed around New York since the end of the war."[51]

When she left the Brooklyn Navy Yard, the *Constellation's* cargo included 1,346 barrels of potatoes, 675 barrels of flour, 1,144 barrels of cornmeal, 150 barrels of oatmeal, 59 cases of canned soup, some miscellaneous provisions, and about 300 suits of children's clothes.[52] Poor wind conditions forced the vessel to anchor off Sandy Hook for two days before heading out across the Atlantic on 30 March 1880. Midshipman Alfred L. Hall kept a journal of the trip and recorded frequent rain, clouds, squalls and strong gales en route.[53] Bad weather failed to deter the ship and the *Constellation* reached Queenstown near Cork on 20 April. In 1847, the cargoes sent on *Jamestown* and *Macedonian* had been distributed by Quakers in Cork and Dublin, but in 1880, the committee created by Gordon Bennett gladly accepted responsibility. President Hayes allowed them a free hand in distributing the privately raised provisions. Secretary Thompson instructed Commander Potter to deliver the cargo of provisions to the *New-York Herald* Irish Relief Fund in Queenstown, near Cork, for "disposition at their discretion."[54]

As soon as the *Constellation* arrived in Ireland, Potter contacted the *Herald's* Irish Relief Fund representatives in Dublin. Rev. Hepworth traveled to Queenstown to meet with Potter and arrange the distribution of the relief. Hepworth also met with other members of the *Herald* committee and Catholic Archbishop McCabe to discuss the issue. The Duchess of Marlborough suggested having Alfred, Duke of Edinburgh, facilitate the distribution of the cargo. The Duke agreed to send his fleet of gunboats to Queenstown to expedite the unloading and distribution of the cargo after Potter explained that the bad weather conditions encountered at sea would require several days to make repairs. Ships in the relief fleet reached Queenstown on 23 April and unloading of the cargo began the next day. Sailors transferred the provisions to the gunboats, including *Lively, Valorous, Amelia, Goshawk, Hawk, Orwell* and *Imogene.* Provisions from America went to Donegal, Galway, Mayo, Sligo and islands off the coast. Tenants and laborers in the west of Ireland, especially those on the islands, appeared most in need of America's bounty because they had limited supplies of food. Also, 150 barrels went to the 1847 poster child for the Great Hunger—Skibbereen in west Cork. By 30 April, the British gunboats had completed their task of transferring the American provisions from the *Constellation* to the needy Irish communities.[55]

Representatives of the British government, Irish political leaders and the Irish public repeatedly thanked the officers of the *Constellation,* the American people, and the United States generally for their generosity. Even before the ship had docked, the people of Cork gathered on the heights overlooking the harbor, cheering repeatedly the arrival of the American warship. The mayors of Cork and Dublin expressed their gratitude for the arrival of the provisions. Mayor Gray of Dublin thanked the United States for "coming to the assistance of the starving peasantry of Ireland." He and several other dignitaries associated with the Mansion House Relief Committee, were present to welcome the *Constellation*.[56] A representation of the people of Queenstown thanked Americans for their repeated benevolence: "Thirty-three years ago ... we had a similar proof of the generosity of your nation. We have not forgotten it ... [this] sympathy for us shall bind a thousand-fold more firmly the bonds."[57] The Board of Guardians of the Cork Union expressed "their gratitude for the generous supply sent by the American nation for the relief of the distress in Ireland."[58] Similarly, the people of the city and county of Cork stated their gratitude for "this mission of noble charity, we greet you warmly, and welcome you, and proffer you the gratitude ... of a poor, downtrodden, and liberty-loving people."[59]

Potter and the American people were repeatedly thanked for the gift of food for the starving Irish. Edward Brooks, the American Consul in Cork, wrote to John Hay, the Assistant Secretary of State, that the arrival of "a Relief Ship has been the occasion of many demonstrations by the Irish people and the official and unofficial classes ... of respect to the Government and people of the United States." The Americans received invitations to balls, banquets, tennis parties, and social entertainments "quite too numerous to mention."[60] As an example, Commander Potter and his officers attended a banquet in Cork on 29 April with the letters "U.S." displayed in the center of the hall. Guests repeatedly cheered the officers and toasted President Hayes, the donors, and crew of the *Constellation*.[61] A few days later, the Americans traveled to Dublin to attend a ball in honor of American benevolence. Fifteen hundred people attended. Representing the people of Dublin, Mayor Gray offered Commander Potter the freedom of the city in a ceremony on the next day. Gray informed Potter that "through you" the people of Dublin wanted to acknowledge "the nation that you represent for its munificent generosity to this country in its hour of need." The Irish remembered, "with feelings of deepest gratitude the way in which the people of the United States helped the starving people of this country in 1847."[62] During the many tributes, Potter steered clear of Irish politics. However, many Irish interpreted the Irish relief movement in the United States as an American acknowledgment of British exploitation of the Irish and American recognition of British misrule. In contrast, Irish spokesmen in speeches and toasts criticized British rule in Ireland. Potter diplomatically refrained from expressing an opinion that would anger either the Irish people or the British government.[63]

After several days of tributes, Commander Potter set sail to the United States and the *Constellation* had an uneventful voyage home. Potter reported to Secretary Thompson on the mission to Ireland. He thanked the Secretary of the Navy for giving him the opportunity to lead a mission of mercy and "to witness the ... heartfelt gratitude of the Irish people to the United States government for assistance; certainly, the attentions to us ... almost overpowering in their demonstration."[64] In turn, Thompson reported to the Senate and Vice-President William A. Wheeler that the public authorities and people of Ireland "were impressed ... that the Government of the United States had fitted out a national vessel upon this mission of benevolence" and had expressed their gratitude. Thompson noted that the Navy had borne the costs of the voyage and that Potter had not drawn on any of the money appropriated by Congress.[65] The report included copies of letters sent by the British government thanking the American government for aiding the Irish poor. In mid-May, Sir Edward Thornton, British Ambassador to the United States, on orders from Earl Granville, British Secretary for Foreign Affairs, informed the Secretary of State, William Evarts, that Queen Victoria and the British government wanted to thank the United States for its generosity in sending the *Constellation*, "loaded with provisions which were so much needed for the relief of the distressed subjects of Her Majesty in Ireland," which were of "substantial aid to them in their affliction."[66]

In the 19th century, Americans emerged as the leaders in international philanthropy. On a number of occasions, Americans had aided the Irish. According to journalist James Redpath, a special correspondent for the *New-York Tribune,* who reported on the Forgotten Famine in Ireland, by August 1880, Americans had sent $5 million to the Irish. Redpath listed 10 different channels used for the purpose.[67] The generosity came from individuals or through temporary public committees. The American government refused to directly help the starving, both in 1847 and 1880, as officials at the national and state levels viewed foreign aid an unconstitutional expenditure of public funds. Presidential and congressional opposition vanished, however, when citizens and members of Congress proposed the use of American warships to carry privately donated food and clothing. In 1847, the *Jamestown* and *Macedonian* sailed on their errand of mercy, followed by *Constellation* in 1880. Ireland was not the only recipient of this benevolence. In 1871, the United States sent the new sloop of war, the *Worcester*, with a cargo of privately donated food, to France during the Franco-Prussian War. During the famine in Russia in 1891–92, the *Constellation* carried a cargo of grain to Russia. Americans throughout the 19th century provided voluntary food, clothing, and money to people abroad who were suffering from famine or other disasters, whether in New Brunswick, Crete, Ireland or Russia.[68]

Americans became the most generous donors to foreign tragedies, whether from Little Beckie Harvey of New York City who sold her toys to donate $30 to Irish relief in 1847, or $4 in 1880 from "a little North Carolina girl who on her deathbed expressed great sorrow for the poor sufferers in Ireland for want of food."[69] What historians Henry Lee and H.A. Forbes wrote about American aid in 1847 also applies to American actions in 1863 and 1880: "This spontaneous and voluntary response comprised ... an act of unparalleled benevolence from one people to another."[70] Historian Rob Goodbody observed that "donations from the United States were so great as to virtually overshadow all other sources."[71] Writing about 1847, historian Christine Kinealy concluded that "a wave had swept across America that prompted people, rich and poor, from all religious persuasions, often with no direct connections to Ireland, to raise money to take food and clothes to Ireland."[72] The same spirit was repeated in 1862–63 and 1879–80. Kinealy noted that in 1863 American donations made the United States "the centre of these activities," and in 1880 "American support was prompt and generous."[73] Contemporary observers made the same points about the importance of American assistance and the gratitude of the Irish people. In March 1847, Jonathan Pim, one of the leaders of Quaker relief in Ireland, described American aid as "one of the most remarkable manifestations of national sympathy on record."[74] The Mansion House Committee in 1880 considered the outpouring of kindness and gratefulness directed at the officers of the *Constellation* as "tokens of the profound gratitude with which all ranks and classes of the Irish people were inspired by the unexampled generosity of America."[75] In 1847, the sending of the *Jamestown* and *Macedonian* and, in 1880, the voyage of the *Constellation*, turned warships into messengers of peace and benevolence from the United States. Their mission was part of a larger campaign of international voluntary philanthropy by America to Ireland. In each case, the people of New York City played a crucial role in the donation of funds and transportation of food and clothing to Ireland.

The author gratefully acknowledges the partial financial assistance of the Sage Colleges for the award of the Harder-McClellan Fellowship for 2015–17.

NOTES

1. Gerard Moran is the leading expert on the Little, Near or Forgotten Famine. See Gerard Moran, "'Near famine:' The Roman Catholic Church and the subsistence crisis of 1879–82," *Studia Hibernica* 32 (2002/2003), pp 155–77; Gerard Moran, "Near famine: The crisis in the west of Ireland, 1879–82," *Irish Studies Review* 5:18 (Spring 1997), pp 14–21; citation from Timothy O'Neill, "Minor famines and relief in the County of Galway, 1815–1925," in Gerard Moran (ed.), *Galway: History and Society* (Dublin: Geography Publications, 1996), p. 465. The full article is chapter 14. Also, see James Green, "American Catholics and the Irish Land League," *Catholic Historical Review* 35:1 (April 1949), 19–42.
2. Moran, "Crisis in the west of Ireland," p. 15.
3. Dublin Mansion House, *The Irish Crisis of 1879–80: proceedings of the Dublin House Relief Committee, 1880* (Dublin: Browne and Nolan, 1881), p. 37.
4. Ibid, p. 5.
5. Ibid, p. 15.
6. Norman Palmer, *The Irish Land League Crisis* (New Haven: Yale University Press, 1940), pp 83–105.
7. W.H. Martin, Chairman, and Paul Leonard, Secretary, Fenian Brotherhood, to Charles Daly, 15 Dec. 1879, Dec. 1879 folder, Box 5, Charles Daly Papers, Manuscripts and Archives Division, New York Public Library (NYPL).
8. "Address of the Irish Relief Committee to the People of the United States, 1880," 24 Jan. 1880, Relief Committee, Ch 1/10/G/522, New York; Mansion House Fund for Relief of the Distress in Ireland, 1880, Dublin City Archives (DCA).
9. Charles Trevelyan, *The Irish Crisis* (London: Brown, Green and Longmans, 1848), pp 22–23.
10. HR 140, 46th Congress, Center for Legislative Archives, National Archives Washington, D.C. holds the handwritten copy of the resolution. See *Congressional Records, 46th Congress, 2nd Sess., 1879, X Pt. 1,* 41, 43. Also, see: Entries for 9 Dec., Mr. Frost, HR 140 #73, 9 Dec., Mr. Gillette, HR 141, # 74, Docket Volume, 14 April 1879 to 28 Feb. 1881, Foreign Affairs, 46th Congress, Records of the House of Representatives, Record Group 233, Center for Legislative Archives, National Archives (NA).
11. Ibid., HR 141, 46th Congress. Gillette was a member of a third political party that sprang up in the Middle West, the Greenback Party, which represented farming interests and their desire for currency reform to help farmers in debt. This suggested that support for the Irish in 1879–80 spanned the American political spectrum.
12. Ibid., HR 177, 46th Congress, for a handwritten copy of the resolution. See *Congressional Record, 46th Congress, 2nd Sess. X, Pt 1,* p. 418.
13. HR 193, 46th Congress, Center for Legislative Archives, NA. This is the original handwritten draft of the joint resolution. Also, see *Congressional Record, 46th Congress, 2nd Sess. X, Pt 1,* p. 649.
14. Memorial of the Saint Paul Chamber of Commerce, on behalf of an appropriation for the people of Ireland, 9 February 1880, Referred to the Committee on Foreign Affairs, 16 Feb. 1880, in HR46A-H9 2; Petitions and Memorials Referred to the House Committee on Foreign Affairs, 46th Congress, Center for Legislative Archives, NA.

15. *Washington National Republican,* 21 Jan. 1880; *Washington Evening Star,* 21 Jan.1880; *Washington Post,* 21 Jan. 1880.
16. "The Irish Famine," Richard Gilmour, Bishop of Cleveland, *Catholic Universe,* 6 Nov. 1879, Courtesy of the Archives of the Diocese of Cleveland.
17. William McCloskey to Rev. McCabe, 12 Jan. 1880, 346/1/II/1, Archbishop Edward McCabe Papers, Dublin Diocesan Archives.
18. *Irish-Canadian,* 17 Dec. 1879.
19. *New York Herald,* 2 Feb. 1880; Charleston *News,* 19, 20, 21, 28 Jan. 1880. See the letter of L. Gillooly, Bishop of Elphin, Sligo, 14 Feb. 1880 to Mayor Courtenay in the *News,* 28 Feb. 1880 expressing his gratitude for the contributions from Charleston, South Carolina.
20. Albany *Argus,* 22 Jan. 1880. See the letter from Mayor Nolan to Bishop Doane, 20 Jan. 1880 and the response of Bishop William Croswell Doane of the same date. Nolan was the first Irish-Catholic mayor of Albany. Doane's father, an Episcopal Bishop in New Jersey, was instrumental in organizing Irish relief in the Garden State during the Great Hunger in 1847. William Croswell Doane was the first Episcopal Bishop of Albany. The Catholic Bishop of Albany, Frances McNierney, in his reply of 21 Jan. 1880, indicated he would call on all his parishioners to contribute.
21. Trenton *State Gazette,* 31 Jan. 1880.
22. Milwaukee Irish Relief Committee to E. Dwyer Gray, Lord Mayor of Dublin, 14 Feb. 1880, 1/11/26, Mansion House Relief Fund, DCA.
23. New York *Freeman's Journal,* 10 April 1880.
24. *Congressional Record, 46th Cong., 2nd Sess.,* pp 393–4, 664–5.
25. *New York Herald,* 6 March 1880.
26. See Christine Kinealy, *Charity and the Great Hunger. The Kindness of Strangers* (London: Bloomsbury, 2013), chapter 10, which explores American aid to Ireland.
27. *Congressional Record, 46th Congress., 2nd Sess.*, pp 1571–72; U.S. Congress, "Relief for the Irish People," Report of the Committee on Foreign Affairs, #465, House of Representatives, 46th Congress, 2nd Sess. (10 March 1880).
28. Ibid. For a summary of American aid to Ireland in 1879–80, see Merle Curti, *American Philanthropy Abroad: A History* (New Brunswick, N.J.: Rutgers University Press, 1963), pp 82–98.
29. Original draft of the Joint Resolution, HR 238, 46th Congress, NA.
30. Curti, *American Philanthropy*, p. 95.
31. Original draft of Ward's, H.R. 4298, 46th Congress, NA. See also, *Congressional Record,* 46th Congress, 2nd Sess., 763 (9 Feb. 1880).
32. *Congressional Record,* 46th Congress, 2nd Session, 938, 963; Citation from Curti, *American Philanthropy,* p. 95.
33. Ibid., 1046, 1065, 1076, 1175; Original Draft of S.R.80 Joint Resolution, Senate Bills and Resolutions (Approved Resolution, 18 Feb. 1880), NA. For the Approved House Resolution, *Congressional Record,* 46th Congress, 2nd Sess., Res. 16, 25 Feb. 1880.
34. R.W. Thompson to Commander Edward E. Potter, 25 March 1880 in the *Washington Post,* 26 March 1880. The *Constellation* is currently a floating museum in Baltimore Harbor. For

the original letter, R.W. Thompson, Secretary of the Navy, to Commander E.E. Potter, 24 March 1880, Letter Copybook, pp 263–64, Thompson Manuscripts, Lilly Library, Indiana University (IU).

35. *Washington Evening Star*, 8 March 1880. There are two histories of the *Constellation*. Geoffrey Footner, *U.S.S. Constellation* (Annapolis, Maryland: Naval Institute Press, 2003), contains a one sentence reference to the trip to Ireland and an 1880 drawing from *Frank Leslie's Illustrated Newspaper*, 29 May 1880, pp 259–60. The drawing is of USS *Constellation*, Cork Harbour, Ireland, 1880. Also, Stephen Bockmiller and Lawrence Bopp, USS *Constellation: An Illustrated History* (Charleston, S.C.: Arcadia Publishing, 2002) contains a drawing of the *Constellation* loading in New York and several photos of the ship and crew in Cork, pp 58–60.
36. Levi Morton to Whitelaw Reid, 17 March 1880, Whitelaw Reid Papers. Morton served in Congress from 1879–81, as Minister to France from 1881–5, Vice-President from 1889–93, and Governor of New York, 1895–96.
37. Levi Morton to the Editor of the *Herald*, 9 March 1880. Published in *Herald*, 10 March 1880. "Cargo for the Famine Ship," p. 1, Political Papers, Box 8, Levi Morton Papers, NYPL. The major biographer of Morton only briefly mentions his role in famine relief. Robert McElroy. *Levi Parsons Morton: Banker, Diplomat and Statesman* (New York: G.P. Putnam's Sons, 1930), p. 92.
38. *Herald*, editorial, 10 March 1880. See, "Cargo for the Famine Ship," page 2, Political Papers, Box 8.
39. William Grace to Edmund O'Brien, 27 Feb. 1880. William Grace Papers, Columbia University (CU).
40. William Grace to Editor, *Herald*, 16 March 1880. William Grace Papers, CU. There are about 25 letters written by Grace about supplying and loading the *Constellation*. There is a brief mention of Grace's role in 1880 in Marquis James, *Merchant Adventurer: The Story of W.R. Grace* (Wilmington, Delaware: Scholarly Books, 1993), pp 140–1.
41. Ibid.
42. "Relief ship *Constellation*," p. 54, Political Papers, Box 8, Levi Morton Papers, NYPL. *Herald*, 27 March 1880. This file contains a mimeographed copy of articles that appeared in *Herald*, 10 March 1880–21 June 1880.
43. Ibid, 36, *Herald*, 23 March 1880.
44. Ibid, 43, *Herald*, 24 March 1880.
45. Ibid, 24, *Herald*, 19 March 1880.
46. Mrs. George De Cunha to the Editor of the *Herald*, 10 March 1880, "Cargo for the Famine Ship," Political Papers, Box 8, Levi Morton Papers, NYPL. See: William Grace to G.H. Nicholas, *Herald*, 27 March 1880, William Grace Papers (CU) for a discussion of contributions by De Cunha.
47. Ibid, "Various Donations," pp 8–10; "Statement of Shipment by W.R. Grace and Consigned to the *New York Herald* Irish Relief Fund Committee, Dublin." In "Relief Ship *Constellation*," pp 53–7, *Herald*, 27 March 1880, Political Papers, Box 8, Levi Morton Papers, NYPL.

48. *Herald,* 19 March 1880.
49. "Relief Ship Constellation," p. 59, *Herald,* 27–8 March 1880; Political Papers, Box 8, Levi Morton Papers, NYPL.
50. Ibid, p. 52.
51. Ibid, p. 60. Also, see *New-York Tribune,* 28 March 1880.
52. *Tribune,* 28 March 1880.
53. See, for example, the entries for 16 March–8 April 1880, Journal of Midshipman Alfred L. Hall, Entry 608, vol. 137. RG 45 Naval Records Collection, NA.
54. Secretary Thompson to Commander Potter, 24–25 March 1880, Letter Copybook, Thompson Manuscripts, Lilly Library, IU. Also, see *New York Times,* 26 March 1880.
55. For details of the unloading of the cargo and the role of the Duke of Edinburgh's (Queen Victoria's second son) relief fleet: "Relief Ship *Constellation*, pp 62–76, 81–2, 93–4, *Herald,* 9, 16, 21–3, 25, 28, 30, May and 21 June 1880, Political Papers, Box 8, Levi Morton Papers, NYPL; *New York Times*, 26 Apr. 1880; Edward Potter, Commander, to R.W. Thompson, Secretary of the Navy, 20, 28, April, 1 May 1880 in R.W. Thompson, Secretary of the Navy to William Wheeler, Vice-President of the United States, "Letter of the Secretary of the Navy Transmitting the Report of the Commander of the Relief Ship *Constellation,* 14 June 1880," 46th Congress, 2nd Sess., Senate, Ex Doc. No. 215, pp 1–4. The total report is seven pages. Timothy Collins," HMS *Valorous:* Her Contribution to Galway Maritime History," *Journal of the Galway Archaeological and Historical Society* 49 (1997), 130–6. The complete article is pp 122–42.
56. *Herald,* 22 April 1880.
57. Stephen Ashlin, Admiral, Chairman, et al, Committee of Presentation, to Commander Potter, 25 April 1880, "Letter...Relief ship *Constellation*," p. 5.
58. Ibid., Nicholas Mahoney, Chairman of the Board of Guardians to Commander Potter, 22 April 1880, p. 4.
59. Ibid., "From the People of the County and City of Cork to Commander Potter, officers, and crew of *Constellation*," undated, p. 5.
60. Edward Brooks to John Hay, 11 May 1880, Despatches of the United States Consuls in Cork, 1800–1906, 10 Jan. 1870 to 22 Oct. 1880, Department of State, NA Brooks also reported a minor annoyance while the Americans were in Ireland. A local customs officer demanded the right to search the vessel for contraband and to charge customs duties. Brooks and Potter complained to British civilian and naval officials who quickly apologized and reprimanded the officer.
61. *Herald,* 4 May 1880. Also, 5 May 1880.
62. Ibid., 6 May 1880.
63. Brooks to Hay, 11 May 1880, Despatches, NA.
64. Edward Potter to R.W. Thompson, 12 June 1880, Letter from the Secretary of the Navy, p. 7.
65. Ibid., R.W. Thompson, Secretary of the Navy to William Wheeler, Vice-President of the U.S., 14 June 1880, p. 1.
66. Ibid., Sir Edward Thornton to William Evarts, 14 May 1880; Ibid., William Evarts to Richard Thompson, Secretary of the Navy, 25 May 1880. Handwritten copies of both

letters can be found in "Letters Received by the Secretary of the Navy from the President and Executive Departments," 1837–86, vols 112–3, 1 Oct. 1879, 30 June 1880, 166, NA. These documents contain a second set of correspondence from Brooks about the protests by Brooks and Potter over the conduct of the customs officer.

67. *Tribune*, 15 Aug. 1880.
68. Curti, *American Philanthropy*, documents multiple cases of American assistance.
69. Alexander Sprunt, Treasurer, Wilmington Irish Relief Committee, to E. Gray, Chairman of the Mansion House Committee for the Relief of Irish Sufferers, 2 June 1880, 1/11/52, Mansion House Relief Fund, DCA. Sprunt, a cotton merchant, was one of the richest men in Wilmington in 1880.
70. Henry Forbes and Henry Lee, *Massachusetts Help, to Ireland during the Great Famine* (Milton, MA: Captain Forbes House, 1967), p. xxi.
71. Rob Goodbody, *Suitable Channel: Quaker Relief in the Great Famine* (Bray, Ireland: Pale Publishing, 1995), p. 82.
72. Kinealy, *Charity and the Great Hunger,* p. 255.
73. Ibid, pp 289–290.
74. Cited in Helen Hatton, *Largest Amount of Good: Quaker Relief in Ireland, 1654–1921* (McGill-Queen's University Press, 1993), p. 126.
75. *The Irish Crisis of 1879–80*, p. 23.

CHAPTER TWELVE

BOSTON AND THE FORGOTTEN FAMINE OF 1879–1882

Catherine B. Shannon

This chapter outlines the enthusiastic moral and financial support that Irish-American residents of New England provided to the west of Ireland between 1879 and 1882, when the area was threatened with a repetition of the horrors of starvation, eviction and mass emigration suffered during the Great Famine. Crop failure in 1877 and 1879, unrelenting bad weather, increasing foreign agricultural competition, and diminishing employment opportunities for the impoverished cottiers, left one million without sufficient resources for rent, food or clothing. Many in Ireland and in Irish America feared a complete social collapse similar to the 1840s. Fortunately, a combination of private relief efforts within Ireland and from abroad, in conjunction with the establishment of the Irish National Land League in October 1879, prevented a repeat of the mortality experienced 30 years earlier. The unprecedented aid from Boston sent on the U.S.S. *Jamestown* in 1847 served as a powerful precedent, and Boston responded positively to this new humanitarian crisis with relief donations sent by individuals, churches, and *ad hoc* fund-raising committees formed by leading Irish Americans. John Boyle O'Reilly, Patrick A. Collins, Patrick J. Flatley and Hugh O'Brien played important roles in launching early relief efforts and they subsequently helped Charles Stewart Parnell secure $300,000 (or £60,000) for famine relief during his 1880 American tour.[1] The establishment of a Land League in America in May 1880 gave Parnell and his lieutenants the resources to fight evictions.

The Land League of America played a vital role in convincing the American public that the flaws of the Irish land system, such as landlord absenteeism, rack-rents, and insecurity of tenure, demanded radical reform that would transform the "tillers of the soil into owners of the soil." Approximately 80 percent of the League's funding came from America, with Boston and the New England Irish among the most generous donors. The visits of Parnell, Michael Davitt, John Dillon, T. P. O'Connor, Rev. Eugene Sheehy and Timothy Healy to New England sparked a sense of Irish consciousness and personal involvement that created a "Greater Ireland" in places of Irish settlement that intensified the pressure on the British government.[2] As Prime Minister William Gladstone admitted in 1890, the Land Act of 1881, which provided statutory acknowledgement of the concept of dual ownership of tenant and landlord, would never have happened without the transatlantic campaign. In addition to providing tenants with the Three Fs (fixity of tenure, fair rents and free sale of their interest), this legislation established a land court to arbitrate rents, which eventually secured reductions of £1.2 million, or about 21 percent for approximately 275, 525 tenants.[3]

Although tenant farmers in Leinster and Munster had experienced a considerable improvement in their economic status between the mid-1850s and 1870s, residents of Connacht, most especially those in Galway, Mayo, Sligo and western Roscommon, experienced little improvement and remained vulnerable when the crops failed as in the late 1870s. The value of Irish agricultural output declined from £43.7 million in 1876 to £35.4 million in 1879, which hurt strong farmers and their laborers. The return of potato blight in 1877 and 1879 caused a sharp decline in potatoes harvested from 4.2 million tons, valued at £14.7 million in 1876 to 1.1 million tons, valued at £6.7 million in 1879. In Connacht, the potato harvest in 1879 was 75 percent below that of 1876.[4] Heavy rains between March and June not only diminished the potato yield, but also reduced the amount of turf harvested for the approaching winter. These conditions were potentially disastrous for large swaths of Galway, Mayo and Sligo, where residents lived on tiny holdings of inferior soil quality and still depended on potatoes as their major food source. Unlike Munster and Leinster, early marriage and large families, along with archaic agricultural methods continued to impoverish the cottiers of this area.[5] The magnitude of the crisis was such that approximately one million out of a population of two and a half million, west of the River Shannon, needed assistance by 1879.[6] As in the 1840s, absenteeism led to under-investment in land as well as indifference among the owners regarding the increasing perils facing their tenants. In County Mayo alone, the five major absentee landowners, Lords Sligo, Dillon, Lucan, Palmer and Arran, drew £100,000 annually in rents. This equaled the amount spent on relief in the county between 1879 and 1881.[7] For decades, wages earned as seasonal agricultural laborers in England and Scotland had been the only cash income available. In Mayo, 17 percent of adult males crossed the Irish Sea annually to keep their families afloat.[8] By 1879, demand for Irish migrant workers had declined sharply. Mayo was most severely affected, experiencing a fall of £100,000 in income earned.[9] Additionally, the loss of supplementary income from the collapsing kelp industry dealt a blow to coastal families, especially in Connemara where income declined from about £10,000 to £2,000 in the late 1870s.[10] The threat of eviction also increased during these deteriorating economic conditions. An estimated 87 percent of Connacht cottiers were tenants at will and many owed two years rent.[11]

As early as May 1879, clergy in counties Galway and Mayo were vocal in warning of an approaching catastrophe unless rent reductions, public works programs and private charity were secured. Appeals increased after July with confirmation of the diseased and depleted state of the potato crop. Always suspicious of Irish exaggeration, the British government, the press and many Irish landlords dismissed these initial warnings.[12] The Local Government Board did not order a comprehensive survey of Irish harvest conditions until 5 September, a task not completed until late October, after the supply of good potatoes in Connacht had been consumed. Rev. Peter J. Nolan of Killala warned, "A disaster unparalleled for thirty years in now at hand," and a few weeks later, Canon James Magee of Castlebar proclaimed that the people must be rescued from "the jaws of famine, the gaunt spectre of which ... was at their doors."[13] In the final of his five reports for the *Freeman's Journal* on the deteriorating situation in Connacht, journalist William O'Brien declared, "I now deliberately raise the cry of famine in Connemara," and called for prompt state action as "a question of life or death."[14] The Catholic Church hierarchy agreed. An episcopal delegation, led by Archbishop McCabe of Dublin, met with the Lord Lieutenant, the Duke of Marlborough, to urge the government to save the people by introducing public works.[15] Between October 1879 and January 1880, 291 similar memorials were sent to the Viceroy.[16] These pleas and the reports of local government inspectors fell on deaf ears, as Dublin Castle refused to provide additional relief or extend the current powers of the poor law unions.

The only positive response came from the Viceroy's wife, the Duchess of Marlborough, who was so moved by reports of widespread hunger that in mid-December she set up her own private charity. Given her roots in County Down and her earlier efforts to promote Irish-made textiles and crafts, the Duchess was more sympathetic to these pleas than her husband or her son, Randolph, who advised against establishing her charity lest it justified the growing Land League agitation in Connacht. Nonetheless, he eventually served on the Duchess's charity fund board, which eventually raised £135,000, mostly from England. Meanwhile, Parnell quipped that the Tory government was "fighting the famine or perhaps the Land League from behind the Duchess's petticoats."[17] Dismissing the Duchess's initiative as an insult, the Boston *Pilot* commented, "The English relief effort for Ireland is the charity of the thief, who gives his victim enough to buy his breakfast from the money he stole from him the previous day."[18] Nonetheless, the Duchess's initiative in providing food and seed potatoes to the most impoverished areas of the west during the spring of 1880, certainly saved lives during the crisis.

On 2 January 1880, two weeks after the Marlborough Fund was established, the newly elected Lord Mayor of Dublin, Edmund Dwyer Gray, MP, moved by increasing reports of near starvation in the west and the political need not to allow the Duchess's fund to dominate private relief efforts, set up the Mansion House Relief Committee. Contributions arrived from all parts of the globe, eventually totaling £181,350, with half coming from the Irish diaspora of Australia, New Zealand and Tasmania. American donations amounted to £37,000, which included £537 from Springfield, Pittsfield and Fitchburg, Massachusetts.[19] Over the next six months, 840 local committees, composed of 9,707 Catholic and Protestant clerical and lay persons, distributed food, primarily Indian corn and oats, to 500,000 people, mostly residents of Donegal, Galway and Mayo. American involvement in sending relief aid and providing moral and financial support to the newly established Irish Land League was also crucial in preventing mortality on the scale of the 1840s. Private relief was particularly important given the inadequate and tardy response by the government and landowners. In January 1880, £5 million had been made available to encourage landowners to apply for Treasury loans for relief works on their estates, but it met with little success with less than 20 percent of the available money being spent.[20] In March, legislation was introduced allowing poor law unions to apply for government loans to purchase seed and initiate public works. In contrast, private charity was direct and responsive to local needs. Aid from the Mansion House Committee's fund, the leader in securing contributions, reached a broader geographical area over a longer period than either the Marlborough Fund or the government.[21] The famed physician, Dr. George Sigerson, travelled to the west in mid-summer 1881, and concluded: "There is no question that the assistance granted by the relief committees has availed to save thousands of human lives."[22]

If the government was slow to acknowledge the evolving crisis in 1879, this was not the case in Boston where news of the dire situation in Ireland came via political and family links. Additionally, the transatlantic cable, laid in 1866, guaranteed that news of Irish developments appeared in the American press quickly, giving readers a sense of the urgency of the unfolding events.[23] The *Boston Globe* devoted considerable coverage to Ireland, while detailed reports were available in Boston's weekly *Pilot* and the New York-based *Irish World.* These weekly newspapers, with a combined circulation of approximately 120,000, helped to make Bostonians and the region's Irish Americans attentive to the distress in 1879 and the necessity of American relief.[24] Irish-American readers, therefore, had detailed information about the deteriorating conditions at home, which energized the American canvas for relief funds. These papers also solicited support for the Land League campaign. As early as June 1879, the *Pilot* reported resolutions from farmers clubs in Cork, Louth and Waterford demanding rent reductions to counter the impact of the agricultural depression. Rent reductions granted by English and Scottish landlords were noted as was a rent abatement of about $40,000, granted by the Earl of Westmeath, as an example to be followed by his peers. Without such reductions, increased emigration would follow.[25]

In July and August, the *Pilot* published reports of meetings and resolutions of Irish clergy in Dungarvan, Galway, Killaloe, Sligo, Tralee and Tuam, predicting disaster unless rents were reduced and relief measures initiated.[26] On 26 July 1879, it published an alarming article entitled "Dark Clouds in Ireland" by an unnamed correspondent. It summarized all the factors that threatened a repeat of 1847, condemning landlords who refused abatements but were demanding "their pound of flesh," as well as the Mayo landlords who had already carried out 800 evictions. Four weeks later, Patrick Ford's *Irish World* declared that Ireland was in a state of famine and promised that Irish America would do everything in its power to prevent a repeat of the 1840s.[27] Other factors explain Boston's and New England's quick response to cries of Irish distress in 1879. First, there was a significant Fenian presence in the area and a desire to move beyond what Michael Davitt had pejoratively decried as a "saloon conspiracy" approach by Irish American republicans.[28] John Boyle O'Reilly, one of the principal planners of the Catalpa rescue in 1876, and now influential editor of the Boston *Pilot*, had been involved in shaping the final terms of the "New Departure" in November 1878 when he met with Michael Davitt and John Devoy during Davitt's first American tour.[29] This plan was designed to unite physical force and constitutional nationalists in a transatlantic alliance to destroy Irish landlordism and eventually secure Irish self-government. Second, there were approximately 370,000 Irish born in New England, with Massachusetts having 226,000, and the greater Boston area having 155,885, divided between Boston and Cambridge.[30] These Irish-born men and women, and their first generation children, had bitter and haunting memories of death, disease and the traumatic flight from Ireland during the Great Famine, while more recent immigrants were aware of the deteriorating conditions at home in the late 1870s.[31] Third, Davitt kept in close contact with O'Reilly after leaving America and acted as the *Pilot's* Irish correspondent. His dispatches kept O'Reilly and *Pilot* readers informed about the growing misery in the west of Ireland, as well as of his efforts to organize the tenant farmers of Mayo to secure rent reductions and major land reforms.[32]

On 10 October 1879, Davitt wrote to O'Reilly urging him to arouse "the wealthy Irish Americans to a generous appreciation of what this national movement demands at their hands, if they care anything at all for Ireland."[33] Davitt's plea for Irish American support in Boston was answered within a month. On 6 October, two weeks prior to the formation of the Irish National Land League in Dublin, O'Reilly and his close associates organized a meeting of Boston Irish at historic Faneuil Hall to consider what to do about the unjust and oppressive land system, which they contended brought only poverty and despair to Ireland's tenant farmers. Patrick A. Collins, who had emigrated as a small boy during *An Gorta Mór*, gave a fiery speech condemning Irish landlordism and announcing Irish-American solidarity: "the heart of Irish America is throbbing with sympathy for the oppression of the Irish tenants and her purse is open to them." After referring to American aid in 1847, Collins proclaimed:

> America will not permit the Irish tenant to starve while the (rent) strike continues, and until their rights are achieved ... I don't care, myself, being born on the soil of Ireland and being the son of a tenant farmer, what the title of a thief landlord is, for it is tainted with fraud. The statute of limitations does not run against an act of spoliation. We must not and will not stand idle and let the people of Ireland fight their own battles.

He ended with the promise that America's 10 million Irishmen would stand behind the leaders of the agitation.[34] Collins' oration resonated deeply with the audience, with loud cheers and applause throughout his address. The meeting concluded with resolutions supporting the tenant farmers and Irish self-government. Together with an announcement that contributions for relief could be sent to the *Pilot* office. Fanny Parnell and her sister, Theodosia, had already sent contributions of $75 and $50 respectively. A report from Dublin on 6 November to the *Pilot*, stated, "The Boston meeting has created great hope on this side and caused no little alarm to the land grabbers and their supporters."[35] Two weeks later, an editorial titled "No Famine Graves this Year" reflected O'Reilly's confidence that American aid and the Land League program would save lives.

The *Globe* editors rejected accusations by its rival journal, the *Boston Daily Advertiser*, that the land agitation was communist in nature and the approaching famine was exaggerated. Citing Ireland's economic underdevelopment and its huge tax burden, the editors informed its 30,000 readers that:

> The reforms must be radical. The tenantry of Ireland will be peaceable citizens only when they are not confronted with hunger or exile. A peasant proprietary is the only hope for the future of Ireland. And we hope the farmers will leave politics alone and keep agitating this till they get it.

Parnell's imminent visit to America was viewed as an opportunity to counter British misinformation and propaganda and to educate the American public on the causes and nature of Irish grievances. It concluded, "Let a substantial contribution be sent from the Parnell meeting to be applied, not in purchasing arms, nor ammunition, nor even land, but food and fuel wherever they are needed."[36] The *Globe* editors labeled government public works as helpful, but insufficient to cure the evils of the land system. They also criticized the *New York Herald's* attack on Parnell and its advice not to contribute funds directly to him.[37] In a strong editorial, the *Globe* proclaimed:

> Whatever may be the political outcome of the (tenant-farmer) agitation now going on, the present terrible fact is that starvation stares many thousand Irish men, women and children in the face, and that the local means of relief are utterly inadequate to save them. This is the trouble to be remedied first; and if England fails to avert from Ireland the horrors of another famine, she will forfeit in the estimation of the world the right to claim sovereignty over a land which cared ably for its own people before coming under English dominion.[38]

Following Parnell's and John Dillon's arrival in New York on 1 January 1880, the *Pilot* and *Globe* published their interviews with the *New York Herald*, which described humanitarian relief as the first priority and then educating Americans, Irish and non-Irish, about the necessity of changing the land system in Ireland.[39] The need for intervention was reinforced by Toronto Archbishop John Lynch's report that "Starvation stares the (Irish) people in the face if they are not succored," warning that at least a million people, especially women and children, were at risk.[40] During autumn 1879 and up to Parnell's January 1880 visit, contributions by individuals and local Irish groups were sent in response to continuing dire news from Ireland. The ever-dependable Irish servant girls of Boston sent 2,250 drafts worth £5,376 through Patrick Donahoe's exchange bureau in December 1879. In January and February 1880, Donahoe's office sent another $36,000 in private donations.[41]

Parnell's visit to Boston on 12 and 13 January 1880 was a huge political and financial success.[42] Over 5,000 people, many non-Irish, attended the official event at Boston's Music Hall, decorated with colorful floral arrangements, banners and Irish and American flags. Mayor F. O. Prince chaired the meeting and gave enthusiastic support to Parnell's relief mission while endorsing the Irish tenant farmers' demands for "ownership of the soil." The renowned Boston abolitionist, Wendell Phillips, described Parnell as "The Man who Made John Bull Listen." Parnell's clear and concise exposition of the tenant farmers' plight and his plan for tenants to purchase their holdings with British government subsidies won plaudits from the *Boston Globe*, while John Dillon's speech reinforced the urgency of the situation, explaining, "If we had not acted there would be famine in Ireland and people would have died of starvation three months ago." Collins urged the audience to declare their subscriptions, with $1593 pledged within 15 minutes. Parnell's mother, Delia, and his sister, Fanny, were in the audience and made numerous appearances over the next two years to mobilize Irish-American support for the Land League. Demand to see and hear Parnell was so great that he appeared the following morning at historic Faneuil Hall where another 5,000 people cheered him and made pledges.[43] Later, he spoke in Lowell, Massachusetts and $3000 was subscribed.[44] Parnell received similar enthusiastic receptions in Cambridge, Fall River, Holyoke, Lawrence, Lynn and Springfield, all in Massachusetts. Other regional cities visited were Providence, Rhode Island, New Haven, Connecticut, and Troy and Albany in New York. John Dillon's appearance in Manchester, New Hampshire, raised close to $3,000.[45] In total, Parnell's 62-city, 16,000-mile tour raised about $300,000 for the Land League relief fund and $50,000 for the political purposes of the Land League.[46]

Three days after Parnell's Boston visit, Archbishop John J. Williams announced a diocesan wide relief collection that eventually netted $37,000. This generous outpouring was helped by reports in the *Pilot* and *Irish World* from Irish clergy that their people were on the verge of starvation.[47] The proceeds from Williams' appeal were sent to Archbishop McGettigan at Armagh, following the pattern of 1847 when Bishop Fitzpatrick sent the proceeds of his collection to Archbishop Crolly. McGettigan also received £5,000 in individual donations from Boston. The Diocese of Hartford sent $22,625 and the Bishop of Springfield, Massachusetts, raised $17, 253 for relief, while the Bishops of Portland, Maine and Vermont sent significant amounts so that the total Episcopal collections from the region equaled $125,378 dollars or £23,973.[48] Worcester's Irish parishes collected $1700 for Irish relief and another $1000 came from others in the city.[49] Over the next few years, the clergy in Boston and its surrounding regions were intimately involved in forming and supporting American Land League branches and many served as treasurers of branches. The American Land League's annual report of April 1882 indicated that clergy in Boston had contributed $1329 in the previous year.[50]

Meanwhile, both the *Pilot* and the *Globe* published detailed reports on good and bad landlords, identifying those who were absentees, rack-renters and evictors, as well who had granted rent remissions and aid to their tenants. Lord Clanricarde was singled out as a bad landlord. Anti-landlord feeling increased in the spring of 1880 with the publication in the Boston press of *New York Tribune* journalist James Redpath's letters from Ireland and his subsequent "Famine and Landlords" lectures.[51] Redpath advised Irish Americans not to contribute a single dollar to a new Mansion House appeal to America and Canada claiming, incorrectly as it proved, that Irish landlords had not contributed either to the Mansion House Committee or the Duchess's fund. Redpath gave four talks on the folly of Gladstone's coercion policy and the limitations of his 1881 land bill.[52]

Another event dedicated to Irish relief was a concert at the Boston Theater, on 22 February, which was organized by sympathetic Yankees hesitant to align with the local Irish leaders. The entire proceeds of $2,302 were sent to James G. Bennett's *New York Herald* Relief Fund, which financed a considerable portion of the relief supplies that the U.S.S. *Constellation* brought to Cork in April 1880.[53] After February, news reports indicated that 87,000 residents of Mayo and Sligo remained in dire distress, the *Globe* editorializing:

> The world has advanced since the great famine of 1847, and it will be a shame to civilization if the horrors of that time are repeated when all the wealth and increased appliances of the world are available for relief. The actions of the several Irish societies in this and other cities, in foregoing their customary annual celebrations and instead contributing to the relief of their suffering brethren is an example which well may be copied. For the peasantry of Ireland are men, women and children of the same human brotherhood as ourselves.[54]

In response to reports of continuing hunger and misery, many Irish groups cancelled their St. Patrick's Day festivities or dedicated all proceeds for Irish relief. The Charitable Irish Society of Boston, following its precedent from 1847, cancelled its 1880 annual dinner and made a donation of $1,000 to the Irish Relief Fund.[55] Proceeds totaling $200 from the annual celebration of Robert Emmet's birth on 4 March, which featured lectures by John E. Fitzgerald and John Boyle O'Reilly, were dedicated to Irish Famine relief, while the St James Catholic Temperance Society and the Lynn Chorus and Band held concerts in aid of Irish relief.[56] Meanwhile, various *ad hoc* local groups raised money for relief. Businessmen in Weymouth, Massachusetts, sent $336 and promised to canvas all the local factories to secure more aid. The Roman Catholic and Congregational churches of East Weymouth sent $264, while checks for $100 were received from Irish groups in Bridgeport, Connecticut, Valley Falls and Warren, both in Rhode Island. Inmates from the Massachusetts State Prison and the boys at the Westboro Reform School contributed $72 and $12. Frank Crowley, a 12-year-old factory hand from Westvale, Massachusetts, collected $25 dollars from his co-workers. By late February, the trustees of the Boston Parnell Relief Fund had received $30,436 and already forwarded $10,000 to Patrick Egan, the Land League treasurer in Dublin. By 24 March, Asa Potter, the Boston treasurer of the relief fund, reported that the total raised had reached $61,307.[57] One of the most poignant contributions came from a poor Irish woman who gave her entire savings of $100 to a priest who tried, but failed, to convince her this donation was beyond her means. When he asked for her name, she replied, "My name, don't mind that sir. Just send them the help and God will know my name."[58]

Convinced that persistent Irish poverty and future famines could only be prevented by the abolition of Irish landlordism, O'Reilly and Collins established the Irish National Land League of the United States in May 1880. Over the next two years, this centralized American committee provided approximately $341,000 to support the League's relief program and the various costs associated with Parnell's prosecution of the Land War.[59] By April 1882, under the leadership of three New Englanders, president Patrick A. Collins, secretary Thomas Flatley, and treasurer Father Lawrence Walsh, the American League had 970 active branches, including 382 in New England, of which 225 were in Massachusetts.

One of the most interesting features of the agitation in Irish America was the growing involvement of Irish-American women. As early as 6 September 1879, Fanny Parnell urged the establishment of an Irish relief fund, and she and her sister, Theodosia, contributed to the initial fund set up in Boston in October. Fanny's poetry was published regularly in the *Pilot*, and her signature 1880 poem "Hold the Harvest," encouraged both male and female engagement in the cause. Fanny and her sister, Anna, had worked tirelessly helping Davitt set up the central Irish National League office in New York in the summer of 1880. On 15 October 1880, Fanny's proposal to harness the energy and empathy of Irish-American women with the establishment of the Ladies' Land League of the United States was implemented in New York City. Her call was answered enthusiastically in the Boston area, especially after Davitt's arrest in February 1881 and the passage of the British government's coercion bill in March. Both the *Boston Globe* and the *Pilot* gave enthusiastic backing to the mobilization of this new organization.[60] Delia Parnell, mother of the Irish leader, and Ellen Ford, sister of *Irish World* editor Patrick Ford, lectured in 16 New England cities in January and February 1881, bringing new recruits to the American movement. Ladies' branches were established in East Cambridge, Charlestown and Woburn, in Massachusetts, Newport in Rhode Island, and Hartford in Connecticut. The *Boston*

Globe's 22 January extensive interview with Delia Parnell and Ellen Ford, detailing the origins of the Ladies' Land League and highlighting the potential of female involvement, provided useful publicity for the whole Irish land movement.[61] Delia's visit to Worcester on 29 February drew 5,000 people and raised $1,400.[62] The enthusiasm of 17 newly organized Massachusetts ladies' branches was apparent by their raising $2,600 between January and April 1881, a little over 10 percent of the total raised in the state.[63] Another factor in the growth of the Ladies' Land League in the Boston area was Fanny Parnell's extended visit in May 1881, when she made 10 appearances. In a lengthy *Boston Globe* interview, Fanny defined the Land League's mission as the creation of a peasant proprietorship through state-assisted purchase, as well as the provision of relief and housing for those who had been evicted or league members imprisoned under the Coercion Act. American financial support remained crucial as weekly relief needs had grown to $10,000 per week.[64] Glowing tributes for Fanny and her sister, Anna, came from O'Reilly, Collins, Flatley and former Fenian, Patrick Meledy. Local clerical support for female involvement was apparent from the presence of a dozen priests among the 2,000 people who heard Fanny speak at St. Mary's Hall in Lawrence in May.[65] Clerical support for the ladies' efforts was also shown by the parish priest of Central Falls in Rhode Island, who donated his entire monthly parish collection of $600.[66] Occasional accounts written by Anna and published in the *Pilot*, describing the activities in resisting evictions and assisting the evicted, contributed to gender solidarity and confidence that women's efforts were helping Ireland.[67] The Worcester branch included a number of middle-class women and raised close to $8,000 for the Irish cause by June 1882. Eli Janis' study of the Woonsocket, Rhode Island, Ladies' Land League underscores the support that Irish working-class single women in New England's industrial cities gave to the cause. This branch had a membership of at least 300 women. Similar numbers were found in other industrial cities like Lawrence, Lowell, and Fall River, where young factory workers agreed with Patrick and Ellen Ford that "the cause of the impoverished tenant in Ireland was the cause of the factory worker in the United States."[68] Since branch meetings often featured singing, recitations and readings, the opportunity for social interaction beyond their homes, parish and work places was undoubtedly attractive to women.

Worcester and Woonsocket were not unique in their enthusiastic support for the American Ladies' Land League as indicated by the formation of 86 branches in the region affiliated with the Irish National League by 1882. Massachusetts had 47 branches, Connecticut 14, Rhode Island four, Maine two, and Vermont one. Boston and Cambridge had 11 branches with a membership of 1,830, while the total membership for Massachusetts was approximately 4,927. Of the $81,706 raised by 207 Land

League branches in Massachusetts between April 1881 and April 1882, the ladies' branches contributed $12,773 or 15 percent of the total. Connecticut ladies raised $2,166 or 13 percent of Connecticut's total return of $16,502, sent to Father Walsh, the Irish National Land League's treasurer.[69] These figures do not reflect branches that were not affiliated with the national league, who sent their donations to Patrick Ford's *Irish World* fund.[70] Ely Janis calculated that the New England region had 72 ladies' branches, representing about one-third of an estimated national figure of 225 branches, and they contributed approximately $22,500 between 31 January and 31 October 1882.[71]

The American movement lost momentum, however, when the threat of famine and arbitrary eviction disappeared, combined with significant rent reductions and tenant protections achieved as a result of the Land Act of 1881 and the Arrears Act of 1882. The sudden death of the energetic Fanny Parnell in July 1882, and the strong opposition of American bishops such as Richard Gilmore of Cleveland to women's involvement, curtailed the activity of the American Ladies' Land League except in branches like Worcester, Massachusetts and Cleveland, Ohio, where the members vowed to continue their efforts to abolish landlordism in Ireland. Davitt's abandonment of his land nationalization policy led working-class radicals and eventually their principal leader, Patrick Ford, to abandon the Land League in October even though the *Irish World* had sent $343,000 to Ireland.[72] Diminishing support was reflected in the 1882 monthly returns sent to the *Irish World,* from a high of almost $45,000 in January, to $5,000 in August, and only $1,500 in September, led Ford to close his fund on 15 October 1882.[73] As Table 1 shows, there was a 50 percent drop in active branches nationally by April 1883 and a huge decline in branch receipts sent to Father Walsh. Massachusetts and Connecticut experienced a smaller reduction with one-third of the $24,261 sent by New England donors designated exclusively for relief purposes. Although Massachusetts and Connecticut experienced fewer reductions, these figures suggest that the dissolution of the Irish National Land League was inevitable.

Six months after Parnell formed the Irish National Land League, at its third annual convention in Philadelphia in April 1883, the Irish National Land League of the United States transformed itself into the Irish National League of America. Its stated mission of providing moral and financial support to its Irish counterpart and to agitate exclusively for Home Rule, rather than for the economic and social transformation desired by Patrick Ford and his followers, reflected the priorities of conservative nationalists like Collins and O'Reilly.

Table 1: Summary of Returns of branches and receipts received by Irish National Land League treasurer for 1882 and 1883.
No. of branches, April 1882. Total receipts, April 1881 to April 1882.
No of branches, April 1883. Total receipts April 1882 to April 1883.

	1882		1883	
State	**State**	**Active and reporting**	**Receipts**	**Active and reporting**
Massachusetts	$81,706.73	225	$15,721.52	140
Connecticut	$16,342.26	88	$6,306.10	49
Rhode Island	$6,906.39	32	$1,499.40	14
New Hampshire	$2,840.92	18	$321.99	6
Maine	$1,436.40	8	$351.98	3
Vermont	$782.35	11	$62.55	3
Regional Totals	$110,014.85	382	$24,263.74	215
National Figure	$272,810.61*	946	$61,976.27	562

Branch returns for this period, $175,632 and $97,177.84, were sent directly to Patrick Egan in Ireland or Paris for the national total of $272,810.61. Thus, the Massachusetts receipts represented 46 percent of national branch returns and 29 percent of total funds collected for the Land League as of April 1882. Massachusetts was the top contributor in 1882, and second to New York in 1883. New England 1882 returns were 40 percent of the national total and in the following year were 39 percent of the national total.[74]

To conclude, given New England's large Irish-American population, it is not surprising that the region was prominent in sending relief during the food crisis of 1879–1880, and in establishing the Irish National Land League of the United States. The time, talent and energy that both men and women expended in gathering moral and financial support for the Irish agitation was unprecedented. Notably, like their fathers and brothers, large numbers of Irish-American women in New England moved beyond contemporary gender roles to secure justice for Ireland. Through their public speeches, writings and interviews, they not only mobilized the region's Irish Americans, but also convinced influential leaders in the wider American community such as Wendell Phillips, James Redpath, Mayor F. O. Prince and Colonel William Taylor, editor and owner of the *Boston Globe*, to become advocates for Irish economic and political justice. The combined support of the Irish National Land League and Patrick Ford's *Irish World* subscribers provided Parnell with the necessary resources and leverage to fight coercion and secure land reform, while tenant farmers were emboldened in their fight against landlordism by knowledge of Irish-American support.[75] Furthermore, the passage of the Land Act and the Arrears Act, which provided for significant rent reductions and dual ownership, essentially conceded that a permanent solution to the Irish land question would require the abolition of landlordism and the creation of a peasant proprietorship. The Tory-initiated Land Acts of 1888, 1891 and 1903 were additional steps towards this goal.[76] Although the broad class and gender alliance that characterized Irish-American support for the Irish Land War was weakened by the move to an exclusively political agenda, Parnell was able to rely on the continued moral and financial support of many of the Irish National Land League male leaders and members in building a strong parliamentary party that would ultimately force William Gladstone to introduce Home Rule in 1886. Despite the defeat of the Home Rule bills of 1886 and 1893, the influence of organized Irish-American nationalism that had begun in 1879 remained an important dynamic in Ireland's continuing struggle to win independence from Britain. Moreover, the significant amount of monies raised also helped to save lives during Ireland's Forgotten Famine.

NOTES

1. For Boston and New England's role in providing relief in 1847, see H.A. Crosby Forbes and Henry Lee, *Massachusetts Help to Ireland During the Great Famine* (Milton: Captain Robert Bennet Forbes House Museum, 1967). Also, Captain Forbes' personal account of the voyage, *The Voyage of the Jamestown on her Errand of Mercy* (Boston: Eastburn's Press, 1847).
2. See Ely M. Janis, *A Greater Ireland: The Land League and Transatlantic Nationalism in Gilded Age America* (Madison: University of Wisconsin Press, 2015) for the most comprehensive account of the creation of "A Greater Ireland" on the national level.
3. Norman D. Palmer, *The Land League Crisis* (New Haven: Yale University Press, 1940), p. 254 and Gladstone's speech of 3 March 1890, 3 *Hansard,* CCXLL, 1686–1687. Paul Bew, *Land and the National Question in Ireland, 1858–82* (Dublin: Gill and Macmillan, 1978) pp 235–36.
4. T.W. Moody, *Michael Davitt and the Irish Revolution, 1846–82* (Oxford University Press, 1981), pp 569–571.
5. For analysis of the persistence of pre-famine conditions in the west of Ireland relating to population density, small holdings, and early marriage, see S. H. Cousens, "Regional Variations in Population Changes in Ireland, 1866–1881," *Economic History Review,* vol. 17, no. 2, pp 301–21 and Brendan M. Walsh, "Marriage Rates and Population Pressure in Ireland", *Economic History Review,* vol. 23, no. 1 (April, 1970), 148–62.
6. Palmer, p. 74; Gerard Moran, "'Near Famine': The Roman Catholic Church and the Subsistence Crisis of 1879–82, *Studia Hibernica,* no. 32 (2002–2003), p. 172. For a comprehensive analysis of the severity of the crisis in County Mayo, see Gerard Moran, "Famine and

the Land War: Relief and Distress in Co. Mayo, 1879–1881" Part I and II, *Cathair na Mart: Journal of the Westport Historical Society,* vol. 5 (1985) 54–66; vol. 6. no. 1 (1986) pp 118–126.

7. Moran, "*Famine and the Land War,*" pp 113–114. Lucan and Arran provided some relief works on their estates, but only to those who refrained from participating in the land agitation. James H. Tuke noted the connection between high rates of distress and absenteeism in his account of his spring tour of 1880.
8. Bew, pp 10, 57.
9. Moran, "Near Famine," p. 157.
10. Gerard Moran, "From Great Famine to Forgotten Famine: The Crisis of 1879–81," *Irish Hunger and Migration: Myth, Memory and Memorialization",* eds. Patrick Fitzgerald, Christine Kinealy, Gerard Moran (Hamden, CT: Quinnipiac University Press, 2015), p. 122.
11. Moody, p. 561. Between 1876 and 1880 evictions in Connacht increased from 101 to 365, and reached a high of 1430 in 1882, p. 564.
12. Palmer, pp 66, 77–79, *The Times,* 17 Sept. 1879, 4 Nov. 1879. For an account of the efforts of the Catholic clergy in warning and acting on the crisis, see Moran, "Near Famine." An exception to Irish landlords' denial of the crisis was Colonel E. R. King-Harman, M.P. His 25 Dec. letter in the *Times* stated, "Our people are on the verge of starvation," and he hoped the government would take action to show that "they may depend in their hour of trial upon English justice."
13. Moran, "Famine and the Land War," p. 111; "Near Famine," p. 161, n. 27.
14. Palmer, p. 70.
15. Ibid., p. 78; Moran, "Near Famine," p. 160.
16. Donnacha Seán Lucey, *Power, politics and poor relief, 1879–82* (Cambridge University Press, 2015), p. 586.
17. Catherine B. Shannon, "Lord Randolph Churchill's Irish Apprenticeship" in Robert McNamara (ed.), *The Churchills in Ireland, 1660–1965: Connections and Controversies* (Dublin: Irish Academic Press, 2012) p. 74. Of the £135,000 raised by the Duchess's Fund, £119,000 was spent on food and relief works, £36,983 for potato and oat seeds, £10,091 on clothing and blankets, and £1,458 to fund emigration and internal migration. The closing balance of £2,000 in October was allocated to help families in densely-populated districts to emigrate. Palmer, p. 89.
18. *Pilot,* 7 Jan. 1880. See Palmer, pp 83–91 for more details on the Duchess' Fund.
19. *The Irish Crisis of 1879–80: Proceedings of the Dublin Mansion House Committee* (Dublin: Browne and Nolan, 1881), p. 27.
20. Moran, "Famine and the Land War," part 2, p. 115. These loans were to be financed by £1,500,000 in the Irish Church Disestablishment Fund, Moody, *Davitt,* p. 367.
21. See Palmer, pp 91–98, for an overview of the work of the Mansion House Committee. For full coverage, see *The Irish Crisis of 1879–80.*
22. Ibid., p. 164.
23. For example, the *Boston Globe* carried the Local Government Report of 10 Nov. that the 1879 "potato crop is everywhere deficient and inferior" and that increased distress and pauperism were expected in winter and fall, on the same day as its Dublin publication. *Boston Globe*, 10 Nov. 1879.

24. Janis, p. 116; Ian Kenneally, *From the Earth a Cry: the story of John Boyle O'Reilly* (Cork: Collins Press, 2011), p. 331, n. 58.
25. The *Pilot,* 7 June 1879, 12 June 1879, 21 June 1879, 28 June 1879.
26. Ibid., 12 July 1879, 19 July 1879, 26 July 1879, 2 Aug. 1879.
27. *Irish World,* 1 July 1879, 30 Aug. 1879.
28. The papers of George Cahill at Boston College's Burns Library contain various notices of Fenian social and business meetings at Boston's Shawmut branch, and Davitt mentioned meeting about 50 Fenians when he visited Lawrence, Massachusetts in 1878. At the height of the American Fenian movement in the late 1860s, there were 65 branches in Massachusetts. Davitt described his evolution and that of American Fenians away from the physical force approach to a moral pressure political campaign in his *The Fall of Feudalism in Ireland* (Shannon: Irish University Press, 1970) pp 120–133. For an account of the *Catalpa* rescue detailing the roles of John Devoy and John Boyle O'Reilly, see Kenneally, pp 205–213 and Ian Kenneally, *From the Earth a Cry: The Story of John Boyle O'Reilly* (Cork: Collins Press; 2011) and Terry Golway, *Irish Rebel: John Devoy and America's Fight for Ireland's Freedom* (New York: St. Martin's Press, 1998) pp 71–86. The Shawmut Fenian branch held a large commemoration of the Manchester Martyrs in November 1879. *Boston Globe*, 25 Nov. 1879.
29. Moody, *Davitt,* pp 263–264; the *Pilot,* 21 Dec. 1878.
30. Based on the 1880 census figures and Oscar Handlin, *Boston's Immigrants, 1790–1880* (Cambridge: Harvard University Press, 1991), p. 261.
31. Davitt's analysis that these haunting memories and hatred of landlordism among the American Irish had potential to mobilize a stronger Irish national movement, see Davitt, *Fall,* pp 120–121.
32. Paul Bew contends that Parnell's support of the land agitation at this point was tentative and only became firm with the establishment of the National Land League in Dublin in October. *Land and Nationalism*, pp 65–70. Bew's distinction probably was lost on Irish-American *Pilot* readers; *Boston Globe,* 7 Oct. 1879. At this juncture, Davitt was a regular correspondent for the *Pilot.* Moody, *Davitt,* p. 227.
33. *Boston Globe,* 7 Oct. 1879.
34. Ibid.
35. *Pilot,* 22 Nov. 1879.
36. *Boston Globe*, 23 Nov., 7 Dec. 1879.
37. Ibid., 17 Nov., 14 Dec. 1879, 11 Jan. 1880.
38. Ibid., 12 Dec. 1879.
39. Ibid., 4 Jan. 1880; *Pilot,* 10 Jan. 1880. O'Reilly and three other members of the local Parnell committee greeted Parnell and Dillon in New York.
40. Ibid., 4 Jan. 1880.
41. *Donahoe's Magazine,* vol. 3, May 1880, p. 437, April 1880, p. 418.
42. An *Irish Times* journalist covering Parnell's visit reported $2,500 in ticket sales and another $2,000 in donations the evening of Parnell's address. *Irish Times,* 14 Jan. 1880.
43. *Boston Globe*, 13 Jan. 1880.

44. *Boston Evening Transcript,* 14 Jan. 1880.
45. *Pilot,* 7 Feb. 1880.
46. Janis, p. 41.
47. For appeals of Galway priests, Fathers Peter Newell and Martin Mellet, see the *Pilot,* 31 Jan. 1880, and that of the Bishop of Galway, Dr. McEvely and other priests, *Irish World,* 31 Jan. 1880.
48. Moran, "Near Famine," pp 169–71. For a more detailed analysis of the American Catholic clergy in sending relief and supporting the Land League, see James J. Green, "American Catholics and the Irish Land League, 1879–1882," *The Catholic Historical Review,* vol. 38, no. 1 (April 1949), 19–42. Five of these six New England bishops were Irish born or sons of Irish-born parents.
49. Timothy Meagher, *Inventing Irish America: Generation, Class and Ethnic Identity in a New England City, 1880–1928* (University of Notre Dame Press, 2001), p. 438, n. 2.
50. *Second Annual Convention Report of the Irish National Land League of the United States, Washington D. C, April 12–13, 1882* (Buffalo, N. Y. 1882), report of the Secretary, pp 16–17. Hereafter INLL 1882 report.
51. *Pilot,* 24 Jan. 1880, *Boston Globe,* 29 Feb. 1880, 18 May 1880. *The New York Tribune* sent Redpath to Ireland in early 1880 to investigate the crisis.
52. *Boston Globe,* 14 June 1880; several Irish landlords did contribute to these relief funds according to Palmer, p. 103. Redpath's critiques on the land bill were given at Lynn, Canton, Charlestown and Peabody, see *Boston Globe*, 7, 14 March, 25, 26 Nov. 1881.
53. *Boston Globe*, 24 Feb. 1880. For the *Constellation* initiative and the response of New York, see chapter by Harvey Strum. The *Times* reported on 31 May 1880 that the total receipts of the *Herald* fund were $341,000.
54. *Boston Globe* 24, 25 Feb. 1880.
55. Ibid., 25 Feb. 1880.
56. Ibid., 5, 29 Feb. 1880, 13 15, 28, 29 March 1880.
57. Ibid., 28 Feb, 18, 24 March 1880.
58. *Pilot,* 15 May 1880.
59. Patrick Egan, the Irish League's treasurer, reported in October 1882 that £59,178, out of £244,829, had been used for relief. Michael Davitt, *the Fall of Feudalism in Ireland* (Irish University Press, 1970), p. 373.
60. *Boston Globe*, 23 Jan. 1881; *Pilot,* 29 Jan. 1881.
61. Ibid., 22 Jan. 1881.
62. Locations included Boston, East Cambridge, Charlestown, South Boston, Fall River, Woburn, Worcester, Holyoke and Springfield, Massachusetts; Newport, Rhode Island and Hartford and Middletown, Connecticut. See *Boston Globe,* 21 Jan. to 3 March 1881, and *Irish World,* 5, 25 March 1881.
63. Quarterly returns of Irish National Land League branches, 1881–1882, George D. Cahill Papers, Box 5, folder 33, John J. Burns Library, Boston College.
64. *Boston Globe*, 8 May 1881.
65. After appearing at the Music Hall on 8 March, Fanny Parnell spoke in East Boston, Lowell, Lawrence, Quincy, East Cambridge, South Boston, Boston Highlands and Lynn,

concluding her visit with a large reception at the Catholic Union sponsored by the city's Central Land League branch. See the *Boston Globe,* 9–20 May 1881 for press coverage of her tour. *The Boston Globe* gave the names of four priests at Lawrence while the *Irish World* reported that a dozen clerics were in attendance. *Boston Globe* 12 May 1881, *Irish World,* 24 May 1881.

66. *Irish World,* 16 April 1881.
67. For the impact of Anna Parnell, see Beverly Schneller, *Anna Parnell's Political Journalism: Context and Text* (Bethesda, MD: Academic Press 2005).
68. Janis, p. 156.
69. These figures are calculated from the *Report of the Second Annual Convention of the Irish National Land League of the United States,* Washington, D. C., 12–13 April 1882. Eli Janis has calculated that there were 72 Ladies' Land League branches in the New England region, p. 145. He also noted that increases in female recruitment tended to follow events in Ireland such as the arrest of Michael Davitt, the passage of the Coercion Act in 1881, and the arrest of Parnell and the British government's suppression of the Land League in 1882; Janis, pp 144–45.
70. *Irish World,* 3 Dec. 1881; 28 Jan., 28 May 1882.
71. Janis, pp 143, 146.
72. Brown, p. 106.
73. Janis, pp 192–94.
74. These figures are based on the Reports of the Second and Third Annual Conventions of the Irish National Land League of the United States held respectively in Washington, DC on April 12, 13, 1882 and in Philadelphia on April 25–27, 1883.
75. For a full analysis of the demise of the INLL of the USA, see Janis, pp 184–197.
76. Catherine B. Shannon, *Arthur J. Balfour and Ireland, 1874–1922* (Washington, D.C.: Catholic University Press: 1988), chapters 2 and 3.

CHAPTER THIRTEEN

THE CONNEMARAS

Despair in the Heartland

Jane Kennedy

This chapter follows the story of a group of Tuke emigrants, disparagingly referred to by a contemporary as "the Connemaras," who experienced poverty and privation both within Ireland and overseas. They started out like many other emigrants. A group of people living in wretched conditions, surviving one famine and facing another, pleaded for an opportunity to find a better life, even if it meant leaving behind their families, most likely forever. While the Connemaras, through the Quaker benefactor, James Hack Tuke, did find a way to a new life, their fate led them to more hardship and suffering. For many of these nomadic Connemaras, their journey to Graceville, Minnesota, and then finally to St. Paul, Minnesota, never truly lifted them from the penury and hardship into which they were born. For every Connemara family that made this trek, and, indeed, for every person who traveled in search of the necessities of life, their story is one that cannot be lost to time.

Never intended for habitation

Located in the northwest corner of County Galway, Connemara lies on the most western seaboard of Europe. Many of the features that draw visitors to the Connemara region today are the very characteristics that contributed to the inhabitants' inability to thrive, such as the rocky terrain, extensive bogs, rugged coastline, and the area's remoteness. Father Patrick Greally, the Catholic administrator of Carna, County Galway, described this region as the "remotest and poorest promontory in

Connemara. It is hemmed in on one side by lofty mountains and extensive bogs, and on the other by the fierce Atlantic, and is forty-nine miles from the City of Galway, our market town."[1] Greally reasoned that the barren land "was never intended by God or nature for the habitation of man."[2]

There is little doubt that the topography of the Connemara region was a major contributor to the adverse conditions in the west of Ireland, yet other components combined, resulting in a snowball effect that left the people bereft of their basic human needs. The weather wreaked havoc on the region beginning in the late 1870s. "Parts of Donegal, Sligo, Galway and Clare are suffering not so much from a failure of the harvest as from the storms and rains of the autumn which spoiled the harvest before it could be gathered in," noted a *Dublin Review* article.[3] The rains brought on potato blight and decimated the harvest. In 1879, the value of the potato harvest was only a third of the 1876 crop.[4] Similarly, the sea kelp market was in serious decline. Sea kelp attracted a number of people to settle on the islands and seacoast of Ireland where it grew. The industry was productive and a financial boon to the area until another compound—Peruvian potash—was discovered in South America. The discovery reduced both the demand and the cost of kelp.[5] Meanwhile, fishing, a third industry that had sustained people on the west coast of Ireland, also began to diminish. "On the coast of Galway as a rule, they have only open boats to meet the heavy weather that is to be met with for two-thirds of the year on that stormy coast; therefore, the fishing is ... a precarious means of support."[6]

This inability to earn an income off the land and sea resulted in people failing to pay rent to their landlords; in some cases, people were in arrears on rent payments for as much as three years.[7] In addition, people owed money to shopkeepers, and when there was no repayment, shopkeepers no longer allowed them to purchase food and clothing.[8] Father Greally described the growing debt as an inescapable situation:

> Those struggling tenants in consequence of bad seasons are steeped in debt to such an extent to landlords and shopkeepers that they can never pay them. It requires, therefore, no great foresight to predict what the future must be ... It is sufficient that accumulating debt is but accumulating misfortune and inevitable bankruptcy.[9]

Finally, a major contributor to the famine in the late 1870s was the growing population in the west of Ireland, including the Connemara region. Not only were there many large families, but people were marrying at young ages. Farms were divided up among so many families that people were unable to make a living off the land.

With food scarce and no money or credit available to purchase food, the people faced starvation and famine fever. Between starvation and death, there is a disease, known generically as "famine fever," brought on by a weakened immune system.[10] The Irish poor's familiarity with this occurrence had given rise to the aphorism, "fever follows famine." On 12 March 1880, Father Greally wrote to Thomas Flaherty of Minneapolis:

> A famine fever has broken out here extensively and has already whole families within its death grip, who have neither bed nor bed-clothes sufficient to preserve life in even the most robust constitution at this inclement season of the year.[11]

The suffering in Ireland was reported in other parts of the United States. A newspaper in Cincinnati, Ohio, described nearly the entire population of Carna—almost 5,000 people—as being on the "highroad to death by starvation. Hunger had overtaken more than one-third of them already."[12] Mothers were depicted as walking shoeless over many miles of rough and rocky terrain in search of Indian meal for their children. In the town of Oughterard, a correspondent for the *Freeman's Journal* described how the school children were without boots and that "a respected gentleman" said he saw "an absolutely naked child haunting the roads."[13] The correspondent noted that sometimes up to nine family members shared a single straw bed.[14]

Although the poor in Connemara were facing a near-death situation, it did not prevent landlords from evicting them. Rev. Patrick Coyne, Catholic administrator of the parish of Killanin in County Galway, at a local Land League meeting denounced the land tenure system as "vicious" and "iniquitous," and warned that unless it was "remodeled," residents in the west of Ireland would not prosper.[15] He noted that landlords in Killanin Parish had raised rents by as much as 150 percent within a six-to-seven-year span. He described one man in the parish as "going out of his mind" over such a steep increase and condemned the cruel eviction practices that were taking place.

If not for private relief organizations, more people would have succumbed to starvation, fever and death. Both the Mansion House Relief Committee and the Duchess of Marlborough Relief Committee helped provide relief to hundreds of thousands of people. Tuke, the English philanthropist and Quaker, also did much to assist the poor. He had been involved in famine relief in 1846 and 1847 and was respected not only for his work in that capacity but also for the reports he wrote regarding conditions in the remote areas of western Ireland. His writings not only "gave an impartial assessment" of the situation, they also were sympathetic to the poor.[16] Tuke's return to Connemara in the spring of 1880 was considered a fact-finding mission. He spoke to a number of sources to see how people were faring and to distribute money he brought with him. He discovered very distressing conditions and later revealed that it was this visit that changed his life and became the impetus for his work to assist the country's downtrodden.[17] In her article, "*A Good Christian*," Rita Nolan stated, "The chief value of [Tuke's] visit lay in the opportunity it afforded him of studying the Irish problem"[18] and finding a permanent solution to addressing the poverty that enmeshed the people. In the short-term, an immediate solution was needed.

The idea of relocating families first came from Rev. James Nugent of Liverpool.[19] He perceived that conditions in the Connemara region were becoming more devastating so he wrote to Bishop Ireland in St. Paul, Minnesota, as well as others, including Bishop O'Connor of Nebraska, who might be able to assist by helping families to move and settle in the midwestern United States. He advised, "It would be a real blessing to help some of these families to emigrate to the Catholic colonies now opening out in America." Rev. Nugent indicated that he would try to find the means to cover the expense of their travel costs, but added, "I consider that if I could only help 100 families to emigrate from Connemara this spring it would be an immense blessing to those who leave the country and would give greater opportunities to those who remain."[20] Neither Bishop Ireland nor Bishop O'Connor were in favor of Rev. Nugent's plan. Moreover, not everyone in Ireland supported the idea of emigration; those who were opposed argued that people in the affected areas did not want to leave. Among those who were against assisted emigration were shopkeepers, Irish nationalists, and some priests who did not want to see the population of Ireland diminished.[21]

Initially, Bishop Ireland informed Rev. Nugent that it was "contrary to all the rules of successful colonization to accept indigent settlers and doubly dangerous to accept persons who were not accustomed to farm life in America."[22] However, despite his misgivings, he agreed that he would first try to see if he could raise money to bring people from Connemara to Minnesota before he rejected Rev. Nugent's plea. Consequently, Bishop Ireland reached out to potential contributors, imploring, "Remember, there is no time to delay, those we will have we must have here in time to make little gardens to help to support them for the first year."[23] Within a short time, $5,000 was raised and the bishop persuaded railroad officials to transport the emigrants from Boston to western Minnesota at no cost. These developments led Bishop Ireland to respond affirmatively to Rev. Nugent. But there was more than benevolence at play—Bishop Ireland was keen on colonizing the Midwest. "The bishop looked on the Irish settlers as a test of his grand plan of colonization ... He knew that their backgrounds as fishermen and garden farmers handicapped them for large-scale farming in the West."[24]

Ultimately, pledges of money from Irish descendants in Chicago, St. Paul and surrounding areas were sufficient to help fund emigration from Connemara. Bishop Ireland ordered 50 farms sites, 160 acres each, to be set aside for the Irish arrivals.[25]

Each site was to have a small house built on it that included some modest furnishings and a cow. Of the 160 acres, five acres would have been broken for planting. "Breaking" of the land was considered a very difficult undertaking:

> Sometimes it was done with huge breaking plows, drawn by four oxen, or with heavy stone boats, equipped with steel prongs to break up the sod...It was necessary to leave the upturned sod exposed to the elements for a whole year before it would rot and break up. If a man could turn and break ten acres a year, he was doing well.[26]

Leaving Ireland

The Connemara emigrants left Ireland on 11 June, embarking from Galway. On the night before their long journey, the emigrants gathered with their clergy to walk to the port where the steamer, *Austrian*, awaited them. Before setting foot on the ship, the emigrants and their accompanying priests attended 6 a.m. Mass at the Cathedral of St. Nicholas. From there, they boarded a steam tugboat to take them out to the *Austrian*. Father Dooley, who deferred his homily during Mass until the passengers were onboard the steamer, delivered a compassionate speech. He compared their parting to a "death" and explained that "as sterile as were the rocks and hills of Connemara, every spot was dear to them." He implored them to never forget Ireland and to continue to speak in their own language, adding that this parting might be the last time they would hear a priest speak in their native tongue. Not surprisingly, the emigrants were filled with anguish when it came time to part from their beloved clergy.[27]

Rev. Nugent had engaged Thomas Campbell of London to accompany the emigrants to their new home. Campbell kept notes on the voyage to America, which he shared with Rev. Nugent. The voyage encountered heavy seas that caused the travelers—and even some crew members—to be sick. The ship passed large icebergs but there were also calm seas that roused the travelers to dance to tunes from an Irish flute. On 22 June, 11 days after departing from Galway, the emigrants arrived in Boston. Bishop Ireland's friend and co-worker, Dillon O'Brien, met the passengers. Exhausted from a long sea voyage, the emigrants were required to stay onboard one more night before departing on the Western Express train the next afternoon. When they arrived in Chicago, Illinois, on 25 June, they were greeted by William J. Onahan, secretary of the city's St. Patrick's Society, who furnished the group with clothing and warm meals. Onahan was appalled at the poverty and suffering of the emigrants, with none of the children, and only some of the women, wearing shoes:

> The famine was visible in their pinched and emaciated faces and in the shriveled limbs—they could scarcely be called legs and arms—of the children. Their features were quaint, and the entire company was squalid and wretched. It was a painful revelation to all who witnessed it.[28]

After observing their impoverished state, Onahan concluded the passengers were not fit for the prairie. Even O'Brien, a friend and defender of Bishop Ireland, came to a similar conclusion after the emigrants reached Graceville. But he was careful not to share his concerns with the bishop.

From Chicago, the Western Express brought the Connemara group to St. Paul in Minnesota, arriving there on 26 June, where they were greeted by crowds of people. Here, 70 young men and women departed from the group for work in the city. Men found work with the railroad, while women took jobs as domestic help and seamstresses. In addition to supporting themselves, the young people also would be expected to send part of their wages to their families in Graceville. From St. Paul, they departed for the last leg of their journey—a two-day, 193-mile trip by train. On 28 June, they arrived in the town of Morris, the end of the line for the railroad. There remained 28 miles to go before they reached their final destination.

> The train arrives at the end of the line in Morris, a frontier town of one thousand. Townspeople, dignitaries of the Masonic Lodge, and rail agents all turn out to witness the most interesting event to occur since the railroad tracks arrived in 1871. Graceville parishioners and "Irish River" members of Morris's Assumption Catholic Church arrive with wagons to transport their new neighbors.[29]

When the poverty-stricken group from Connemara finally reached Graceville, they had traveled a total of 3,721 miles. They had journeyed by tugboat, steamship, train and wagon to arrive at their destination that looked nothing like their homeland. They were in the prairie of western Minnesota where the land was flat and the late June temperature considerably warmer than they were accustomed to at home. In addition to clothing, essential furnishings for their homes and credit for food, the newcomers were given a year's supply of seeds and farming implements. Yet, here they were, skeletal from near starvation and so unlike the well-fed Midwest farmers and their families who lived off the land and their livestock. It was easy to see why Bishop Ireland's friend, Onahan, in a private letter to Omaha's Bishop O'Connor, wrote about the newcomers, "A more wretched lot of people I never saw."[30]

Off to a late start

Farmers in western Minnesota and elsewhere generally finished their planting in late April. In the Midwest, the corn crop was usually knee-high by 4 July, but by that date in 1880, the Connemara emigrants were just getting settled and trying to adjust to their new surroundings. While they had seeds for planting, the emigrants could only make use of five of their 160 acres because that was all of the soil that had been broken for planting. Within a few short months of their arrival in Graceville, rumors circulated that all was not well in Graceville with the new emigrants. The Irish newcomers claimed they had little to eat and insufficient clothing. The Connemara men were more interested in taking jobs as day laborers, not farmers of lands much larger than what they were accustomed to. Some Graceville residents accused the immigrants of being lazy and relying solely on handouts from Bishop Ireland and the clergy.

By mid-August, the *Morris Tribune* wrote about rumors of discontent in Graceville.

Visitors from Morris were troubled when they saw the Connemaras' condition so they took to the Morris newspaper to level criticism at Bishop Ireland and Graceville's Father Ryan:

> Surely there must have been some fund for the support of these people until a crop is harvested another season. It does not seem possible that large numbers of poor families were brought here late in the season and left to starve and freeze to death on the prairies...their condition is deplorable, and if what we hear is true, a terrible blunder, or worse, has been made.[31]

Bishop Ireland's response was swift. He visited Graceville in September and, while he thought the Connemara immigrants were doing well enough, "their common mutters of discontent alarmed and angered him."[32] He learned that some emigrants favored day labor work over farming and were complaining about treatment by their employers and the low wages they were earning. Enraged by this, Bishop Ireland initiated a system of public works, financed by the dioceses, that would pay the workers \$1 a day; they had been earning up to \$2 per day. To make matters worse, the bishop said that anyone who could not find employment to suit him in the public works program or as a farmer would have his credit for provisions cut off.[33]

Things were about to get even worse for the Connemaras. Winter began early with a blizzard that lasted from 15 to 18 October. While blizzards were not rare on the western Minnesota prairie, October blizzards were uncommon. Research by Barbara Boustead has confirmed that "the Hard Winter emerges as one of the worst since European-descended settlers arrived in the region and began documenting weather."[34] The winter of 1880–81, when the members of the Connemara group were trying to settle into their new environment, has been categorized among the top five in terms of severity. Dealing with the cold and snow was one thing, but the deep snow drifts over the railroad tracks curtailed railroad travel for months, preventing food and fuel resources from getting to the area's residents. Boustead noted, "Accounts are pretty consistent in that people were pretty much cut off from the outside world. There was some horse and sleigh travel." She considered it remarkable that there were very few fatalities from the severe winter but observed that most people had no choice but to remain in their small houses. [35]

The weather only exacerbated the growing discontent. In November, the *Morris Tribune* continued to report on conditions in Graceville and, by early December, the Morris Board of Trade appointed Henry Hutchins to go to Graceville and make a report. Hutchins returned in a week to inform the board of his findings, his report also being published in the Morris newspaper. It detailed interviews Hutchins had conducted with 25 Connemara families and candidly described the deplorable conditions they were facing.[36] The report also blamed Graceville's Father Timothy Ryan, who had been appointed by Bishop Ireland to oversee the transition. The report was telegraphed to Minnesota Governor John Pillsbury, and to Bishop Ireland in St. Paul. In no time, the report's findings made it into newspapers in St. Paul and Minneapolis, as well as Chicago, Boston and New York. While a number of headlines were scathing about the emigration scheme, other reports defended the project. Father Ryan was quoted in New York's *The Sun* as saying there was no suffering among the Connemaras, "I consider them among the best provided for of any people in this colony."[37]

The Morris report angered Bishop Ireland so much that he dispatched his friend, O'Brien, along with Leonard B. Hodges, to visit Graceville and investigate the condition of the emigrants. Prior to conducting their investigation, O'Brien said of Hodges, "...there was no one in Minnesota I had greater respect for."[38] But the two men ended up traveling to Graceville separately, and despite O'Brien's urgings for them to jointly investigate the settlement, Hodges met separately with the people. Ultimately, the two issued separate reports on their findings and their conclusions differed dramatically. O'Brien accused the Connemara emigrants of pretending that they had nothing and were suffering from little to eat, when in fact they were hiding clothing and money from O'Brien when he arrived. "Many of them are wholly unreliable, and have all the cunning which a life of pauperism gives," wrote O'Brien in his report, which was published in the Minneapolis newspaper. He told of two little boys who had shoes on when O'Brien and his partner entered a home but a little later, both boys were barefoot. The men later located the shoes under a bench in the house. O'Brien also accused the Connemaras of hiding the extra income they received from young family members working in St. Paul. Meanwhile, Hodges accused O'Brien of consorting with Graceville's Father Ryan. Hodges wrote, "Bishop Ireland blundered when he imported the Connemaras, blundered in leaving them to the tender mercies of Ryan, and blundered in his unfortunate letters and telegrams concerning me."[39] Hodges frankly described their suffering:

> I have seen with my own eyes a condition of squalid poverty and human suffering rarely found in any civilized community, disgraceful alike to the State, to the Colonization Bureau, and the resident priest.[40]

He described women and children as "more or less frozen in their shanties for the want of fuel. Some have told me that they went for two days in the worst weather without either food or wood."[41]

Rather than produce a conclusion, the separate investigative reports only created more angst. By now, Bishop Ireland reached boiling point. He did not hold back when he submitted a letter to the St. Paul newspaper just two days before Christmas that lambasted the Connemaras and described them as not the kind of people he had bargained for.

> Both Father Nugent ... and myself [sic] ... had supposed that we would have as objects of our beneficiana [sic], industrious, sober, hard-working people ... The parties in the west of Ireland whom Father Nugent requested to select families for the colony, sent us for the most part paupers of long standing, totally demoralized and unmannered by years of suffering, and unaccustomed to provide for their own wants. It would have been folly, under these circumstances, to do more for them than I did.[42]

When the Connemara emigrants responded by pleading to be allowed to move to St. Paul where they could find jobs at which they were skilled, the Bishop finally relented. In March 1881, he funded their transportation to St. Paul and found many of the men railroad jobs.

In writing about Bishop Ireland and the Connemaras many years later, James P. Shannon wrote that none of the small number of emigrants who chose to remain in Graceville realized a profit during their first years of farming due to the arduous task of breaking the soil. "it took years of patient labor to get the western soil in condition for intensive farming."[43] Biographers of Bishop Ireland refer to this experience as "the greatest grief of his life."[44] But Marvin O'Connell noted, "in the absence of direct evidence, one may be permitted to doubt that this failure, bitterly disappointing as it may have been, loomed quite so large in the firmament of a man for whom hyperbole was stock in trade."[45]

Another new home

The Connemara emigrants ultimately made their home in St. Paul in a section referred to as the "Connemara Patch." The area was located just to the east of downtown St. Paul and the broader area around the "Patch" was home to a number of European settlers, particularly Swedes and Italians. From a geographical standpoint, the area was opposite to the plains of western Minnesota. Instead, the Patch was little more than a ravine with 70-foot bluffs adjacent to it that contributed to flooding. The "homes" in the Patch were tiny huts with little more than a foot between each one. Six years after the Connemaras settled in the Patch, a reporter for the *St. Paul Globe* accompanied a relief worker to one particular hut. "It is small, contracted and unfit for any human to live in. Many people would blush to house their cow within that hastily and rudely constructed shanty."[46] In this particular home lived a widow with three children. Her husband had died recently and only the oldest daughter, age 10, could speak English. The shanty, with a floor that tipped at an angle, was "so narrow ... that 1 or 2 would find difficulty in lying lengthwise in it."[47] Just two years later, the paper reported on a young girl, Agnes O'Hara, who four years earlier attempted to rescue her baby brother from a "flying team of horses."[48] Not only did the infant die, but Agnes suffered a severe spinal injury that left her confined to "a wretched pallet bed in a still more wretched shanty."[49] To earn her keep, she made artificial flowers that her younger sister sold. After the turn of the century, a reporter noted about the Connemara Patch: "The sturdiest ... worked their way up, climbed the forbidding bluffs and are now enjoying independence."[50] Still, a small number had been left behind in the Patch "too indifferent or too disheartened to make the slightest attempt at climbing."[51]

The emigrants from Connemara who had left Ireland destitute but hopeful continued to experience hardships throughout their lives. But they had two things that motivated them to persist and aspire—one, their community of Irish friends and neighbors who were with them on their journey, and two, the hope that their children would be able to escape the abject poverty that defined their parents' entire lives. The Connemara story signifies hope and endurance. History may not judge them fairly—or always accurately—but their descendants can be gratified that their families remained determined to seek a better future.

NOTES

1. *Minneapolis Tribune*, 31 March 1880.
2. Ibid., p. 1. Greally is also spelled as Grealey or Grealy.
3. *Dublin Review*, vol. IX, Jan.-April 1883.
4. Gerard Moran, *Fleeing from Famine in Connemara* (Dublin: Four Courts Press, 2018), p. 13.
5. Report from Captain Digby Morant, HMS *Valorous,* Command 379 271, Aug. 1880.
6. Ibid.
7. *The Contemporary Review*, vol. 41, A. Strahan, 1882, p. 704.
8. Ibid., p. 132.
9. *Minneapolis Tribune*, 31 March 1880.
10. World Health Organization, "*Famine and Health*," www.who.int/emergencies/humanitarian-emergencies/famine/en/.
11. *Minneapolis Tribune*, 31 March 1880.
12. *Cincinnati Daily Star*, 9 Feb. 1880.
13. *Freeman's Journal*, 29 Oct. 1879.
14. Ibid.
15. Speech by Rev. Patrick Coyne, at a local Land League meeting, *The Nation*, 22 Nov. 1879.
16. Moran, *Fleeing from Famine*, p. 21.
17. Ibid., p. 23.
18. Rita Nolan, "A Good Christian," *Rabharta*, Kilmore Parish Magazine, 2001–2002.
19. Kathleen Villiers-Tuthill, *Beyond the Twelve Bens: A History of Clifden and District, 1860–1923* (Dublin: Connemara Girl Publications, 1990), p. 80.
20. Rev. James Nugent to Bishop John Ireland, 19 Feb. 1880. Published in *Saint Paul Sunday Globe*, 21 March 1880.
21. *Dublin Review*, vol. IX, Jan.-April 1883.
22. *Minnesota History*, March 1957, p. 206.
23. Bishop Ireland in *Saint Paul Sunday Globe*, 21 March 1880.
24. James P. Shannon, "Bishop Ireland's Connemara Experiment," *Minnesota History*, March 1957. The article is drawn from Shannon's doctoral dissertation on the subject of "Catholic Colonization on the Western Frontier."
25. How Bishop Ireland acquired the land, his role as a "contractor," and his treatment of those who remained on the land in Graceville, remained controversial for several decades.
26. *Benson Times,* 5 June 1876, as quoted in *Minnesota History*, p. 10.
27. Ibid.
28. *Catholic Review*, 1 Jan. 1881, quoted in *Minnesota History*, p. 208.
29. Bridget Connelly, *Forgetting Ireland: Uncovering a Family's Great Secret History* (St. Paul: Borealis Books, 2003), p. 5.
30. Onahan to O'Connor, 1 July 1880, Chancery Archives, Omaha, NE, quoted in *Minnesota History*, p. 208.
31. Connelly, *Forgetting Ireland*, pp 93–94.
32. Marvin R. O'Connell, *John Ireland and the American Catholic Church* (St. Paul: Minnesota Historical Press, 1988), p. 151.

33. *Minnesota History*, March 1957, p. 209.
34. Barbara E. Boustead, *The Hard Winter of 1880–1881: Climatological context and communication via a Laura Ingalls Wilder narrative*. Ph.D. dissertation, 2014, School of Natural Resources, University of Nebraska-Lincoln.
35. Interview with Barbara E. Boustead of Norman, OK, 25 Nov. 2019.
36. Connelly, *Forgetting Ireland*, p. 98.
37. *The Sun* (New York), 21 Dec. 1880. Chronicling America: Historic American Newspapers. Library of Congress: https://chroniclingamerica.loc.gov/lccn/sn83030272/1880–12–21/ed–1/seg–1/.
38. *Minneapolis Tribune*, 21 Dec. 1880.
39. Ibid.
40. *Chicago Tribune*, 18 Dec. 1880.
41. Ibid.
42. *St. Paul Pioneer Press*, 23 Dec. 1880.
43. Shannon, *Minnesota History,* p. 210.
44. Humphrey Moynihan, "Archbishop Ireland," *Acta et Dicta*, vol. VI, no. 1, Oct. 1933.
45. Marvin R. O'Connell, *John Ireland and the American Catholic Church* (Minnesota Historical Society Press, 1988), p. 152.
46. *St. Paul Globe*, "In Homes of Want," 2 Dec. 1887.
47. Ibid.
48. *St. Paul Daily Globe*, "One Phase of Life, A Pathetic Scene of Existence on the Connemara Flats," 30 June 1889.
49. Ibid.
50. *St. Paul Daily Globe*, 16 March 1902.
51. Ibid.

CHAPTER FOURTEEN

IMPACT OF THE TUKE EMIGRATION SCHEME

From County Mayo to Cleveland

Margaret Lynch

Scholars of the Great Famine will be familiar with the selfless role played by the young English Quaker, James Hack Tuke. More recently, attention has been paid to his heroic role during the Forgotten Famine of 1879–81. In the forefront of the scholarly resurgence of interest is historian Gerard Moran. His research has illuminated the importance of Tuke's assisted emigration schemes in counties Galway and Mayo in the 1880s.[1] Public organizations have also called attention to Tuke's impact. In 2013, *Ionad Deirbhile* Heritage Centre in Eachléim in Belmullet, County Mayo, created a memorial garden and developed a searchable database that focused on the Tuke-sponsored immigrants who left from Blacksod Bay.[2] Inspired by the pioneering work of both Moran and Rosemarie Geraghty of the Heritage Centre, Clifden and Connemara Heritage Society similarly highlighted the effect of the Tuke scheme in Connemara.[3] The websites of these three organizations provide both historians and descendants of Tuke-sponsored passengers with a vehicle for learning and sharing information about their ancestors. Furthermore, in March 2019, Ireland's Great Hunger Institute at Quinnipiac University opened a year-long exhibition dedicated to Tuke and his legacy.[4] In June of the same year, at its biannual international conference on the theme of "Famines in Ireland Before 1845 and After 1852," one day was dedicated to examine Tuke's role in relief efforts during the Forgotten Famine. Both historians and descendants of the original emigrants participated.[5]

It has long been recognized in Cleveland that a disproportionate number of Irish immigrants to the city hailed from County Mayo, especially Achill Island. The 15 sailings that left from Blacksod Bay carried 3,267 individuals from local communities, including families from Achill and its adjoining parishes. Today, Cleveland has an active Mayo Society and sponsored the international Mayo Society Convention in 2014, where the work of *Ionad Deirbhil*e was promoted. In addition, the communities of Cleveland and Achill initiated a twinning relationship in 2003, and the counties of Mayo and Cuyahoga, where Cleveland is located, followed suit several years later.[6] The Tuke story also connects with the mission of the Irish American Archives Association (IAAS). To assist in the work of recovery, the IAAS approached John Carroll University (JCU), for help in discovering and documenting the Tuke-assisted immigrants from Blacksod Bay who settled in Cleveland. The university had an established study-abroad exchange program with the National University of Ireland in Galway, sponsored by the Mayo Society of Greater Cleveland. Receptive to the request, the History Department identified students to serve as IAAS research interns every spring semester since 2016.[7] In the first five years of the project, six students, five from JCU, contributed to the effort.

Passenger manifests can provide information about passenger destinations. Transcriptions of all 15 sailings from Blacksod Bay have been completed, indexed and are available to be searched online. However, onward destinations were not provided on all of the manifests, and some families did not end up where they said they were headed. To gain a more accurate picture of who settled in Cleveland, it is necessary to search for all 3,267 passengers in United States' records. Combing through census, birth, marriage, and death records is tedious work. The structure of the project is that the students take the "first pass" at finding the passengers. Their work is reviewed, suggestions made and additional research conducted when they hit roadblocks. Passengers on four sailings have been documented to date. While Cleveland is the primary focus, the long-term goal is to develop a database of information about the Blacksod Bay passengers that could aid family history researchers as well as historians. Additionally, descendants continue to add information as they discover information about individual passengers.

The *Ionad Deirbhile* website was designed for descendants, not for scholars; nonetheless, it reveals overall patterns of general interest. The *Ionad Deirbhile* transcription project relied on passenger lists that were compiled when the passengers embarked from Blacksod Bay. Passenger lists for the same sailings on Ancestry.com represent a different set of manifests, which were apparently compiled when the passengers disembarked at the ports of Boston or Quebec.[8] The passenger manifests frequently recorded onward destinations for each passenger. When an onward destination was listed, that information was included as part of the passenger record in the website's database. Of the 3,267 individuals who set sail from Blacksod Bay in 1883 and 1884, onward destinations were specified or can be inferred for 2,140 passengers.

Although more than 1,000, or about a third, of the passengers went to unspecified destinations, the recorded destinations do reveal trends. The Blacksod Bay immigrants were headed toward 23 destination states. However, only four destination states attracted more than 100 immigrants, with Pennsylvania and Ohio far exceeding the others:

Destination state	# of passengers	% of total passengers
Pennsylvania	756	23%
Ohio	490	15%
Massachusetts	135	4%
Wisconsin	111	3%

Looking at regions within states, the top three destinations were:

Destination sub-region	# of passengers	% of total passengers
"Southern Tier" PA Coal Region (Schuylkill and Columbia counties)	396	12%
Cleveland	346	10.5%
"Northern Tier" PA Coal Region (Lackawanna and Luzerne counties)	313	9.5%

Focusing on individual communities, the top three destinations were:

Destination community	# of passengers	% of total passengers
Cleveland, OH	346	10.5%
"Lost Creek" (West Mahanoy), PA	171	5%
Scranton, PA	127	4%

Even without accounting for passengers whose destinations were not specified or who subsequently changed destinations, Cleveland emerged from this initial analysis as significant.

When searching for Tuke-assisted passengers in public records, familiar challenges apply. Names were spelled inconsistently, misinterpreted by clerks or indexers, or transformed entirely. The ages and dates supplied were frequently inconsistent. The 1890 U.S. census records were largely destroyed by fire, leaving a 16- or 17-year gap between the arrival of the sponsored immigrants in the U.S. and the next census in 1900. City directories that could fill the gaps are not easily available. Marriage and death records, while potentially helpful, are not uniformly accessible online and do not always contain enough identifying information. All of these challenges have resulted in a "can not find" rate of up to 25 percent. However, new resources are continually becoming available. Recently, the Irish government's Department of Arts, Heritage and the Gaeltacht launched a website that provides indexed and searchable scans of Irish Civil Records of birth, marriage and death.[9] The birth records, commencing in 1864, give the names of both parents, including the mother's maiden name. Since American marriage and death records sometimes provide the same information, the Irish records can help to confirm a match. Consequently, the "can not find" list is constantly revisited.

Irish Civil Records also shed light on family relationships. This is particularly helpful where individual family members cannot be found. Family groups were an important part of the "Tuke Assisted Emigration Scheme," with priority given to families. As Tuke overseer Sydney Buxton reported:

> I made it also a rule, in cases of families, that the whole family should go, or none. An inclination was occasionally shown to leave one or two members of the family behind on the land—an old father or mother, a brother, or someone; an idea which had to be sternly resisted if any permanent good were to accrue to the country.[10]

The idea was that a family's vacated land could enlarge and improve the sustainability of the holdings of families that stayed behind.

Passenger manifests offer only limited clues about family relationships. Family groups were sometimes bracketed on the manifests, and a married woman might be identified as a "wife." Unmarried women were designated as "spinsters" or "domestics," while men, married and single, were undifferentiated as laborers. Extended family relationships—such as mother-in-law or grandchild—were rarely specified. Relying on scarce clues from the manifests, *Ionad Deirbhile* has organized the passenger names into family groups, designated as "sailing parties." However, additional research sometimes warranted revision of the family groups. For instance, the Irish Civil Records have been useful in confirming that several older women were grandmothers traveling with the families of married daughters, or that several seemingly unaccompanied teenagers were traveling with an aunt. Research also revealed that people who were blood relations were not always going to the same destination. Birth records for the children of McLane (#313–316) and McNulty (#317–320) families on the 1884 *SS Canadian* sailing revealed that both families came from Kilcommon Parish and that both mothers had the same maiden name, Killker.[11] While it is highly likely that the two women were relatives, if not sisters, the two families were going to separate locations—the McLanes to Pennsylvania and the McNultys to Wisconsin. The probable relationship was noted, but they were classified as two family groups, not one. A family group was defined as people related by blood who had the same destination in North America. For statistical purposes, each individual who did not have a discernible family connection with other passengers was assigned as a single-person "family group."

Preliminary observations about the research can be drawn from a sample sailing—that of the *SS Canadian*, departing Blacksod Bay on 13 April 1884, and arriving in Boston on 24 April 1884. A total of 279 sponsored passengers boarded the *Canadian* in Blacksod Bay in 1884: 56 were assigned as family groups. All of the onward destinations were in the U.S. (some sailings to Quebec stayed in Canada). The primary question was: Where did the passengers end up? The corollary was: Did they end up where they said they were going? This is an overview of the passenger destinations:

- 26 family groups (48%) were found in the city named as their onward destination.
- 6 family groups (10%) were found in the same county, though not the city named. This tended to be the case in the agricultural "Great Plains" states.
- 5 family groups (8.5%) were found in the same state, though not the city named. This tended to be the case in western mining states such as Montana and Colorado.
- 5 family groups (8.5%) were found in other destinations entirely, including three Belmullet families who went to Holyoke, MA—a popular Belmullet destination—rather than to their stated destination.
- 14 family groups (25%) were not found.

The passengers who ended up in Cleveland were categorized as follows:

- 20 of 56 family groups (35%) stated Cleveland or Newburgh (a Cleveland neighborhood) as their destination.

- 100 percent of the family groups who hailed from Achill parish listed Cleveland as their destination, as did three of six families from neighboring Burrishoole parish.
- All but two of the families who stated Cleveland as their destination were found in Cleveland.
- Two Achill families went to Cleveland initially but later went to Nebraska.

The following observations were noted about the composition of the *SS Canadian* family groups in 1884:

- 30 family groups (55%) consisted of two parents traveling with children. Three of these groups also had additional relatives traveling with them.
- 17 family groups (30%) consisted of "single parents"—16 were mothers traveling with children. A higher number of the single parent groups—six— had other relatives with them.
- Three family groups (5% each) consisted of:
    - Teenage or young adult siblings
    - Husbands and wives without children or other relatives
    - Women without discernible family connections with other passengers.

In addition, 144 passengers, almost 52 percent, were 18 years or younger. The youngest, Kate Lally (#197–2), daughter of Anthony and Honor Monaghan Lally from Kilcommon Parish, was only 2 days old. The youth of so many passengers must have made travel all the more challenging.

While tracking the Tuke-assisted immigrants in U.S. public records, it became apparent that the impact of the scheme did not stop with the passengers themselves. Parents from 15 of the 1884 *SS Canadian* families subsequently had additional children. Although they were born in the United States, those children could have been shaped by their family's experience of hunger and poverty. Several of the groups had a family member who had emigrated ahead of the rest of the family. At least three of the women who were traveling on their own with children were not widows but joining husbands who had preceded them. Others were joining grown children. As Buxton explained, one of the conditions for selection was, "That those only should be sent to the States who could produce recent letters from friends willing and anxious to receive them out there."[12] It is possible that some family members went ahead specifically so that they could send back such letters.

One family group on the *SS Canadian* exemplified many of the varied family circumstances and complexities. There was a family (#292–296) consisting of a mother on her own, Bridget Hogan, and three children under the age of 6. The birth records for her children indicated that her maiden name was Corduff, and her death record revealed that her parents were Michael and Margaret Joyce Corduff. A Michael and Margaret Corduff (#289–290), on the same sailing and both in their 50s, were undoubtedly her parents. A teenage girl, Kate Moore (#291), was listed between the two parties. All were going to the coal mining town of Centralia, PA. Bridget Hogan was reunited with her husband James, a coal miner, and the couple had at least four more children. In the 1900 census, the Hogans were listed in Conyngham, another coal-mining town in Columbia County. They lived close to people whose last names were prevalent in Belmullet—Kilker, Mooney, Padden—and a Gaughan family who had sailed on the *SS Scandinavian* in 1883. The elder Corduffs and the teenaged Kate Moore could not be found in public records. Other Corduff families were found in neighboring towns; it cannot be ruled out that the Corduff parents may have lived with other relatives. The Corduff parents, Kate Moore, and Bridget Hogan and her children, were categorized as three separate "family groups" because Kate Moore's family connection could not be established, nor could it be demonstrated that the parents and their married daughter shared the same trajectory in the U.S.

Like the Hogans in Pennsylvania, many of the Tuke-assisted passengers settled near family or friends from home. The impulse to stay together was still evident 20 or 30 years later. In the 1910 census for Cleveland, four neighboring households on one street included individuals with connections to the 1884 *SS Canadian* sailing, encompassing nine passengers, children born in the America, and in-laws. The composition of the households was:

- Household 1: Widowed mother Catherine Mangan (#110); Catherine's unmarried young adult children—Patrick (#111), Rose and Catherine (both born in the U.S.); married daughter, Mary Mangan English (#113); Mary's husband, John English, and their two young daughters.
- Household 2: Margaret English, a married daughter of Catherine Mangan, born in the U.S., with Margaret's husband, Joseph English, and her two young sons. (Margaret and her sister Mary married two brothers.)
- Household 3: Widowed mother Catherine Gallagher (#75); adult son, Martin Gallagher (#78); married daughter, Celia Gallagher Mangan (#77), with Celia's husband, James, and five children; married daughter, Catherine Gallagher Foley (#79), with Catherine's husband, Bernard, and one child; and two boarders who were possibly cousins. The relationship between Celia

Gallagher Mangan's husband and the husband of the widowed Catherine Mangan who was living in Household #1 has not been documented.

- Household 4: Widowed mother Catherine Burke (#81); and married daughter, Anna Burke McIntyre (#85) with Anna's husband, Dennis, and one child.

Clearly, many of the Tuke-assisted passengers came from the same communities in Ireland and went to the same communities in the U.S. Thus, it is not surprising that marriages took place between them. For instance, Edward English (#73), who was 8 years old when he sailed with three older brothers on the 1884 *SS Canadian* and settled in Cleveland, subsequently married Celia (Sabina) Kilbane (#120), who had sailed with her family on the *SS Canadian* in May 1883. Celia Kilbane's older brother, James (#115) also married a Tuke-sponsored immigrant, Margaret McManamon (#34), who had left with her family on the *SS Scandinavian* in April 1883. The English, Kilbane and McManamon families all departed from Achill and could have known each other in Ireland.

Merely finding Tuke-assisted passengers in public records does not reveal everything about the emigrants' new lives. Details from public records need to be placed in a larger context in order to discover what happened to them. Unique factors shaped their experiences in each place where they settled. Since Cleveland is the primary focus of this study, it was important to identify factors shaping this city.[13] When the Tuke immigrants arrived, Cleveland was one of the country's fastest growing industrial centers. From a population of 43,417 in 1860, just before the outbreak of the Civil War, Cleveland's population almost quadrupled by 1880 to 160,146. In the next decade, the population soared to 261,352. Located at the junction of a river and a Great Lake, Cleveland had already established itself as a transportation hub before 1860. By the 1880s, the city had become dominant in steel making and shipbuilding. For an unskilled Irish immigrant arriving, Cleveland offered plentiful opportunities for backbreaking work.

Cleveland's geography also influenced settlement patterns. Cleveland sits on the southern shore of Lake Erie, and the Cuyahoga River roughly bisects the city. A northern tier of railroad lines runs east-west along the lakeshore, connecting with Buffalo, Detroit and Chicago, and another set of railroad lines comes up from the south, connecting with the coal fields of Pennsylvania and West Virginia. Iron ore was shipped from Upper Michigan and Minnesota. The iron ore docks, along with railroad and shipyards, were located at the junction of the river and the lake, on the west side of the river. The iron works—and later steel mills—were located along the east side of the river, south of the city center, where land was more plentiful when the first iron rolling mill was built in 1857. The neighborhood along the lake was home to the docks and shipyards, called "The Angle," while the steel center to the south, originally an independent village that had been annexed in 1873, was known as Newburgh.

Both neighborhoods offered work for unskilled laborers and were "points of entry" for incoming Irish immigrants. A small wave of Achill immigrants had come to Cleveland in the early 1860s escaping from a series of bad weather and poor harvests in those years.[14] They split between the Angle and Newburgh. Through chain migration, family and friends of the 1860s' immigrants arrived in Cleveland throughout the ensuing decade. Anecdotally it seems, Newburgh may have gained more ground with new arrivals after the iron works converted to steel making in 1868. In any event, when Tuke provided the opportunity for immigration in the early 1880s, family connections prompted Achill people to choose Cleveland as a destination, with some even specifying Newburgh by name. However, labor conflict possibly steered some of the immigrants away from the steel mills of Newburgh. In May 1882, steel workers, many of whom were Irish, walked out of the Cleveland Rolling Mills, the largest employer in the area, to demand higher pay and better working conditions. The owners shut the workers out and hired Polish and Czech workers as low-cost strikebreakers. Although some of the striking workers were eventually rehired—and there were other jobs in the Newburgh railroad yards or with other steel companies—tensions remained high for several years, with another violent strike taking place in 1885.[15] In 1883 and 1884, therefore, Newburgh was a less promising place for newly arriving Irish immigrants than it had been. It appears, therefore, that a greater portion of the Tuke-assisted immigrants made their way to the Angle than to Newburgh.

The Angle was a fan-shaped neighborhood that sloped down toward the Cuyahoga River, and the most gently slopes were settled first in the 1860s. When the Tuke immigrants arrived, they crowded onto the only available hillside—the steepest and least hospitable—within a small "triangle" of streets crisscrossed by narrow alleys. In 1890, a local newspaper, *The Plain Dealer*, reported: "The three-sided bit of ground lies between Old River, Hanover, and Division streets upon the side of a steep hill and 400 people lodge nightly in its twenty odd houses."[16] *The Plain Dealer* was reporting on conditions in the "Triangle" in 1890 because it was gaining notoriety as an Irish ghetto, the city's first. Packed into low-quality housing on steep, narrow lots at the edge of industrial tracts, the recent immigrants lacked education and suffered from a high mortality rate. There was work on the iron ore docks, but only on a day-to-day basis. Crippling and fatal accidents were frequent. Outsiders began to associate the Angle with drinking, brawling and lawlessness. As *The Plain Dealer* claimed, "Ignorance, hot blood and poverty lead to the prevalent disorder through a path of overindulgence in the few pleasures at the command of the people. With the ignorance of fear they regard the police as their common enemy."[17]

The Plain Dealer did not indicate awareness of any specific wave of immigration but the Irish-American community in Cleveland knew about the "Forgotten Famine." In February 1880, the city's Irish organizations canceled the upcoming St. Patrick's Day Parade and applied the money that would have been spent on it "to the relief of the destitute in Ireland."[18] Land League chapters formed in Cleveland in the early 1880s to raise funds for famine relief and to promote Irish independence and a more just system of land management. The city's Irish Americans had also heard about "assisted emigration." In February 1883, Clevelander Patrick Smith, a pre-Famine immigrant who was a prominent member of St. Malachi Parish in the Angle, joined a national Irish-American delegation to President Chester Arthur to protest against "assisted emigration" and "the policy of the English government in first reducing the Irish peasantry to abject poverty and then sending them penniless to the United States." Among other points, the delegates argued:

> That emigration from Ireland is political oppression, and not a natural necessity is apparent, because, although 18,000,000 of her 20,000,000 acres are cultivable, only 8,000,000 are under tillage. The obvious remedy is the distribution of the people over new land in their own country.[19]

The influx of destitute Irish immigrants was noted in Cleveland. Each year, the pastor of every Roman Catholic parish had to make a report to the bishop of the diocese. On 29 January 1884, Father James P. Maloney, pastor of St. Malachi Parish in the Angle, submitted his report for 1883. Of 580 families in the parish, 270 had not made any financial contribution to the church that year. Father Maloney explained, "The number of poor Emigrants that settled here last year was very great."[20]

The Tuke-assisted immigrants were not responsible for all of the poverty, crowding and under-employment in the Angle—or the urban ills that resulted—but the "Triangle gang" had Tuke connections. Michael and Patrick Gorman had sailed with their parents and siblings (#471–479) on the *SS Austrian* in 1883, when Patrick was 16 and Michael was 12. Michael, nicknamed "Foxy," was named by the *Plain Dealer* as a "Triangle boy." The family moved out of the Angle in 1891 to a new development that replicated the small lots and inferior housing of the Angle. In the new neighborhood, the Gorman brothers and friends, dubbed the "McCart Street Gang," were frequently in the news for petty theft.[21] During the bootlegging 1920s and 1930s, the name of James "Shimmy" Patton was legendary in Cleveland; Patton was born in the U.S., but his mother and two oldest brothers (#245–247) had left on the *SS Manitoban* among the "poor Emigrants" who came to St. Malachi Parish in 1883.

To counteract the pull of the streets, St. Malachi Parish formed a club for boys and young men, whether or not they were able to attend the parish elementary school. The LaSalle Club offered boxing, tumbling and other activities. World champion boxer Johnny Kilbane was a product of St. Malachi's LaSalle Club, even though he had to quit school at age 10 to work as a water boy on the docks.[22] The boxer's father had immigrated to Cleveland about 1879, and his grandmother, Bridget Kilbane, uncle Patrick Kilbane, and several McGinty cousins (#87–91) immigrated on the *SS Canadian* in 1884. At that time, many Irish-American priests and bishops were concerned that newly arrived and destitute Irish immigrants would flock to industrial cities and succumb to the urban vices as depicted in *The Plain Dealer* story about Cleveland's Angle neighborhood. A group of priests, prelates and lay supporters formed the Irish-Catholic Colonization Association in the Chicago area in 1879. Inspired by then-Bishop John Ireland's promotion of Irish settlement in Minnesota in the 1870s, its goal was to encourage Irish immigration to "healthful" agrarian states in the Midwest.

Bishops John Lancaster Spalding, of Peoria, and James O'Connor, of Omaha, were particularly active in promoting farmland in Nebraska as an antidote to crowded industrial cities.[23] Some of the Tuke immigrants heeded their call. An extended McManaman family that hailed from Tonatanvally in Achill came to Cleveland first but left quickly for Nebraska. An older step-sister who had settled in Nebraska a decade earlier encouraged the move. Sisters Grace McManaman (#424–430) and Honor McManaman Henne [Haney] (#431–434) and their children all sailed together on the *SS Austrian* in 1883. Their brother, James (#452), unmarried at the time, sailed on the *SS Phoenician*, also in 1883. Another brother, Patrick McManaman, along with his wife, children and mother-in-law (#122–127) were on the *SS Canadian* in 1884. Michael McManaman, the final sibling to immigrate, came without assistance in about 1890 and went directly to Nebraska. The McManamans settled initially in a hard-scrabble area near Lincoln in Greeley County, Nebraska, and many moved subsequently to richer farmland in Spalding County when Bishop O'Connor purchased land there.

The McManaman trajectory illustrates another crucial source of information for finding out what happened to the Tuke immigrants in the United States—the testimony of descendants. The *Ionad Deirbhile* website provides a gateway for families to share stories and photographs of their ancestors.[24] Without the personal testimony of descendants, a researcher may never have thought to look in certain sources. Untangling complicated family relationships among passengers also sometimes requires "insider" information. For instance, regarding passengers (#48–54) who boarded the *SS Scandinavian* in a row: Anne Doogan, age 28; James Doogan, age 25; Anne Doogan, age 5; Mary Doogan, age 3; Patrick Doogan, infant; Bridget Gallagher, age 7; and John Gallagher, age 18, we now know that the party consisted of a widowed, remarried woman; her second husband; two children (Anne and Mary) by her first husband (traveling under the name of her second husband); an infant by her second husband; her oldest daughter (Bridget Gallagher) by her first Gallagher husband; and a step-son, John, son of her Gallagher husband by previous marriage.

Public records can only provide limited information. They show that Anne Dugan (the spelling adopted in the United States) gave birth to several more children, that the family kept a saloon, and that her youngest daughter, May, eventually took over the saloon. But the records will not reveal that May Dugan was so well regarded in her community that a Cleveland social service center was named after her in 1974.[25] The fact that Thomas Masterson, who arrived with his family on the *SS Manitoban* (#184), worked for the city park system can be derived from census records, but not the fact that he helped to found the West Side Irish-American Club in Cleveland in 1930.[26] A death record reveals that Martin Lynch (#327), who traveled with his family on the *SS Waldensian*, died at the age of 41, but not that his fatherless son, James, would serve as the "voice" of Cleveland's St. Patrick's Day Parade for many years.[27]

While public records are only part of the picture, they contain details that suggest directions for further study, including information about literacy, occupation and home ownership. How quickly were the Tuke-sponsored immigrants able to buy their own homes? Were the younger passengers able to obtain more skilled jobs than their parents were? Could the mortality rates of those who availed of Tuke's assistance be compared with those who stayed behind? A full picture of what happened to the Tuke immigrants will draw on all available resources—public records, local history research, and descendant stories and vintage photographs. Such photographs frequently reassemble the living members of the original sailing parties years later. Their "Americanized" clothing, their formality, their access to a camera—all bespeak their aspirations and testify to their resilience.

At the end of the day, did the Tuke Assisted Emigration Scheme enable better lives? The definition of success is up for debate—and the appropriate timeframe for judging it. The benefits of assisted immigration may not have seemed clear-cut when Michael "Foxy" Gorman responded to limited opportunities by turning to a life of petty crime *c.*1890, but may have seemed more evident when his granddaughter, Patricia Gorman Kern, was serving as president of a local division of the Ladies Ancient Order of Hibernians in Cleveland in the 1970s. The Tuke Assisted Emigration Scheme provides a fruitful case study for Irish immigration, and the IAAS hopes to make a lasting contribution by assembling information that can be used for further research.

NOTES

1. Gerard Moran, *Sending out Ireland's Poor* (Dublin: Four Courts Press, 2004); Gerard Moran, *Fleeing from Famine in Connemara: James Hack Tuke and his Assisted Emigration Schemes in the 1880s,* Maynooth Studies in Local History, No. 135 (Dublin: Four Courts Press, 2018).
2. "Blacksod Bay Assisted Immigration Sailings," www.blacksodbayemigration.ie.
3. "Clifden and Connemara Heritage Society, Connemara and Her People," www.clifden-heritage.org
4. Ireland's Great Hunger Institute, "Fleeing from Famine," Quinnipiac University, curated by Christine Kinealy and Gerard Moran, Hamden, CT. It subsequently travelled to other locations in Ireland and North America.
5. Conference, Ireland's Great Hunger Institute, "Famines in Ireland before 1845 and after 1852," Quinnipiac University, Hamden, CT.
6. Special thanks to Rosemarie Geraghty whose passion for recovering the stories of the Tuke passengers is an invaluable resource.
7. Daniel Kilbride, Ph.D., Professor of History, coordinated the IAAS internship for JCU in 2016–17; Rodney Hessinger, Ph.D., Associate Dean for Humanities & Social Sciences and Professor of History, in 2018–19.
8. Telephone call, 12 June 2019, with Rosemarie Geraghty, principal researcher for *Ionad Deirbhile*, confirmed the use of embarking manifests for the transcriptions, and that there are discrepancies between the embarking and disembarking manifests.
9. "Irish Genealogy," www.irishgenealogy.ie
10. "Mr. Sydney Buxton's Report," *Emigration from Ireland; Being the Second Report of the Committee on 'Mr Tuke's Fund'* (July 1883), pp 20–21, in *Reports and Papers Relating to the Proceedings of the Committee of "Mr. Tuke's Fund," for Assisting Emigration from Ireland, During the Years 1882, 1883, and 1884,* at: www.blacksodbayemigration.ie
11. In the Blacksod passenger database, each passenger is assigned a number. This paper relies on the passenger numbering used on www.blacksodbayemigration.ie. However, on a few of the sailings, some family members became separated from other family members and the passenger numbers do not align with family units. There are also several discrepancies between passenger numbering on the embarking and the disembarking manifests. A revised standardization of passenger numbers may be needed in the future.
12. "Report of the Committee," *Second Report of the Committee 'Mr Tuke's Fund,'* p. 4, in *Reports and Papers Relating to ... the Years 1882, 1883, and 1884.*

13. For an overview of the history of the Irish in Cleveland, as seen through the lens of the city's annual St. Patrick's Day Parade, see Margaret Lynch, *The Day We Celebrate: 175 Years of Cleveland's St. Patrick's Day Parade* (Cleveland: IAAS with United Irish Societies of Greater Cleveland, 2017).
14. Theresa McDonald, *Achill Island* (Tullamore: I.A.S. Publications, 1997), pp 198–204.
15. For an account of the Cleveland Rolling Mill strikes in 1882 and 1885, see "Cleveland Rolling Mill Strikes," Encyclopedia of Cleveland History. At: https://case.edu/ech/articles/c/cleveland-rolling-mill-strikes.
16. *The Plain Dealer*, 6 March 1890. The name "Triangle," later shortened to Angle, originally referred to the 3-street area, which inhabitants dubbed "Achill Patch," but came to be applied to the whole larger neighborhood.
17. Ibid.
18. *The Plain Dealer*, 23 Feb. 1880.
19. "Assisted Emigrants," *The Plain Dealer*, 25 June 1883.
20. St. Malachi Parish Report, 1183, submitted to the Catholic Diocese of Cleveland, 29 Jan. 1884.
21. See, for example, a newspaper item about stolen beer kegs in "McCart Street Gang," *The Plain Dealer*, 9 Oct. 1891.
22. See, "Johnny Kilbane," www.johnnykilbane.com for an account of Kilbane's growing up in the Angle and his career as a boxer.
23. See, Sister Mary Evangela Henthorne, *The Irish Catholic colonization association of the United States; its origin and development under the leadership of the Rt. Rev. John Lancaster Spalding, bishop of Peoria, president of the association, 1879–1892* (Champagne, IL: The Twin City Printing Company, 1932).
24. I have McManamons from The Valley in my own family background and exchanged family information with a Nebraska lawyer named Kevin McManaman—the Nebraska family members spelled their last name with an "a" rather than an "o." He and I discussed and confirmed which of his ancestors arrived on Tuke-assisted sailings. Personal correspondence with Kevin McManaman, Lincoln Nebraska, via email on 9/25/2016 and 10/1/2016.
25. "May Dugan Center," www.maydugancenter.org/about-us/
26. Lynch, *The Day We Celebrate*, p. 78.
27. Ibid., p. 118.

CHAPTER FIFTEEN

THE REAL FAMINE QUEEN?

Maud Gonne and Famines in the 1890s

Christine Kinealy

Because Maud Gonne is frequently defined as muse to, and the unrequited love interest of, the poet, W.B. Yeats, her accomplishments as an advanced nationalist, artist, actor, lecturer, polemist, writer and social activist are often marginalized.[1] In particular, her role in assisting with the perennial poverty and intermittent subsistence crises that dogged Ireland in the final decade of the 19th century has largely been ignored. This chapter examines Gonne through her engagement with localized famines in the west of Ireland during the 1890s and its influence on her subsequent political activities.[2]

Born in England in 1866, an acknowledged beauty who was independently wealthy, articulate and a master at manipulating media to her own benefit, Gonne lived her adult life in the public eye, easily traversing the distances between England, Ireland, France and North America. She also had an alternative—and more private—life in France, where she had an impassioned relationship with married journalist and right-wing activist, Lucien Millevoye. Their secret liaison would result in the births of a son and a daughter. Only three months after giving birth in Paris, in January 1890, to Georges Sylvère, the dashing, public Gonne was in Tipperary, speaking out against evictions.[3] She was part of a delegation of English members of the Home Rule League. Throughout this fact-finding mission, they were followed by hostile policemen, "who sang indecent songs and used offensive expressions in the presence of the ladies."[4] From Ireland, Gonne traveled to England to speak on behalf of a Home Rule candidate during a July by-election in Barrow-in-Furness. One Irish newspaper praised

Gonne's role and her "fascinating and irresistible enthusiasm."[5] By August, Gonne was back in Ireland, speaking in counties Galway and Kildare. Earlier in the year, Clongorey in Kildare had been the location of a number of high-profile evictions, which had resulted in arrests, including that of the local parish priest.[6] Gonne was again accompanying a delegation of British male politicians who were members of the Home Rule Association.[7] Regardless of her youth and gender, Gonne was allowed to share the platform and speak as their equal. Moreover, despite her upper-class English accent and upbringing, she referred to herself as "an Irish woman," which was also accepted and even met with cheers.[8] Unusual for a young, single woman, Gonne had inserted herself into local Irish politics—local politics that were being played out on both national and international stages. These appearances marked the commencement of her prolonged and passionate engagement with the poor of Ireland. That she had been accepted in this role was apparent when one newspaper described her as being "universally known here."[9]

At the end of 1890, Gonne returned to the west of Ireland to speak out against evictions. At this stage, it was clear that this part of the country was facing another subsistence crisis. Although nothing matched the scale, longevity or deadliness of the Great Famine of the 1840s, during the decades that followed, crops, notably potatoes, frequently failed in Ireland. When combined with bad weather, a poor corn harvest, indebtedness, depression in the prices of dairy products and cattle and lack of employment opportunities elsewhere, the failures often resulted in localized famines, with concomitant higher levels of evictions, emigration, disease and, occasionally, excess mortality. The most severe crises occurred in the years 1860-62 and 1879-81, but the final decade of the century was also marked by intermittent crop failures and evictions, despite a year of agitating for land reforms and some piecemeal legislation having been passed.[10] In 1886, in response to bad weather and agricultural depression, some of the more militant followers of Charles Stewart Parnell, in a move to revive the land agitation, launched the Plan of Campaign, calling on landlords to reduce rents by between 20 and 40 percent. They enjoined tenants to withhold their rent payments if demand was not complied with.[11] Although the campaign was intended to raise the morale of tenants, the fact that it coincided with a series of poor harvests made tenants more vulnerable.

The first potato harvest of the 1890s was not auspicious. In August, blight and "blackening crops" were reported on Achill Island. At that time of year, most of the able-bodied men, and some women, were in Britain, undertaking their annual journey to assist with the harvest.[12] According to one newspaper:

> There will be no potatoes for them to dig when they get back. The seed sown before they left Achill in May and June is rotting in the ground; and the total failure of the crop in the island is a matter of sad absolute certainty.[13]

It was not just the islands where the prospects looked gloomy. In large stretches of the nearby Ballina Union, the crop was a complete failure. The Poor Law Guardians passed a resolution asking that employment be provided in extending the train lines, "since, apart from public purposes, it will serve to stave off the danger of threatened famine in the most extensive and congested and poorest districts of Mayo."[14] In November, a "special correspondent" for the *Freeman's Journal* toured west Cork, the site of so much suffering in 1846 and 1847. He concluded that:

> Reports on the condition of the potato crop in south and west Ireland are almost as discouraging as those received from Mayo and Donegal ... when the small farmers and fishermen from Clonakilty to Crookhaven, and round by Bantry, always excepting Baltimore and its immediate neighbourhood, find the potatoes completely exhausted, they will be resorting to the towns in a starving condition, as in '47 and in a less degree, '69.[15]

To address concerns about exaggeration and deception by the Irish poor—a claim made by the authorities during every famine—a Scottish agriculturalist visited the west of Ireland "to get to the true facts as to the blight" and provide an "impartial" assessment. He travelled from Cork to Donegal. Regarding to the latter, he reported:

> I think there can be hardly any doubt that in Donegal the loss from the potato plague will be heavier than in any other county in Ireland. Nowhere have I seen the crop so universally deficient ... This was attributable to the fact that the wet and cold character of the summer continued longer in Donegal than in any other part of Ireland. In their weed-covered, water-logged, ill-made beds, the Donegal potatoes soon fell a prey to the enemy.[16]

The distress in the west of the country was raised in the House of Commons by several Irish politicians, including James O'Brien, MP for South Mayo. The Chief Secretary, however, was dismissive, responding, "The Government do not apprehend anything of a nature which could be described as famine in the district referred to."[17]

Similar to 1879-81, this period of shortages coincided with increased nationalist activity both in Ireland and North America. Just as Parnell had visited America in 1880 to raise money for famine and for the Land League, in 1890, John Dillon and William O'Brien crossed the Atlantic to solicit support for the latest famine and their Plan of Campaign. Dillon, MP for East Mayo since 1885, informed attendees at a large meeting in Philadelphia that his constituents numbered 52,000, "all poor and threatened with starvation." He added, "The question is not how to feed the starving Irish, but how to remove the cause of starvation. We come here not asking for food but help to enable the people to feed themselves." At this meeting alone, $13,000 was raised, a pattern replicated wherever Dillon and O'Brien visited.[18] Once again, private charity, especially from overseas, saved lives in Ireland, in contrast to the apparent indifference of the government.[19]

As had been the case previously, evictions accompanied the food shortages, thus combining hunger with homelessness. They were particularly severe in Falcarragh and Ardsmore in County Donegal, land owned by Wybrants Olphert, a fierce opponent of the Plan of Campaign. Olphert's ruthless evictions attracted the attention not only of Irish nationalists, but also their sympathizers in Britain and America. Intense media scrutiny kept the evictions in public view. One newspaper referred to those evicted as "half-famished, half-naked, feeble peasants," while Olphert was "the old tyrant with a heart of lead." It further explained:

> The armies of Attila sweeping over Europe were not more destructive in their way than the proportionate ravages of this hoary old hypocrite. The emissaries of Olphert flung out under the drenching rain and the fierce Atlantic mid-winter blasts poor women weak from recent childbirth and poor old men blind and tottering into the grave from the weight of patriarchal years.[20]

Reminiscent of the work of James Mahoney during the Great Famine, a sympathetic artist, J.D. Reigh, traveled to Donegal and created powerful visual images, many to be given free with the *United Ireland* newspaper.[21]

At the end of 1890, Maud Gonne travelled to Donegal, building on her reputation as a champion of the poor and oppressed. Although she was accompanied by other nationalist women, it was Gonne who repeatedly took to the stage and who inevitably garnered the most publicity. In addition to urging people not to pay their rents and resist evictions, she also spoke on behalf of political prisoners in British prisons.[22] One of Gonne's companions, Norma Borthwick, was an English-born artist and avid *gaeilgeoir*, who created sketches of the evictions on the Olphert estate.[23] The women were singled out for praise in the *Flag of Ireland*:

> When it tried the nerve and endurance of the men of the Royal Irish Constabulary, what can we say of the devoted ladies from England who came over to witness the horror, and saw it through from the opening to the close! Ireland ought never to forget the services of those brave women—Mrs. and Miss Amos, Miss Borthwick, Miss Maud Gonne, and Miss Mary [sic];[24] and if we had such an institution as the Legion of Honour they would certainly claim its highest decoration for their chivalrous service in Donegal.[25]

Two of the women—Gonne and Borthwick—were immortalized in an illustration by Reigh, entitled, "Mr. Golfour's [Balfour's] Method of 'Protecting the Weak'," which was given as a free supplement with *United Ireland*. In the text, Gonne (who was incorrectly referred to as Maud Gorme [sic]), was described as "an Irish sympathiser," and Borthwick as "an English sympathiser." The paper informed its readers that, "The cartoon is more than double the size ordinarily presented to our readers, and neither trouble, skill nor expense have been spared in its production."[26] Inevitably, unionist papers were less impressed with Gonne's interventions; the *Londonderry Sentinel* in early November described the female visitors as "birds of evil omen." They claimed they had not heard of Gonne before but, "She seems to be a person of some authority." They also noted that when urging people to break the law, she announced that she was willing to go to prison with them.[27] A week later, the *Sentinel* stated that the local people had been "goaded into resistance by the harangues of such fire-eaters as Miss Maud Gonne."[28] What did the local people feel about having so much international attention focused on them, and having a beautiful, fearless woman as their champion? According to Gonne, the people of Donegal, and later Mayo, believed she was a *Sidhe*—a mythical fairy that could live in the real world. Gonne used the people's superstitions to her advantage, subsequently claiming, with some self-aggrandizement, that, "In Donegal, being the woman of the *Sidhe* helped me to put evicted families back in their homes and to release prisoners."[29]

However much she divided opinion, Gonne's rise to celebrity status was rapid. Only weeks after agitating in Donegal, a "striking likeness" of Gonne was displayed at the annual meeting of the Hibernian Academy.[30] When she returned to Paris, her movements were followed in the Irish and British press. In 1891, Gonne was interviewed by a correspondent for the *Daily Telegraph*, "upon whom she seems to have made a great impression." His reference to her as belonging to "the softer sex," was mocked by the London *Globe*, who also noted that Gonne was delivering a series of lectures in France on "English atrocities in Ireland."[31] In March 1892, the *Globe* reported that while there was little interest in her lectures, "her portrait is to be seen in every photographer's shop."[32] In contrast, Irish papers commented favorably on her lectures, which had all been given in French. An article that appeared in several newspapers described her as the "beautiful Irish Home Ruler" adding, "She is young and fervidly earnest, and her views on the Irish question are so strong and thorough that they have won for her high place in the favour of the Irish Nationalists." They pointed out that her lectures had raised large amounts of money for Irish distress and for political prisoners.[33] A description of her activities, written by Yeats, was even more complimentary, he averring that, "she has made her voice heard where so many have failed. Every speech has been a triumph, and every triumph greater than the one that went before it." He pointed out that not only did thousands of people attend Gonne's lectures in France, but that they were followed by newspapers as far away as Egypt.[34] The besotted Yeats referred to Gonne as "The New Speranza"—a reference to a woman nationalist poet whose poem, "The Famine Year," written in 1847, had castigated the British government for deliberately starving the Irish poor.[35] Tellingly, the persistence of famine continued to inform Gonne's lectures, she evocatively describing to French audiences what had taken place in Ireland in 1848:

> Men and women ate the dogs, the rats, and the grass in the field, and some even, when all food was gone, ate the dead bodies ... Ireland was heroic in her suffering. Whole families, when they had eaten their last crust, and understood they had to die, looked once upon the sun and then closed up the doors of their cabins with stones, that no one might look on their last agony. Weeks afterwards men would find their skeletons gathered round the extinguished hearth. I do not exaggerate, gentlemen. I have added nothing to the mournful reality. If you come to my country every stone will repeat to you this tragic history. It was only fifty years ago. It still lives in thousands of memories.[36]

When Gonne returned to London in July 1892 for the inaugural meeting of the Irish Literary Society, hosted by veteran nationalist, Sir Charles Gavan Duffy, she was "warmly greeted all round." The meeting was attended by 300 leaders of Irish society in Britain, including many politicians and writers, among whom were Oscar Wilde and Bram Stoker, but Gonne was the only person singled out for such a mention.[37] Still aged only 26, she already had taken her place in the pantheon of strong female nationalists.

For the next few years, Gonne frequently lectured in France and England on the plight of evicted tenants and political prisoners, but she constantly returned to the horrors of the Great Famine.[38] By 1897—the 60th anniversary of Queen Victoria acceding to the throne—her focus had changed to look at the condition of Ireland under the reign of Victoria. She drew a comparison with an earlier English Queen, Elizabeth I, who had been advised by Edmund Spenser to starve the Irish into submission, so that they would have to eat each other.[39] In regard to Victoria, Gonne averred that her ministers had advised a similar solution:

> During the short period of ten years—namely, from 1841 to 1851—three millions of Irish firesides had been laid waste. In the terrible year of the famine, when all other countries were contributing to aid the unfortunate people of Ireland, the Sultan of Turkey not excepted, England was draining the country of its life's blood; and it was a mark of the wonderful vitality of the Celtic race that it had survived all Anglo efforts to destroy it.[40]

In Manchester in the north of England, Gonne informed an audience, "It would take a great number of revolutions stamped out in blood before the death toll reached one million, and yet this number had died of hunger and famine in Ireland during the reign of Victoria."[41] When lecturing to a Young Ireland group in Paris, she alluded to the cost of making Victoria the Empress of India, while people were starving in another part of her empire.[42]

By this stage, nationalists were planning for the centenary of the 1798 Rising—and Gonne was in the forefront of the preparations.[43] She was also arranging to visit America to call for the release of political prisoners.[44] Concurrent with Gonne preparing to travel, people in the west of Ireland were facing the prospect of another season of localized famines. As usual, the government prevaricated in allowing the guardians to provide additional relief, only relenting in December. Furthermore, as one Irish newspaper warned its readers:

> It is just possible that the Government have in mind the plan of making to the Guardians not a grant, but a loan of money. The latter, certainly, has been the traditional shape which the Government's generosity to the distressed districts of Ireland has taken. We can only say that, if this is the shape which it is to take now, protest against it cannot be too strong.[45]

Gonne's tour of the United States was successful both in attracting publicity and raising funds. She spoke before large audiences and made a considerable impact.[46] In New York, some of the audience were visibly sobbing when listening to Gonne's emotive words. Amongst other things, she criticized Queen Victoria's Jubilee celebrations:

> Well did the Irish people know that in celebrating sixty years of Victoria's reign, the English people were celebrating sixty years of successful murder, rapine, plunder and piracy ... during the past century more than 1,000,000 Irish souls died of starvation and destitution, driven out by English agents of English lords. It is a part of England's policy to exterminate people by its so-called methods of civilization, and then make them think it is the divine finger of Providence.[47]

Gonne sailed home to Ireland on Christmas Eve 1897.[48] She later recalled that upon landing, she was surrounded by newspaper reporters, but that she, "turned the tables on the reporters trying to interview me by asking them for news." The news was disheartening:

"Not too good," said the reporter of the *Freeman's Journal,* "Potato blight in the West," and he handed me a copy of his paper which contained the insolent reply of Balfour to a question in the House of Commons in regard to deaths from starvation in County Mayo and the inadequate relief measures.[49] Balfour had produced doctors' certificates of 'death from heart-failure' and then said: 'You can't expect us to supply your farmers with Champagne.'[50]

Gonne then traveled to Dublin where she met with her close friend, James Connolly. In response to the reappearance of famine in the west, they jointly wrote a leaflet entitled "The Rights of Life and the Rights of Property."[51] They used the words of the Catholic hierarchy to show the injustice of hunger, while invoking the memory of the Great Famine:

> In 1847 our people died by the thousands of starvation though every ship leaving an Irish port was laden with food in abundance. The Irish people might have seized that food, cattle, corn and all manner of provisions before it reached the seaports—have prevented famine and saved their country from ruin, but did not do so, believing such action to be sinful and dreading to peril their souls to save their bodies. In this belief, we know now they were entirely mistaken. The very highest authorities on the Doctrine of the Church agree that no *human* law can stand between starving people and their RIGHT TO FOOD including the right to take that food whenever they find it, openly or secretly, with or without the owner's permission.[52]

Money raised by Gonne in America paid for printing the leaflet and for Connolly to travel to Kerry to assist with relief. Gonne, in turn, traveled to Mayo to continue work on the 1798 centenary preparations and to observe the distress first-hand.[53] Her stay was brief, as in February 1898, she embarked on a punishing schedule of lecturing in England and France.[54] Although her mission was to talk about the centenary, she repeatedly returned to the topic of famine, pointing out that during the reign of Victoria, while the population had been reduced by one half, taxation had increased by nearly £4,000,000 annually. She also spoke of her recent experiences:

> On my return from America, I travelled in the West of Ireland. I find it difficult to convey an idea of the terrible misery and poverty of the people, or the indifference of the English Government to it. In certain parts of the country the peasants, having sold their last rag for food, are ashamed to go out, and hide in their wretched cabins awaiting death from hunger. Every day the famine spreads, while England looks coldly on, or rather rejoices in the extermination of the Celt.[55]

Gonne then returned to County Mayo, lecturing in Ballina on the 1798 commemoration. Instead of returning to Dublin afterwards, she visited the remote and impoverished district of Erris.[56] Throughout her travels, she maintained correspondence with her friend, Yeats, informing him of the splits within the '98 movement and adding, in a post-script, "the poverty here is AWFUL." She also shared her concerns about the low wages on the relief works, which she believed were slowly starving the poor.[57] Gonne also sent articles to the Irish press, to raise awareness and to encourage donations. Her first letter appeared in the *Freeman's Journal* on 9 March, and was entitled, "Relief Works in Erris." Gonne explained, "What shocked me most on the relief works was that women should be engaged on them. There they were; old, bent women of sixty; young, slight girls of sixteen, working away with pickaxes and spades under the pouring rain." Similar to Fanny Parnell a decade earlier, Gonne concluded by appealing to "my sisters, women of Ireland." She asked that they shake off their indifference and help the starving women of Erris.[58] In a separate article, she commenced by admitting:

> I have kept silent a long time—perhaps too long—on the subject of Irish distress. A feeling akin to shame kept me from uncovering the wounds of our motherland to the careless or pitying gaze of the world, and made me feel it were perhaps better to accept the veil of silence which England hypocritically cast over her hideous work in Ireland.[59]

Gonne spent almost a month in Mayo, mostly in Ballycastle and Belmullet. Her tenacious appeals through the press resulting in donations being sent to the area.[60] Her graphic descriptions of the suffering led the *Irish Independent* to ask, "Must it ever be thus in this country? Must history be ever repeating itself, and must the black record of starvation go on generation after generation?"[61] Gonne's efforts were praised by William O'Malley, MP for the Connemara division of County Galway, for providing accurate eye-witness accounts. He also praised her for her political analysis of the causes of the starvations. O'Malley informed the nationalist press that "the Irish Parliamentary Party is anxious that more publicity should be given to the distressing facts, known only to those who are straining every nerve to help the people in their sore need in Western Ireland."[62]

In her 1938 autobiography, Gonne included a chapter entitled "Famine," which outlined her role in County Mayo, 40 years earlier. While some of the details were inaccurate, and Gonne placed herself in a heroic role, what cannot be denied is that, unlike many other sympathizers, she placed herself in harm's way by living in a disease-ridden area and interacting with desperate people. The publication described how Gonne had persuaded the men on the public works to stop working, on the grounds that, "The people must be taught to be afraid of nothing, neither death nor war, if the famine was to be stopped." She had also chastised them:

> You are worse than sheep-stealers if you allow one of your children to die of hunger when there is food to be taken. Sheep can be killed and made into soup which will keep your wives and children alive and if you go to jail for it, you will go as honorable men, for a decent cause, but if you are clever, no one will go to jail. Who is to stop you on these lonely mountains! Be men. Go out hunting!

The way in which the local people responded to Gonne puzzled her. Two young priests explained why some people seemed afraid of her, explaining the story of Brian Ruadh and his prophecies.[63] One of his predictions had been that:

> ... there would be famine and that a woman dressed in green would come and preach the revolt. After that, men would rise and there would be fighting and many killed but that the English would in the end be driven out ... now there is a famine and you have come and are wearing a green dress; so you are the woman of the prophecy—the woman who is to bring war and victory. Do you wonder that some of the women are afraid of you and that the men are ready to follow you anywhere?'[64]

Gonne used her influence over the people as leverage to confront the local guardians and convince them to give higher wages and more relief. She was successful, much to the delight of the local people and clergy.[65]

Following her success, Gonne visited Dublin from where she penned a long letter to the *Freeman's Journal*, which opened, "I am powerless to describe the suffering I have witnessed," and went on to outline the distress of the people, especially the children. She insisted it was a lie to say that people were dying of disease: the truth was, they were dying of starvation. She praised the Mansion House Committee and the Manchester Committee for their work in the west, but stressed that they were being "hampered by the idiotic system of Government relief works." Similar complaints had been made during the Great Hunger and in subsequent famines, namely, that by forcing the head of the house to work for low wages at some "generally useless road from the morning till 5 in the evening," he was unable to do the necessary preparations for his own crop of potatoes, thus damaging the prospects of the following year's harvest.[66] The ever-practical Gonne, ended her long letter with an appeal:

> Surely there are Irishmen and women whom the cause of humanity would interest sufficiently, and whose sympathy would permit them to volunteer their services in going round at their own expense and visiting the stricken districts, making reports of the suffering of the people, and of what is being done for them ... An immense amount of good might be done in this way. It would encourage the downhearted people to feel that their fellow countrymen are interesting themselves in them, and not leaving them to their fate. It also stimulates poor law guardians, relieving officers, and those who are apt to get slack to the keener sense of duty to the people. Women of Ireland—will not some of you find time for this important work? The gratitude of the people and the help you will be able to render them, will more than repay you for the trouble and hardships you may meet with.[67]

Gonne's "admirable suggestion" was praised in the Irish nationalist press.[68] While in Dublin, Gonne also worked with the Mansion House Committee to establish a fish curing station and a school feeding system in Mayo. She then briefly returned to the west to assist in putting them in place. An exhausted Gonne then traveled to France:

> I was worn out when I got back to my little flat in Paris where I stayed lazily in bed for a fortnight, reading novels and answering no letters, but I had stopped the famine in Mayo, and, I think, saved many lives. Talking in the British House of Commons would never have done it.[69]

While Gonne's assertion, made four decades later, may have been exaggerated, her role in bringing money to, raising public awareness of, and lifting local morale in, famine-ravished County Mayo is difficult to dispute. Moreover, throughout these months, Gonne was suffering from a recurring lung problem, a disorder that she had inherited from her late mother.[70] In placing herself at the heart of an impoverished, demoralized, diseased and hungry people, Gonne demonstrated considerable bravery and, as is clear in her writings, considerable compassion. She thus became part of a group of heroic champions of the Irish poor, that included Count Paul Strzelecki, Asenath Nicholson, the Grey Nuns of Montreal and James Hack Tuke.

In France, Gonne did not rest for long, almost immediately lecturing and raising money. In April, she spoke at the Paris Young Ireland Society, giving "a touching description of the distress she had witnessed in the famine-stricken districts of Ireland." The secretary of the society reported that, as a result of Gonne's labors, she had "received letters and donations from French sympathisers with the victims of England's organised famine in Ireland."[71] At the end of the month, Gonne lectured on "The Irish Cause" in Amiens to the *L'Association Démocratique conférencière de la Somme*. When introducing her, the president expressed "his sympathy and the sympathy of the people of France with Ireland at a moment like the present." Gonne responded with "a graphic and touching description" of the sufferings of the Irish poor from her own observations. The newspaper report concluded by saying, "Miss Gonne, who, we regret to say, looked much fatigued, returned to Paris the same night."[72] Gonne's intention to return to County Mayo in June was thwarted by "the severe accident I have met with."[73] Instead, she donated £10 to the Mansion House Committee, asking that it be used to feed children in the National Schools—"when I remember the poor little skeleton forms and the hollow famine brightened eyes I saw two months ago in the schools of the West, I am haunted by the fear that from lack of money you will be forced to stop the supply of bread." In a long letter, she pointed out:

> We know that little Irish children are dying from—well, we may say, 'weakness brought on by insufficient food.' As Mr Balfour says, there is no starvation in Ireland. In countries ruled by a civilized Government, like France, poor children

> have the right to a daily meal in their schools; but in Ireland we can only appeal to private charity, for we live under a hard and barbarous Government, which understands how to make poverty, but not how to soften it or end it. I trust therefore that Irish charity will help these Irish children.[74]

The impact of Gonne repeatedly drawing attention to the suffering children clearly had an impact. In July, Gonne forwarded the Mansion House Fund a further £61 13*s*, from the proprietor the *Boston Pilot*. Sir Thomas Brady responded to this donation:

> In many places, although they [potatoes] are being dug in small quantities, they are utterly unfit for food for the poor children, and may, if eaten by them, bring on dangerous illness. The *Boston Pilot* contribution is, therefore, doubly welcome at this time. It means 14,796 good luncheons for these poor wee mites, of whom there are at the present moment on the Lord Mayor's list receiving this daily allowance over 12,000. With any regard to the children's health, this list could not be reduced much less than to about 5,000 till the middle of August, when it is hoped there will be plenty of ripe potatoes of good sound quality for them.[75]

Following this, Gonne was not involved directly in helping to relieve famine. These experiences, however, had a lasting impact on her subsequent activities, in which hunger and famine featured prominently.

As the 20th century opened, Britain was fighting the Second Boer War in South Africa. The war had two consequences: in early 1900, Gonne returned to the United States to raise funds for the Boer Hospital Fund; in April of the same year, Queen Victoria traveled to Ireland to enlist more Irish troops. Despite divisions with the nationalist movement, Gonne was warmly welcomed in the States.[76] In Boston, reference was made to her earlier visit and her "noble efforts" to stop "the advance of the dreadful spectre of famine."[77] In April, Queen Victoria undertook her fourth and final visit to Ireland. The visit prompted Gonne, who had just returned from the United States, into actions that were to have a lasting impact.[78] Defining Victoria's relationship with Ireland through the prism of famine, Gonne penned a powerful condemnation, initially published in France, but that appeared in the *United Irishman* of 7 April 1900. It was a blistering attack on a monarch—moreover a female monarch—who Gonne accused of hating Ireland, and "whose inhabitants are the victims of the criminal policy of her reign, the survivors of sixty years of organized famine." For Gonne, Victoria's gender made her even more reprehensible, she saying of the 81-year-old visitor:

> ... after all she is a woman, and however vile and pitiless and selfish her soul may be, she must sometimes tremble as death approaches when she thinks of the countless Irish mothers who, shelterless under the cloudy Irish sky, watching their starving little ones, have cursed her before they died.[79]

Inevitably, the paper was seized by the authorities, but the damage had been done. Gonne's article was discussed by even those who disagreed with it. In an article subtitled, "A Disloyal and Seditious Print," the London-based *St James' Gazette* described Gonne as "an American-Irishwoman [who] has made herself prominent as a hater of the English and all things English."[80] The *Newry Reporter*, described it as "coarse and insolent to a surprising degree," adding the gendered opinion that its "vehemence" was "hysterical."[81] Regardless of the confiscation of the *United Irishman*, and the *ad hominem* attacks on Gonne, the article's title, "The Famine Queen," proved to be enduring.

The monarch's visit also was being watched by nationalists in North America. The *Boston Globe*, admirers of Gonne, reprinted "The Famine Queen," informing its readers that when Victoria appeared in public in Dublin she had been treated with "respectful aloofness."[82] Undaunted by the furor, two weeks later, Gonne again attacked the queen in the columns of the *United Irishman*, questioning why it was "illegal to write about this famine queen," but not illegal to "burn down the houses of the starving peasants?" She justified her actions by explaining:

> I today only wrote about her subjects, and humbly hope that I may not again have the misfortune to offend the richest woman in the world, whose proud boast is to reign over more starving millions of human creatures than any queen in history has ever done.[83]

Victoria's time in Ireland coincided with a severe famine in another part of her vast empire—India. The Indian famine of 1900 had been triggered by monsoons in the previous year, which had a disastrous impact on a population still recovering from famine only three years' earlier. Excess mortality was in the region of one million, but some estimates gave it as four times higher.[84] The consensus was that intervention by the British government had been woefully inadequate.[85] Gonne took a similar position on famines in India as she took on those in Ireland. Again, using the columns of the *United Irishman*, she castigated the debates taking place in the London parliament opining, "The death by starvation of millions of Irish and of Indians have never moved them. Why should it?"[86] She reminded her readers that neither the richest woman in the world, nor the richest empire in history, were interested in saving the lives of their poor subjects, wherever they were located.[87]

Famine was at the center of other projects that kept both Gonne in public view. Hunger was at the heart of the 1892 play, *The Countess Cathleen,* which Yeats dedicated to Gonne.[88] Early on in the play, Teig uttered the ominous lines:

> They say that now the land is famine-struck.
> The graves are walking.[89]

At the end of scene three, Cathleen explained that she was hearing "wailing in unnumbered hovels ... men and women mad from hunger." Just as Gonne had done in Donegal and Mayo, the countess's role was to rescue famished people and lead them to independence, even if the cost was her soul. When playing the eponymous lead in Yeats' 1902 play, *Cathleen ni Houlihan*, Gonne was cast as savior of the Irish nation, leading men to their death with the promise of being remembered forever. Gonne's autobiography, *A Servant to the Queen*, was published in 1938.[90] In it, Gonne wrote of the famine of 1897 and 1898 but, it was possibly inevitable at a distance of 40 years, with some inaccuracies regarding dates. The publication has been described as "one of the many texts through which she is mythologized, in this instance by herself."[91]

Having turned down multiple marriage proposals from Yeats, in 1903, Gonne married the Irish hero of the Boer War, John MacBride. The following year, their son, Seán, was born. A few months later, Gonne, now married and known as Maud Gonne MacBride, wrote *Dawn,* "a play in one act and three tableaux—sunset, night, and dawn." It appeared in the *United Irishman* and was written for *Inghinidhe na hÉireann* (the Daughters of Ireland).[92] The short play combined elements of both the Countess and Cathleen, with famine, death, starvation, the Stranger and redemption at its core. It was set during an unidentified famine. The central characters—and the hope for Ireland's redemption—were women. Throughout, the divisions between the dead and the living, the past and the present, were porous. To end constant death from starvation, death from rebellion was necessary. The play's descriptions of relief works and evictions echoed Gonne's own experiences in counties Donegal and Mayo. Brian Ruadh's prophecies, which Gonne had heard of while in Mayo in 1798, were also referenced.[93]

Only months after the birth of Seán and the publication of *Dawn*, Gonne initiated a prolonged, public and bitter divorce from MacBride. One consequence was to cast her to the margins of politics in Ireland:

> The scandal ruinously damaged her position in nationalist circles. In 1906 she was hissed in the Abbey Theatre: a mere four years earlier she had been rapturously received in Cathleen Ni Houlihan.' She was never again to be at the centre of advanced politics ... When she next entered politics after 1916 it was as a widow and a mother.[94]

In order to keep custody of Seán, Gonne relocated to France, only returning to Dublin in 1918, John having been executed for his role in the 1916 Rising.

According to one biographer, "If one reads Gonne's autobiography, one might be forgiven for misconstruing the year 1903 as the end of Gonne's political career."[95] In reality, despite being ostracized by some former colleagues, Gonne remained a presence in Irish politics. In particular, she continued to agitate for ending childhood poverty in Ireland. Victoria's visit in 1900 had prompted Gonne to help to mastermind a more direct protest by founding *Inghinidhe na hÉireann*, which emerged from an attempt to discourage Dublin schoolchildren from attending a picnic in honor of the visit. Born out of protest, it became an important tool for promoting Irish traditions and cultural nationalism, especially amongst children. Gonne's concern with feeding school children, which she had done so effectively in the west of Ireland, had a practical and lasting impact. In 1910, she established the Ladies' School Dinner Committee to deal with what she termed "school-day starvation."[96] As she had done before, she used the press to draw attention to this issue. In an article titled "The Children Must be Fed," published in May 1910, she drew on her own experiences as a mother:

> People look at things a long time with unseeing eyes; suddenly something makes them see and understand.
>
> I only understood when I was watching my own little boy in St Stephen's Green throwing bread to the ducks. A party of bare-footed children came and looked longingly at the bread. My child thought they wanted to feed the ducks, too, and held out half of his bread to the eldest of them. It was not for the ducks that they wanted it, and as I saw them sharing that bread and looked at their eyes and pale faces and their thin little hands, I understood; and once one has seen and understood one cannot forget.[97]

Gonne's committee provided hundreds of dinners daily to inner-city Dublin children. Significantly, these actions led to a legislative change in the provision of school meals in 1914.[98]

Following her full-time return to Ireland in 1918, Gonne and her two surviving children, Iseult and Seán (Georges had died as an infant), agitated on behalf of Irish republicanism while drawing attention to the failings of the new Free State especially, but not exclusively, in regard to women's rights.[99] For her actions, Gonne was imprisoned a number of times, going on a hunger strike in 1923. In May 1946, aged almost 80 and bedridden, she wrote an impassioned plea to the *Irish Times* appealing to the Irish government on behalf of Irish political prisoners—it was a poignant request given that almost 60 years earlier, she had campaigned on behalf of political prisoners incarcerated by the British government.[100]

Maud Gonne was part of a generation of remarkable nationalist women who not only acted autonomously from their male counterparts but did so in a visible way. Being frequently defined by her appearance and her exoticism, rather than by her activism, disguised the fact that for many decades Gonne was at the forefront of political and cultural debates in Ireland, especially during the pivotal period between the fall of Charles Stewart Parnell and the Easter Rising. She combined nationalism and feminism with a demand for social justice, repeatedly showing by her actions that they were not incompatible. Referred to variously as "the new Speranza," "the Irish Joan of Arc" and "the Maid of Erin," throughout the 1890s, her bravery and contributions were frequently commemorated publicly. This included many poetic tributes, including one by M. Barry Delaney that appeared in *Shan Van Vocht* in 1896:

> Uncrowned save by a nation's love, our island's maiden Queen ...
> Yet well too is she known at home, in cottages that fear
> The vengeance of the evictor cursed, that ever hovers near.
> Well is our Maid of Erin known to solace there and cheer.[101]

Mary Trotter has argued that, at the turn of the century, Irish women activists could only transcend rigid gender roles and constraints, and escape from the private to the public sphere, by becoming "extraordinary women," but doing so in a way that did not threaten men or challenge ideals of femininity. Gonne—beautiful, charming, independent and intelligent—was at the forefront of this offensive, "characterized by feminine ideals of beauty, performative skill and accomplishment."[102] These attributes allowed her to enter into the male sphere, but also facilitated her dismissal by later commentators. However, over six turbulent decades of political engagement, Gonne developed as a sophisticated and inspirational political thinker and writer.

Gonne's death in April 1953, aged 88, was widely noted in the Irish newspapers.[103] She was still referred to as Madame Gonne MacBride, part of her fame coming through her long dead ex-husband, and, latterly, her son, Seán MacBride TD, then Minister for External Affairs.[104] Gonne, so often remembered and defined by her beauty as a young woman, or for her unconventional relationships with four powerful men, should also be recognized for her multiple political contributions, including her life-long concern with Irish poverty, especially that of children. Tellingly, her role in helping the poor was not forgotten by those whom she had helped. On her death, Letterkenny Urban Council passed a vote of sympathy to her son, adding "Madame Maud Gonne had spent her life in the service of the country, and in particularly the people of Donegal, whom she had not forgotten in their days of distress."[105] A further legacy of her interventions was a spinning wheel that she kept in her living room in her home in Clonskeagh in Dublin. It was, "a gift made to her by the grateful peasants of County Mayo, whom she saved from starvation and death."[106] Gonne, perhaps more than any other individual, responded to the famines in the 1890s, and, in doing so, kept them and the accompanying evictions in the public eye. For this, and many other reasons, she deserves the honorable title of Famine Queen.

NOTES

1. William Butler Yeats (1865–1939) met Gonne in 1889. She was then involved in a relationship with a Frenchman, with whom she had two children. Yeats proposed to Gonne several times.
2. The Famine Queen was the title of a polemical piece of writing by Gonne that first appeared in *L'Irlande Libre* and was reprinted in the *United Irishman* on 7 April 1900, to coincide with Victoria's visit to Ireland. The authorities in Dublin Castle seized the paper.
3. Georges died in Aug. 1891. Gonne was heartbroken. Her daughter, Iseult, was born in 1894 and died in 1954, a year after her mother.
4. "How Ireland is Ruled," *Boston Guardian*, 19 April 1890.
5. No title, *Flag of Ireland*, 23 Aug. 1890.
6. The arrests, and the ruthless manner in which they were carried out, were raised in the House of Commons on a number of occasions, but Chief Secretary Balfour, an implacable enemy of Irish Home Rule, remained impervious to all appeals, See, questions by Thomas Sexton, then MP for West Belfast, and James Care, MP for North Kildare, "ARRESTS AT CLONGOREY," *House of Commons Debates, Hansard,* 24 Feb. 1890, vol. 341, cc. 1026–28.
7. The Galway evictions were on the Clanricarde Estate, "Meeting near Woodford," *Freeman's Journal*, 22 Aug. 1890.
8. "The Clongorey Estate", *Kildare Observer and Eastern Counties Advertiser*, 23 Aug.1890. In an article, "On their best behavior," 23 Aug. 1890, the *Flag of Ireland* described Gonne as "a patriotic Irish lady."
9. "The Clongorey Estate," *Tablet,* 23 Aug. 1890.
10. These Acts were, the Landlord and Tenant (Ireland) Act (1870); Land Law (Ireland) Act (1881); Irish Land (Purchase) Act (1885); Land Act (1887). Although collectively they gave tenants more rights and made money available for land purchase, they were limited and accompanied by complicated legal restrictions. The Land Purchase (Ireland) Act (1903) was more successful.
11. "Three Oxford liberals and the Plan of Campaign in Donegal, 1889," *History Ireland*, issue 33, vol. 19 (May/June 2011), 34–37.
12. See chapter by E. Moore Quinn.
13. "THE POTATO BLIGHT. BLACKENING CROPS. DISEASE SPREADING. Famine Threatened," *Flag of Ireland*, 23 Aug. 1890.
14. Ibid.
15. "Alarming Spread of the Potato Blight," *London Daily News*, 18 Aug. 1890.
16. "The Potato Plague," *Londonderry Sentinel*, 20 Nov. 1890.
17. Question by J.F.X. O'Brien, House of Commons Debates, *Hansard*, 27 Nov. 1890, vol. 349, cc. 132–3.
18. "THE AMERICAN MISSION. GREAT MEETING IN PHILADELPHIA. 13,000 DOLLARS SUBSCRIBED," *Dublin Weekly Nation*, 15 Nov. 1890.
19. See chapters by Catherine Shannon and Harvey Strum. See also, Christine Kinealy, *Charity and the Great Hunger. The Kindness of Strangers* (London: Bloomsbury, 2011).

20. *Flag of Ireland*, 29 Nov. 1890.
21. John Dooley Reigh (1851–1914) was an Irish cartoonist whose work often focused on Irish nationalism. It included, "The Fight for Bare Life on the Olphert Estate," *United Ireland*, 12 Jan. 1889. See, Lawrence W. McBride; "Nationalist Constructions of the 1798 Rebellion: The Political Illustrations of J. D. Reigh" in *Éire-Ireland*, vol. 34, no. 2. Summer 1999, 117–134.
22. The treatment of political prisoners was a cause that Gonne would return to over many decades. She was imprisoned on a number of occasions, the first time in 1918, when she was arrested in Dublin and spent six months in a prison in England. See, Karen Steele (ed.), *Maud Gonne. Irish Nationalist Writings, 1895–1946* (Dublin: Irish Academic Press, 2004), pp 1–38.
23. Borthwick had been born in Chester in the north of England in 1862. She identified with her Scottish-Gaelic lineage and developed an interest in Irish culture, especially the Irish language. She and Mairead Ni Raghallaigh founded an Irish language printing press in 1900.
24. Probably May Gonne, Maud's cousin.
25. *Flag of Ireland*, 29 Nov. 1890.
26. This image appeared in *United Ireland*, 22 Nov. 1890. The original graphic is now available in National Library of Ireland: http://catalogue.nli.ie/Record/vtls000220335
27. "Editorial," *Londonderry Sentinel*, 11 Nov. 1890.
28. Ibid., "The evictions in Falcarragh," 20 Nov. 1890. See also, "IRELAND—EVICTIONS AT GWEEDORE AND FALCARRAGH—THE BATTERING RAM;" House of Commons Debates, *Hansard,* 24 Feb. 1890, vol. 341, cc. 1025-6.
29. In Maud Gonne MacBride, *A Servant of the Queen: Reminiscences* (London: V. Gollancz, 1938), p. 231. A chapter in the book is titled "Woman of the Sidhe."
30. "Hibernian Academy," *Drogheda Argus and Leinster Journal*, 28 Feb. 1891.
31. "Miss Maud Gonne," *Globe*, 31 Dec. 1891.
32. Ibid., 22 March 1892.
33. "YOUNG LADY Maude Gonne, beautiful Irish Home Ruler," *Derry Journal*, 17 June 1892; *Irish Independent*, 16 June 1892.
34. "THE NEW 'SPERANZA' by W.B. Yeats," *Wexford People*, 13 Aug. 1892.
35. Born Jane Elgee (1821-1895), but more commonly known by her pen-name, Speranza, she started writing poetry for the *Nation* newspaper in 1845. Lady Wilde, as she became in 1864, continued to write into late life. She was mother of Oscar Wilde. See, Amy Martin, "'The Skeleton at the Feast': Lady Wilde's famine poetry and Irish internationalist critiques of food scarcity,'" in Christine Kinealy, Jason King and Ciarán Reilly, *Women and the Great Hunger* (Hamden, CT and Cork: Quinnipiac University Press, 2016), pp 149–60.
36. Ibid., *Wicklow People*, 13 Aug. 1892.
37. "Sir Charles Gavan Duffy Founds a Literary Society," *Evening Herald* (Dublin), 25 July 1892. In his welcome, Duffy referred to the genius of Young Ireland but that "The famine of 1846 paralyzed many forces in Ireland, and none more disastrously than our growing literature."
38. "MISS MAUD GONNE IN PARIS. HELP FOR THE EVICTED TENANTS," *Irish Independent*, 25 March 1893.

39. See chapter by Peter Murphy.
40. "Gonne lecturing in Paris on state of Ireland under Queen Victoria," *Dublin Weekly Nation*, 24 April 1897.
41. "Convention at Manchester. Maud Gonne main speaker," *Flag of Ireland*, 9 Oct. 1897.
42. "Meeting of Paris Young Ireland," *Dublin Weekly Nation*, 17 April 1897.
43. "Jubilee celebrations," *New Ross Standard*, 26 June 1897.
44. "Convention at Manchester. Maud Gonne main speaker," *Flag of Ireland*, 9 Oct. 1897.
45. "Distress in the west," *Irish Independent*, 30 Dec. 1897.
46. During her 1997 tour of the U.S., Gonne was referred to as the Irish Joan of Arc. Amongst other things, she was seeking amnesty for Irish political prisoners, "Reception to Miss Maud Gonne," *Boston Globe,* 14 Dec. 1897.
47. "ENGLAND HOTLY ARRAIGNED: Miss Maud Gonne Addresses the Irish National Alliance at the Grand Opera House. AN ENTHUSIASTIC AUDIENCE," *New York Times,* 25 Oct. 1897.
48. Also Anglicized to Cove, it was a main transatlantic passenger port in the 19th century.
49. Arthur James Balfour (1848–1930) was a British Conservative politician. In 1887, he was appointed Chief Secretary for Ireland, by his uncle, Lord Salisbury. Balfour immediately showed himself to be tough on crime and opposed to Home Rule. In 1890, he helped create the Congested Districts Board for Ireland. The following year, he became leader of the Conservative Party in the Commons. Balfour served as Prime Minister from 1902 to 1905. His younger brother, Gerald (1853–1945), served as Chief Secretary for Ireland from 1895 to 1900. He was associated with the second phase of "constructive unionism."
50. Referred to as his "champagne speech," Chief Secretary Gerald Balfour not only persistently denied the existence of suffering and famine in parts of Ireland, but stated that the poor "could not be supplied with champagne and sent to the South of France." He was criticized by nationalists for his insensitivity. See House of Commons Debates, *Hansard*, 13 May 1898, vol. 57, cc. 1239–40.
51. This manifesto was published in March 1898. Around this time, Connolly spent three weeks in County Kerry, reporting on the approaching famine for the socialist *Weekly People* in New York.
52. Henry Edward Manning (1808–1892) was an English convert to Roman Catholicism. He was appointed a Cardinal in 1875. While conservative on theological matters, he developed a Catholic doctrine of social justice.
53. In the *Servant of the Queen,* the chapter on the 1798 famine suggests Gonne traveled to the west once, but from contemporary newspaper reports it is more likely that she went twice—in January and returning either late in February or early in March.
54. In late February, Gonne lectured in Liverpool with Yeats, "Meeting of Centenary Committee," *Flag of Ireland*, 26 Feb. 1898.
55. Ibid., "The Irish Cause in France."
56. "RELIEF WORK IN ERRIS. BY MAUD GONNE," *Freeman's Journal*, 9 March 1898.
57. Gonne, Belmullet, to Yeats, dated "late February" 1898, in Maud Gonne, Anna MacBride White, *The Gonne-Yeats Letters, 1893–1938* (Syracuse University Press, 1994), pp 84, 85.

58. "Relief Works in Erris," *Freeman's Journal*, 9 March 1898.
59. "Famine in the West," *Irish Daily Independent*, 10 March 1898.
60. "Famine! My experiences in County Mayo," *Daily Nation*, 10 March 1898.
61. "THE FAMINE-STRICKEN WEST. APPALLING STATE OF AFFAIRS," *Irish Independent*, 30 March 1898; *Weekly Freeman's Journal*, 2 April 1898; "THE DISTRESS IN THE WEST. AN ENGLISH LADY'S DESCRIPTION TO THE EDITOR OF THE FREEMAN'S JOURNAL," *Freeman's Journal*, 5 April 1898.
62. Letter from William O Malley, House of Commons, 2 April 1898, reprinted in "THE DISTRESS IN THE WEST. AN ENGLISH LADY'S DESCRIPTION TO THE EDITOR OF THE FREEMAN'S JOURNAL," *Freeman's Journal*, 5 April 1898.
63. Brian Ruadh was thought to have been born in 1648 in the parish of Kilcommon in Erris. Passed down through oral tradition, it was not until 1906 that his stories were collected and written down, in Irish.
64. Gonne, *Servant of the Queen*, p. 234.
65. Ibid.
66. "THE DISTRESS IN THE WEST. LETTER FROM MISS MAUD GONNE, dated 29 March," *Freeman's Journal*, 30 March 1898.
67. Ibid.
68. "The New Famine," *Dublin Daily Nation*, 30 March 1898.
69. Gonne, *Servant of the Queen*, p. 246.
70. Gonne's mother, Edith, had died of tuberculosis in 1871 and, when a young woman, Gonne had suffered from a collapsed lung. In June 1898, the ever-vigilant Yeats shared his concerns with Lady Gregory about Gonne's health on the grounds, "she has been very ill this spring with her old trouble in her lungs, and was looking pale and ill," White, *Gonne-Yeats Letters*, p. 91. Gonne's daughter, Iseult, also suffered from weak lungs. Ibid., Gonne to Yeats, July 1901, p. 100.
71. "Paris Young Ireland Society," *Flag of Ireland*, 23 April 1898.
72. "THE IRISH CAUSE IN FRANCE," *Dublin Weekly Nation*, 14 May 1898.
73. "DISTRESS IN THE WEST. THE SUFFERING CHILDREN. Maud Gonne to Sir Thomas Brady. Schools. Children's Bread Fund Committee. Mansion House," *Dublin Daily Nation*, 15 June 1898. In early June, Gonne had travelled to the unveiling of a memorial tablet in honor of Lord Edward Fitzgerald (of 1798 fame) in Dublin. When a horse stumbled, she was thrown from her carriage and broke an arm and had cuts and bruises on her face. A concerned Yeats wrote to Lady Gregory on 14 June 1898 saying, "I cannot leave her now," White, *Gonne-Yeats Letters*, p. 91.
74. Ibid.
75. "Letter from Thom Brady to Editor of Boston *Pilot*," *Irish Independent*, 30 July 1898.
76. "Miss Gonne Greatly Pleased," *Boston Globe*, 12 Feb. 1900.
77. Ibid., "Miss Gonne's Reception," 19 Feb. 1900.
78. At this stage, Britain was fighting the Second Boer War. Gonne, who was urging Irish men not to fight in it, was raising funds for the Boer Hospital Fund. This project led to her fateful meeting and subsequent marriage to John MacBride, the commander of

the Irish Brigade in the Boer Army. For more on her reception in the U.S., see, "Maude Gonne at Lowell," *Boston Globe*, 11 Feb. 1900; Ibid., "About 2,500 Persons Listen to an Address by Miss Maud Gonne," 13 Feb. 1900.

79. Gonne, "The Famine Queen," *United Irishman*, 7 April 1900.
80. "Suppression of an Irish Newspaper," *St James's Gazette*, 7 April 1900.
81. "The 'United Irishmen' Suppressed," *Newry Reporter*, 9 April 1900. Traditionally, it was believed only women were hysterical: www.smithsonianmag.com/science-nature/history-of-the-hysterical-man-43321905.
82. "Maud Gonne's Scathing Words to Her Majesty," *Boston Globe*, 8 April 1900.
83. Gonne, "Her Subjects," *United Irishman*, 21 April 1900.
84. "The Effect of Famines on the Population of India," *The Lancet*, vol. 157, no. 4059, 15 June 1901, pp 1713–14.
85. Brian Fagan, *Floods, Famines and Emperors. El Nino and the fate of civilizations* (New York: Perseus Books, 2009); Sashi Tahroor, *Inglorious Empire: What the British did to India* (London: Hurst and Co., 2017).
86. "Gonne 'India,'" *United Irishman*, 12 May 1900.
87. In May 1900, Gonne was also fighting a court case, having accused the editor of the *Figaro* of libel, for suggesting that she was in the pay of the British government. See, "Dublin Political Libel. Miss Gonne Complainant," *Cork Examiner*, 5 May 1900. In July, she was a part of a delegation to Paris, where she was singled out for her "beauty, grace and patriotism," "French Sympathy with Irish Claims," *Dublin Daily Nation*, 17 July 900.
88. The first edition appeared in 1892. It was first performed in the Abbey Theatre in Dec. 1911, with Maire O'Neill playing the Countess.
89. These are the first lines in the play and were spoken by Teig, aged 14.
90. Only one year later, a German language version was published: Maud G. MacBride; Ruth Weiland, *Im Dienste einer Königin: eine Frau kämpft für Ireland* (Bremen: Schünemann, 1939).
91. Margaret O'Callaghan and Caoimhe Ní Dháibhéid, "Maud Gonne MacBride," Dictionary of Irish National Biography online, at: www.ria.ie/news/dictionary-irish-biography/revolutionary-women-and-wider-world-maud-gonne-macbride.
92. *Dawn* appeared on 29 Oct. 1904 and was about 4,000 words in length. The Daughters of Ireland had been formed by radical woman nationalists in Dublin on Easter Sunday 1900. Gonne was the President. One of their aims was to promote Irish culture, while discouraging English influences. See, Margaret Ward, *In Her Own Voice: Women and Irish Nationalism* (Dublin: Attic Press, 1995), p. 20.
93. Gonne, *Servant of the Queen*, pp 252, 253.
94. Margaret O'Callaghan and Caoimhe Ní Dháibhéid, "Maud Gonne MacBride."
95. Steele, *Nationalist Writings,* pp xxiii–xxv.
96. Gonne, "Responsibility," *Irish Review* 1, no. 10 (Dec. 1911), p. 483. Quoted in Ian Miller, "Nutritional Decline in Post-Famine Ireland, c.1851–1922," in *Proceedings of the Royal Irish Academy: Archaeology, Culture, History, Literature*, vol. 115, C (2015), 307–23, p. 320. Gonne published frequently on this topic.
97. Gonne, "The Children Must Be Fed," *Bean na hÉireann*, May 1910.

98. Ibid., pp 320–321; Provision of Meals (Ireland) Act, 1914 (7).
99. Gonne, "1937 Constitution," *Prison Bars*, July 1937.
100. Gonne, "A Request," letter to the *Irish Times*, 10 May 1946.
101. *Shan Van Vocht*, 7 Feb. 1896, p. 33. *Shan Van Vocht* (a phonetic rendition of *An tSeanbhean Bhocht*) translates as "The Poor Old Woman," a traditional name for Ireland.
102. Mary Trotter, *Ireland's National Theaters: Political Performance and the Origins of the Irish Dramatic Movements* (Syracuse University Press, 2001), pp 78–79.
103. "Death of Madame Maud Gonne MacBride," *Irish Independent*, 28 April 1953.
104. Margaret Ward shows how, after 1916, Gonne was viewed as the widow of a hero of the Easter Rising, Margaret Ward, *Maud Gonne. Ireland's Joan of Arc* (London: Pandora, 1990).
105. "Condolence on death of Maud Gonne," *Strabane Chronicle*, 16 May 1953.
106. "The story of Maud Gonne," *Longford Leader*, 10 Nov. 1951.

Hunger after 1900

CHAPTER SIXTEEN

"A SPECTACLE OF OUR PEOPLE IN A STRANGE LAND"

Irish Women's Food Experiences in Scotland's Tattie-Hoking Fields in the 20th Century

E. Moore Quinn

The title of this paper addresses a painful memory by a former Irish laborer. When reminiscing about his days spent harvesting potatoes abroad, he acknowledged that from the very first day one "humiliating" image lived on in his thoughts: the "spectacle of our people in a strange land."[1] With these words, Peadar O'Donnell opened up a nearly tabooed subject, that of the experience of leaving Ireland temporarily to work in the fields of England and Scotland. Known as "tattie-hokers,"[2] or "tattie howkers,"[3] those women and men were referred to by various other names, too, such as "harvesters"[4] and "tattie squads."[5]

O'Donnell's deep-seated understanding of what he had to do to make a living in his earlier years was shared by other Irish migrants. Testimonials collected by the Bessborough Commission of 1881 repeatedly revealed former migrants' awareness of their marginalized status within society. One person summarized it well: "We are like wild geese, your honour."[6] This acknowledgement endured, Shannon Dunn noting in 2008:

> Unfortunately, the practice is still considered humiliating ... and for that reason surviving former migrants, who are now elderly, are not only hesitant but sometimes refuse to admit or to discuss the practice and their experiences associated with it, often because of embarrassment or painful memories.[7]

My own fieldwork among former women harvesters in Donegal confirms the accuracy of these sentiments. For instance, one woman who had shared some of her experiences subsequently denied ever having traveled to Scotland in order to "hoke" potatoes. Moreover, so deeply buried are seasonal migratory experiences in Irish history that many Irish women and men told me that they did not know about or had never heard anything about those who had sought to "turn a penny" by laboring in English and Scottish potato fields.[8]

All the more important and significant, then, are testimonials from those willing to share their experiences. This chapter brings together folkloric and archival materials on seasonal migration from County Donegal, interspersed with the words of several "tattie-hoking" women with whom I conducted open-ended and informal interviews. The women were in their 80s and 90s. Hailing from Glenties and Gweedore in particular, they recalled their youthful participation as members of migrant streams that, for them, took place in Ayrshire, the Lothians and Perthshire.[9] Although the testimonials are complicated by the temporal corruption of memory and circumscribed by an awareness of outsiders' perceptions of them, they provide a richer understanding of the meaning of Irish women's experiences of migration and hunger than what has hitherto been reported. For example, one elder, when asked how she fed her large family, especially if a new mouth to feed arrived at her table, perfunctorily retorted, "We added another quart of water to the soup." Yet, in conversation, she admitted that such jocular "tricks of the trade" could only take her and her family so far. Although such statements were couched within wider discourses of self and self-making, ultimately this woman confided that the cooking method she and members of her family utilized to stretch food proved insufficient as a means to alleviate the pain that accompanied their undernourishment. Like many other Irish women caught within webs of seasonal hunger, she came to embrace the necessity of leaving home to procure work. Pivoting to the subject of obtaining staples, this woman expressed that not only were eggs cheap in Scotland, but dairy commodities could be purchased for little money: "You got milk for a penny a pint on the farm."[10] Just as they had for migrating women who left the western marginalized areas of Ireland in earlier times, this woman's migratory movements, although "occupationally concentrated along a much smaller spectrum of choices,"[11] made sense within the cultural milieu in which she functioned. Moreover, her seasonal movements align with our understanding of how famine and famine-like conditions reconstituted women's roles during and after *An Gorta Mór*. Due to that catastrophe, women were forced to travel farther for food and to become "active procurers of it." In these ways, they transcended their "traditional association with food preparation and preservation."[12] It is interesting to note that those behaviors continued to operate after the onslaught of the Famine.

It is well-attested that temporary migrations function as safety valves for the sending societies. In the late 19th century, in the economically compromised western areas of Ireland, certain push factors like poverty and social dislocation endured.[13] Although seasonal migrants often differed from landless famine victims in the sense that they were in possession of small plots of land, those holdings might best be described as no more than "hard scrabble" tracts. Indeed, it was difficult, if not impossible, for their owners to eke out enough food to sustain their families.[14] Seasonal migration, then, relieved the pressure of having other mouths to feed.[15] By the early 20th century, members of Donegal families not only continued to be imbricated within inequitable patterns of global economic development, they continued to serve as inexpensive sources of labor upon which receiving communities could draw. As Jonathan Bell notes, "Families in Donegal early this century depended greatly on money sent home by migrants."[16] Moreover, "gender play[ed] a central role in the decision to migrate and in the composition of the migration flows."[17] Female-centered households in particular benefited from such household adjustment, which was highly dependent on remittances from family members who had seasonally migrated.[18] In the words of one former tattie-hoker from Glenties: "We were always hungry."[19] Such statements from former tattie-hoking Donegal women make it possible to develop an awareness of how women's lives and movements were embedded within the macro-economic world within which they functioned, and even more, within their own communal systems. From the women's testimonies, we become apprised of their personal food experiences within Scotland's tattie-hoking compounds. For instance, the women discussed such details as their "discovery" of food, its gathering, its rationing, its preparation and even its use as "devilment" for teasing and playfulness. In addition, sometimes food precipitated both hurt and shame. These categories align with Mary Corcoran's observation that food represents not only material culture; it is also a symbolic measure of social and class status and a measure of one's cultural capital.[20]

Seasonal migrants are defined as "those who travel once a year, either as complete or partial families, or as single adult individuals, to areas in which great numbers of workers are needed temporarily in such occupations as harvesting or processing of raw food items."[21] This perspective on global flows, themselves the product of specific historical conditions, need to be more carefully outlined in terms of particular regions and more succinctly placed within larger contexts of supply and demand.[22] Moreover, the definition deserves to be tweaked in terms of issues relating to women, their bodies, their migratory patterns and their labors. Addressing the paucity of attention paid to these categories in social science literature, Monica Boyd and Elizabeth Grieco argue that the lack of concerted theoretical approaches to women's patterns of migration in the past has led to problems in terms of itemizing the conditions that impelled women to migrate, the duties and obligations required of them abroad and the particularized working environments into which they were thrust. In short, Boyd and Grieco advocate for more attention being paid to women's overall "gender-specific migration experiences."[23] This chapter takes a step in that direction.

The spread of the Industrial Revolution increased the need and desire for labor in England and Scotland. "From early in the eighteenth century it had been customary for small bands of [Irish] peasants from the West and South, after the potato stock was exhausted in the summer, to migrate to England and Scotland for work in the harvest fields."[24] This type of seasonal migration was a fundamental dimension of Irish pre-industrial labor in Britain; migrants traveled from small subsistence holdings to the much larger agriculturally capitalized farms of Britain. In mid-19th-century Ireland, "the vast majority of the population lived in the countryside and what skills it had were agricultural in nature."[25] Although internal seasonal migration to the greener pastures of eastern Ireland took place, and employers drew from the entire Celtic fringe, by and large they relied upon cottier farmers from Ireland's impoverished western counties—Donegal, Galway, Mayo and Roscommon—"the most agriculturally underdeveloped regions of the country."[26] For Irish males, the "main marketable commodity ... was their abundant labour power."[27] However, the practice of tattie-hoking for Irish women, having begun in the mid-19th century, was equally significant, increasing the opportunities to work in the potato fields of Scotland.[28] As one consultant revealed, "Some girls went at 14; some boys went at 12." Yet, women's migratory flows in the post-Famine years differed from those of their male counterparts in that they followed what was known as the "gaffer system."[29]

David Fitzpatrick has argued that an eagerness for Irish seasonal workers, called *spailpíní*, existed among the hiring community; the Irish were sought out for their diligence, their thrift, and their work ethic.[30] Moreover, southern English agricultural wages were an indubitable pull factor for Irish men, being more than double the level prevalent in Ireland.[31] In certain places, farm employment could be counted on at other times of the year.[32] Due to the fact that the small holders were available for employment during and sometimes even beyond the summer months, their movements were "long distance and long-duration."[33] Several push factors were also at work. Despite Roman Catholic Church disapproval of seasonal migration, which, according to Kenneth McNally, was motivated as much by concern that its authority might be weakened as by fear that families might suffer from long periods of separation, the necessity for seasonal migration endured.[34] Its maintenance extended well beyond the Great Hunger, due in large part to the economic and demographic adjustments that occurred in the west of Ireland.[35] Of course, entrenched and enduring economic distress continued to motivate Irish emigration of all kinds, and permanent migration from Ireland paralleled seasonal migration. F.S.L. Lyons averred that, although "some improvements in the wage-structure [in Ireland] did occur between the Famine and the First World War, yet it cannot be too heavily stressed that they were insufficient to conceal the existence of deep abysses of poverty."[36] Cormac Ó Gráda has argued that "the search for subsistence" constituted a crucial part of the need for seasonal migration.[37] Gerard Moran goes further, noting that the prime mover that drove Irish from the west to "the edge of extinction" in the 19th century, was the recurring "problem of famine."[38] Thus, for mainly Irish language speakers who were famished, poor and nearly landless, seasonal migration enabled communities on the fringe to continue.[39] The pattern of external migration to England and Scotland became "the cornerstone of a social system whose equilibrium otherwise could have been maintained only by massive permanent migration."[40]

Irish women in the post-Famine years dominated the migration flows from Ireland. Hasia Diner noted: "In the years 1871 through to 1880 men and women [between the ages of fifteen and twenty-four] arrived in exactly equal proportion. From 1881 through to 1890, 30 percent were women and 27.4 percent were men, and from 1891 until the end of the century, 35.4 percent were women and 24.5 percent were men."[41] This emigration pattern continued into the mid-20th century: "Between 1926 and 1951, about 52,000 women left southern Ireland for the United States and a further 180,000 went to Britain."[42] Although Diner focuses on women who migrated permanently, what is important is that over 50 percent of tattie-hoking seasonal migrants were also women.[43] Their migratory flows, functioning according to the gaffer system, took place within a subcontracting arrangement in which certain men specialized in recruiting and mobilizing their laborers. The gaffer was a middleman, a go-between, a useful intercessory between the workers he gathered and the established class he served.[44] For Donegal women, the system was described in the following manner:

> The potato raisers are generally employed by potato merchants, who sometimes find employment for 100–150 throughout the whole season. The merchants have a number of foremen or 'gaffers' as they are called ... who collect the labourers and are employed supervising the work ... The labourers work in squads of twenty to thirty, and are paid in pairs ... Thus two girls alternatively digging and picking would receive 5*s*. per day as their joint wage ... In addition to the cash wages, they get housing, bedding, coal, potatoes and sometimes a little milk, so they have only their groceries to buy ... [45]

The women interviewed confirmed these details, elaborating on the tattie-hokers' movements from place to place. One former harvester, detailing how her specific female migratory chain operated, explained: "Ayrshire was the starting point, then on to The Lothians in Edinburgh. Perthshire was the finish up place." Other revelations had to do with how women's lives were embedded within larger social contexts, such as how the women's particular squads operated, how the tattie-hokers traveled, and how they remitted their wages home to their mothers. In light of the call for more theoretical research expounded by Boyd and Grieco, all of these experiences deserve thoughtful attention; however, the remainder of this chapter focuses more specifically on the words of former tattie-hoking Donegal women and the meaning of their expressions in terms of hunger, work, food, and personal bodily experiences.

Just as the tattie-hoking women discussed their own work travail, so too did they emphatically recall their mothers' labors in caring for the family's food supplies in their absence. The specifics of how such duties and obligations unfolded in the lives of seasonal migrants in Donegal families align with how Irish patterns and attitudes functioned in terms of gendered duties and obligations. Timothy Meagher, in his exploration of women "born in Ireland and nourished by working class conditions [abroad]," asserts, "The wife's role was to be a mother, the daughter's role was to work."[46] Such a statement recognizes that "[e]conomic conditions [at home] were very important ... in shaping conceptions of the roles of [Irish] single women" elsewhere.[47] Expressing an awareness of their mothers' existence within the larger social system, former tattie-hoking women reminisced about the ritual of leave-taking and how it affected local mothers. From early June into the early weeks of November, those mothers were bereft of their offspring. The heart-wrenching experience at "the going"—the time to say goodbye in order to take up harvest employment—became a rich aspect of Irish folk memory; in fact, leave-taking loss is preserved in lines recorded in 1938:

> Now the winter is all over and the spring is coming on
> When all the girls around must go and leave their mams [to mourn][48]

Indeed, in light of the work that had to be done by stay-behind Irish mothers, apart from the loss of their children's company for extended periods of time, at least some mothers' anguish at separating from their hardy teenage children must have been in contemplating the nearly single-handed work that awaited them in the coming months. According to one scholar, the contribution of children's labor "to the economy of the rural poor can hardly be sufficiently stressed."[49] When chances were available in the calendrical year, children "assisted in such work as sowing potatoes, haymaking, harvesting corn, and tending livestock."[50] Anne O'Dowd quotes one of her consultants recalling:

> The women worked very hard here at that time. They did all the work after [the tattie-hokers] went away ... in the line of looking after turf and looking after crops and everything. They had to do all that and they used to rear pigs and hens and that's how most of us kept going.[51]

Some scholars go so far as to suggest that Irish women worked "more like slaves than labourers."[52] Bell corroborates the women's reminiscences by noting, "It was harder for the [stay behind] women. The woman would have to go out and set the potatoes, delving and dunging them ... She would have to harvest the corn and potatoes and look after the cows"[53] It is little wonder, then, that "massive grieving and crying took place" at leave-taking. Mothers' practices and behaviors at times of parting remain palpable in the memories of former tattie-hoking Donegal women. One recalled that she could hear still the mothers "crying and howling" as they sent their children off to the tattie-hoking fields. Another explained, "They were all losing their children." Moreover, Meagher correctly recognizes the necessity for migrants' labors and that, "Irish families ... encouraged—even expected—single Irish women to work because of 'the force of circumstances,'"[54] yet parents worried about the prejudices and biases their migrating children were likely to encounter. Such attitudes were summarized by Dominique Vidal who, following Piore, asserted:

> All the migrants ... look the same ... They are uprooted and are treated like social strangers. The locals frequently make fun of their languages and manners. They regularly have to face ostracism for simply being newcomers and looking different. They are easy targets for the local thugs ... Sometimes, they do their best to be invisible.[55]

Arguably, Vidal's observations amount to additional reasons why left-behind mothers bemoaned their children's travels.

In large measure, Vidal's insights are confirmed by Fitzpatrick, who quotes a reference to Irish seasonal migrants as "peculiar tramping people." The modifier "peculiar" singles out Irish workers as, at best, strange, odd and unusual, but at worst, weird, bizarre, abnormal and "other." Clearly, these linguistic items reinforce the well-entrenched ideological prejudices regarding the Irish in England and Scotland. Although intermittent objections to the "low Papish Irish" with their "debasing habits" surfaced in English and Scottish news sources, the solicitation of Irish workers persisted.[56] Then too, although denigrating terms like spalpeen and tramp—and arguably, even tattie-hoker itself—persisted, they were less important within the capitalist-oriented realms of Britain. It was there that "astute Scottish farmers and marketing merchants placed too high a value on their Irish labourers to pay heed to religious or class prejudice."[57] Eventually, the label spalpeen was used to reference not only working migrants but any Irishman deemed dirty, degraded and deprived."[58] Tramp, on the other hand, was applied to Irish harvest workers in a variety of ways. For instance, in addition to the reference to "peculiar tramping people", E.J.T. Collins quotes a description of "Irish tramps ... bringing pestilence on their backs, famine in their stomachs,"[59] while Arthur Redford refers to Irish women "tramping out for miles in the early morning to their work."[60]

The belief that the English and Scottish locals resented the presence of Irish workers was born out in reality. "Sectarianism, lack of education, and the fact that some Irish workers spoke only Irish, prevented them from working in highly paid and skilled trades."[61] As one former harvester complained, "The farmers think that we're pigs."[62] These derogations are a reminder of the larger connotation of the word "spectacle" that opens this chapter; likewise, the deprecatory comments suggest additional reasons for the hesitation to talk about former tattie-hokers' lives and experiences. Although Patrick MacGill, when speaking about the typical Irish woman harvester, noted that "the work challenged the life in her, and the dash of it excited her,"[63] yet tattie-hoking women's encounters with reality soon checked their enthusiasm. In addition to the labels foisted upon the harvesters, unfamiliar surroundings and disconcerting circumstances contributed to what Fitzpatrick calls the seasonal migrants' "cultural alienation" abroad.[64]

One particularly poignant anecdote illustrates a former tattie-hoker's lack of cultural knowledge. Having left Donegal at the age of 15, she did not know what sausages were until then. She went on to detail her passion for sweets as well as her inability, coming from an all Irish-speaking world, to ask for a pot of jam in a shop where workers could obtain provisions such as biscuits, chocolate, crisps and cigarettes.[65] She explained:

> My request for it [the pot of jam] came out in such a garbled way, so much so that the lady in the shop took pity on me, saying, loudly and slowly, 'It's called 'POT OF JAM,' and [she] gave me more than what I could pay for. I think she felt sorry for me.

In this brief anecdote of language differentiation, a highly personal and in some ways painful recollection of a former tattie-hoking girl in a host culture, one becomes apprised of the kinds of encounters that could produce cultural alienation. Indeed, until the Second World War, many in the marginalized areas of Ireland were monoglot Irish language speakers. The need to master different social codes in order to acculturate into life abroad was but one of the many hurdles that Irish seasonal migrants faced.[66] Heather Holmes quotes consultants who admitted, "We hadn't much English,"[67] one even confessed, "[we] had to learn English in a hurry."[68] Such constant exposure to two societies and cultures equates to what Pedraza calls the living of "double lives" which, compounded by disruptions, separations and losses, took its toll on women's mental health.[69]

In the Donegal case, loss of self-esteem was but one of the long-term effects on women's health. Others were more physical in nature. Peadar O'Donnell describes the contorted physical countenances of some harvesters; one was said to have had "teeth bare and buried in her under lip and a twisted smile on her face;" moreover, O'Donnell provides an auditory sense of Irish women's bodies at work: "[T]here was not a word in the field; there was an occasional grunt; now and then a gasp. Some digger said something to a gatherer and a sob was heard. After it came a general titter."[70] For gregarious individuals, silence in gathering food may have produced further distortion of self. Some former harvesters, their postures permanently compromised, confessed difficulty in standing and/or walk erect; the constant stooping that their former harvesting endeavors demanded had placed a nonremedial strain on their once young and still developing bodies. As for the diet of these "birds of passage," as Piore characterizes temporary workers abroad, it resembled that of the native Irish who resided in the west of Ireland prior to the Famine, consisting mainly of potatoes, which were consumed almost to the exclusion of everything else. The refrain:

Prátaí ar maidin,
Prátaí ar nóin,
Is dá néireoinn san oíche
Prátaí a gheobhainn[71]

reflected the reality of Irish country life. Even within the migratory sphere in which tattie-hokers operated, there was little to differentiate the meals that were eaten abroad from those that were consumed at home. Although one woman recalled that sometimes on offer were "Bread and a cup of tea for brekkie," another added, "Sometimes [there was] no breakfast at all". One woman, when asked about the food supplied to "the 'hokers,'" as she self-represented herself and her squad, responded: "You got potatoes and milk for dinner;" another, however, corrected her by saying, "Just potatoes." There was, in truth, other food available to the seasonal harvesters, yet "It was all rationed." One-quarter pound of butter and six ounces of sugar were supplied; they were supposed to last for a week. Keeping the harvesters working was the goal. Heather Holmes notes:

> Employers had reasons for giving food. In the East Lothians, precious and valuable time was said to be saved during the day as workers did not have to spend it by returning home to eat; work could also start promptly after they had eaten their meal.[72]

However, one Donegal interviewee remembered that the time for lunch depended on one's closeness to the living quarters, called bothies, which were, in effect, mere byres. "If we were close, we went to the bothy for lunch and got an hour; if farther away in the field, we only got half an hour."

Even tea breaks were restricted. Another former harvester recalled, "The 'bothy woman' [the person tasked with providing rations and the like to the harvesters] would come out with a can of tea." Although this revelation might suggest that cultural contact occurred between employers and employees—and even among Irish and Scots workers—the opposite was the case, for Irish seasonal workers abroad continued to function according to the habitual "livelihood from within" pattern to which they were accustomed: "Even in the 1930s, nearly a century after the bulk of the Irish-speaking, nearly landless laborers had disappeared from the landscape, the economic life of the small farmer could be described as "a livelihood little connected with the outside world."[73] Furthermore, migrant workers of different backgrounds rarely interacted with one another: "There was little association between Irish girls and Scotch women. They kept different sheds and were apart in their leisure hours."[74]

The sheds were little more than mean animal shelters, or in MacGill's words, "byres, pig-stys [sic] and barns."[75] So abhorrent were they that the editor of the *Donegal Democrat* averred that "legislation governing [the] housing of pigs and cattle provides these brute beasts with habitations that are often palaces compared with those allotted to 'tattie hokers.'"[76] Despite these and numerous other accounts regarding conditions within which the potato harvesters were housed, it fell upon them to make the best of it. Donegal women spoke of the ways they tried to set up house within their respective byres, ascertaining that everyone, especially the younger boys, were cared for and fed. They also talked about the nature of their cooking situations: "We cooked outside [over] a big round fire."[77] Additional coping mechanisms and strategies for survival included learning how to respond to being the butt of the joke when "devilment" was all the rage. "They would throw a dirty potato at you for sport," confided one woman, "but you couldn't get angry or it would be worse." This statement demonstrates an awareness of how Irish women migrants understood and operationalized what Pedraza calls, "strategies of resistance, accommodation, and consent."[78] Although the consultant did not elaborate on women's mechanisms for "righting the wrong," yet embedded in other discourses are statements that showcase the rationalization of the conditions in which they found themselves. For instance, referring to the dirty potato practice, one former harvester attested that such "devilment was ok, because [we] didn't know anything else." This justification is consistent with Patrick MacGill's revelation that tattie-hokers were inclined to "tak[e] life as we found it."[79] A sense of fatalism is yet another coping strategy for strangers in strange lands.

Several former Donegal tattie-hokers discussed the practical and moral dilemmas caused by their living arrangements and their attempts to actively find solutions for them; these included defecating without facilities for doing so, keeping clean, and finding ways to robe and disrobe. The latter effort was deemed particularly awkward if boys and girls were housed within the same facilities, a situation which occurred more often than not. In O'Donnell's experience, much was the same. Corroborating the revelations of the Donegal women, he recalled how "[w]e slept in byres and shook out straw for ourselves. Boys and girls slept in the same open shed."[80] In such circumstances, the tattie-hokers took turns at the tasks of sheltering and protecting one another. Such admissions suggest how Donegal women harvesters asserted their agency, collectively and individually, within the delimited social strictures in which they found themselves.[81] Notwithstanding their best efforts, however, sheltering and protecting were not always successful. One consultant spoke of having been abused at the hands of a man who had raped her and left her pregnant. Such was her shame that she hid the fact—and the truth of her child's identity—from her mother for 10 years. Understand this woman's decision demands knowledge of Irish culture, for, as O'Dowd writes, when discussing women in such a condition, people said that they returned home "with their bellies up to their chins."[82] Moreover, they would be spoken of derogatorily with words like: "He paid her well, she got five pounds for the trespass; she'll go back and do another term with him."[83]

Returning for another season was yet another coping and survival strategy in the sense that it allowed women to continue to "mind the job" and to fulfill their larger intent to provide for those at home. Understanding that larger familial goal was crucial, for as difficult as seasonal labor was, and although significant improvement in many tattie-hokers' lots in life failed to materialize, yet, as Moran observed, the group was preserved.[84] Pedraza goes further, suggesting that, notwithstanding that seasonal migration for women amounted to "employment without liberation," and although "we might not easily understand today the satisfaction of those who lived for and through others," what those migrating women offered to their families, coupled with their personal sacrifices, left a deep impression.[85] In many ways, the practice of tattie-hoking protected the workers and their communities from hunger and permanent emigration.

To conclude, the working lives of women tattie-hokers who labored in the potato fields of Scotland in the earlier decades of the 20th century lies at the intersection of ethnicity, class and gender, while addressing gender-specific migration experiences largely overlooked in social science literature. Food within the context of seasonal hunger is addressed, yet there is much more to be said and emphasized about the lives of women harvesters. For instance, their interpretation of the status of their work as lowly, their friendships with one another, the nature of their travel to and from their workplaces and the venues they preferred and despised. Finally, the tattie-hokers' memories reveal much in terms of the deeply political nature of food, hunger and women's health. What emerges most significantly is the crucial role played by migrating women in staving off the total collapse of their communities. The fulfilling of women's roles was stimulated in large part by what the women themselves deemed their responsibilities to their families and communities in Ireland. Staring down the humiliating ideological "spectacle" imposed by outsiders, women who hoked the 'tatties' appear to have clung to the dictates of their upbringing by fulfilling their families' expectations that they migrate each season. This adhesiveness is particularly remarkable in that, unlike their sisterly counterparts who entered permanent migration flows, it resulted in little personal advancement or gain—and sometimes, even the opposite: opprobrium and shame. Neither the receiving society nor the sending one provided avenues for escape. Women tattie-hokers' motivation for their family's survival served as their goal, especially for County Donegal families and communities that had been driven to "the edge of extinction" by hunger and near-famine, and that impetus superseded their need for personal self-actualization.

NOTES

1. Peadar O'Donnell, "Achill, Arranmore, and Kirkintillock," *Ireland To-day* 2, no. 10 (1937), p. 46.
2. Anne O'Dowd, *Spalpeens and Tattie Hokers: History and Folklore of the Irish Migratory Agricultural Worker in Ireland and Britain* (Dublin: Irish Academic Press, 1994), p. 52.
3. Heather Holmes, "Remembering their History: Memories of Irish Migratory Agricultural Workers in Scotland," *Human Affairs* 12, no. 2 (2002), p. 140.
4. Kenneth McNally, *Achill* (Newton Abbot: David & Charles, 1973), p. 86.
5. Ibid. McNally notes that Achill Island laborers were referred to more generally as "harvesters."
6. *Report of H. M. Commissioners of Inquiry into the Working of the Landlord and Tenant (Ireland) Act, 1870 and the Acts Amending the Same* (Bessborough Commission) (C 2779), 1881, xviii and xix. Item 17155.

7. Shannon Monique Dunn, "'Little More than a Winter Home:' An Historical Archaeology of Irish Seasonal Migration at Slievemore, Achill Island." Unpublished Ph.D. dissertation, Syracuse University (2008), p. 313.
8. Quoted in Stephen A. Royle, "Settlement, Population and Economy of the Mayo Islands (including Inishbofin)," *Cathair na Mart: Journal of the Westport Historical Society* 9 (1989), p. 124.
9. According to Sara Goek, as late at 1937, Glenties continued to operate seasonal migration, constituting the third highest total of all the areas counted. See note 7, "Na Spailpíní: Irish Seasonal Labourers in Britain in the 20th Century," The Dustbin of History (Blog), 18 March 2018. https://thedustbinofhistory.wordpress.com/2013/03/18/na-spailpini/
10. Anonymous Donegal consultant interviewed in June 2019.
11. Silvia Pedraza, "Women and Migration: The Social Consequences of Gender," *Annual Review of Sociology*, 17 (1991), pp 313–314.
12. E. Moore Quinn and Cara Delay, "Bounty, Moderation and Miracles: Women and Food in Narratives of the Great Famine," *New Hibernia Review* 21: 2 (2017), p. 119.
13. Hasia Diner, *Erin's Daughters in America: Irish Immigrant Women in the Nineteenth Century* (Baltimore: John Hopkins University Press, 1983), p. 29; see also Pedraza, "Women and Migration," p. 312.
14. This situation was made more difficult following the passage of the draconian "Quarter-acre Clause", which denied relief to any family occupying more than this amount of land. The Poor Extension Act had been passed in 1847; known as "Black '47." The main legislation was: "An Act to make further Provision for the Relief of the destitute Poor in Ireland" (8 June 1847), 10 Vic., c.31.
15. Pedraza, "Women and Migration," p. 307.
16. Jonathan Bell, "Review: Migratory Labourers from Donegal," *Saothar* 9 (1983), p. 105.
17. Pedraza, "Women and Migration," p. 321.
18. Ibid., p. 311.
19. Anonymous Donegal consultant interviewed in June 2019.
20. Mary Corcoran, "The Political Economy of the Urban Food Landscape": Keynote lecture delivered at the "Irish Famines before 1845 and after 1852," presented at Ireland's Great Hunger Institute Conference, Quinnipiac University, 13 June 2019.
21. Nancie L. Solien de Gonzalez, "Family Organization in Five Types of Migratory Wage Labor," *American Anthropologist* 63, no. 6 (1961), p. 1265.
22. Alessandro Monsutti, "The Contribution of Migration Studies and Transnationalism to the Anthropological Debate: A Critical Perspective," in Cédric Audebert and Mohamed Kamel Doraï (eds), *Migration in a Globalized World* (Amsterdam University Press, 2010), p. 120.
23. Monica Boyd and Elizabeth Grieco, "Women and Migration: Incorporating Gender into International Migration Theory" (Washington, DC: Migration Policy Institute, 2003): www.migrationpolicy.org
24. Thomas N. Brown, "Nationalism and the Irish Peasant, 1800–1848," *The Review of Politics* 15, no. 4 (1953), 413; see also E. J. T. Collins, "Migrant Labour in British Agriculture in the Nineteenth Century," *The Economic History Review* 29, no. 1 (1976), p. 38.

25. Peter M. Solar and Malcolm T. Smith, "Background migration: the Irish (and other strangers) in mid-Victorian Hertfordshire," *Local Population Studies* 82 (2009), p. 45.
26. Gerard Moran, "'A Passage to Britain': Seasonal Migration and Social Change in the west of Ireland" in *Saothar* 13 (1988), p. 24.
27. Kennedy, "The Rural Economy", p. 33; Moran, "A Passage to Britain," p. 28, and Jonathan Bell and Mervyn Watson, "Emigrant Irish Farming Implements & Practices" in *Material Culture of Donegal Communities Abroad* Donegal Heritage Series 2 (Lifford: County Donegal Heritage Office, 2014), p. 16.
28. O'Dowd, *Spalpeens*, p. 41.
29. Cormac Ó Gráda, "Population Adjustment and Seasonal Migration in the West of Ireland" in L. L. Cullen and F. Furet (eds), *Ireland and France 17thto 20th centuries: Towards a Comparative Study of Rural History* (1981), p. 111.
30. David Fitzpatrick, "'A Peculiar Tramping People': The Irish in Britain, 1801–1870" in W. E. Vaughan (ed.), *A New History of Ireland*, vol. 5 (Oxford University Press, 1989), p. 645.
31. Peter M. Solar and Malcolm T. Smith, "Background migration: the Irish (and other strangers) in mid-Victorian Hertfordshire," *Local Population Studies* 82 (2009), p. 45.
32. Ibid.
33. E.J.T. Collins, "Migrant Labour in British Agriculture in the Nineteenth Century," *The Economic History Review* 29, no. 1 (1976), p. 45.
34. McNally, *Achill*, p. 91.
35. Cormac Ó Gráda, "Seasonal Migration and Post-Famine Adjustment in the West of Ireland," *Studia Hibernica*, 13 (1973), pp 55–56.
36. F.S.L. Lyons, *Ireland Since the Famine* (London: Fontana Press, 1985), p. 69.
37. Ó Gráda, "Seasonal Migration," p. 61.
38. Moran, "A Passage," p. 22.
39. Ibid., p. 24.
40. Collins, "Migrant Labour," p. 45.
41. Hasia Diner, "The Search for Bread: Patterns of Female Migration" in Alan Hayes and Diane Urquhart (eds) *The Irish Women's History Reader* (New York: Routledge, 2001), p. 176.
42. Sharon Lambert, "Irish Women's Emigration to England 1922–1960: The Lengthening of Family Ties" in Alan Hayes and Diane Urquhart (eds) *The Irish Women's History Reader* (New York: Routledge, 2001), p. 181.
43. Heather Holmes, "Remembering their History: Memories of Irish Migratory Agricultural Workers in Scotland," *Human Affairs* 12, no. 2 (2002), p. 151.
44. Pedraza, "Women and Migration," p. 316.
45. M. G. Wallace, "The Earnings of Irish Migratory Labourers in England and Scotland, Season, 1904," cited in Jonathan Bell, "Donegal Women," p. 80. For more on the "gaffer" system on Achill, see McNally, *Achill*, pp 86–7. McNally notes that the gaffer "was usually notified beforehand by his Scottish employer as to the number of workers required and the sailing date."
46. Timothy Meagher, "Sweet Good Mothers and Young Women out in the World: The Roles of Irish American Women in Late Nineteenth and Early Twentieth Century Worcester, Massachusetts," *U.S. Catholic Historian* 5, no. 3/4 (1986), p. 342.

47. Meagher, "Sweet Good Mothers," p. 342.
48. Anne O'Dowd, "Rabbles and Runaways, Church Gates and Street Corners: Temporary Workers and How They Found Work," in Alan Gailey and Dáithí Ó hÓgáin (eds), *Gold Under the Furze: Studies in Folk Tradition presented to Caoimhín Danachair* (Dublin: Glendale Press, 1982), p. 73.
49. Kennedy, "The Rural Economy," p. 33.
50. Ibid.
51. O'Dowd, *Spalpeens*, p. 172.
52. Kennedy, "The Rural Economy," p. 33.
53. Jonathan Bell, "Donegal Women as Migrant Workers in Scotland" in *Review of Scottish Culture* 7 (1991), p. 74.
54. Meagher, "Sweet Good Mothers," p. 342.
55. Dominique Vidal, "Living in, out of, and between Two Cities: Migrants from Maputo in Johannesburg," *Urban Forum* 21, no. 1 (2010). https://link.springer.com/article/10.1007/s12132–010–9080-y#Fn6_source.
56. Fitzpatrick, "A Peculiar Tramping People," p. 631; see also Sara Goek, "Irish Seasonal Labourers in Britain in the 20th Century," The Dustbin of History (Blog), 18 March 2018. A respondent to Goek's blog site noted, "The Irish word '*spailp*' means a short period of time or a spell. '*Spailpín*' was literally a very short period and became the name for someone spending short periods of time at a job—a casual worker. In later years, it took on a pejorative flavour."
57. McNally, *Achill*, p. 91. For the Roman Catholic clergy's opposition to seasonal migration, see McNally, p. 91.
58. Fitzpatrick, "A Peculiar Tramping People," p. 624.
59. Collins, "Migrant Labour," pp 49–50.
60. Fitzpatrick, "A Peculiar Tramping People," p. 636; Arthur Redford, *Labour Migration in England, 1800–1850* (Manchester University Press, 1926), p. 157.
61. *Slán go Deo: Mná as Dún nan Gall Ar Imirce A Long Farewell: The Emigration of Donegal Women 1845–1950* (Letterkenny: Donegal County Museum & Donegal County Archives, 2018), p. 18.
62. MacGill 1986: 154; quoted in Holmes, "Remembering their History," p. 150.
63. Ibid., p. 151.
64. Fitzpatrick, "A Peculiar Tramping People," p. 644.
65. Holmes, "As Good As," p. 93.
66. Vidal, Dominique, "Living in, out of, and between Two Cities: Migrants from Maputo in Johannesburg", *Urban Forum* 21, no. 1 (2010). https://link.springer.com/article/10.1007/s12132–010–9080-y#Fn6_source.
67. Quoted in Holmes, "Remembering their History," p. 143.
68. Ibid., "Constructing Identities," p. 45.
69. Pedraza, "Women and Migration," pp 319–20.
70. Quoted in Holmes, "Remembering their History," p. 150.
71. "Potatoes at morning, potatoes at noon ... and if I arose in the night, it's potatoes I would get."

72. Holmes, "As Good As," p. 92.
73. Robert Scally, *The End of Hidden Ireland: Rebellion, Famine and Emigration* (Oxford University Press, 1995), p. 135.
74. O'Donnell, 1929, 187; quoted in Holmes 2002, p. 149. Holmes discusses Scottish women's antipathy toward Irish girls and the complaints lodged by them.
75. Patrick MacGill quoted in Holmes, "Remembering their History," p. 149; see also Bell, "Review: Migratory Labourers," p. 104.
76. Quoted in Holmes, "Remembering their History," p. 148.
77. Anonymous Donegal consultant interviewed in June 2019.
78. Pedraza, "Women and Migration," p. 317.
79. Patrick MacGill quoted in Holmes, "Remembering their History," p. 149.
80. Holmes, "Remembering their History," p. 146.
81. Pedraza, "Women and Migration," p. 308.
82. O'Dowd, *Spalpeens*, p. 134.
83. Ibid., p. 396.
84. Moran, "A Passage," p. 24.
85. Pedraza, "Women and Migration," p. 319.

CHAPTER SEVENTEEN

FAMINE IN ART: IMAGERY, INFLUENCES AND EXHIBITION IN MID-20TH-CENTURY IRELAND

Works by Lilian Lucy Davidson and Muriel Brandt in the Centenary Commemoration of Thomas Davis and Young Ireland, 1946

Niamh Ann Kelly

In August 1946, *Gorta* (also known as *Burying the Child*), 1946, by Lilian Lucy Davidson (Image 1) and *Famine*, 1946, by Muriel Brandt (Image 2) were exhibited at The Exhibition of Pictures of Irish Historical Interest at the National College of Art, Kildare Street in Dublin.[1] The exhibition was the last in a series of cultural events in the Centenary Commemoration of Thomas Davis and the Young Ireland Movement that had commenced in 1945.[2] This chapter positions these two paintings as images of history made by artists who had clear biographical and artistic differences, but whose working lives overlapped in a number of ways. Davidson (1879–1954) was born in Wicklow and lived with family there before settling with two of her sisters in Dublin. She was reliant upon teaching and commissions for economic survival. Even so, she crossed disciplinary boundaries through her writing and design work. Brandt (née McKinley) (1909–1981) was born in Belfast and moved to Dublin as a young adult. Married, she undertook a variety of visual commissions to supplement the sale of her non-commissioned works. Both artists were highly active in arts organizations, committed to the art of others through education, guidance and leadership, and highly productive in their artistic outputs and pursuit of public exhibition. This chapter explores the evolution of their 1946 famine paintings by assessing the

Image 1: Lilian Lucy Davidson, 1946, *Gorta* (also known as *Burying the Child*). Oil on canvas, 70 x 90 cm, Coll: Ireland's Great Hunger Museum, Quinnipiac University, Hamden, CT.

crossovers between the social and historic contexts in which they produced their art. The topical focus is principally upon aspects of changing patterns of food consumption—commercially and culturally manifested—in Ireland from the post-mid-19th-century famine adjustment period up to and during the artists' lifetimes. The first part of this paper advocates the significance of works by these two artists for the historiography of hunger, and food politics more broadly, in Ireland in light of the potential of art to contribute to historical understanding. The combined influences of temporary open submission exhibitions as the pillar for the public display of art in Ireland in the mid-20th century and the impact of the artists' oeuvres on the imagery of their 1946 famine works form the second and third parts of this study, respectively.

Analyses of the complexity of influences on the making and public accessibility of works of art and in turn, an artwork's capacity to contribute to historical understanding, suggest that art is not merely illustrative. Rather, images can be actively historiographical, indicative not only of an artist's attitudes and interests but also

Image 2: Muriel Brandt, 1946, *Famine* (also known as *An Gorta*).
Oil on canvas, 89 x 119.5 cm, Coll: National Museum of Ireland.

of those of their wider contemporary society. Writing on 19th-century "historical painting" of the global north, Peter Burke notes two features. Firstly, a tendency for the subject-matter of such painting to be, more often than not, informed by nationalistic sentiment or themes. Secondly, a common trend toward focusing on social history or "the social aspects of politics" that reflects a desire by artists to move from modalities of formal history painting to more popularly readable genre art.[3] In reading Davidson's and Brandt's works as images of history, their art offers evidence of social and cultural life in Ireland at a time of early, and fraught, national assertion. In their 1946 famine works this is two-tiered as the artists set about historical retrospection on a time known to their parent's generation, while simultaneously informed by their contemporary experiences and observations of ordinary life which, in turn, were framed by the period in-between. Their 1946 genre informed historical paintings are thus, among other descriptors, cultural artefacts embedded in 100 years of food politics in Ireland.

An Expanded Archive of Food Politics in Ireland: Tea, Bread and Art

> [...] [W]e have moved away from the History (capitalized and in the singular), as it has been normally studied in the halls of the academy, and find ourselves in the realm of histories (in lower case and inevitably in the plural), which reflect the myriad ways in which the past is routinely recalled in discreet social and cultural interactions, some of which are barely noticeable to outsiders.[4]

Guy Beiner's thesis on the significance of what he terms "social forgetting" in vernacular historiography is centred on, for example, the gathering of stories and intangible forms of heritage, often articulated either casually or informally, and promotes multiple histories to counter monolithic approaches to the past. Refocusing historiography on polyphonic forms "... necessitates the compilation of a wide range of sources, effectively creating an alternative custom-made archive ... most of the sources for such ... are to be found outside of state and institutional archives."[5]

By embracing and thus generating an expanded notion of archive, the net is effectively broadened as to who, or by extension what, might be a form of witness to the past. Reading images, including art, as "historical evidence", in Burke's terms, is potentially a comparable scoping of an expanded archive.[6] This conception of visual culture mitigates against repeatedly implied "condescension towards images," where history-writing has conventionally overlooked, to its loss, the potential of images: instead of regarding photographs, printed illustrations and art works as "mere illustrations" they can be explored as pieces of history.[7] In a further elucidation of his contention on the uses of images as sources of information, Burke cites cultural historian Johan Huizanga: "What the study of history and artistic creation have in common is a mode of forming images."[8] This provides a theoretical point of departure for the exploration of the 1946 commemorative artworks by Davidson and Brandt in the context of the imaging of food politics from the late 19th to the early 20th century. While Davidson's and Brandt's works are retrospective and thus "after-images" of the mid-19th-century Irish Famine, in their execution in the mid-20th century, the impetus and imagery of each work reflect on a range of social, economic and cultural influences of the interim 100 years.[9]

The latter decades of the 19th century saw subsistence crises in parts of Ireland that threatened to recall the severity of the catastrophic famine begun in the 1840s. Gerard Moran notes the periodic crises of the early 1860s, 1879–83 and the 1890s and that the "western seaboard suffered most on these occasions because local landowners were often absentees and did little to assist tenants overcome destitution and poverty."[10] In 1880, the *Illustrated London News*, *The Graphic* and *Harper's Weekly* printed illustrations of suffering that variously echo the conditions imaged at the time of 1840s famine.[11] These news weeklies were the mainstays of text and image accounts of the effects of economic distress in Ireland in the public domain with a readership largely outside of Ireland. Moran suggests that a catastrophe was only averted in 1877 because of credit extended by local shopkeepers.[12] Ian Miller describes that "[f]rom the 1870s [...] a national network of urban and rural retailing was established that encouraged the less affluent to rely increasingly upon food purchased from shopkeepers and, in many instances, to accumulate considerable debt."[13] On the relative rise of traders outside of Dublin and Belfast at the turn of the century, Liam Kennedy writes:

> For the country as a whole, the large number of outlets, particularly from 1890 onwards, ensured that local monopolies were generally not possible. However, in isolated rural areas, mainly in the west of Ireland, probably a not uncommon market form before 1890 was one of a limited number of sellers, each with a degree of monopoly power, and shielded in part by transport and information costs from contiguous markets.[14]

In exploring the links between agriculture and rural traders, he suggests the "very probably [...] the social origins of rural traders lay to a considerable extent in the farming community," elaborated though kinship links and patronage and he quotes a report from 1914 that remarked "many shopkeepers in Ireland are themselves farmers."[15]

It is not surprising, therefore, to find the crucial role of shopkeepers in social and economic life across rural Ireland examined in art. Claudia Kinmonth discusses Davidson's work in terms of wider Irish genre painting that draws attention to social spaces such as public houses, shops, markets and fairs and describes Davidson's painting *Fair Day in Miss O'Dowd's*, c. 1945, as an "enthusiastic and colourful depiction."[16] Davidson's theatrically populated shop is thought to have been in Roundstone, Connemara, County Galway.[17] Using a richly-hued palette, she presents an animated scene with a sense of the bustle of a fair day. There is a clear interest in imaging cultural history with much emphasis placed upon the traditional clothing of the elderly female patrons in the shop. None of these figures nor the younger female shopkeeper look out of the canvas. Kinmonth notes the viewer's perspective from the back of the shop, with a view out its door, as well as the bleeding of internal space between the shopkeeper and customers which suggests a social mixing.[18] The image is detailed in its observation of the shop interior which typically sold diverse produce from consumables to hardware, often hung from the ceiling as well as arranged along wall shelving. The interior in Davidson's shop is well-stocked and the countertop is "piled high with white baker's bread of various sizes."[19] An elderly woman sits behind the counter and appears to sip from a bowl or saucer, while a full teacup sits on the ground at her feet.

Such village and market town shops typically served some food and drink, but the pictorial prominence given to white bread and tea speaks to Davidson's observation of social life as economically and culturally bounded. The shop is a meeting place, but, perhaps more significantly, it had also become in the early 20th century an increasingly central locus for rural dietary survival as food distribution networks altered the flow of food to and from rural Ireland. An outcome of this was a dietary shift. Miller quotes the *Freeman's Journal* of 6 December 1893: "White bread and tea have now taken the place of the humble but more strengthening oatmeal, stirabout and milk."[20] Patricia Lysaght writes that:

> Increased consumption of tea among all the social classes ... is shown to be the result of reduced prices for tea occasioned somewhat by the reduction in grocers' licences and the increased facility of purchasing tea in the little shops which were springing up in many rural areas.[21]

Miller highlights that by the late 19th century the preponderance of this dietary dependence was considered problematic: "... the Irish poor seemed undernourished and underfed as they now subsisted upon nutritionally insufficient diet dominated by tea and white bread."[22]

Tricia Cusack analyses the social mores and class segregation enacted by tea cultures: "as tea drinking spread across society in Ireland, differences in the manner of making and taking tea were associated with social status."[23] Cusack outlines the perceived links between good tea habits, which implied social aspirations for betterment and indications of propriety, and bad tea habits, specifically of poor and laboring-class women, which were linked to slovenliness and distemper wrought by indulgent and addictive behavior. Lysaght discusses that "the descent of tea" took two centuries; it was the 1880s that "tea would become firmly established in the daily diet of all classes in Ireland."[24] Cusack looks to visual art for evidence of historical and class-based tea cultures and though she finds imaging of "respectable farmers" and middle- to upper-class families, "there is scant visual imagery of the tea-drinking habits of the poor, which are repeatedly deplored in medical writings and improvement tracts."[25] The pile of large white loaves prominently displayed in Davidson's shop interior is brightly rendered and a focal point in the image. The figure of the crouched tea-drinking women defies all decorum associated with refined tea cultures as performed to dictums of social aspiration. Davidson's imaging of the social space of the country shop in the 1940s is thus as much a historical document on the socially-charged nutritional habits fostered by expanded access to imported products, altered networks of food distribution and trade, as it is a nostalgic lingering on diminishing cultural traditions in rural Ireland.[26]

Miller notes that the over-consumption of cheap white bread and perceived excessive tea-drinking led to a "moral panic" about tea-drinking in the late 19th century.[27] While there was an embedded class-based prejudice within these outlooks, there were also social health benefits by way of increased knowledge and awareness on the importance of improved and varied diet. Indeed, the desire to improve nutritional health led, in 1900, to domestic education becoming a compulsory school subject for girls.[28] Cusack recounts how tea-rituals among the middle- to upper-classes came to be viewed by some women as simultaneously a sign of civil society and a mechanism of limitation on women's potential as political beings.[29] Arguably, similar might be said for the impact of domestic education as the preserve of women.

The devastating links between women and dietary habits were more starkly defined among the poor and laboring-classes in urban areas, where child mortality was eventually linked to the nutritional health of mothers and babies. The making of tea was unlikely where there was no access to running water and little to heat it with, even by 1945, Dan Buckley writes, only one in four had running water.[30] As outlined by Miller, significant improvements in nutritional health at the start of the 20th century were pushed along by voluntary groups. In 1907, Lady Aberdeen founded the Women's National Health Association, which was primarily aimed at infant health and encouraged the use of pasteurized milk.[31] In 1910, Maude Gonne established the Ladies' School Dinner Committee to deal with "school-day starvation."[32] The committee provided hundreds of dinners daily to inner-city Dublin children and eventually led to the provision of school meals through legislation in 1914.[33]

During and after the national and international political turbulence of the first decades of the 20th century, the dynamics of food distribution changed significantly in Ireland and food shortages were intermittent and geo-politically defined. The 1916 Rising temporarily compounded food poverty for inner-city Dubliners, giving rise to short-lived but severe food shortages.[34] While through 1924 and 1925, a number of local, national and international newspapers reported near famine conditions in the west of Ireland, Adrian Grant describes that "poverty and distress were acute in the west", and itemizes contributory factors including a post-war economic slump that hit cottage industries, combined with excessively wet weather that led to repeated crop failures and unusable turf.[35] Subsequent decades were also difficult, particularly in expanding urban areas. Alvin Jackson notes the rising cost of living between 1937 and 1945 when: "industrial wages rose by 30 per cent, while prices rose by 74 per cent," amid shortages caused by the effects of the war.[36]

In Brandt's post-war painting on the 1916 Rising she focused on the distribution of bread during the food crisis it precipitated and titled the work *The Breadline, 1916*,

c. 1950.[37] The painted scene is a busy one. The Daughters of Charity of St. Vincent de Paul distribute white bread from baskets to a poor population amid the ruins of Dublin city center, while in the background, British soldiers survey the damage on Sackville Street (now O'Connell Street). Well-dressed passers-by moved through the scene, but, as in many of Brandt's works, the main focal points were the children who both actively assess the scene and visually engage the viewer. Sighle Bhreathnach-Lynch terms the image an "historical genre painting" that celebrates "the unobtrusive gallantry" of those "unwittingly caught in the fray" and notes "the attitude of the children is pathetic yet humorous." She further suggests that Brandt "remains aloof from her subject" when compared to works by Kathleen Fox or Seán Keating.[38] However, both Fox and Keating had direct experiences of 1916, whereas Brandt was then a 7-year-old, living in Belfast. In this regard, her imaging is overtly commemorative in form, rather than directly observational, and its inspiration is presumably drawn from archival, biographical and artistic sources.[39] The painting has resonance not least in its insistence on retrospective social documentary and the depiction of charity encapsulated in the distribution of an increasingly common food product: white bread.

Around this time, Brandt painted populated streetscapes with her focus trained upon a more contemporary subject: the sociality and spectatorship of urban shopping cultures. *Window Shopping*, N.D., images a rapidly altering consumer landscape where more specialist shops became accessible to a wider social descriptor.[40] Painted from a viewpoint of inside a butcher's shop, the picture's composition draws attention to the people who pass by and peer in at the elaborate display of meat products on the window. *Christmas Eve (Figures on Moore Street)*, N.D., though different in style, is similarly focused upon the social and visual aspects of new consumer spaces where desire overtakes need within the modernist shopping environment, fueled by the spectacle of shopping itself.[41] This colorful scene of one of Dublin's best known shopping streets, noted for its stalls of fresh produce and range of food stores, is depicted at a slightly overhead angle filled with figures, balloons, toys and a somewhat jaded air of expectation. Children are rendered with particular attention and seem overawed by intense seasonal excitement.

By the mid-20th century, Ireland was in economic and political transformation. Buckley terms the 1940s as "a decade of war and want—and change."[42] The consumer change was exemplified, nationally, by the opening of Dunnes Stores in Cork in 1944, which denoted the advent of a shift towards self-service grocery shopping in Ireland presented in the coded visuality of a department store. An international dimension was epitomized by the launch of Shannon Duty Free in 1947, a first in the world. Such changes in the dynamics of retail trade and supply chains had a huge impact on the organization and distribution of food networks in Ireland. Brandt's post–1946 works on consumer streetscapes bear witness to that changed urban environment of shopping. Davidson's work visualizes earlier altering patterns of urban-rural networks and related socio-cultural implications through the prism of the country shop.

When Thomas Davis published in the *Nation* in July 1843, his Hints for Irish Historical Painting, he not only presented a rationale, but he supplied a list of heroic content for the establishment of a national art. The significance of Davis' text, as Brendan Rooney outlines, was perhaps most apparent in its subsequent aspirational appropriation for nationhood for Ireland. As articulated through the Loyal National Repeal Association, a political organization founded by Daniel O'Connell in 1840, such art would be "for future decoration of the Irish Parliament house."[43] Despite these public statements, artists remained largely reticent to embrace, or at least exhibit, what might be construed as political works and "well-established exhibition orthodoxy, dominated by portraiture and landscape painting remained intact."[44] In the main, from the mid-19th to the mid-20th century, "historical subjects remained, for the most part, the stuff of passive conversation and editorial comment. Moreover, Irish political paintings proved consistently unmarketable."[45] Even so, Rooney outlines three factors which indicated subtle shifts in the appearance of history subjects in Irish art as the 19th century progressed. Firstly, an increase emerged in response to "nationalist momentum"; secondly, changes occurred in the "cultural profile of the artistic community," and lastly, there was a shift in patronage from Anglo Irish to "a professional, and often Catholic, elite."[46] By the start of the 20th century, some artists had engaged with ambitious largescale works to indicate historical gravitas of certain subjects.[47] John Turpin explains from the period 1916 to 1923, " ... several artists responded to the violence of the day in creating images from a national point of view," noting Fox, Jack B. Yeats and Keating in particular.[48] Despite this, the continued lack of curatorial, critical or market appetite for such works dictated the ongoing invisibility of nationally or culturally resonant historical subjects in art in Ireland. Turpin writes that the rising Catholic middle-class "wished to be socially assimilated into established Protestant social conventions and taste" and thereby had no desire for art that might appear nationalistic.[49] Thus, debates on what might constitute national art stalked art education and public exhibition practice well into the mid-20th century.

Public Art Exhibitions in Mid-twentieth-century Ireland

By the time of the 1946 Exhibition of Pictures of Irish Historical Interest, the international aesthetics of Modernism was the crux around which many debates on art revolved. As artists from Ireland travelled to absorb European Modernism in particular, new paradigms of art became fuel to a backlash against the perceived rigidity of academy traditions associated with the National College of Art (NCA) and its linked professional public output in the Royal Hibernian Academy of Art (RHA) exhibitions.[50] An account of the 1946 exhibition is thus clarified in light of the contemporary reigning debates on artistic styles and the primary outlet for their articulation: open submission and, usually annual, public exhibitions.[51] In mid-20th-century Ireland, these large-scale fora were the mainstay of the artistic calendar and the lifeforce of an artist's economic survival and professional recognition. The key exhibitions in Dublin were organized by the RHA, from 1826; the Water Colour Society of Ireland, from 1871; the Oireachtas Art exhibition, intermittently from 1905 and annually from 1943, the Irish Exhibition of Living Art (ELA).

Up to the 1940s, the RHA had demonstrated a consistently academic outlook, reflecting the bastion of art school education in Britain, known as the South Kensington System, which had prevailed at the Dublin Metropolitan School and later the NCA.[52] The RHA's first building in Lower Abbey Street had been ruined by fire during the 1916 Rising and it found a modernist home in 1985 in the purpose-built Gallagher Gallery at Ely Place, designed by Raymond McGrath. Between 1916 and 1985, exhibitions alternated between the NCA and the NGI. From 1914 until her death in 1954, Davidson exhibited 135 works at the RHA.[53] In 1940, she was voted an associate member.[54] Also an active member of the RHA, Brandt was elected an associate in 1948 and a full member in 1961.[55] She exhibited over 145 works there over a 40-year period starting in 1938, a great many of them portraits.[56]

The Water Colour Society of Ireland was founded in 1870 and held its first exhibition the following year in Lismore, County Waterford.[57] From 1874 onward, the Society typically held two exhibitions a year—"one in the provinces and one in Dublin."[58] Davidson exhibited with the society annually from 1912 to 1953, totaling 188 works. From 1934, she served on their committee.[59] From 1943 up to her death in 1981, Brandt exhibited regularly with the society, showing 41 works.[60] The Oireachtas Art exhibitions were established as part of the Irish language festival that Oireachtas had begun in 1897. In the mid-20th century, its significance was mostly in its links to State sponsorship. The event's demise in 2003 was lamented in some quarters as a lost opportunity for artists to exhibit in the public arena.[61] Both Davidson and Brandt exhibited regularly at the Oireachtas Art exhibitions. In 1946, for example, Davison had two exhibits and Brandt had four. In 1967, Brandt was awarded the President Hyde gold medal for the best "Irish historical painting" for her work *Carrickfergus Castle, where William III landed in 1690*.[62]

The ELA began when two paintings by Louis le Brocquy were rejected by the RHA for exhibition in 1942 and again, with works by other artists, in 1943.[63] Le Brocquy, Mainie Jellett, Jack Hanlon and Norah McGuinness began the actions that resulted in the establishment of the annual exhibition. Whilst the 1943 exhibition was regarded as a watershed in the history of art in Ireland, and the divisions between academy tradition and Modernism were at times caustically expressed, the ELA did not promote division, inviting academicians to exhibit.[64] So, while raising a debate on Modernism and inversely on what was national art, many artists continued to exhibit across the public fora. There is no record of Davidson exhibiting with the ELA, though her work with the Dublin Painters' Society is proffered as evidence of a tacit support of Modernist trends.[65] Brandt exhibited with the ELA in 1958.[66] The ELA had chosen the National College of Art as its venue and so, in summer of 1946, they had no exhibition in Dublin as the venue was taken by the Exhibition of Pictures of Irish Historical Interest.[67]

This exhibition was the final event in the Centenary Commemoration of Thomas Davis and the Young Ireland Movement that had begun in the previous year. A pamphlet combined photographs, textual description, excerpts from speeches and lists of organizing committees in an account of the commemorative events of 1945. These included formal parades and plaque unveiling to broader cultural celebrations of music, theater and literary events and three loan art exhibitions.[68] The pamphlet had a photograph of the Painting Committee tasked with organizing the exhibition. They were, Dr. M. Quane, Dept. of Education; Dr. George Furlong, Director, National Gallery of Art; Lucius O'Callaghan, R.H.A.; Henry Mangan; Thomas McGreevey; M. de Burca, A.R.H.A National College of Art; Joseph Brennan and John Burke. The project's aims were: "to encourage the production of pictures based on some aspects or episodes in Irish History during the past century facilities will be afforded for the holding in the Autumn of 1946 of an exhibition of original paintings of Irish Historical interest," with a view to purchasing some for government buildings.[69]

Of the 87 works listed in the catalogue, 47 were selected from the open submission process, with the rest loaned from various national collections.[70] The *Irish Times* declared the art in the exhibition "mournful and depressed."[71] In view of the 1946 exhibition's wider context, Rooney's assertion of its brief as "anachronistic" can be understood.[72] In many senses, the overtly commemorative agenda of the project appeared out of time with dominant art debates of the day. However, a number of the exhibited works were a complication of the project's curatorial assumption and, of interest here, are the emergent relationships between art and historical understanding magnified by some of the works. Many of the artists had a number of paintings exhibited and some have since been considered seminal historical works including Yeats' *Men of Destiny*, 1946, which was shown for the first time in Ireland.[73] A work by Sir John Lavery was listed as: *The Trial Of Roger Casement, London, 1916*, with a note: "Sir Roger Casement (1864–1916) was tried for high treason in May and June, 1916, convicted and executed on August 3rd, 1916."[74] Given that Donal O'Donnell has noted that Lavery's painting *High Treason: The Appeal of Roger Casement, 1916*, 1916–c.1930, is often thus "mis-described," this listing suggests 1946 was the first intended public exhibition of an extraordinary monumental work that proved as controversial as its subject.[75] Another large-scale exhibited work that was based on a different kind of court scene and which also remained out of public view in subsequent decades was *Republican Court, 1921*, 1946, by Keating.[76] The painting depicts the titular scene re-enacted for the artist in a kitchen in a house in north Cork, described by Kinmonth as an "authentic location."[77] Among other works by Keating listed in the 1946 exhibition catalogue was the now iconic painting, *Men of the West*, 1916.[78]

Davidson and Brandt were the only two of the eight exhibiting women who chose to depict a famine theme. The other women were Fox, Nano Reid, Norah McGuiness, Lily Williams, Sarah C. Harrison, Dawn Maureen Steele. Among the male artists, Hanlon, le Brocquy, Michael O'Farrell, Cathal MacLuain, Geo F. Campbell, Padraic Woods, Muiris MacCongaill all presented works on famine-related themes.

The Pictorial Histories of *Gorta* and *Famine*

Davidson was born in Bray, County Wicklow in 1879, her family being "as poor as church mice."[79] Her mother died when she was 9-years-old and her father in 1897. In the same year, she received a scholarship from the Royal Dublin Society. This carried free studentship at the Dublin Metropolitan School of Art, which she had attended from the age of 16, winning prizes there in 1895 and 1896. After her father's death, Davidson and her sisters moved to Rathmines in Dublin to live with an aunt. Cahill suggests her brothers emigrated, possibly to Canada.[80] By the 1911 census, just Davidson and her two sisters were living in Gulistan Terrace.[81]

Kinmonth describes Davidson as a prolific artist and Cahill terms her a "journeyman artist."[82] Though Davidson was diverse in her cultural output—she designed costume displays for Switzer's Department Store and, later, set designs. She also wrote poems, short stories and plays under the pseudonym Ulick Burke—by necessity, however, she chiefly earned her living from teaching art.[83] In 1920, she co-organized with her friend, Mainie Jellett, a joint exhibition of their work in Dublin. The exhibition was described in the *Irish Times* as: "[…] in these troublesome times […] a tonic which can be safely recommended to the worried citizen."[84] Davidson's depictions of the environment—its ambience, colors and textures—is particularly evident in her paintings of boats and waterways, with much attention given to qualities of light and its varied reflections on water. A friend of Yeats, Davidson's reputation as an artist was limited by comparisons to him; an association that, arguably, continues to sideline her in histories of art. An artistic legacy of their friendship exists in the form of a warm portrait by her of Yeats, which she bequeathed to NGI.[85] By the 1930s, she had clearly distinguished her artistic focus on distinctive genre studies of rural life that took account of the environments and social forms of fading cultural traditions.

A number of Davidson's works in the 1920s and 1930s show an influence from continental European art. Though she did not possess the financial resources to stay for sustained study periods abroad as her better-known contemporaries did, she visited France, Belgium and Switzerland on painting holidays in the 1920s. Working under the "South Kensington" influence from her days of study at the Dublin Metropolitan School of Art, Davidson amalgamated other artistic influences—both earlier and contemporary to her.[86] She harnessed these stylistic and thematic interests upon Irish subject choices, such as in *The Flax Pullers,* 1921 and *The Potato Harvest*, 1931.[87] The harvesting of flax for the Ulster linen industry is depicted on a sun-drenched hillside, and potato harvesting is portrayed in an earth-toned field, bathed in evening light. Each recall the figurations of laborers presented, for example, by Jean François Millet and Honoré Daumier in a previous century with a similar "naturalism" dominating the works.[88] During this period, Davidson also produced her "Western peasant cycle" of paintings, based on her travels to counties Donegal, Galway and Mayo.[89] This tour of the west of Ireland influenced many of her works thereafter, and included thematic explorations such as *The Holy Well* and *Bringing Home the Turf,* both undated.[90] *The Holy Well* depicts an elderly man and woman paused in prayer at a sacred site on the landscape. Such sites were associated with earlier religious practices, where people would rest in the course of their agricultural labor or make a pilgrimage to, perhaps on a saint's day. The diffused lighting of *Bringing Home the Turf* denotes a growing emphasis on light in her works.

Arising out of her early visits to the western seaboard and prior to the brighter more animated works of the 1940s, such as *Fair Day in Miss O'Dowd's Shop* and *Fashions at the Fair*, Davidson produced an atmospherically elegiac set of works.[91] Marianne

O'Kane Boal writes that in her "night studies," Davidson demonstrated her remarkable ability to "capture the mystery and nuances of colour, light and shadow."[92] The tonal quality of these works indicate a dramatic, almost expressionistic, use of color that prefigures her depiction of Famine in 1946. The mood of works such as *Night at Claddagh*, c. 1933 and *Cottages, Keel, Achill*, 1938, capture the closing of the day. In each, lone figures washed in blue-purple tones walk rough lanes towards cottages from which leak warmly-glowing light, calling the walkers out of the cool and misting fall of night. Cahill suggests the Keel painting recalls a line from a Davidson poem, *A Night*: "The sky itself like a purple cloak."[93] Heavily pictorial, rather than documentary in content, the works' evocations of temporality imply a symbolic, and romanticized, meditation on a passing way of life. Cahill comments on Davidson's empathy with her subjects as most "potent" in her "night scenes."[94] There is a considerable portion of twilight and night-time scenes in her oeuvre, which implies many evening study excursions. Her command of tonal expressiveness, empathy with rural subjects coupled with observations of pictorial landscapes and figurations all served to heighten the effect of her most arresting imaging of the past: *Gorta*, 1946 (Image 1).

The harshly unsettling and confrontational image of *Gorta* presents a devastating scene of three emaciated people burying the body of a dead baby. The lack of markers in the bleakly autumnal landscape suggest this is not a formal graveyard. This is either a hurried burial at a roadside or ditch, or perhaps, given Davidson's *Holy Well* painting, it is a locally-known site with former religious association such as old church or well. Such symbolic sites were often chosen for burial during the haste precipitated by famine conditions.[95] If the baby was not baptized before death, it might be the site of a *cillín*, a type of burial ground for unbaptized children and other "individuals considered unsuitable for burial in consecrated ground by the Roman Catholic Church in Ireland," evident in Ireland since the early 17th century.[96]

The figures are visually striking, in somber dress with bodily demeanors of despair. The woman holding the wrapped tiny body appears on the verge of collapse. Unusually for Davidson, the male figure looks straight out of the canvas, as if to challenge the viewer, and a mourning elderly woman with rosary beads catches the viewer's gaze as she appears to lean back with her eyes half-closed, perhaps to start an exhausted keen, a traditional lament for the dead led by women.[97] The inclusion of these overt gazes and carefully rendered facial expressions distinguish the painting among Davidson's genre works where faces are rarely depicted in any detail and they further suggest her pictorial choices in *Gorta* were indicative of the gravity with which she approached the historical subject as an artist. Davidson died eight years later and is buried with her sisters in an unmarked grave in Mount Jerome's cemetery in Dublin.[98]

Famine, 1946, Muriel Brandt

Brandt was born in Belfast, Northern Ireland. She studied at the Belfast School of Art and in 1934, she won the Sorella Scholarship to attend the Royal College of Art (RCA) in London. As part of her course at the RCA, she studied mural painting under the tutelage of Gilbert Spencer.[99] She returned to Ireland in 1937 and settled in Sutton, Dublin. She was active across the Dublin art scene, including as a member of the United Arts Club and had her first solo show in the Dawson Gallery in early 1960s. She travelled and, "never let her pen rest."[100] Brandt married Frank Brandt, a designer and art advisor for the Electricity Supply Board (ESB) Ireland, in 1935 and they had three children.[101] Her design work included a *Fógra Fáilte* poster and the state-sponsored commission of the first postage stamp to mark the official declaration of the Republic of Ireland in 1949.[102] She is best known for her portraits and fellow artist and friend James Nolan observed her as "... a compulsive draughtsman [who] sketched like lightening, achieving in minutes those likenesses of her contemporaries."[103] Among her sitters were key figures in Irish cultural life, including Lady Christine Longford, Micheál MacLiammóir, Hilton Edwards and Sinéad de Valera.[104] Along with personal commissions, she had formal ones, on which she relied to support her art, such as *Major General Liam Egan*, c. 1961, the Chief of Staff of the Defence Forces, 1952–54.[105]

Throughout her career, Brandt demonstrated a consistent interest in imaging outdoor life in Ireland with a particular focus on social gatherings, apparent in such paintings as *A Courting in the Meadow* and *The Road Bowler*, thought to be based on a festival in County Antrim.[106] These bright and busy bucolic scenes are rendered in light-washed tones and, though their figure-filled compositions have a staged quality, the images document by turn generational distinctions and gender segregation in aspects of the cultural formations of social life. In the same series, *The Spirit Grocery* depicts a lively crowded shop, painted from a similar viewpoint to Davidson's, the back interior of the shop.[107] Brandt has rendered a notable mix of gender and ages and great detail is given on the produce for sale, as well as on the customers' and shop workers' clothing and animated interactions. In other works, her painted depictions of land- and sea-scapes demonstrate fluidity in the use of watercolor as well as oils, and suggesting an artistic sensibility informed by environmental awareness. Some of her topographical works on Ireland were published intermittently in the *Irish Times* and included heritage ruins. She also produced drawings on topographical features of other countries she visited. This sustained element of her oeuvre highlights her extraordinary skill at observational drawing and the depth of draughtsmanship underpinning her work. Some works, like the *Daisy Market, Dublin,* N.D.

harken a mural influence, perhaps from Spencer's teaching, while others appear more consciously driven by documentary interests.[108]

Alongside her portraits, Brandt was noted in her lifetime as a keen observer of children and in many of her figurative paintings it is children who carry the viewer's gaze. The children are the primary bearers of meaning in *Breadline, 1916*, where they not only signify aspirational symbolism, but reflect on the historic social reality and poverty of inner-city Dublin.[109] Brandt's many studies of her own children and of wider family and friends are indicative of a powerful strength in portraiture, which she often deployed in other works. However, this artistic emphasis on figuration and visualizing children may have mitigated against her work harboring the serious critical engagement it deserved in mid-20th century.[110]

Brandt's manifold use of children in her works was often highly affective: the direct, intense gazes of children, that are rarely given or held past adolescence, were frequently appropriated to full pictorial potential, as exemplified in her 1946 painting, *Famine*. The visual impact of *Famine* references another iconographic influence on her work: Renaissance religious art. Blaithin O'Ciobhain draws attention to Brandt's close study of early Renaissance painting on her travels to Italy, suggesting that this may have tailored her use of children.[111] Brandt gave expression to this aspect of her artistic studies in her first major commission: a series of scenes from the life of St Anthony for the Franciscan Church of the Immaculate Conception, better known as Adam and Eve's Church, on Merchants Quay, Dublin. She began work on the seven large paintings in 1938.[112] In their general compositional orders and her imaging of children within them, the paintings reflect on her study of early Renaissance art.[113] Her depiction of Irish elements of landscape in the scenes offer further insight into *Famine*. The trees, house, bridge and mountain horizon in the 1946 commemorative work all echo details of the topography Brandt presented at Adam and Eve's Church.

Though the gloomy mood of *Famine* is highly differentiated from her genre works which were largely upbeat in tone, there are commonalities. As in her Antrim scenes, *Famine* is set out of doors and defined by an array of observed social customs: here, the wake and related burial and mourning rituals, greatly diminished by the 1840s Great Famine, are depicted. Furthermore, as in many other of her works, all the figurative elements are embedded in a carefully rendered Irish landscape. The image's affective atmosphere of defeat is evoked by the weariness in the woman's face and the fear depicted across the children's expressions. This bereaved, and perhaps now homeless, family are overwhelmed by the circumstances in which they find themselves. A religious connotation is lent by the pieta-like composition of the woman with children in foreground. At the time of painting *Famine,* Brandt was

37-years-old, a prolific artist, a committed arts organizer and a mother to young children. In later years, Brandt was a governor of NGI and a board member of National College of Art and Design.[114] She remained a proactive contributor to art until her death in 1981.

Imaging Hunger

The imaging of social life in Ireland generated in the art of Davidson and Brandt articulated various temporally defined cultural tropes, such as the country shop, out-of-doors social events and historically specific Irish topographies. The influences upon their works were complex. Place and circumstances of childhood shaped the artistic paths they set upon as young adults. During their later adult lives, personal, as well as socio-economic shifts occurring in Ireland impacted upon their artistic themes and mode of outputs. With contrasting results, their art was defined by their individual experiences and observations of early-20th-century life in Ireland, and aesthetically framed by the wider expanse of shifting artistic currents around them. Various aspects of their works take account of dietary and related consumer and cultural changes in Ireland in the early to mid-20th century, thus effectively expanding the archive on the socio-economic realities of food politics.

Davidson's and Brandt's distinctive responses to the call for submissions to the 1946 Exhibition led to the making of two extraordinary images of history. *Gorta* and *Famine* are the result of entanglements of social, economic, cultural and personal experiences of the artists. Davidson and Brandt applied these experiences as forms of knowledge to produce retrospective views on a past that preceded them and by so doing, reinvigorated the scope of historical painting with nuanced genre informed observations.

NOTES

1. *Gorta*, oil on canvas, 70 x 90cm. Coll: Ireland's Great Hunger Museum; *Famine*, oil on canvas, 89 x 119.5 cm. Coll: National Museum of Ireland.
2. Along with Charles Gavan Duffy and John Mitchel, Thomas Davis (1814–45) was a leader of the Young Ireland movement, which was initially aligned with Daniel O'Connell's Repeal movement. In 1842, they launched a weekly newspaper, *The Nation*.
3. Peter Burke, *Eyewitnessing: The Uses of Images as Historical Evidence* (London: Reaktion Books, 2001), pp 158–159.

4. Guy Beiner, "Introduction: Sites of Oblivion," *Forgetful Remembrance: Social Forgetting and Vernacular Historiography of a Rebellion in Ulster* (Oxford University Press, 2018), p. 5.
5. Ibid., p. 14.
6. Burke, *Eyewitnessing*, p. 9.
7. Ibid., p. 10. This approach is underway in some historical writing on Ireland's past as evident in work by Claudia Kinmonth and Tricia Cusack, for example. Claudia Kinmonth, *Irish Rural Interiors in Art* (New Haven, CT: Yale University Press, 2006); Tricia Cusack, "'This pernicious tea drinking habit.' Women, Tea, and Respectability in Nineteenth-Century Ireland," in *Canadian Journal of Irish Studies*, 41, The Food Issue (2018), 178–209.
8. Burke, *Eyewitnessing*, p. 11.
9. "After-images" references James Young's use. James Young, *At Memory's Edge: After-Images of the Holocaust in Contemporary Art and Architecture* (New Haven, CT: Yale University Press, 2000) pp 3–4. Art on famine as after-images is discussed in Niamh Ann Kelly, *Imaging the Great Irish Famine: Representing Dispossession in Visual Culture* (London: Bloomsbury, 2018).
10. Gerard Moran, "'Near Famine': The Roman Catholic Church and the Subsistence Crises of 1879–82," in *Studia Hibernica*, 32 (2002/2003), pp 155–56.
11. The crisis of the late 1870s was a result of both potato failure and a fall in seasonal migration to Britain, due to increasing mechanization, coupled with an influx of American grain. Moran, "Near Famine," p. 157.
12. Ibid., p. 156.
13. Ian Miller, "Nutritional Decline in post-Famine Ireland, c. 1851–1922," in *Proceedings of the Royal Irish Academy: Archaeology, Culture, History, Literature* 115C, Food and Drink in Ireland (2015), pp 313–14.
14. He adds: "In cases of such limited local monopolies, underinvestment or too few resources committed to retailing was the problem ...." Liam Kennedy, "Traders in the Irish Rural Economy 1880–1914," in *The Economic History Review, New Series* 32, no. 2 (May 1979), p. 206.
15. Ibid., pp 209, 205.
16. Oil on canvas, 71 x 91.5 cm. Exhibited RHA 1945. Kinmonth, *Irish Rural Interiors*, pp 234–235.
17. Katherine Cahill, "In the Mainstream of Irish Naturalism: The Art of Lilian Lucy Davidson, 1879–1954," in *Irish Arts Review Yearbook* 15 (1999) p. 45.
18. Oil on canvas, 71 x 91.5 cm. Exhibited: RHA 1945. Kinmonth, *Irish Rural Interiors*, pp 234–235.
19. Ibid., p. 235.
20. Qtd. in Miller, "Nutritional Decline," p. 315.
21. Patricia Lysaght, "'When I makes Tea, I makes tea....': Innovation in Food – the Case of Tea in Ireland," in *Ulster Folklife*, 33 (1987), p. 48. Also: "Allied to tea consumption was the increasing use of baker's bread which the memoirs [Ordnance Survey memoir material] show to be a response to market forces." Ibid., p. 45.
22. Miller, "Nutritional Decline," p. 307.
23. Cusack, "this pernicious tea," p. 183.

24. Lysaght, "When I makes Tea," p. 49.
25. Cusack, "this pernicious tea," p. 203.
26. Brendan Rooney comments that painting "is strikingly theatrical in composition." National Gallery of Ireland, *A Time and A Place: Two Centuries of Irish Social Life* (Dublin: National Gallery of Ireland, 2006), p. 147. Davidson's *Fashions at the Fair*, c. 1940s (oil on canvas, 71 x 92 cm. Coll: NGI) demonstrates her interest in rural social life and in the tonal exploration of texture and textiles. See: National Gallery of Ireland, *A Time and A Place*, pp 145–147.
27. Miller, "Nutritional Decline," p. 315.
28. Ibid., p. 319.
29. Cusack, "this pernicious tea," p. 183.
30. *Irish Examiner*, 9 March 2015.
31. Miller, "Nutritional Decline," p. 312.
32. Maude Gonne, "Responsibility," *Irish Review* 1, no. 10 (Dec. 1911), 483. Quoted in Miller, "Nutritional Decline," p. 320. See chapter by Christine Kinealy.
33. Ibid., pp 320–21.
34. Food queues outside bakeries were noted by John Gibney, *Irish Independent*, 15 April 2016. Contemporary reports on food shortages and distributions in *Daily Mail*, 3 May 1916; *Cork Examiner*, 3 May 1916.
35. Adrian Grant, "'Workers to the rescue:' Workers' International Relief in Ireland, 1925," in *History Ireland* 19, no. 1 (Jan/Feb 2011), p. 38.
36. Alvin Jackson, *Ireland 1798–1998* (Oxford: Blackwell Publishing, 1999), p. 305.
37. Oil on board, 61 x 38cm. Coll: Crawford Art Gallery, Cork.
38. Sighle Bhreathnach-Lynch, "The Easter Rising 1916: Constructing a Canon in Art and Artefacts," *History Ireland* 5, no.1 (Spring, 1997), p. 39.
39. Press clippings from the era show great similarity between Brandt's retrospective depiction of children and photographs of inner-city children printed in newspapers contemporary to 1916. Bureau of Military History (1913–21), "1916 Press Cuttings," at: www.militaryarchives.ie.
40. Oil on board, 41 x 53 cm. Coll: Waterford Municipal Art Collection, purchased by the Haverty Trust, 1955. Peter Jordan, *Waterford Municipal Art Collection: A History and Catalogue* (Cork: Waterford Institute of Technology and Waterford City Council, 2006), p. 126.
41. Oil on boards, 43 x 29 cm. Exhibited: Dawson Gallery, 1963. Coll: private. For an account of the designed spectacle of modern urban consumer spaces, see, Aaron Betsky, "All the World's a Store: The Spaces of Modern Shopping," in Jane Pavitt (ed.), *Brand New* (London: V & A Publications, 2000), pp 110–41.
42. *Irish Examiner*, 9 March 2015.
43. Brendan Rooney, "'If the artist be as national as the minstrel:' Irish History on Display" in Brendan Rooney (ed.) *Creating History: Stories of Art in Ireland* (Dublin: Irish Academic Press, 2016), p. 4.
44. Ibid., p. 6.

45. Ibid., p. 16.
46. Ibid., p. 10.
47. Ibid., pp 17–18.
48. John Turpin, "Irish History Painting," *The GPA Irish Arts Review Yearbook* (1989/1990), p. 242.
49. Ibid., p. 240.
50. The NCA was known as the Dublin Metropolitan School up to 1936, and from 1971, as the National College of Art and Design.
51. Through the second half of the 20th century, these were augmented and then overtaken by burgeoning networks of both public and private galleries, augmented by a growth in the internationalization of art through increased participation in biennales and art fairs. In the 1940s, private galleries such as the Victor Waddington Galleries, on Anne St, from 1927 and the Dawson Gallery on Dawson St, opened in 1944 by Leo Smith, were supporting a market for contemporary art in Ireland.
52. Turpin describes the pedagogical approach of James Brenan's Headmaster at the Dublin Metropolitan Schools, 1889–1907, as "pure mid-Victorian theory of South Kensington." Brenan advocated for design to "enter more largely into our teaching" and "the application of art to industry in the past, and a constant reference to nature." John Turpin, "The South Kensington System and the Dublin Metropolitan School of Art 1877–1900," in *Dublin Historical Record* 36, no. 2 (March 1983), p. 48. The South Kensington System refers to both administrative and ideological aspects of the Dublin Metropolitan School of Art. The school remained under the Department of Science and Art, South Kensington until 1900, and its curriculum was perceived to be influenced by its founding aim in 1853, to primarily encourage design for industry. Ibid., p. 42. In a review of the 1944 Oireachtas exhibition, Thomas MacGreevy commented on the RHA, who had selected the exhibition, that the "secularist and middle-class South Kensington tradition ... still prevails at the Academy and at our schools of art," underlying the close association between the RHA and the Dublin Metropolitan School of Art. *Irish Times*, 23 Oct. 1944.
53. Theo Snoddy, *Dictionary of Irish Artists* (Dublin: Wolfhound Press, 1996), p. 94.
54. John Turpin, *History of the Royal Hibernian Academy of Arts, Volume Two 1916–2020* (Dublin: Lilliput Press, 2018), p. 166.
55. Ibid., p. 626.
56. Snoddy, *Dictionary*, p. 34.
57. Patricia Butler, *The Silent Companion: An Illustrated History of the Water Colour Society of Ireland* (Woodbridge: Antique Collector's Club, 2010), p. 16.
58. Ibid., p. 17.
59. Kinmonth, *Irish Rural Interiors*, p. 39.
60. Whytes, "Whytes Irish and British Art Auction listing, 28 September 2009," at: www.whytes.ie.
61. Gerald Davis, "Demise of Oireachtas Exhibition", *Irish Times*, 17 July 2003. Davis (1938–2005) was a Dublin-based artist and gallerist based.
62. *An Chomhairle Ealaion* (The Arts Council), *Sixteenth Annual Report and Accounts, from 1 April 1967 to 3 March 1968* (Dublin: An Chomhairle Ealaion, 1968), pp 4–5.

63. Fionna Barber, *Art in Ireland Since 1910* (London: Reaktion Books, 2013), p. 104.
64. Robert O'Byrne refers to the 1943 exhibition as "a milestone in the history of Modernism in Ireland." Robert O'Byrne, "Irish Modernism: The Early Decades," in Irish Museum of Modern Art, *The Moderns: The Arts in Ireland from the 1900s to the 1970s* (Dublin: Irish Museum of Modern Art, 2011), p. 21. The beginnings of the ELA are discussed in: Riann Coulter, "Hibernian Salon des Refuses," in *Irish Arts Review* 20, no. 3 (Autumn 2003), 80–85. S.B. Kennedy, *Irish Art and Modernism 1880–1950* (Belfast: The Institute of Irish Studies, 1991), 115–133. Jellett, an active advocate of Modernism, died the following year. Also, in 1944, the IELA committee voted to include non-Irish artists.
65. Katherine Cahill writes, "given her involvement with The Dublin Painters' Society, whose aim was 'to encourage artists whose tendencies are in harmony with contemporary world movements', her interest in the *avant-garde* is unquestioned." Cahill, "In the Mainstream," p. 36.
66. National Irish Visual Arts Library File: Muriel Brandt, Ref. IE/NIVAL AR/293.
67. Kennedy, *Irish Art*, p. 132.
68. Michael Quigley, "Pictorial Record: Centenary of Thomas Davis and Young Ireland," in: Government Publication Sales Office, *Illustrated Centenary Volume: Thomas Davis and Young Ireland 1845–1945* (Dublin: The Stationery Office, 1945).
69. Quigley, 'Pictorial Record', 1945.
70. National College of Art, *Thomas Davis and the Young Ireland Movement Centenary: Exhibition of Pictures of Irish Historical Interest* (Dublin: National College of Art, 1946).
71. As this is dated 23 July 1946, it may have been a preview text. Quoted in, Niamh O'Sullivan (ed.), *Coming Home: Art and the Great Hunger* (Hamden, CT: Quinnipiac University, 2018), p. 109.
72. Rooney, "If the artist," p. 18.
73. Oil on canvas, 51 x 69 cm. Coll: National Gallery of Ireland. Yeats' painting was exhibited at Society of Scottish Artists 52nd Exhibition, Royal Scottish Academy Galleries, Edinburgh, in Spring 1946.
74. National College of Art, *Thomas Davis*, p. 16. Oil on canvas, 194.5 x 302.5 cm. Coll: Government Art Collection London, on Loan to the Honorable Society, King's Inns, Dublin. Lavery took more than 10 years to complete the work. Catherine Marshall, "'Of all the trials not to paint…": Sir John Lavery's painting *High Treason, Court of Criminal Appeal: The Trial of Roger Casement 1916*, in Lisa Godson and Joanna Brück (eds.), *Making 1916: Material and Visual Culture of the Easter Rising* (Liverpool University Press, 2015), p. 228.

    Fintan O'Toole and Catherine Marshall point out that Lavery had bequeathed the work to the National Portrait Gallery in London and the Royal Courts of Justice, but neither institution wanted it: "If Darling commissioned it, he did not pay for it: it remained in Lavery's studio until his death, in 1941. […] After years in storage at the NPG it was hung in the office of the senior clerk of the court of criminal appeal in London, removed from the public gaze, for fear of arousing the wrong kind of attention from 'people who considered Casement a martyr.'"

    The painting was lent to the Honorable Society of King's Inns in Dublin, in 1951. The message from the lord chancellor's office accompanying the loan said, "We can adopt the suggestion of lending it to the King's Inns on indefinite loan, which means that we can forget to ask for its return." *The Irish Times*, 21 Feb. 2015.

75. Donal O'Donnell, 'High Treason: The Appeal of Roger Casement' in Dublin City Gallery the Hugh Lane, *High Treason: Roger Casement* (Dublin: Dublin City Gallery the Hugh Lane, 2016), p. 38.
76. Oil on canvas, 172.8 x 289.6 cm, Coll: Collins Barracks Cork. Kinmonth, *Irish Rural Interiors*, p. 69.
77. Ibid., pp 69–70.
78. Oil on canvas, 97 x 125cm. First exhibited: RHA 1917. Coll: Dublin City Gallery the Hugh Lane. Éimear O'Connor outlines the extraordinary impact of the image, which was produced as a limited-edition poster and sold to raise funds for families affected by "the political turmoil" following the 1916 Rising. Éimear O'Connor, *Seán Keating: Contemporary Contexts* (Cork: Crawford Art Gallery, 2012), p. 13.
79. Cahill, 'In the Mainstream', pp 34–45.
80. Ibid.
81. Census of Ireland 1901/1911, "Residents of a house 13 in Gulistan Terrace (Rathmines & Rathgar East, Dublin), 5 May 1911," at: www.census.nationalarchive.ie.
82. Kinmonth, *Irish Rural Interiors*, pp 34–45.
83. John Turpin writes "Switzer's employed Miss Davidson to draw costume designs." Turpin, "The South Kensington System," p. 60. Katherine Cahill discussed her literary work including her play *Bride*, performed at the Gate Theatre in 1931 "directed by Hilton Edwards with costumes and set design by Michael McLiammoir [sic]." Cahill, "In the Mainstream," pp 39, 45.
84. Quoted in Bruce Arnold, *Maine Jellett and the Modern Movement in Ireland* (New Haven, CT: Yale University Press, 1991), pp 43–44.
85. *Portrait of Jack B. Yeats (1871–1957)*, N.D. Oil on canvas, 93 x 74 cm. Coll: National Gallery of Ireland.
86. See note 52.
87. Oil on canvas, 66 by 76cm. Exhibited: RHA, 1921. Coll: private; Oil on canvas, 76.2 x 101.6 cm. Coll: private. Exhibited: RHA, 1931.
88. Cahill writes: "She remained firmly in the mainstream of Irish naturalism, using Irish landscape, seascape and genre scenes as her raw material, material she used with remarkable facility." Cahill, "In the Mainstream," p. 44.
89. Ibid., p. 36.
90. Oil on canvas on board, 30 x 25 cm. Coll: private; Oil on canvas, 57.15 by 73.66cm. Coll: private.
91. Re: *Fashions at the Fair*, see note 26.
92. Marianne O'Kane Boal, "Lilian Lucy Davidson, *Boats at Wicklow, Dusk*," in *Adam's, Adam's Important Irish Art Catalogue* (Dublin: Adam's, 30 Sept. 2015), Lot 21.
93. Cahill, "In the Mainstream," p. 39.
94. Ibid., p. 36.
95. This is discussed in, Niamh Ann Kelly, *Ultimate Witnesses: The Visual Culture of Death, Burial and Mourning in Famine Ireland* (Hamden CT: Quinnipiac University, 2017).

96. Colm J. Donnelly and Eileen M. Murphy, "The Origins of Cillini," in *Archaeology Ireland* 22, no. 3 (Autumn 2008), 26–29.
97. Patricia Lysaght, "*Caoineadh os Cionn Coirp*: The Lament for the dead in Ireland," *Folklore* 108, no.1–2 (1997), 65–82.
98. Cahill, "In the Mainstream,' p. 44.
99. Spencer (1892–1979) was Professor of Painting at the R.C.A., 1932–48 and an Official War Artist in Britain, 1940–3. He was the younger brother of better-known painter muralist, Stanley Spencer (1891–1959).
100. *Irish Times*, 13 June 1981.
101. Their eldest child was born in 1936, a year before Brandt completed her exams for the ARCA diploma. Snoddy, *Dictionary*, pp 34–35.
102. One of the posters is held at the National Museum of Ireland, Museum of Country Life, Castlebar, County Mayo.
103. Nolan is quoted in Snoddy, *Dictionary,* p. 35.
104. Among these are: *Micheál MacLiammóir (1899–1978).* Oil on canvas, 66 x 86.3 cm. Coll: NGI; *Christine, Countess of Longford.* Oil on canvas, 53 x 76 cm. Coll: NGI and: *Sinead, Bean de Valera.* Oil on board, 37 x 30cm. Coll: private.
105. Oil on canvas, 74 x 60cm. Coll: McKee Barracks, Dublin John de Vere White writes that "she struggled to make a living out of art" and relied on her portrait commissions. De Vere, *De Vere's Irish Art Auction, 22 May 2012* (Dublin: de Vere's, 2012), p. 84.
106. Both: Undated; Watercolour and ink, 33 x 46 cm. John de Vere White writes that these are part of a watercolour series that "show scenes from a rural Irish festival and may well be her interpretation of the Ould Lammas Fair, Bally Castle, Co. Antrim, that has been going for over one hundred years." De Vere, *De Vere's Irish Art*, p. 84.
107. Watercolour and ink, 28 x 39cm. Coll: private.
108. Oil on board, 42 x 57cm. Exhibited: RHA, 1960.
109. The symbolism of the children is emphasized in writing by Cristín Leach, *The Sunday Times* (Ireland), 13 March 2016.
110. The complexities of ethnic, class-based and gendered exclusions were actively at play in the climate of art criticism from 1960s to 1980s. See, Róisín Kennedy, "Lhote's wives – Scapegoating Women Artists, 1962–84," in Éimear O'Connor (ed.), *Irish Women Artists 1800–2009: Familiar but Unknown* (Dublin: Four Courts Press, 2010), pp 168–178.
111. Blaithin O Ciobhain, *Irish Press*, 12 June 1981.
112. Crawford Municipal Art Gallery, *Irish Art 1900–1950: An exhibition in association with Rosc Teoranta* (Cork: Rosc Teoranta, 1975), p. 18. She painted seven scenes from the life of Saint Anthony, six of which survive, one being destroyed by fire shortly before her death. Snoddy, *Dictionary*, pp 34–35. She also painted two largescale works for the church's mortuary chapel.
113. A poignant study for this, *A Child Standing beside Saint Anthony* is in the NGI collection. Graphite on paper, 39.8 x 17.7 cm Coll: NGI.
114. Turpin, *History of the Royal Hibernian Academy*, p. 284. Houses of the Oireachtas, "Written Answers—State Board Appointments, Dáil Éireann Debate, Tuesday, 7 Nov. 1978," at: www.oireachtas.ie.

CHAPTER EIGHTEEN

HUNGRY FOR CHANGE

Civil Society Responses to Food Insecurity in 21st-Century New Haven, Connecticut

Mary P. Corcoran

The politics of food

> The reproduction of human subjects, their habitus, cultural ethos and the material basis of capitalisms are strongly interconnected with the way food is produced, bodies are fed, economies turn and ecologies disrupted.[1]

Food is central to our everyday lives although many of us take it for granted. Food is multidimensional. It has a material quality—it is life giving and its absence is life threatening. Food also has an important symbolic quality—it signifies social class and cultural preferences (posh food versus junk food; slow food versus fast food; organic food versus processed food). Food confers status (e.g. Michelin starring system for restaurants) and informs life-style choices (note the proliferation of vegetarian, vegan, pescatarian and flexitarian diets). Food and its consumption are a measure of cultural capital (expressed through food literacy, knowledge of food provenance, food production skills and food taste). The rise of a new type of food consumer—the "foodie"—is evident in the success of television programs that demonstrate (or fetishize) food skills—The Great British Bake Off, Nigella Lawson and Anthony Bourdain on The Taste, MasterChef, Chef's Table, Diners, Drive-Ins and Dives. The list goes on.

More importantly, consuming food is a deeply social and political process. It is mainly through the sharing of food that we come into communion with each other. The preparation, serving and consumption of meals nurtures social bonds, reinforces relationships, socializes children, and encourages reciprocity (we do not appreciate guests who fail to bring a gift to the table!). Food also gives us the opportunity to exercise our innate creativity and capacity as human beings. However, inequality of access to nutritious food is closely linked to social and economic vulnerabilities and is deeply consequential for people in terms of their health, their mortality and morbidity rates and their opportunities to fully participate in society. Disparities arise as a consequence of the institutional arrangements in place in the wider economy and polity. Analyzing the links between environmental justice, social equity and public health, Rachel Morello Frosch refers to the "political economy of riskscapes."[2] The social context of structural inequality, racial segregation and discriminatory policies interacts with particular racial, ethnic, class, income and gender demographic profiles to produce disparities in exposure to environmental and health risks, and social vulnerability. This has been brought into sharp relief during the COVID–19 pandemic. African Americans and Latinos have experienced disproportionately high infection and death rates, reflecting the fact that "Today's disparities of health flow directly from yesterday's disparities of wealth and opportunity."[3]

Such riskscapes are also evident in the context of food hunger. Bearing witness to the impact of periodic famines in 17th-century Ireland, Brendan Scott notes, "the utter undoing of the people"[4] without access to food that would sustain them. Today, in the city of New Haven food hunger is a live issue. In two recent studies, food insecurity was shown to impact one third of adults in the city's lowest income neighborhoods; Latinx communities are most likely to be affected by food insecurity as are those who are unemployed or underemployed. Over 56 percent of New Haven children live in households that participate in the government-funded Supplemental Nutrition Assistance Program (SNAP). Not surprisingly, those who are food insecure are more likely to report health problems.[5] Preliminary data from the New Haven Mayor's office on COVID–19's impact in the city "indicates that black and brown New Haveners have tested positive, been hospitalized, and died from the coronavirus at higher rates than their white counterparts."[6] One of the main reasons that these communities are more susceptible to the virus is that so many are engaged in front-line work such as transport, sanitation, healthcare and retail—jobs that are essential to the economy but generally low paid, and do not afford the luxury of self-isolation. In the United States, many of these groups fall into the category of "working poor," characterized as Asset Limited, Income Constrained, Employed (ALICE) households. Approximately 30 percent of Connecticut households have earnings above the federal poverty level, but below a basic cost-of-living.[7] As one service provider in New Haven familiar with the concept of ALICE explains:

> Folks are not getting their basic needs met and really food is kind of the hidden one that goes first. 'I've got to pay my mortgage, my cell phone, or I'll put money for that, my kids' needs. What can I cut? I can cut my food budget, we just won't eat as much food this week.' I feel like that is what is happening with our ALICE folk.[8]

The genesis of food hunger lies in structural issues of inequality and the pernicious effects of a food political economy that is primarily market-driven and profit oriented. In April 2019, the Hamden Food Security Task Force presented its report on Food Hardship at Ireland's Great Hunger Museum in Hamden, Connecticut. A local journalist remarked on the important symbolism afforded by the venue for the launch writing that, "hunger is not a distant problem but rather a harsh reality for many Hamden residents."[9] In fact, the story of the Irish Famine is a salutary reminder of the terrible consequences that flow from the pursuit of an economic model based on extraction, with scant regard to the well-being of those most vulnerable in the population. Historian Christine Kinealy's path-breaking work on the Great Hunger enables us to view contemporary issues of hunger in a wider socio-historical context.[10]

In 19th-century Ireland, the Great Hunger resulted from over-reliance on a single crop, an outcome of the political economy of colonial rule that prevailed at that time. The British state refused to provide a program of aid to the Irish peasantry when the potato crop failed (with some notable local exceptions) opting instead to let market forces prevail. The colonization of Ireland involved the extraction (and exploitation) of raw materials and native peoples in pursuit of a profit motive. Irish peasants cultivating land as tenants in the mid-19th century were systemically and intentionally impoverished through a system of rent increases and through repeated soil depletion. There was little or no investment in agriculture by the landlords who were concerned only with profit—rental income was the main driver of accumulation.[11] As peasant production was overtaken by agriculture organized on capitalist principles, eviction and forced emigration followed in post-Famine Ireland. This amounted to a process of dispossession of the people and consolidation of holdings (through property or land rights).[12] Those twin motifs—of a market-driven approach to food production and consumption, and a process of dispossession from nature and land—continue to resonate down the centuries, and are evident in the adjoining municipalities of Hamden and New Haven.

To an unprecedented extent, urban dwellers have been dispossessed of the capacity to produce, distribute and consume food for themselves within the context of their localities. That is because food *production, distribution* and *consumption* are now organized on an industrial scale and almost wholly with a profit motive in mind.

This has led to massive over-production, homogenization, the rise of "convenience food" that has a de-skilling impact on our capacities to make food ourselves, and a global food market that has major implications for climate and ecology in terms of sustainability and food miles. Serious inequities have arisen in relation to food that mirror inequities in the wider society. For some sectors of the population, there are problems of access and affordability of food, even in the richest countries of the Global North, where:

> The working poor, the homeless, the dispossessed are hungry and unable to provide for themselves. Food knowledge, food skills and food production have been largely removed—as a fundamental component of social reproduction—from human daily life.[13]

Moreover, we are witnessing a less visible dispossession from the land, itself characterized by Brett Christophers as a kind of modern enclosure movement that distances people "economically, socially and politically-from the land they inhabit."[14]

Local responses to global food trends

A hegemonic global food industry connects almost all countries. Academics, journalists, and those working the land at grassroots level increasingly question and challenge the industry's extractive approach, counterpointing with an agroecological approach to stewardship of land and its produce. The latter views agricultural areas as ecosystems and is concerned with the ecological impact of agricultural practices. Research has shown that agroecological farmers and communities across the Global North and South are engaging in practices that not only offer an alternative to the dominant food economy model, but also seek "to actively dismantle disempowering and oppressive processes, disabling arrangements and unjust systems."[15]

In response to emerging *riskscapes*, highlighted by those concerned about the over-extension of the industrial food system and the threats posed to ecological sustainability, both states and international bodies have had to assume much more proactive roles in monitoring and policing food provenance, food safety and food standards. Furthermore, states are increasingly coming under pressure to develop policies and technologies that can address pressing environmental challenges, particularly in the context of accelerating climate change and, more recently, the threat posed by pandemic viruses. However, these challenges are occurring at a time when, to a considerable degree, states themselves have rolled back services, adapting market (rather than public good) strategies as a way of reducing state spending and promoting individualized and privatized approaches to service provision.

Against this backdrop, this chapter focuses on the potential role of civil society to effect change. Specifically, it examines how non-profit groups and organizations in the city of New Haven have committed to environmentally sustainable ways of living, as well as how urban food cultivation and food justice attempt to reshape the urban food landscape. In 1961, Robert A Dahl, a Yale political scientist, noted that New Haven [then] was "in many respects typical of other cities in the United States."[16] This remains the case. Several study respondents drew my attention to the Data Haven 2016 report, whose author, Mark Abraham, points out that the city is the most representative urban area in the nation if you look at it demographically—that is, it is more similar to the U.S. average than any other city in America.[17] This insight is something of a statistical artifact—every place has its uniqueness and the idea of an "average" place makes little sense. However, it does confirm that New Haven is not an outlier city. Its profile is representative of the nation in terms of its class, and its racial and ethnic composition.

To address the research issue, 28 people were interviewed who were involved in a range of sustainability initiatives mostly, although not exclusively, focused on food in the New Haven area. They included academics, practitioners, municipal personnel, directors of non-profit organizations, activists, and students.[18] I also visited /volunteered at a range of community gardens, the Yale Farm Project, farmers' markets, food pantries and soup kitchens in the New Haven area, and attended policy and advocacy meetings. The research was carried out during the Fall of 2018. The following sections detail the nature of the civil society sector that has mobilized around issues of food hunger and food justice; explore the relationships between the civil society sector, the municipality and Yale University; and identify the core tensions in the sector that produce both political and de-politicized responses to hunger in the contemporary city.

Civil society food activism

New Haven is distinguished by a high degree of civil society activism—evidenced in the existence of between 800 and 1,000 (by respondent estimations) non-profit organizations (NPOs) on the ground. In the specific context of the food landscape, the NPO sector acts (1) as a loose network of interconnected agents that keep the issue of food "live" in New Haven and (2) performs crucial advocacy, mediation and political organizing functions linking the population of the city with the municipality, and with the state. NPOs are involved in a wide spectrum of activities ranging from providing meals to vulnerable populations to advocating for self-sustaining, self-determining local food systems, and everything in-between. I provide an indicative—but not exhaustive—classification of those activities in Table 1. Though categorized in terms of their primary mission, some combine a number of different activities in their work.

Table 1: Civil society NPOs and the food/urban agriculture sector in New Haven, CT

Pragmatic food provisioning to the vulnerable, support for greening initiatives in community	Pedagogic teaching and learning activities in schools and beyond	Eco-entrepreneurial business oriented interventions	Political interventions aimed at capacity-building and political change
DESK (Downtown Evening Soup Kitchen) Food pantry and soup kitchens; FISH (Food In Service to the Homebound); CT Food Bank; Fresh produce prescription program at NH Farms; Common Ground School's mobile pantry; Land Trust Community gardens; Urban Resources Initiative (Yale)	Lelia Day Care Center nature curriculum; Common Ground School leadership program; Yale Farm Program; Leon Sister Cities project; Love Fed education program	CitySeed farmers markets; City Seed food business incubator; Land Trust Growing Entrepreneurs initiative; Community Supported Agriculture (CSA); Peels and Wheels composting.	CT CORE (Community Organizing for Racial Equality) food justice platform; Witnesses to Hunger; Love Fed home gardening; Citizen's Campaign for the Environment.

Such organizations are linked by their broad commitment to food justice, which may include fostering social inclusion, promoting health and well-being, and inculcating the values of environmental stewardship/ agroecological sustainability in the city more generally. Civil society-driven activities grounded in the American *communitarian tradition* emphasize interactive and reinforcing relationships between groups of individuals who have a clear commitment to particular set of values, norms and meanings.[19] Those leading and managing the sector frequently share a common trajectory: they have a history of commitment to social justice, evident in their track records of volunteering; further education and upskilling in their chosen field; and experience obtained in a variety of NPO posts. There is significant networking between all of the actors involved: "Everybody knows everyone, and everyone has worked for everyone ... You've gotta be very careful and not burn bridges in this town. You gotta know when you are going to need someone else."[20]

Another interviewee suggested that this high level of integration was a function of the relatively modest size of the city and the relatively high level of civic engagement:

> The density of connections within the civil society sector feels much more possible because of the scale of the city New Haven is. It is large enough to have a carrying capacity of non-profit organizations where there are a lot of actors who care about the same issues, but it is small enough that you can look at the city as a scale and wrap your arms around that but know each other.[21]

Urban policy-making that deals with food and agriculture is relatively new for municipal administrations and that presents its own challenges in terms of garnering the financial and other supports required by NPOs.[22] Not surprisingly, the impetus for greater food justice emanates almost wholly from within the civil society sector—the main driver of innovation and change. However, the sector's dependence for survival on volunteerism and fund-raising from government, individual, philanthropic and corporate sources seriously curtails its capacity to act. Consequently, most organizations spend a considerable amount of their time grant writing, advocating and developing "story narratives" to capture the imagination of potential donors. One interviewee characterized this organizational model as a "begging economy."[23] Moreover, because funding is always contingent, it militates against more long-term or joined up strategic thinking in the sector. Some of the interviewees did reflect on the fragmented nature of the sector and the problems that flow from that, including the disjointed nature of their efforts in the absence of well-funded government agencies in the field, and the need to foster greater collaboration thereby eliminating the potential for duplication and achieving economics of scale: "I personally think that we shouldn't have so many non-profits and we should join and be much more effective. It's more a question of how effective could we be versus how effective we are."[24] To reinforce this point:

> We know that there are more non-profits here per capital than there probably should be compared to other places ... I think most of the innovation going forward will be more about consolidation, and more assistance from the local and state government in terms of leadership.[25]

This observation brings us to the thorny issue of the role of the city in advancing food policy and food justice in New Haven.

Elephants in the room: The city and the university

The New Haven municipality has a commitment to advancing a sustainable and socially just urban food system. The New Haven Food Policy Council (NHFPC) is a volunteer advisory council of the City of New Haven, consisting of 12 members appointed by the mayor and the board of aldermen, who represent various parts of the local food system. Members of the public are welcome to attend these meetings. The NHFPC, which held its inaugural meeting in 2007, addresses issues concerning local and regional food systems and their connection to individuals, communities, businesses, the environment and local government.[26] The 2013 Food Action Plan set out an ambitious set of goals including increasing access to healthy food; strengthening the local food economy; and encouraging healthy food choices through education and marketing efforts (all of which are functions currently carried out by the NPOs in the sector). The Food Access Working Group (FAWG) is a sub-committee of the NHFPC that brings a range of stakeholders from across the city together to focus specifically on food access and develop joined up approaches to their work programs.[27] It is largely through these fora that different civil society organizations communicate with each other. Regular meetings allow for information sharing, exchanges of views and forward planning. Those involved represent a relatively broad cross section of New Haven residents in terms of gender, generation, race, class and ethnicity. There is also a broad range of views expressed at the meetings reflecting the varying roles, passions and missions of the participating organisations. New Haven is a pioneer in that the position of food system policy director, inaugurated in 2016, was the first of its kind in Connecticut and among just 20 similar jobs (at that time) across the United States. Moreover, the municipality's creation of a Food Policy Council remains relatively unusual in both the American and European contexts.[28] Despite the existence of this strategic policy infrastructure, interviewees expressed concerns about the efficacy of the NHFPC. From their perspective, the municipal response to the challenges of food hunger and food justice is undermined by (a) limited funding and resources, and (b) an "arms-length" approach to food security that has the effect (even if unintended) of de-politicizing hunger.

New Haven's municipal budgets are extremely tight and there has been a series of cuts to funding in recent years. While the city acts as a partner on several projects and funds on a small scale, there is deep unease across the sector about the dire financial straits in which the municipality finds itself. Two interviewees put it succinctly: "New Haven has a lot of financial issues. There is not enough of a tax base to pay for everything it needs ... the city has no money"[29] and, "The city is starving for a source of revenue and you can only do it through taxation."[30] As a consequence of the precarious state of affairs, policy directorates have insufficient resources in terms of budgets and personnel to drive the policy goals outlined in the City of New Haven Framework Plan.[31] While the food policy directorate exists, funds are not forthcoming either to properly resource the unit, or to publicly fund innovative food growing initiatives and environmental interventions. The city cannot drive the change required:

> Last year they finished a sustainability framework, consulted everybody ... Is this going to be linked to a programme, to a Department, to a budget? Who is going to push this agenda because then you have to make it happen? Otherwise, you gather people you get them excited and nothing happens ... There is not a lack of ideas, of enthusiasm, of energy of young people involved. It is a question of how you make this program sustainable ... we know that planning is not enough, because the plans are there—the Sustainability Framework, the Food Policy Council recommendations. These are things someone has to take-in-charge, whether an office, an institution, a private organization, a non-profit and make it happen. Because it is not going to happen from the city.[32]

There is a recognition that someone has to be responsible and accountable for implementation. These issues are, of course, not unique to New Haven or even to North America. The neo-liberal winds of change that have been blowing around the globe since the 1980s brought in their wake a greater emphasis on slimmed-down government, in some cases a diminution of the role and function of municipal authorities, and a new concern with the third sector or civil society domain between state and market. Public sector provision has been de-emphasized "whereas the 'societal' and 'voluntary' side and the 'market' dimension of the local arena of the 'community space' has been re-accentuated and expanded."[33] The contemporary scenario of a depleted municipality stands in stark contrast to the situation prevailing 60 years ago when the burghers of New Haven acted boldly and decisively, to implement an urban renewal plan in the city. Then, Dahl noted that, "to pass from ideal to reality every proposal required an expenditure of critical resources—money, time, energy, attention, skill and political support."[34] The then mayor, supported by a dedicated development administrator, secured the necessary approval from others. In the absence of sufficient critical resources, bold ambitions of that nature are much less likely to succeed today.

The state (at both the federal and local level) has been reluctant to recognize the political dimension to growing hunger and has not taken a lead in championing the right to food. Rather it has divested itself to a significant extent for responsibility for food security. That responsibility has largely devolved to agencies and organizations operating in the civil society sector. For instance, the number of food banks has increased dramatically in the United States over recent decades. When President Reagan assumed office in 1980, there were 200 food banks in the US; today there are more than 40,000.[35] As one interviewee noted:

> The onus is being shifted from the government to people then people do like this 'charity' model which goes back to the dignity part. It does not solve anything. It is a hole in a big tank of water, and you are putting a piece of gum in there and hoping for the best.[36]

Given the huge demand for supplementary food aid among the local population, the municipality's approach is viewed by interviewees as skewed toward emergency provision rather than toward the development of a political and strategic food agenda that might address broader systemic inequities:

> Emergency food access is a piece that gets a lot of attention and resources on one side, and often isn't a big part of the conversations about grassroots justice ... the way the emergency food industry operates, it doesn't leave a lot of room for self-determination or even addressing system issues about why people are hungry in the first place.[37]

If emergency provision always takes precedence, the time and space for standing back and thinking more strategically about the right to food, is automatically curtailed. This drift towards a de-politicization of hunger has taken place under the municipality's watch largely as a result of limited resources, a lack of leadership and a concomitant lack of imagination. This is eloquently expressed by one interviewee who asks:

> What should a food policy be based on: To feed your people, a goal to find food and give it to people? Or to build more resilience in our regions so that you can secure and grow your own food?[38]

The choice is between a reactive and a radical food policy approach, a sticking plaster solution versus transformative change.

Complicating matters further for the municipality and the communities it serves is the relationship with Yale University, the richly endowed institution that stands across New Haven Green from City Hall. Dahl's *Who Governs?* noted the important role of Yale in the city and the university continues to be a power-broker to the present day. Dahl observed rather wryly that the university was not only one of the largest property owners in the city, it also was the largest owner of tax-free property. This, he believed, made Yale officials sensitive to expressions of local hostility and fearful of becoming embroiled in disputes with locals.[39] The relationship between the city and the university remains underlined by this core tension.

In all kinds of ways, Yale reaches out to the city and communities of New Haven, contributing resources largely in the form of cultural and social capital. A significant number of Yale graduates stay on and remain actively involved in their communities through paid work, volunteering or a combination of both. They also tend to have multiple affiliations within the civil society sector. One respondent characterized this human capital resource in terms of a "Yale intelligentsia." The university has extended its efforts to connect with the municipal and civil society sectors to contribute to advancing a sustainability agenda. For instance, the Yale School of Public Health and the Yale School of Management provides supervised graduate research students to conduct research for non-profit organisations involved in emergency food provision in the locality. The Yale Farm Program has a mission to grow a generation of food literate leaders and is developing a New Haven Food Fellows program that will provide New Haven-based organizations with Yale interns over the summer months to work on specific projects. Its farm is open to the public and it runs a science curriculum program, Seed to Salad, for second graders in public schools. The Yale Office of Sustainability is involved in GoNHGo, which promoted a bike-sharing initiative, has contributed to the drafting of the municipality sustainability framework plan, and it is working on a resilience plan for Yale that connects with New Haven and the wider region. The Urban Resources Initiative is a non-profit program affiliated with Yale that creates opportunities for Yale students to foster community-based land stewardship and promote environmental education. The members work with New Haven community groups and residents to restore, replant and reclaim the urban environment.

Yale has worked hard through its extension programs to win over hearts and minds. Nevertheless, there is considerable unease about the extent to which Yale is seen as "a hoarder of land and capital;"[40] and, in the view of some residents, Yale is engaged in the "colonization of the city ... and is unwelcoming to the wider community of New Haven."[41] Several interviewees made similar points focusing on the financial loss to the city of a restricted tax base:

> Yale University does not pay taxes. Every year they buy a new building and that takes that building out of the tax net. Yale says: 'we are creating jobs, we are already paying'... they pay a fraction of what they potentially could pay in local taxes. If you are in there, you are in heaven. But if you are outside, there is resentment because they don't pay their taxes.[42]

And:

> We need to deal with the elephant in the room here if this city is going to survive. And we all know what that is: Yale needs to pay more money ... Yale is smart and

> they will say you want us to pay more money to the city. Right, but we are going to have to cut the number of people that we employ here, so you will lose your job. That is the bind we are in right now.[43]

There is at the very least an uneasy town and gown relationship. The benefits of the university's presence in New Haven are visible in the outreach programs, particularly the ones that have a direct impact on the community such as the Urban Resources Initiative. They are also evident in the high caliber Yale graduates who work across the civil society sector demonstrating commitment to urban sustainability, food security and social justice. But that has to be set against the widespread view that Yale's ever-expanding footprint in New Haven, shrinks the tax base and, therefore, the capacity of the municipality to work in the public's interest. Finally, while Yale's housing policy supports staff to buy homes and put down roots in the New Haven area, it simultaneously engages in informal redlining by approving some neighborhoods for the home purchase scheme and excluding others.

Re-politicizing hunger in New Haven

Access to land and the opportunity to own property are central to the capitalist system upon which American democracy is based. However, property markets in the United States have historically been distorted by power relations that ensured that racial inequality was built into the very structure of society, extending from the time of slavery right to the present day. Under this system, African Americans and other people of color have been dispossessed of land, excluded from property ownership, or subject to systematic discrimination by banks and other mortgage lenders. In an essay on the thorny issue of reparations and how the United States might respond to past wrongs, Ta-Nehisi Coates observes, "no statistic better illustrates the enduring legacy of our country's shameful history of treating black people as sub-citizens, sub-Americans, and sub-humans than the wealth gap."[44] In the specific context of the pandemic and the disproportionate impact of COVID-19 on people of color, Janelle Bouie contends that "racialized inequality reflects the character of American capitalism itself, a deep logic that produces the same outcomes again and again."[45] The wealth gap is very visible in New Haven where African Americans and people of color suffer multiple disadvantages. The more radical within the civil society sector seek to re-politicize the issue of hunger in New Haven as a way of generating debate around wider racial and class disadvantage.

Focusing specifically on a food justice agenda in the contemporary city, Tornaghi argues for a politics of engagement, capability and empowerment, which would extend citizens' control over social reproduction.[46] This is of particular relevance to those people in the city whose lives are deeply impacted by "underlying racial and class dynamics which perpetuate structural inequity."[47] African-American activists are acutely aware of the systemic inequities—historical and contemporary—that structure their lives. They recognize that their faces and their voices are marginal within the civil society sector. They have identified food justice as one arena where there is potential to develop a much more powerful leadership role:

> Almost all of the non-profits that are successful are white led. The ones that are headed by people of color tend to stay at grassroots group level and not necessarily move to an established non-profit funded organisation. And there are reasons for that that are structural and systemic in the way that funding works.[48]

Furthermore,

> Being born and raised in New Haven and being black we just felt especially with existing non-profits there is a lack of leadership of color ... [and] there is definitely a lack of connection to the community that they are trying to help.[49]

CT CORE (Campaign Organising for Racial Equality) is a highly political NPO active in the food sector that has as a core goal to move people of color to lead on racial justice and equity issues. To this end, it seeks to remove barriers to self-advocacy for people of color. It organizes state-wide to create coalitions and networking using a people of color lens. CT CORE has produced a racial justice platform as well as a food justice guide. From CT CORE's perspective, an authentic community initiative is one grounded in an understanding of the suffering of the past, focused on organizing in the present with a view to moving toward a transformed future. Their point of departure is an acknowledgement that "food systems disparities grow out of historically inequitable power relationships that in turn, confer social and economic advantage to some over others."[50] A CT CORE interviewee expressed the desire to move beyond these historically structured barriers and create new, more inclusive social arrangements. This would require a radical transformation of political economy:

> Systematic inequities and disparities are not a modern phenomenon. They have always existed and are baked into how our country was always meant to function and was never meant to allow for equal opportunities for everyone ... and so our approach is to look at the food system and figure out how we can use our organizing approach and our liberation frame to put in place a just food system.[51]

Another activist group, Witnesses to Hunger, takes a similarly political approach to food justice. They identify the value in bearing witness to the everyday lived experience of hunger and deprivation, through telling their own stories and presenting visual and verbal testimonies to legislators, at academic and policy conferences and so on. As one member noted:

> We are empowering ourselves to tell legislators that what they propose isn't working. We put you in we can put you out. We tell stories, and we tell them through pictures: the trouble of getting to a food pantry, to a soup kitchen, with a 16-year-old who won't go because she is embarrassed.[52]

The focus on empowerment, finding voice and making demands, echoes the call by Karen Washington, the New York City food activist, that people must have access to opportunity, capital and land in order to take control of their own narrative.[53] Land, in particular, is important because its value dictates the cost of development, the price of housing, and the fiscal base. Mostly land tenure for growing in the city is contingent—short-term leases and tenancies to ensure that if the value of the land increases it can be "cashed in" for its development value. In many cities across the Global North and South, there is not enough land available. Moreover, land that is available may be poisoned by industrial toxins making it either unsuitable for cultivation or too expensive to treat in order to restore the soil. The barriers for entry may be too high in terms of the requirements for access to capital and resources, that will disproportionately impact African American, Latino and Native American groups. Yet, the right to access farmland and the desire to preserve farmland for socialized uses as a basis for radical transformation of the food landscape was a key theme that emerged in the interviews:

> You should have protected farmlands that you cannot sell, leave for fallow, or give away for development. Because that is the main source of food sovereignty. But a lot of the land is being developed as, for example, parking lots.[54]

And:

> Looking at the work of folks currently ... and even some of the aspirations of our black ancestors, indigenous ancestors wanting to reconnect to the land. You can trace the roots of systemic oppression but also in there is the source of healing and liberation, and that connection to the land, how we relate to the land, to each other as stewards of the land and the environment. If we can get that right, the systems we build out of that will also be in that vein.[55]

Groups like CT CORE and Witnesses to Hunger among others are politicising food hunger in the city and offering an analysis that raises fundamental questions about the current political-economic arrangements in place. This thinking goes beyond reformist or even progressive innovations in the food sector to question the very basis of land markets. It requires a radical re-imagining that would "place urban soil care centrally within land policies, nourish the communing of urban resources in ways that allow communities to exercise control of their social reproduction."[56] Re-thinking the food landscape in this way holds out the promise of moving from dispossession to repossession. It also holds out the prospect of moving beyond what some interviewees described as "food apartheid" in the city, an epithet that could just as accurately be applied to the situation prevailing in colonialized Ireland during periods of famine.

In the city of New Haven, the NPOs in the civil society sector make interventions across the spectrum from emergency food services provision through to radical social movement activism. In between, a range of educational, awareness raising, and sustainable entrepreneurship programs, build greater food literacy and contribute to enhanced eco-social capital among the citizenry. The NPOs involved in the sector find ways of coalescing through the municipality supported Food Policy Council. However, the sector does not have a single view or purpose. Running a food bank or soup kitchen is a different intervention to radical grassroots organizing aimed at transcending systemic inequities. This tension is not unusual in that opposing positions within the civil society sector more generally "encapsulate the contradiction between acting as consensual glue to avoid civil disorder and acting independently to promote critical or dissenting voices."[57]

The food landscape in the city is not a purely recreational, environmental or ecological issue. It is fundamentally structured through powerful political and social processes. Civil society seeks to challenge existing ways of doing things on the one hand, and to contribute to nurturing inclusive and sustainable food practices on the other. A civil society sector that seeks to connect food growing, food consumption, food distribution and food waste within the contours of socially just and racially equitable frameworks has a key role to play in advancing a more sustainable vision of the city of New Haven. These issues have taken on even greater urgency in the context of the COVID–19 pandemic and its impact on people of colour in New Haven, Hamden and beyond. As epidemiologist, Dr. Camara Jones notes, the virus is "unmasking the deep disinvestment in our communities, the historical injustices and the impact of residential segregation."[58]

NOTES

1. Chiara Tornaghi and Michel Dahaene, "The prefigurative power of urban political agroecology: Rethinking the urbanisms of agroecological transitions for food system transformation," *Agroecology and Sustainable Food Systems*: DOI: 10.1080/21683565.2019.1680593 2019, p. 6
2. Rachel Morello Frosch, "Environmental Justice, Social Equity and Public Health," presented at the School of Forestry and Environmental Science, Yale University, 24 Oct. 2018.
3. Jamelle Bouie, "Why Coronavirus is killing African-Americans more than others" in the *New York Times*, 14 April 2020.
4. Brendan Scott, "Famine and Poverty in Early Modern Ireland," presented at Irish Famines before 1845 and after 1852 conference, Ireland's Great Hunger Institute, Quinnipiac University, 13 June 2019.
5. DataHaven, "Greater New Haven Community Indicators," New Haven, CT (2016); Alycia Santilli and Kathleen O'Connor Duffany, *The State of Hunger in New Haven 2017–18*, New Haven, CT: CARE and NHFPC (2018) pp 2–3. See also: *Facts and Faces: Food Hardship in Hamden*, United Way of Greater New Haven (2019).
6. Thomas Breen, "Covid Updates: Black And Brown New Haveners Hit Hardest; Hotel Deal Struck" in the *New Haven Independent*, 8 April 2020.
7. 2018 ALICE Report Executive Summary Connecticut: United Ways, at: http://alice.ctunitedway.org
8. Interview with United Way Greater New Haven staff member (12 Nov. 2018).
9. Sam Gurwitt, "1 in 8 go hungry in Hamden," in *The New Haven Independent*, 25 April 2019.
10. Professor Christine Kinealy is founding director of Ireland's Great Hunger Institute at Quinnipiac University. She has published extensively on the Great Famine, including the award winning, *The Great Calamity. The Great Famine in Ireland* (Dublin: Gill and Macmillan, 1994 and 2007).
11. Eamonn Slater, *Marx on Ireland: The dialectics of colonialism,* Maynooth University: NIRSA—National Institute for Regional and Spatial Analysis Working Paper Series, no.73 (2013).
12. Ibid.
13. Chiara Tornaghi, "Urban Agriculture in the Food Disabling City: (Re)defining Urban Food Justice, Reimagining a Politics of Empowerment," *Antipode,* vol. 49, issue 3 (June 2017) pp 781–801, p. 794.
14. See Brett Christophers, *The new enclosure: The appropriation of public land in Britain* (London: Verso, 2018) reviewed by Ian Jack, "Why Did We Not Know?" in *London Review of Books*, vol. 41, 23 May 2019.
15. Tornaghi and Dahaene, *Rethinking the Urbanisms*, p. 5.
16. Robert A. Dahl, *Who Governs? Democracy and Power in an American City* (New Haven, Connecticut: Yale University Press, 1961) p. v.
17. David Holohan, "Number crunching," New Haven: 17 Data Points, *Hartford Courant*, 1 Dec. 2016.

18. For reasons of confidentiality, I have anonymized the data. Issues raised in interviews included questions such as, who are the key actors and what are their motivations? Who are the stakeholders—the beneficiaries of civil society activities and initiatives? What is the role of the municipality? To what degree is the sector formally or informally organized and how does it integrate with the municipality? To what extent do different civil society actors partner with each other to achieve common aims?
19. Amatai Etzioni, "Communitarianism," *The Encyclopaedia of Political Thought*, Michael T. Gibbons (ed.), John Wiley & Sons, Ltd. 2015. Available at: https://icps.gwu.edu/sites/icps.gwu.edu/files/downloads/Communitarianism. Etzioni.pdf
20. Interview with United Way Greater New Haven staff member (12 Nov. 2018).
21. Interview with member of the staff, Common Ground School (25 Oct. 2018).
22. Kristin Reynolds and Nevin Cohen, *Beyond the Kale: Urban Agriculture and Social Justice Activism in New York City* (University of Georgia, 2016), p. 93.
23. Interview with a member of the New Haven Bioregional Group (26 Sept. 2018).
24. Interview with New Haven Land Trust staff member (3 Oct. 2018).
25. Interview with Downtown Evening Soup Kitchen staff member (19 Oct. 2018).
26. New Haven Food Policy Committee, Food Action Plan (City of New Haven, 2013)
27. As of Feb. 2020, the FAWG has been disbanded and reabsorbed into the NHFPC
28. As of 2016, there were over 200 active Food Policy Councils throughout the United States: John Hopkins Center for a Liveable Future. Food Policy Council Report.
29. Interview with member of Yale Office of Sustainability (11 Oct. 2018).
30. Interview with member of the New Haven Bioregional Group (26 Sept. 2018).
31. The City of New Haven published *A Climate and Sustainability Framework* in Jan. 2018, which incorporated the core policy goals of the Food Policy Council.
32. Interview with member of the New Haven Bioregional Group (26 Sept. 2018).
33. Helmut Wollman, "Good Local Government and the Local Community," presented at the Resurgent City Conference. London School of Economics, 19–21 April 2004. See also: Mary P. Corcoran, "Urban partnership and community development: A European perspective," in *Economic and Social Review*, Special issue on governance, vol., 37, no. 3, Winter 2006, 399–422.
34. Dahl, *Who Governs*, p. 128.
35. Larry Romanoff, "The Richest Countries Empty Plates. 50 million hungry Americans:" www.globalresearch.ca/richest-country-empty-plates/5698008
36. Interview with Food Policy Director (5 Oct. 2018).
37. Interview with CT Community Organizing for Racial Equality (CORE) (22 Oct. 2018).
38. Interview with member of the New Haven Bioregional Group (26 Sept. 2018).
39. Dahl, *Who Governs?* p. 138.
40. Interview with member of the NHFPC (14 Oct. 2018).
41. Contribution by a local resident at the Soil And Social Justice Conference, Yale University (6 Sept. 2018).
42. Interview with member of the New Haven Bioregional Group (26 Sept. 2018).
43. Interview with local activist, Fairhaven, New Haven (14 Oct. 2018).

44. Ta-Nehisi Coates, "The Case for Reparations," *The Atlantic Monthly* (June 2014) https://www.theatlantic.com/magazine/archive/2014/06/the-case-for-reparations/361631/
45. Bouie, "Why Coronavirus is killing African-Americans more than others."
46. Tornaghi, "Urban Agriculture."
47. Reynolds and Cohen, *Beyond the Kale*, p. 10.
48. Interview with member of CT CORE (22 Oct. 2018).
49. Interview with co-founder of Love Fed New Haven (26 Oct. 2018).
50. Reynolds and Cohen, *Beyond the Kale*, p. 41.
51. Interview with a member of CT CORE (22 Oct. 2018).
52. Contribution at the Soil and Social Justice Conference, Yale University (6 Sept. 2018).
53. Karen Washington speaking at the Soil and Social Justice Conference, Yale University (6 Sept. 2018).
54. Interview with member of the New Haven Bioregional Group (26 Sept. 2018).
55. Interview with a member of CT CORE (22 Oct. 2018).
56. Tornaghi and Dahaene, *Rethinking*, p. 5.
57. Linda Milbourne and Ursula Murray (eds), *Civil Society in Turbulent times: A gilded web?* (Stoke on Trent: Trentham Books, 2017), p. 15.
58. Akilah Johnson and Talia Buford, "Early Data Shows African Americans Have Contracted and Died of Coronavirus at an Alarming Rate" in *Propublica*, 3 April 2020.

Making History Visible

CHAPTER NINETEEN

THE IRISH POVERTY SPECIAL COLLECTION AT THE ARNOLD BERNHARD LIBRARY, QUINNIPIAC UNIVERSITY

Robert A. Young, Jr.

As a librarian at Quinnipiac University's Arnold Bernhard Library, I oversee and assist researchers wishing to access materials in the Lender Family Special Collection, which is dedicated to the history of Ireland's Great Hunger. I therefore have responsibility for many unique sources that explore the history of this tragedy.[1] While the primary focus and purpose of the Lender Collection was originally to collect and make available to scholars primary and secondary sources related to the years of that catastrophe, the collection has grown to be far broader than this topic alone, containing primary and secondary sources that document Irish history before and after the decade of the 1840s. This includes a sub-collection within the larger collection that has been designated as "The Irish Poverty Collection." The publications within it provide information about how those who governed Ireland dealt with issues surrounding poverty and food shortages as far back as the 17th century and as late as the second decade of the 20th century.

The Irish Poverty Collection is a relatively recent addition to the Lender Collection. In 2014, when Irish historian, Christine Kinealy, was in her second year as director of Ireland's Great Hunger Institute, she was contacted by Kennys Bookshop in Galway. They offered the Institute a collection of over 70 items that they had labelled "The Irish Poverty Collection." By this stage, Kennys had established a longstanding relationship with Quinnipiac dating back to the late 1990s. They had provided the university with many unique and rare books, documents, letters, etc.

related to the Great Hunger. They also had been responsible for acquiring the original artwork that would, in 2012, form the core of the Great Hunger Museum. The Poverty Collection, which had been assembled by Kennys, contained documents dating from 1683 to 1914, and covering topics related to charity, education, health, landlord and tenant relations and emigration. Publication formats included parliamentary papers, pamphlets, scrapbooks, sermons and speeches.

Recognizing the significance and importance of this collection, it was decided that it should be acquired and added to the Lender Collection. To make the case for acquisition, Dr. Gerard Moran, a researcher at the Social Science Research Centre at NUI, Galway, was asked to review and submit a report on the collection. Having published extensively on the history of social conditions in Ireland, Moran was able to provide an insightful and positive critique of the collection, highlighting the reasons why they should be acquired by the Institute. Several of the items from the collection mentioned in this chapter were the ones that Moran specifically singled out in his report. He explained what he found to be significant about the Irish Poverty Collection and why it would be a good fit for Quinnipiac University:

> What makes the collection impressive is the time span covered: while the concentration mainly covers the nineteenth century, it also includes some rare and extremely important material on the question of poverty in the seventeenth and eighteenth centuries. The material on the nineteenth century is not just confined to the Great Famine, indicating that poverty was a major issue for Irish society, commentators and the authorities for much of the century and thus was a major concern for philanthropists, social reformers and a section of the political establishment. This is highlighted by the several crises in the 1879–1898 period which, while localised in many instances, on other occasions affected large tracts of the country as with the Forgotten Famine of 1879–81. Some items in the collection not only deal with poverty and the Great Famine, but also other periods of crisis. For example, the pamphlet produced by the Trustees of the Mansion House Relief Committee in August 1822 for improving the condition of the poor in Ireland.[2] This document has relevance to the famine of the early 1820s which impacted on the Munster region in particular.[3]

Moran also noted that some of the items were extremely rare and only available in physical format in a small number of specialized libraries such as the British Library in London, the Bodleian Library at Oxford and the National Library of Ireland.[4] Moreover, by searching for the items in WorldCat, it became apparent that while a few titles were available in microform or digitally, there were indeed very few institutions that held original copies.

The collection is extensive and diverse and what follows is a brief description of its highlights. One of the rarest, and also the earliest, items in the collection is a pamphlet by William Petty, *Observations upon the Dublin-bills of Mortality, MDCLXXXI, and the State of that city by the observatory on the London Bills of Mortality*.[5] Petty was an English economist, physician, scientist and philosopher. He first became prominent serving as physician-general with Oliver Cromwell in Ireland in the 1650s. Later, in the 1660s, he settled in Ireland, living there for 20 years.[6] The pamphlet, published in 1683, deals with such items as accommodation and housing in Dublin, including birth and death statistics for various diseases. Few copies of this pamphlet exist and besides Quinnipiac, only three libraries are listed in WorldCat as having actual paper copies. The three libraries are all in Europe. Interestingly, a later item in the collection which complements this work and gives a review of Petty's views on Ireland is W.H. Hardinge's monograph titled *Observations on an unpublished essay on Ireland by Sir W. Petty (A.D. 1687)*.[7] This publication examines Petty's proposal to use emigration as the solution to the perennial problem of poverty in Ireland. As Moran noted in his review, Hardinge's work was published at a time when emigration from Ireland was on the increase in the wake of the agricultural crisis of the early 1860s—the most serious subsistence crisis since the Great Hunger. It also coincided with a period when the emigration of the poorer sections of the population to the colonies was once again being advocated.[8]

The collection includes material from the 18th century which has great value, most notably David Bindon's *An Abstract of the Number of Protestant and Popish Families in the Several Counties and Provinces of Ireland: Taken from the Returns made by the Hearthmoney collectors, to the Hearthmoney Office in Dublin, in the Years 1732 and 1733*.[9] Its significance is that it provides statistics just prior to the major famine of that century which occurred in the 1740s. The inclusion of statistics related to "hearth money" (hearth tax) is also important. The hearth tax had been introduced to Ireland in 1662 and was collected twice a year. Fireplaces (hearths) were regarded as a proxy measure of wealth. The records list the names of householders who were liable to pay tax at the rate of two shillings on every hearth, or fireplace, they owned. The records, which were arranged by county, parish (Anglican) and townland, are regarded as census substitutes for the 17th and 18th centuries. The originals were destroyed by a fire in the Four Courts in Dublin in 1922, but the Presbyterian Historical Society of Ireland had made copies. Hearth tax records provide historians and genealogists with an indication of the size of each assessed house at the time the tax was collected. Bindon's publication provides a rare insight into Ireland on the eve of the famine of 1740 to 1741, remembered as *Bliain an Áir*, or "The Year of Slaughter," which killed up to 20 percent of the population.[10]

The topic of emigration appears throughout the collection in several publications that appeared in the decade before 1845. Robert Wilmot-Horton's, *Correspondence between the Right Honourable Sir Robert Wilmot-Horton, and J.B. Robinson, upon the subject of a pamphlet lately published entitled Ireland and Canada* was published in 1839, and is the transcription of the written communications between Wilmot-Horton and J.B. Robinson, a Canadian official, regarding emigration to Canada of the Irish poor.[11] Wilmot-Horton was a British politician, sociopolitical theorist and colonial administrator. He was under-secretary of State for War and the Colonies between 1821 and 1828, and Governor of Ceylon between 1831 and 1837. He is most widely known today for his writings on assisted emigration to the colonies of the British Empire. In regard to Ireland, he was the instigator of the Peter Robinson assisted emigration scheme from the Blackwater region of North Munster to Peterborough, Ontario, between 1823 and 1825, which was widely regarded as the most successful planned emigration scheme from Ireland in the early 19th century.[12] It would serve as a model for later assisted schemes, including the James Hack Tuke's Assisted Emigration Scheme of 1882–84. *The Colonization of South Australia* by Robert Torrens was published in 1835.[13] Torrens, who was born in Derry in the north west of Ireland, viewed emigration as a solution to the question of poverty. To quote Moran again, "this publication fits in with the proposal, popular in many quarters, that colonization and assisted emigration should be seen as the solution to poverty and destitution in Ireland."[14] Both Robert Torrens and his son, also named Robert, were very much involved with the early colonization of South Australia. The elder Torrens, author of the 1835 book, was a political economist, British MP, and owner of the influential *Globe* newspaper, which was published from 1803 to 1921.[15]

A number of items in the Poverty Collection deal directly with questions relating to modifying the poor laws in the immediate pre-Famine period. They provide coverage of the extensive debates about poverty and its causes, which would lead to the reform of the English and Scottish Poor Laws and, a few years later, the introduction of a Poor Law to Ireland in 1838. Among these publications is Nassau William Senior's, *A Letter to Lord Howick on a Legal Provision for the Irish Poor, Communication of Tithes and a Provision for the Irish Roman Catholic Clergy* which was published in 1831.[16] Senior was an English lawyer and economist. He had a reputation as a valued government adviser on economic and social policy and wrote extensively.[17] In 1868, he published *Journals, conversations and essays relating to Ireland.* George Poulett Scrope's, *Plan of a Poor-Law for Ireland: with a Review of the Arguments for and against it*, which was published in 1833.[18] In addition to being a British political economist and politician with an interest in the management of Ireland, Scrope was a geologist whose studies of volcanoes revolutionized that area of study.[19]

The most in-depth volume relating to the Poor Law and Ireland is Michael Thomas Sadler's 414-page opus from 1828, *Ireland, its Evils and their Remedies*.[20]

Sadler was an English Tory member of the British Parliament, whose Evangelical Anglicanism and experience as a Poor Law administrator in Leeds led him to oppose Malthusian theories of population and their use to decry state provision to the poor.[21] Based on his experiences, in 1831 he proposed that the English Poor Laws should be extended to Ireland. His suggestions were defeated. Instead, in 1838, a Poor Law was introduced in Ireland, which was far more draconian that the Poor Laws in England, Scotland and Wales.[22] These publications reveal the concern with Irish poverty, population and emigration in the decades preceding the Great Hunger. They also complement Quinnipiac's collection of British Parliamentary Papers for the 19th century, which consists of approximately 4,500 individual items that document how Ireland was governed following the Acts of Union of 1800.

Acquiring the Poverty Collection has provided Quinnipiac with a number of documents directly relating to the Great Hunger, which augment its already extensive holdings. For example, a published sermon delivered by James Martineau entitled, *Ireland and Her Famine: A Discourse Preached in Paradise Street Chapel, Liverpool, on Sunday, January 31, 1847*.[23] Martineau was an English religious philosopher who was influential in the history of Unitarianism. For over four decades, he was professor of Mental and Moral Philosophy and Political Economy at Manchester New College, which was the principal training college for British Unitarianism. He was also the brother of social theorist and Whig writer Harriet Martineau, who is often cited as being the first female sociologist.[24] Harriet visited Ireland on two occasions, in 1832 and 1852. Her later visit coincided with Ireland's slow recovery from the Great Hunger.[25] Perhaps the most important document in the Poverty Collection pertaining the crisis of the 1840s is a copy of *The Irish Poor Law Relief Extension Act*, which contains the infamous Quarter Acre Clause or, as it is often referred to, "The Gregory Clause," which stipulated how relief was to be provided both in and outside workhouses for those living on a quarter acre or less.[26] Cruelly, it forced those who had survived the first two years of famine to make a choice between trying to survive on their small holdings, or obtained Poor Law relief.

This brief review of documents in the Poverty Collection concludes by presenting a one-of-a-kind item. A unique aspect of Quinnipiac's relationship with Kennys Bookshop has been that they have always had an eye out for any rare documents that they believe will be an asset to the Lender Collection. There are a few personal scrapbooks in the larger collection that contain news clippings about the Great Hunger years. They are a 19th century version of a digital file folder, in which you would keep a collection of PDFs of articles on a particular subject. The only scrapbook in the Irish Poverty Collection was created by Robert Blakey. Blakey was an English writer and academic, a Chartist Radical and journalist. He also had a passion for fishing and he wrote a number of popular books on the sport.[27] The scrapbook is made up of an assortment of articles published in the late 1830s and early 1840s on the Poor Law, Factory Act, and Negro Slavery. Interspersed within the scrapbook are handwritten observations by Blakey. The scrapbook is labeled as being No. 3, which indicates that Blakey had a number of scrapbooks on various topics. This is the only Blakey scrapbook in the Poverty Collection.[28]

Additionally, there are additional documents in the collection that address a number of other subjects. There are publications on education that span the entirety of the 19th century, beginning in 1800 and ending on the eve of the 20th century. There are also publications dealing with aspects of health and disease, and crime and prisoners. As mentioned at the beginning of this essay, the publications contained within the Irish Poverty Collection provide significant information and insight about how Ireland dealt with issues surrounding poverty and food shortages from the 1700s to the early 20th century. As shown by the above examples, many of these works were written by influential leaders in government, business and religion. To have this collection available for students and scholars at Quinnipiac University, as well as outside researchers of Irish history from around the world, has proven to be invaluable.

In conclusion, the Irish Poverty Collection is just one of several important collections housed at the Arnold Bernhard Library that focus on Ireland's history and culture. The Lender Family Special Collection was established in 1997 to be a foundational repository for understanding poverty and famines in Ireland. It includes hundreds of primary and secondary materials related to the history of *An Gorta Mór*. Since the establishment of Ireland's Great Hunger Institute and the establishment of an Irish Studies minor at Quinnipiac University, the Irish collections have grown significantly. In addition to the Poverty Collection, other collections of note have been added during the past decade. For example, the Irish American Cultural Institute Collection (consisting of 4,000 books on Irish literature, history, culture and society); the letters of Lady Sligo of Westport House (over 400 hand-written documents that span three centuries); and a collection of Home Rule political cartoons from the late 19th century. Taken as a whole, Quinnipiac houses one of the most important collections on Irish history and culture in the United States.

NOTES

1. Robert A. Young Jr. is the public services librarian at the Arnold Bernhard Library at Quinnipiac University. He assists scholars and researchers who wish to access materials in the Lender Family Special Collection, a repository of primary and secondary resources related to the history of the Great Hunger and it causes and consequences. Additionally, he deals with questions related to copyright and Fair Use. He also serves as library liaison to several academic departments and has collaborated with Ireland's Great Hunger Institute on various projects and exhibitions.
2. Committee of Management, *Trustees for improving the condition of the poor in Ireland* (Dublin, 1822).
3. Gerard Moran, *Report on The Poverty Collection, Kennys Books, Galway*, p. 1. Unpublished assessment submitted to Ireland's Great Hunger Institute at Quinnipiac University, 2014.
4. Ibid.
5. William Petty, *Observations upon Dublin Bills of Mortality, MDCLXXXI, and the state of that city by the observatory on the London Bills of Mortality* (London: Printed for Mark Pardoe, 1683).
6. "William Petty," in *World of Sociology*. Detroit, MI: Gale, 2001. *Gale in Context: Biography*, at https://link.gale.com/apps/doc/K2427100048/BIC?u=a13qu&sid=BIC&xid=63c107db.
7. W.H. Hardinge, *Observations on an unpublished essay on Ireland by Sir W. Petty (A.D. 1687)* (Dublin: M.H. Gill, 1866).
8. Moran, *Report on The Poverty Collection, Kennys Books, Galway*, p. 1.
9. David Bindon, *An abstract of the number of Protestant and Popish families in the several counties and provinces of Ireland: Taken from the returns made by hearthmoney collectors to the Hearthmoney Office in Dublin, in the years 1732 and 1733* (Dublin: M. Rhames for R. Gunne, Bookseller, 1736).
10. David Dickson, *Arctic Ireland: The Extraordinary Story of the Great Frost and Famine of 1740–41* (Belfast: White Row Press, 1997); James Kelly, "Coping with Crisis: The response to the Famine of 1740–41," *Eighteenth-Century Ireland / Iris an dá chultúr*, vol. 27 (2012), 99–122.
11. Robert Wilmot-Horton, *Correspondence between the Right Honourable Sir Robert Wilmot and J.B. Robinson, upon the subject of a pamphlet lately published entitled Ireland and Canada* (London: John Murray, 1839).
12. "Wilmot-Horton, Sir Robert Wilmot (1784–1841)," *Australian Dictionary of Biography*, National Centre of Biography, Australian National University: http://adb.anu.edu.au/biography/horton-sir-robert-wilmot-2199, published in hardcopy in 1966.
13. Robert Torrens, *Colonization of South Australia* (London: Longman, 1835).
14. Moran, *Report on The Poverty Collection, Kennys Books, Galway*, p. 2.
15. Robert Torrens (1780–1864), *Australian Dictionary of Biography*, National Centre of Biography, Australian National University, http://adb.anu.edu.au/biography/torrens-robert-2740/text3873, published in hardcopy in 1967.
16. William Nassau Senior, *A letter to Lord Horwick on a legal provision for the Irish poor, commutation of tithes, and a provision for the Irish Roman Catholic clergy* (London: John Murray, 1831).
17. "Senior, Nassau William," *International Encyclopedia of the Social Sciences*, edited by David L. Sills, vol. 14 9Macmillan, 1968), 169–172.

18. George Poulett Scrope, *Plan of a Poor-Law for Ireland: With a review of the arguments for and against it* (London: J. Ridgway, 1833).
19. "Scrope, George Julius Poulett," *Complete Dictionary of Scientific Biography*, vol. 12, Charles Scribner's Sons, 2008, pp 261–264, at: https://link.gale.com/apps/doc/CX2830903939/GVRL?u=a13qu&sid=GVRL&xid=cf0da33c.
20. Michael Thomas Sadler, *Ireland, its evils and their remedies: Being a refutation of the errors of the emigration committee and others touching that country* (London: John Murray, 1828).
21. "Sadler, Michael Thomas," *Encyclopaedia Britannica*, Encyclopedia Britannica, Inc. 2019, at: https://www.britannica.com/biography/Michael-Thomas-Sadler.
22. Christine Kinealy, *A Disunited Kingdom. England, Ireland, Scotland and Wales, 1800–1949* (Cambridge University Press, 1999).
23. James Martineau, *Ireland and her famine: A discourse preached in Paradise Street Chapel, Liverpool, on Sunday, January 31, 1847* (London: John Chapman, 1847).
24. "James Martineau (1805–1900)," biographical entry at The Martineau Society, https://martineausociety.co.uk/the-martineaus/james-martineau/.
25. Deborah Anna Logan (ed.), *Harriet Martineau and the Irish Question: Condition of Post-Famine Ireland* (Bethlehem, PA: Lehigh University Press, 2011).
26. *The Irish Poor Relief Extension Act: 10 Vict., Cap. 31: An act to make further provision for the relief of the destitute poor in Ireland* (passed 8 June 1847) (Dublin: Alexander Thom for H.M.S.O., 1847.
27. "Blakey, Robert," Dictionary of National Biography, 1885–1990, vol. 5, https://en.wikisource.org/wiki/Blakey,_Robert_(DNB00).
28. Robert Blakey, *Writings on the Poor Law Act, the Factory Act and Negro Slavery in the years 1838, 1839, and 1840, Vol. 3: Cuttings book and holograph, compiled by Robert Blakey.*

CHAPTER TWENTY

TEACHING THE GREAT IRISH FAMINE

Alan Singer

The Great Irish Famine curriculum derived from legislation passed by Albany policymakers and signed into law by Governor George Pataki in late 1996. The initial controversy, which resulted in a robust exchange of letters between Pataki and the then British ambassador to the U.S., John Kerr, subsided when the task of developing the curriculum was given to Dr. Maureen Murphy of the Department of Curriculum and Teaching at Hofstra University. Together with a team of historians and classroom teachers, which included Alan Singer, material was developed as part of the New York State Human Rights Curriculum. The final version, which was over 1,000 pages in length, was described as:

> A curriculum for all subjects, based on the New York State Learning Standards, using primary sources, literature, dance and music, mathematics, history, science, art and theatre, geography, economics, government, career development, and technology.[1]

A college-level course or a high school-level unit on the Great Irish Famine provides a case study of the impact of colonization, industrialization, and capitalism on the lives of ordinary people, and offers insights into 19th-century ideas about "progress." Study of the Great Famine introduces students to major historical and social studies themes and the continuing problems of hunger, inequality and powerlessness in the world today.

When teaching a course on the Great Irish Famine to undergraduate students at Hofstra University (in Hempstead, New York), I commence by having students explore contemporary debates over the causes of famine in the world today, focusing on conflicting claims made by Indian economists Amartya Sen and Vandana Shiva. Sen, a Nobel Prize winner, argues that while the primary cause of endemic hunger and malnutrition is poverty, the transformation of hunger into famine requires a non-responsive government, either national or colonial, that does not address the needs of its people. According to Sen, "No famine has ever taken place in the history of the world in a functioning democracy."[2] Shiva, director of the Research Foundation for Science, Technology and Ecology in India, challenged Sen's conclusions, arguing that globalization and trade liberalization policies imposed on nations by the World Bank and the World Trade Organization have effectively robbed nominally democratic governments of the power to prevent famine, especially if political democracy in these counties is divorced from economic democracy.[3]

A course or unit on the Great Irish Famine sheds light on the causes of famine, not just in Ireland, but in other areas of the world, both past and present. Themes included:

(a) The British government's response to famine in Ireland, which was a colony governed by the London parliament after 1801. Britain's treatment of Ireland before, during and after the Great Irish Famine shaped colonial policy in the rest of its vast empire, especially in sub-Saharan Africa and in "British" India.[4] Study of British policy during the Famine exposes the ideology and operation of capitalism and imperialism.

(b) The Great Irish Famine occurred in a period when Great Britain, especially England, other countries in Europe, and in the United States, were industrializing. Peasants were being driven off the land into the cities. Ireland did not go through this process of industrialization, but Irish laborers became a significant portion of the urban industrial work force in other countries, working in factories, in mines, on the docks, and on construction projects. As a result of mass emigration from Ireland, the Irish diaspora transformed the United States, Canada, Australia, and Britain.

(c) The Great Irish Famine occurred while Great Britain and other European nations were focused on expanding and defending empires in Africa and Asia. Students explore "horizontal history," that is, how events in Ireland and British policies were influenced by global circumstances and how they influenced the broader world as well.

(d) Famines, exacerbated by climate change, threaten to reshape human civilization in the 21st century. Study of the Great Famine helps students understand environmental vulnerability, and the lingering impact of food shortages on child health, mortality, and development and on the psychological health of a nation.

Recent developments in epigenetics have revealed that the trauma of famine is transgenerational and can linger for up to five generations.[5]

(e) Study of the Famine engages students in discussions of human nature, human rights, government responsibility, and international obligations. Students can compare what happened in Ireland with the United Nations Universal Declaration of Human Rights (1948a) Section 21, which declares "Everyone has the right to take part in the government of his country, directly or through freely chosen representatives" and Section 25, which declares that "Everyone has the right to a standard of living adequate for the health and well-being of himself and of his family, including food, clothing, housing and medical care and necessary social services, and the right to security in the event of unemployment, sickness, disability, widowhood, old age or other lack of livelihood in circumstances beyond his control." Students also can debate whether events in Ireland and British policy constitute genocide as defined by the United Nations in the Convention on the Prevention and Punishment of the Crime of Genocide (1948b).[6]

According to Article II of the convention:

> ... genocide means any of the following acts committed with intent to destroy, in whole or in part, a national, ethnical, racial or religious group, as such: (a) Killing members of the group; (b) Causing serious bodily or mental harm to members of the group; (c) Deliberately inflicting on the group conditions of life calculated to bring about its physical destruction in whole or in part; (d) Imposing measures intended to prevent births within the group; (e) Forcibly transferring children of the group to another group.[7]

The Irish Famine intensified political discussions that continue today. In the decades preceding it, the British Parliament debated the responsibility of the government to meet the needs of impoverished and starving people and whether the poor deserved their fate. A switch in parliamentary rule from Conservative Tories who recognized some degree of *noblesse oblige* and governmental responsibility to care for the general population to free-market Liberal Whigs in the summer of 1846 meant that even limited relief efforts were abandoned or made more stringent, just as the demand for relief was increasing sharply. In October 2018, Jeremy Corbyn, then leader of Britain's opposition Labour Party, issued a call to finally correct the history curriculum in British schools so that students would explore the country's checkered colonial past, including its treatment of Ireland.[8]

Government assistance to starving populations during the Famine was minimal and often oppressive to discourage "unworthy" aid-seekers. Aid from Protestant religious charities, what we would now call NGOs or non-governmental agencies, sometimes was accompanied by the requirement that the poor, who were largely Roman Catholic, acquiesce to proselytizing in exchange for food. The Quakers, however, deserve special recognition for their "non-denominational" relief efforts. The role of religious organizations in providing emergency global relief has been eclipsed since World War II by supra-national organizations such as the World Bank and the International Monetary Fund, but, like earlier religious charity, assistance still comes with conditions attached. Countries that find themselves in debt to these organizations because of loans and bailouts are often forced to accept outside management of their economies and sharp restrictions on social investment.[9]

As a historian and history teacher, and also as an informed citizen, I try to uncover and explain patterns in world events by asking a few basic questions. What is the connection between causes and effects? Which causes are the underlying roots of an event and which are more immediate? What is the interaction between different historical causes? How are events, places, and eras similar and different? When, if ever, does an "event" become inevitable? How did the past produce the present and how does an understanding of past and present create possibilities for shaping the future? Study of the Irish Famine allows students to think about all of these questions.

The underlying causes of the Famine are long and complex, stretching back to 12th century when Pope Adrian IV (the only English man to have occupied the Papal throne) granted King Henry II of England sovereignty over Ireland, making Ireland its first colony. In 1169, England's Normans rulers, at the invitation of deposed Irish King, Diarmait Mac Murchada, invaded Ireland and established control over a divided island. Later, under the Statutes of Kilkenny of 1366, they outlawed cultural exchanges between the Irish and Anglo-Normans and, at the end of the 15th century, they started to enforce mercantilist laws that required all imports and exports to and from Ireland to pass through English ports. When Henry VIII broke with the Roman Catholic Church in 1534, it set off periodic rebellions by Irish nobility and increasingly savage English reprisals. In 1584, England seized the lands of Irish nobility who challenged the British crown's authority and, in 1601, at the Battle of Kinsale, it soundly defeated Irish forces. This was followed by centralizing authority, the colonization of Ulster with Scottish Presbyterian settlers and increased restrictions on Irish trade.

Between approximately 1650, when British Protestants led by Oliver Cromwell routed Irish-Catholic forces, stripped away remaining land-holdings of Irish-Catholic nobles, and drove a large part of the population west onto unproductive lands, until the final defeat of Irish insurgents at the Battle of Boyne in 1690, Ireland was increasingly dominated by absentee governors and landlords, a plantation pattern Britain exported to the rest of its colonial empire. A rebellion by the United Irishmen was quashed in 1798 with its leaders arrested and either executed or exiled. Britain responded to this rebellion with the Acts of Union, which effectively took away all local authority to address potential disasters. In the wake of this legislation, there were further subsistence crises including crop failures in 1816–17, 1822 and 1831. They were usually accompanied by typhus fever epidemics.[10]

Dependence on single-crop potato agriculture to feed the Irish peasant population was the second underlying ingredient for demographic disaster. The potato was both a blessing and a curse for the Irish living under the heel of British colonialism. There was a major crop failure in 1741 because of extreme weather, with an estimated 10 percent of the population dying in the *Bliadhain an Air*, or the Year of the Slaughter. Conditions in Ireland were at times so drastic that in 1729, Anglo-Irish author Jonathan Swift, an opponent of British misrule in Ireland, had sarcastically suggested that the Irish poor sell their children as food to wealthy people.[11]

In 1772, Benjamin Franklin visited Ireland while he was a colonial representative in London. In a letter to a friend in America, Franklin wrote: "I have lately made a tour through Ireland and Scotland. In those countries, a small part of the society are landlords, great noblemen, and gentlemen, extremely opulent, living in the highest affluence and magnificence. The bulk of the people are tenants, extremely poor, living in the most sordid wretchedness, in dirty hovels of mud and straw, and clothed only in rag."[12] Nevertheless, between 1700 and 1841, as the result of a potato diet, the population of Ireland rose from an estimated 2.5 million to over 8 million. It is estimated that the average Irish adult male ate about 14 pounds of potatoes a day.

By 1841, nearly half of the Irish were tenant farmers to British landlords, many of whom were absentee. The average family lived on holdings of less than five acres and in some counties, especially in the west, arable land holdings were even smaller. The poorest Irish were forced to plant their potatoes on rocky plots covering seed with seaweed. Families raised pigs to pay their rent, but rarely ate meat. There were fish in the streams, some wild game, and fields with grain, but these all belonged to the landlords. In a phenomenon that is seen in contemporary Haiti, overpopulation led to trees disappearing from the landscape. These underlying factors contributed to an impending disaster. Population outstripped available resources, resources that were either limited by natural phenomenon or by government decision, inaction or incompetence. Similar factors also produced famine in China in the 1870s, Russia in 1921, the Ukraine in the 1930s, Bengal in 1943, China in the 1950s, North Korea in the

1990s, and in the Sahel region of Africa today.[13] Amartya Sen blamed the 1943 famine in Bengal, where as many as three million people died, on British policy that diverted food away from the region as part of the war effort and its failure to rein in inflation, speculative buying and hoarding.[14]

The immediate cause of the Great Irish Famine was the destruction of the 1845 harvest by potato blight, which arrived in Europe from North America where it had appeared three years earlier. The blight was caused by a fungus or water mold, *Phytophthora infestans*, that spreads quickly, kills the potato plant, and feeds on the tubers. W. Steuart Trench, an Irish land agent and cultivator, described the reemergence of the potato blight in 1846, the second year of the Famine:

> On August 1st of that calamitous year, 1846, I was startled by hearing a sudden and strange rumour that all the potato fields in the district were blighted; and that a stench had arisen emanating from their decaying stalks. I immediately rode up to visit my crop, and test the truth of this report; but I found it as luxuriant as ever, in full blossom, the stalks matted across each other with richness, and promising a splendid produce, without any unpleasant smell whatever. On coming down from the mountain, I rode into the lowland country, and there I found the report to be but too true. The leaves of the potatoes on many fields I passed were quite withered, and a strange stench, such as I had never smelt before, but which became a well-known feature in 'the blight' for years after, filled the atmosphere adjoining each field of potatoes.[15]

Irish farmers were especially vulnerable to the blight because they primarily planted one high-yielding variety, the "lumper." In other European societies, peasants could turn to grains for survival, but in Ireland, the grains belonged to the largely absentee landlords who shipped grain to British industrial cities and, in Ireland, used it to brew porter (a popular stout) and distill whiskey.

According to Irish nationalist John Mitchel, while "The Almighty sent the potato blight," it was British "principles of political economy" that "created the famine."[16] British colonies in Africa, Asia, the Americas, and Ireland, operated under an economic system, mercantilism, that was a version of commercial capitalism. Under this system, trade was regulated so that the economies of colonies served the needs of the imperial center. Colonies provided raw materials and served as markets. All trade went through imperial center ports where taxes were collected for revenue and goods were then reshipped to other markets. It was taxation without representation and trade restrictions similar to those that pushed the British colonies in North America into rebellion.

Under the Conservative/Tory government of Robert Peel, there was at least a limited sense of British responsibility to address events in Ireland, however, when a Liberal laissez-faire government took control in June 1846 under Prime Minister John Russell, assistance to Ireland was rationalized and monetized. In April 1847, Isaac Butt, a leading Irish political economist, demanded more British aid for the Irish poor and greater landlord control over its spending. In "A Voice for Ireland. The Famine in the Land," Butt argued:

> Can we wonder if the Irish people believe, and believe it they do, that the lives of those who have perished, and who will perish, have been sacrificed by a deliberate compact to the gains of English merchants and if this belief has created among all classes a feeling of deep dissatisfaction, not only with the ministry but with English rule ... All our measures are based upon the principle that this calamity ought to be regarded as an imperial one, and borne by the empire at large. If this be not conceded, if the state be not, as we have said, our government, if we are not to receive the assistance which government can render upon such an occasion, what alternative is there for any Irishman but to feel that the united parliament has abdicated the functions of government for Ireland, and to demand for his country that separate legislative existence, the necessity of which will then be fully proved.[17]

However, Charles Trevelyan, Assistant Secretary of the British Treasury, the official responsible for implementing British policy in Ireland, claimed that Ireland was being treated fairly as a part of the United Kingdom. He wanted famine relief—and consequently famine taxation—to be handled at the local level. According to Trevelyan:

> Ireland is not the only country which would have been thrown off its balance by the attraction of 'public money.' This false principle eats like a canker into the moral health and physical prosperity of the people. All classes 'make a poor mouth,' as it is expressively called in Ireland. They conceal their advantages, exaggerate their difficulties, and relax their exertions. The cottier does not sow his holding, the proprietor does not employ his poor in improving his estate, because by doing so they would disentitle themselves to their 'share of the relief' ... The commonwealth suffers both by the lavish consumption and the diminished production. There is only one way in which the relief of the destitute ever has been, or ever will be, conducted consistently with the general welfare, and that is by making it a local charge."

Trevelyan thanked an "all-wise and all-merciful Providence" for the opportunity the Famine offered for "a true consummation of their union" between Ireland and Britain.[18] British policy was strongly endorsed in the editorial columns of the London *Times*. In September 1846, the newspaper condemned the "preference of the Irish for relief over labour" and accused the Irish of denouncing "human agency" for a "calamity inflicted by Heaven ... Such are the thanks that a Government gets for attempting to palliate great afflictions and satisfy corresponding demands by an inevitable but a ruinous beneficence ... The Government was required to ward off starvation, not to pamper indolence; its duty was to encourage industry, not to stifle it; to stimulate others to give employment, not outbid them, or drive them from the labour market."[19]

For Ireland, colonization meant productive land was owned by landlords who lived on lavish estates or in Irish and British cities. They hired estate managers, or agents, to bleed maximum profits through rents and labor from the Irish peasantry. It was the landlords who served, first in the Irish Parliament, and after the Acts of Union, in the British Parliament. When Britain tried to tax landlords to support poor relief during the Famine, the landlords responded by driving people off their lands or even subsidizing emigration on "coffin ships" to North America. In December 1848, the *Illustrated London News* reprinted a report from the *Tipperary Vindicator*:

> The work of undermining the population is going on stealthily, but steadily. Each succeeding day witnesses its devastations ... We do not say that there exists a conspiracy to uproot the 'mere Irish'; but we do aver, that the fearful system of wholesale ejectment, of which we daily hear, and which we daily behold, is a mockery of the eternal laws of God—a flagrant outrage on the principles of nature. Whole districts are cleared. Not a roof-tree is to be seen where the happy cottage of the labourer or the snug homestead of the farmer at no distant day cheered the landscape. The ditch side, the dripping rain, and the cold sleet are the covering of the wretched outcast the moment the cabin is tumbled over him ... Those who laboured to bring those tracts to the condition in which they are—capable of raising produce of any description—are hunted like wolves, or they perish without a murmur ... The agonies endured by the 'mere Irish' in this day of their unparalleled affliction are far more poignant than the imagination could conceive, or the pencil of a Rembrandt picture. We do not exaggerate; the state of things is absolutely fearful; a demon, with all the vindictive passions by which alone a demon could be influenced, is let loose and menaces destruction.[20]

Irish emigrants often traveled as "human ballast" below deck in returning ships that had transported lumber to Europe. Frequently, they were deposited in fever sheds on *Grosse* Île in the St. Lawrence River where they died of exposure or disease, most frequently typhus. One passenger who traveled from Dublin to Quebec published a detailed account of the voyage in 1848, *The Ocean Plague: The Diary of a Cabin Passenger* by Robert Whyte. There is some question about whether that was his actual name or a pseudonym. According to Whyte, "dreadful disease" was sweeping through passengers living below deck:

> For once having shown itself in the unventilated hold of a small brig, containing 110 living creatures, how could it possibly be stayed without suitable medicines, medical

> skill and pure water to slake the patients' burning thirst. The prospect before us was indeed an awful one, and there was no hope for us but in the mercy of God.[21]

The vessel arrived at Grosse Île at the end of July and passengers were held at a quarantine station. Whyte wrote that he "could not believe it possible that here, within reach of help, we should be left as neglected as when upon the ocean. That after a voyage of two months' duration we were to be left still enveloped by reeking pestilence, the sick without medicine, medical skill, nourishment or so much as a drop of pure water."[22]

There is similar European exploitation and mistreatment of colonized peoples in Africa and Asia and it is often attributed to racism. British cartoonists liked to depict the Irish as sub-human, a different species from the lordly British. But the people of Ireland, Britain's first colony, were white Europeans, which introduces the question of whether racism was the cause of colonial exploitation or a justification. Ironically, recent scientific studies show the overwhelming genetic similarity between the British and the Irish, with the Irish, if anything, more Germanic than the supposedly Anglo-Saxon British.[23]

If you were living in Ireland, the multi-year collapse of the potato crop and consequent famine would have been the transcendent event in your life. This was not the case for people living outside of Ireland and it may not have even been a major event if you were a non-Irish representative in the British Parliament. During this period, the governors of Imperial Britain faced crises and opportunities all over the world that they gave priority to. Great Britain was involved in wars in Afghanistan, India, China, New Zealand, Burma, southern Africa and Crimea. Domestically, between 1838 and 1857, Chartist petitions and demonstrations across England demanded universal manhood suffrage and an end to property qualifications to serve in Parliament. There were strike waves, factory investigations, a railroad boom and bust, and epidemic diseases in crowded urban slums. If you were an Irish family dependent on the potato crop for survival, the blight was the defining factor of your life. But for the lords and industrialists of Britain, many other issues took priority.[24]

The Irish Famine introduces students to other historical themes that continue to be major issues in the world today.

(1) Human migration in response to war, oppression, poverty and natural disasters. Today, European countries and the United States face political upheaval over how to respond to people fleeing failed states and collapsing food supplies in the Middle East, sub-Saharan Africa and Central America.

(2) The impact of geography on history. As the human population grows, it places stress on the ability of locations like 19th-century Ireland to support its population. We see this today in Haiti, Bangladesh and in many sub-Saharan countries.

(3) Environmental catastrophe. Environmental catastrophes have decimated populations and destroyed civilizations in the past. Now, as a result of human-induced climate change, new weather patterns, and a rising sea level, wide swathes of the Earth, including areas with high population density, face monumental changes.

(4)Capitalist ideology. The 19th century saw the discovery of economics as a distinct discipline and, utilizing the "dismal science," scholars, industrialists, financiers, governments, and revolutionary movements tried to understand the transformation of society that was taking place around them. Thomas Malthus argued that humankind was destined to periodic catastrophe as population outstripped food supplies, a theory partly based on his observations on Ireland. David Ricardo promoted unhindered international trade and viewed capitalist society as a constant battle for supremacy with the end result being social inequality. John Stuart Mill elucidated laissez-faire economic principles that shaped British policy in Ireland during the famine years.[25] Karl Marx rooted many of his explanations of political economy on British treatment of Ireland and the Irish. In an 1867 speech, Marx remarked that British economic and political policy between 1847 and 1867 had replaced over a million Irish with almost 10 million sheep that provided wool to the British textile industry.[26]

(5) Responsibility of Government. As in 19th-century Ireland, catastrophe today leads to debate over the responsibility of government to respond both at home and abroad and to resistance against forces and institutions that are seen to be ignoring the situation or making it worse.

In her introduction to the New York State Great Irish Famine curriculum, Maureen Murphy, the director of the project, argued that "the most compelling reason to study the Great Irish Famine is that hunger and homelessness are still with us; that there is want in a world of wealth ... The lessons of the Great Irish Famine have a claim on our fundamental humanity; they remind us that we have an opportunity to help our neighbors who face similar suffering. Students studying the Great Irish Famine in the context of other famines will develop a better understanding of the factors which contribute to famine in today's world and will, as a result, become actively concerned about the human right to adequate nourishment."[27] These remain the most important reasons to study the Great Irish Famine.

This essay is based on a chapter in Teaching Global History, *2nd edition (Routledge 2020) and presentations at Ireland's Great Hunger Institute at Quinnipiac University and the 2019 International Conference on Learning in Belfast. The New York State Great Irish Famine curriculum is available online at: www.nysed.gov/curriculum-instruction/great-irish-famine-curriculum.*

NOTES

1. The Great Irish Famine Curriculum, at: www.nysed.gov/curriculum-instruction/great-irish-famine-curriculum. Also see, Maureen Murphy, "Creating the Great Irish Famine Curriculum in New York," in Christine Kinealy, Jason King and Gerard Moran (eds), *Children and the Great Hunger in Ireland* (Hamden and Cork: Quinnipiac and Cork University Press, 2018), pp 227–242.
2. Amartya Sen, *Democracy as Freedom* (New York: Random House, 1999).
3. Vandana Shiva, "The real reasons for hunger," *Guardian*, 23 June 2002.
4. "Famine Codes" were developed by British colonial administrators in India in the 1880s. They identified three levels of need: near-scarcity, scarcity, and famine.
5. See Oonagh Walsh, "'An Invisible but Inescapable Trauma:' epigenetics and the Great Famine," in Christine Kinealy, Jason King, and Ciarán Reilly (eds), *Women and the Great Hunger* (Quinnipiac University Press and Cork University Press, 2017), pp 173–184.
6. United Nations (1948). The Universal Declaration of Human Rights, at: www.un.org/en/universal-declaration-human-rights/index.html
7. United Nations (1948 b). Convention on the Prevention and Punishment of the Crime of Genocide, at: www.un.org/en/genocideprevention/documents/atrocity-crimes/Doc.1_Convention%20on%20the%20Prevention%20and%20Punishment%20of%20the%20Crime%20of%20Genocide.pdf.
8. Pippa Crerar, "Jeremy Corbyn vows to increase teaching of black history in schools," *Guardian,* 11 Oct. 2018.
9. Jeffrey D. Sachs (ed.), *Developing Country Debt and the World Economy* (Chicago, IL: University of Chicago Press, 2007).
10. Christine Kinealy and Gerard Moran, *Fallen Leaves of Humanity: Famines in Ireland before and after the Great Famine* (London: Routledge, 2019).
11. Dr. Swift, *A Modest Proposal For preventing the Children of Poor People From being a Burthen to Their Parents or Country, and For making them Beneficial to the Publick* (Dublin: S. Harding, 1729). See also chapter by Peter Murphy.
12. Benjamin Franklin, *The Life and Letters of Benjamin Franklin* (Eau Claire, WI: E. M. Hale and Co., 1940).
13. Cormac Ó Gráda, *Famine: A Short History* (Princeton NJ: Princeton University Press, 2009).
14. Amartya Sen, *Poverty and Famines. An Essay on Entitlement and Depravation* (Oxford: Clarendon Press, 1981).

15. William Steuart Trench, *Realities of Irish Life* (London: Longmans, Green and Co. Trench, 1869) p. 100.
16. John Mitchel, *The last conquest of Ireland* (perhaps) (Glasgow: Washbourne, 1861), p. 219.
17. Isaac Butt, "The Famine in the Land," *Dublin University Magazine*, XXIX, April 1847 (Dublin: James McGlashan), p. 20.
18. Charles Trevelyan, *The Irish Crisis* (London: Longman, Brown, Green & Longmans, 1848), p. 185.
19. "Indolent Preference of Relief to Labour," *Times,* 22 Sept. 1846.
20. "Evictions of Peasantry in Ireland," *Illustrated London News*, 16 Dec. 1848.
21. Robert Whyte and J. Mangan (ed.) *Robert Whyte's 1847 Famine Ship Diary: The Journey of an Irish Coffin Ship* (Cork: Mercier Press, 1995), p. 28.
22. Ibid., p. 64.
23. Nicholas Wade, "English, Irish, Scots: They're All One, Genes Suggest," *The New York Times*, 5 March 2007.
24. Bernard Grun, *The Timetables of History, a Horizontal Linkage of People and Events* (New York: Touchstone, 1975), pp 408–419.
25. Robert L. Heilbroner, *The Worldly Philosophers* (New York: Simon and Schuster, 1967); Joel Mokyr, "Malthusian models and Irish history," *The Journal of Economic History,* XL, March 1980 (1), 159–166.
26. Karl Marx, *Ireland and the Irish question: A collection of writings* (New York: International Publishers, 1972).
27. Maureen Murphy, *et al*. "The Great Irish Famine Curriculum" (Albany, NY: State Depart= ment of Education, 2000), at: www.nysed.gov/curriculum-instruction/great-irish-famine-curriculum, p. 32.

ABOUT THE CONTRIBUTORS

MARY P. CORCORAN is Professor of Sociology at Maynooth University. She was a Fulbright-EPA Scholar at Ireland's Great Hunger Institute, Quinnipiac University in 2018-19. Her latest publication is an anthology, co-edited with Dr. Pauline Cullen, *Producing Knowledge, Reproducing Gender: Power, production and practice in Ireland* (Dublin: UCD Press, 2020).

TIMOTHY S. FOREST is an associate professor in History at the University of Cincinnati–Blue Ash. His research focus is in modern British and French history, with specializations in imperialism, more specifically government-sponsored migrations of marginalized populations between the late Victorian and the interwar periods.

NIAMH ANN KELLY'S research areas are contemporary art, the history of art and commemorative visual culture. She is author of *Imaging the Great Irish Famine: Representing Dispossession in Visual Culture* (Bloomsbury, 2018) and lectures at the Dublin School of Creative Arts, Technological University, Dublin.

JANE KENNEDY, a proud Tuke descendant, lives in St. Paul, Minnesota and enjoys researching Irish history and sharing her findings. She is pleased to have connected with many Tuke descendants with whom she will always share a special connection.

CHRISTINE KINEALY is the founding director of Ireland's Great Hunger Institute at Quinnipiac University. She has lectured and published extensively on the Great Famine, and more recently has researched on the experiences of black abolitionist who visited Ireland in the 19th century.

JASON KING is Academic Coordinator of the Irish Heritage Trust. He is author of many publications that look at the intersection between the Irish Famine, emigration to Canada, memory and memorialization.

MARGARET LYNCH (PhD, University of Chicago) is Executive Director of the Irish American Archives Society of Cleveland, Ohio.

MARK G. MCGOWAN is Professor of History at the University of Toronto and is Principal Emeritus at St. Michael's College. He has published extensively on the Catholic Church and the Irish in Canada and is currently completing a monograph on Irish Famine orphans in Canada, which includes the chronicle of 271 assisted migrant families from Strokestown, County Roscommon.

EILEEN MOORE QUINN is a Professor of Anthropology who teaches Folklore, Irish and Irish American Studies, and Anthropology at the College of Charleston, South Carolina. Presently co-editing *Women and Pilgrimage*, a work to be published by CABI in 2021, Quinn continues to examine Irish women at the intersection of hunger, migration, and ideology.

GERARD MORAN is a senior researcher at the Social Science Research Centre at NUI Galway and has lectured in the History Department at NUI Galway and Maynooth University. He has published extensively on 19th-century Ireland, most recently, *Fleeing from Famine in Connemara: James Hack Tuke and his Assisted Emigration Scheme in the 1880s* (2018)

PETER MURPHY has a B.A. in European History from the University of California, San Diego and an M.A. in American History from Trinity College in Hartford, Connecticut. He is currently researching the history of the Emmet family, who are originally from Cork.

CIARÁN REILLY is a historian of 19th and 20th century Irish history at Maynooth University. His publications include *Capard: An Irish Country House & Estate* (Dublin, 2019); *The Irish Land Agent, 1830-60: the case of King's County* (2014); *Strokestown and the Great Irish Famine* (2014) and *John Plunket Joly and the Great Famine in King's County* (2012).

BRENDAN SCOTT holds a PhD in early modern Irish history. He is the manager of the Irish Family History Foundation and teaches history at Maynooth University.

CATHERINE B. SHANNON is Professor Emerita of History at Westfield State University. Her publications include studies of 19th and 20th century Anglo-Irish relations and Boston's Irish-American community and its response to Irish famines.

ALAN SINGER is a historian and teacher educator at Hofstra University, Hempstead, NY. He was co-director of the New York State Great Irish Famine Curriculum.

ROBERT SMART is Dean of the College of Arts and Sciences at Quinnipiac University. He is the author of a number of publications looking at Gothic Literature in Ireland.

LAURA J. SMITH is a historian of the Irish religion, politics, and settlement in early Canada. She is an administrator at McMaster University in Hamilton, Ontario.

KAREN SONNELITTER is an Associate Professor of History at Siena College. She is the author of *Charity Movements in Eighteenth-Century Ireland: Philanthropy and Improvement* (Boydell & Brewer, 2016) and *The Great Irish Famine: A History in Documents* (Broadview, 2018).

HARVEY STRUM is a professor of history and political science at Russell Sage College in Albany and Troy, N.Y. His areas of research and publication are American and Canadian responses to the Irish famines, the War of 1812, American Jewish history, and anti-Irish nativism.

ROBERT A. YOUNG JR., the Public Services Librarian at Quinnipiac University, assists scholars and researchers who wish to access materials in the Lender Family Special Collection. He is an avid collector of vintage photographs of men and is currently writing a book about a collection of 1950s snapshots documenting the life of a gay couple who lived in New York City.

INDEX

IRELAND'S GREAT HUNGER INSTITUTE AT QUINNIPIAC UNIVERSITY

Ireland's Great Hunger Institute is a scholarly resource for the study of the Great Hunger, which is also known as *An Gorta Mór*. Through a program of lectures, conferences, course offerings and publications, the institute fosters a deeper understanding of this tragedy and its causes and consequences.

To encourage original scholarship and meaningful engagement, the institute develops and makes available the Great Hunger Collection, a unique array of primary, secondary and cultural sources, to students and scholars.

Ireland's Great Hunger Institute was established in September 2013 and its founding director is Professor Christine Kinealy.